Stranger in Two Worlds

Stranger in Two Worlds

JEAN HARRIS

MACMILLAN PUBLISHING COMPANY

New York

58138 September 1986 94

Macmillan Publishing Company
866 Third Avenue, New York, N.Y. 10022
Collier Macmillan Canada, Inc.

Library of Congress Cataloging-in-Publication Data
Harris, Jean (Jean Struven)
Stranger in two worlds.
1. Harris, Jean (Jean Struven)   2. Tarnower, Herman.
3. Crime and criminals—United States—Biography.
4. Murder—New York (State)—Purchase.   I. Title.
HV6248.H183A37 1986   364.1′523′0924 [B]   86-103
ISBN 0-02-548330-7

Grateful acknowledgment is made to the following for permission to reprint previously published material from:

The Joke by Milan Kundera, translated by Michael Henry Heim. English translation copyright © 1982 by Harper & Row, Publishers, Inc. Original title *Zert* copyright © 1967 by Milan Kundera. By permission of Harper & Row, Publishers, Inc.

Collected Poems by Edna St. Vincent Millay, Harper & Row, Publishers, Inc. Copyright © 1923, 1931, 1951, 1958 by Edna St. Vincent Millay and Norma Millay Ellis.

Man's Search for Meaning by Viktor Frankl, Beacon Press. Copyright © 1962 by Viktor Frankl. By permission of Beacon Press.

"The Physician as Expert Witness" by A. Bernard Ackerman, M. D., *Medical Heritage*. By permission of A. Bernard Ackerman and W. B. Saunders Co.

Photo credits appear on page 388.

Macmillan books are available at special discounts for bulk purchases for sales promotions, premiums, fund-raising, or educational use. For details, contact:

Special Sales Director
Macmillan Publishing Company
866 Third Avenue
New York, N.Y. 10022

10 9 8 7 6 5 4 3 2 1

Designed by Mary Cregan
Printed in the United States of America

This book is for my sons,
David Michael Harris, and James Scholes Harris, Jr.,
with my love.

Contents

*"I beseech ye in the bowels of Christ,
think that ye may be mistaken." I should
like to have that written over the portals of
every church, every school, and every
courthouse, and may I say of every legislative body in the United States. I should
like to have every court begin, "I beseech
ye in the bowels of Christ, think that we
may be mistaken."*

Judge Learned Hand

Acknowledgments

The many kindnesses that have been shown me over the past six years are beyond anything I could have imagined. Thousands of people from all over America, and all over the world, have written, wishing me well. I'm happy to say their letters will become part of the archives of Smith College. I hope that someday a young graduate student will read them, and find in them a piece of Americana, proof positive that in spite of what has happened to me, there was goodness abroad in the land.

That I am here is not because many good people have not wished and worked and prayed to have me free. They have bestowed upon me love and trust, and given their time and energy, and patience, and understanding and expertise, and money in my behalf. I am proud to call each one friend.

The list that follows cannot be complete. It would be too long. To each of you who has smiled and reached out a hand I am deeply grateful. Your kindnesses have spilled over into the lives of many other women here, as well as into mine.

My special appreciation and deep affection go to Sister Elaine Roulet, Arlene Levkoff, and William Riegelman, three very dear human beings who unquestionably have helped me to retain my sanity in this grim, terrible place. Sister Elaine is head of the Children's Center where I work here at Bedford Hills Correctional Facility, a top security prison for women in the State of New York. At the risk of not making life easier for her by having me sing her praises, there is no way to tell of my life in prison without saying how deeply I admire her and how grateful I am that she is here. I think all of us who work closely with her share this feeling. The days she isn't here are colorless and dull. She brings life and humor and a sense of purpose into our lives.

Bill Riegelman was a virtual stranger to me the night Hy died. He was called in the middle of the night to come and help me until others could arrive. He was there beside me in a tiny room in a Westchester jail when a policeman told me in a casual voice: "Dr. Herman Tarnower? Oh, he passed on." He was there beside me for the next three years, until his own death. He cheered me in every way he could, and kept me informed about what was happening in my case when others were too busy. He handled my private legal matters for me, without being asked and without ever sending a bill. I said to him one day, "I figure on an hourly basis I must owe you about two million dollars by now. Do you want to flip, double or nothing?" He laughed and said, "You don't owe me anything." He made me laugh and he made me cry and he made me angry, and he calmed me down with, "Don't be so hyperbolic, Jean." He used to promise, "I'll live to see you out of here." I wish we both could have made it.

Arlene Levkoff, over the years, has become like a daughter to me, always full of life and funny stories, and heartwarming loyalty, no matter how hard the media was beating on me. No request, however busy she may be, is too large or too small for her to run right out and fill for me. Whether it is a spool of thread and a hairnet I need, or a robe and a nightgown, or toys for the Children's Center, or clothes for Sister's Thrift Shop, or Christmas shopping for David and Jim, she is always there with a smile. She has mailed endless things for me so they wouldn't sit for weeks in the prison mail room, or just disappear, and she has indulged me in charming and ridiculous and heartwarming ways. Best of all she has shared her children, Jodi and Brett, and her dearest friend, Janet Levkoff, with me. Together they have done many kindnesses for the Children's Center, and they are much loved by us all.

My sisters, Mary Margaret Lynch and Virginia McLaughlin, and my brother Robert Struven, though living far away, have stood staunchly beside me when they could, and have been with me in spirit always, never wavering in their loyalty and offers of help.

ACKNOWLEDGMENTS

Three kind women took me into their homes during the year after Hy died, so that I would be living, as I was ordered by the court to do, in Westchester. I lived for nine months with Frances Braxton in her wonderful old house by the duck pond, and came to know and love her family. She even welcomed my big, shedding, lovable golden retriever, Cider. Linda Cohen befriended me in a hundred different ways, and it was she and Rebecca, and Matthew and Seth who bought and trimmed a Christmas tree for me that first Christmas far away from home.

Roz Riegelman's kindness helped to ease the trauma and tension of those eight long days while we waited for the jury's verdict.

Shana Alexander's gifts to me are unique. I have not read her book about me. I do not wish to hear in detail what she thinks about Hy or me. It is enough to know that we are kindred souls, that she understands what makes me tick, that I trust her, and that when I call her in the middle of the night, as I sometimes have, and say, "Shana, just talk. Please, just keep talking so I'll know that something still makes sense," she will.

Sue Cullman's visits mean something special to me because she knows, perhaps better than anyone else, the hurt that I have lived through. Her kindnesses come from the heart, and in their quiet, low key way have touched the lives of every woman in here. It is in part through her generosity that I have been able to keep alive a small program for ladies in the mental ward here.

Ann Lenox, a great headmistress and a great friend, has worked long and hard to establish a defense fund in my behalf. Alice Lacey has worked beside her in this endeavor and her gifts of friendship and beautiful yarns from Hillside Farm have given pleasure not only to me but to many of the women here, and to their children.

Michael and Eleanora Kennedy are two kind and caring people who came late into my life, but thank heavens they came. Michael has exhausted every possible legal avenue for winning me a new trial, but they refuse to let me give up. If effort and selfless determination can set me free, they are the two people who will make it happen. How does one measure gratitude?

Leslie Jacobson was the lawyer I called the night Hy died. He came at once to help, and continued to help in many ways though he is not a criminal lawyer. He and his wife, Marjorie, had introduced me to Hy fourteen years earlier. My friendship with Marjorie spans almost sixty years, and many happy, funny times. I hope we will both live long enough to see so much sadness fade.

Carol Potts, the kind, competent lady who was secretary and friend to me at the Madeira School, helped me to salvage needed records and papers and continues to cheer me with her visits and news of her family. Jackie Barnes, the special lady who filled the same role in Philadelphia, writes, and visits when she can, and mothers me and chides me when I don't call to tell her how I am.

Audrey and Seymour Topping have sent me my window on the world, *The New York Times*, all these years. I am deeply grateful. Sally Duncan has befriended me, and in doing so has become friend to many others here. She seems to have a sixth sense about when we need more colored felt in the Center, or magic markers, or Christmas tree ornaments, and her gifts of personal kindness to me are un-numbered.

Dr. Bernard Ackerman was one of the medical experts who gave testimony at my trial. We were strangers, but he shared with me his disbelief and disillusion at what can happen in a court of law. It was a first, for both of us. He has, at his own expense, written widely on the subject of expert testimony and the medical testimony in my trial in particular. The strength of his integrity, that rarest of all qualities, delights my soul.

Herbert MacDonell studied the physical evidence in Hy's room far more carefully than anyone else involved in the case, and explained to the jury in clear and accurate terms what the physical evidence indicated. That they chose not to believe him is a frustration we share. He is kind enough to come and visit from time to time, and to express again his belief that I told the truth. It would be hard to put into words how much that means to me.

I am grateful to Mrs. Lisa Zumar, a member of my jury who has written to wish me well, to tell me of the depression she felt after the trial, and who has expressed the hope publicly that I will be granted a new trial.

Laura Haywood has sent me a book almost every week for five years, among them all the works of Loren Eiseley, which I had treasured for years and hadn't hoped to see again. She has also helped me to put together a collection of studies about women in prison, published and unpublished works that have broadened my knowledge of incarcerated women far beyond the barbed wire of Bedford. These, too, are gradually going to Smith.

I have said little in this book about two lawyers who have worked in my behalf, Joel Aurnou and Herald Price Fahringer, not because I am ungrateful for their efforts. I am grateful. Both of them wanted to help me. Both of them worked hard in my behalf. Joel believed the truth would set me free, which I now know was naive in the extreme, but at the time it seemed quite logical to me. They did much to give me hope, even when there wasn't any. They were kind to me. They are, I know, sorry that I am here. What else can one say? Life goes on.

There is one other group of friends I have never met, but to whom I am deeply indebted. They are the cast and script writers of *M*A*S*H*. They walk the human tightrope between tragedy and comedy with so much style and so much caring. They have made me laugh on some of the grimmest days, and for that I owe them all a genuine, heartfelt thank you.

I would like to describe the kindnesses of so many others, but I can only mention a few, Kay Carstons, Midge and Ed Clark, Wilma Drysdale, Donna Gilton, Do and Jiggs Johnson, Bruce Jordan, Ann Kinzie, Ed and Cynthia Lasker, Susie and Tom O'Neil, Ad Penberthy, Joel Rothman, Bob Scripps, Ellen and Peter Strauss, Dr. Abraham Halpern, Joy Harris, Peg and Peter Kinney, Kristi Witker, and Robert Stewart, a very kind editor who had to separate the wheat from the chaff, without hurting my feelings. To all of you, and many more, my thanks. You have helped to make me strong.

JEAN HARRIS
January 1986

Introduction

*Slowly I came to realize that there was
no power capable of changing the image of
my person lodged in the supreme court of
human destinies, that the image in question
(even though it bore no resemblance to me)
was much more real than my actual self;
that I was its shadow and not the other
way round; that I had no right to accuse it
of bearing no resemblance to me, because I
bore the guilt for the lack of resemblance;
that the lack of resemblance was my cross,
to bear on my own.*

Milan Kundera
The Joke

1.

It is spring as I begin to put the pieces of a book together. Six springs have gone by since Hy died. Until now, I haven't accepted the reality of that. Only the sheer weight of numbers forces me to accept it now—now, when the hurting should be going away, I feel it still. Until today, the only comfort had been not to think about either of us. Anything that touched upon Hy or me was an open wound. But it's time the wound were attended to. That is part of my reason for writing, but only part.

I live today in a top security prison in Bedford Hills, New York, convicted of murdering Dr. Herman Tarnower, Hy as his friends knew him, and sentenced to stay here for fifteen years to life. To live each day with the knowledge that I am responsible for Hy's death, that a man who loved life, and one who appreciated the gift of life more than anyone I have ever known, died because of me is the worst punishment of all. It was my gun. I brought it loaded to Hy's room. To be the instrument of death and to be a murderer are two quite different things. But Hy is no less dead and no one can feel his death as I do. There hasn't been a day I haven't mourned him. There hasn't been a day I haven't missed him. There hasn't been a day I haven't inadvertently called someone else Hy. There hasn't been a day I haven't wished him back.

But wishing is for candles on birthday cakes. Wishing is for children, and children play a role in this book too, an important role. I wish so many things for children and many days those wishes seem almost as hopeless as wishing Hy back on the eighteenth tee at the Country Club, or back on the salmon stream at Runnymede, or back in the office in Scarsdale, being what he loved most to be, a good doctor.

Children are the true parents of this book, my own and the children of women I have come to know during these excruciating six years. Indeed most of the mothers confined here with me in the Bedford Hills Correctional Facility are younger than my own children. I think of them as children too, our children, yours and mine.

Fortunately, I cannot imagine what it must feel like to have your mother, someone who had been the center of your life, someone you loved and were proud of—and affectionately teased and called Big Woman—suddenly turned into a public freak, called by every grim name the media could contrive, from "Diet Doc Junkie" to "Blue-Blooded Butcher." Overnight I became a cottage industry. Everyone had something to say about me and it was all for sale. *True Detective* magazine carried a lurid twenty-page monstrosity about "The Scarsdale Diet Doc and the Socialite Headmistress." *New York* magazine repeated the same headline, and *Hustler* magazine reduced me to a lewd cartoon, side by side with Charles Manson. *Mad* magazine found the aging mistress and the "Diet Doc" genuine knee-slappers, as did Don Imus on morning radio. Four books were written. I was "the woman scorned," the "power-hungry headmistress," and, finally, as frosting on the cake, "the fornicator." That last touch was added by *Washington* magazine, quoting, of all people, Barbara Keyser, the woman who preceded me as headmistress of Madeira. What follows will hardly be a list of all the things that I am not, but perhaps, for good or for ill, it will help expose the mother of David and Jim Harris as the woman she is. It is late, and little enough to do for them.

Hy fared little better in the press than I did, because the people who knew us least talked the most. He could have shrugged off *Time's* choice of adjectives about him: "brilliant, austere, humorless, ego-tistical"—even rather liked them. But he'd have gagged at Samm Sinclair Baker's statement, "He was a perfect gentleman. Why, I never saw him make any passes at the other women when he came here for dinner." How had the mighty fallen that this should be his epitaph. Hy had probably stopped pinching fannies at the age of thirteen. He had also stopped inviting Samm, author of *The Complete Scarsdale Medical Diet Book*, to his home for dinner after the first invitation.

The all-time high in reportorial folly, and there were hundreds of qualified applicants, came in an article by Sam Rosensohn of the *New York Post*. In the fourth of a series of articles about me, Rosensohn "revealed" to the reading public that Mrs. Harris had stolen the doctor from another woman. He wrote, "Dr. Herman Tarnower, who remained a bachelor to his death, was seeing Zhou Enlai when he met Jean Harris about 14 years ago." And nobody laughed. Zhou Enlai is, of course, the phonetic spelling of Chou En-Lai, former premier of China. Hy did have dinner with him when he went to China in 1973, but they were hardly "going together" when we met in 1966.

As a matter of fact, Hy was between ladies when we met. The last one had grown weary of waiting for a wedding ring and left him to marry someone else. She came back into his life when the marriage didn't work out, but I didn't learn that until the trial. There are many stories that I have learned since his death which I would most happily not have heard. If every man were judged on the basis of his treat-ment of women alone, history would be a sorry tale indeed. That doesn't make it good or bad, it only makes it true.

It was my mother who asked, "How can you sit by and let others write about you? It's your life. You lived it." One has little or nothing to say about what is written about you, or by whom, but she was right. I suppose somewhere in the back of my mind the intention has always been there. But there is so much to tell now, such a jumble of caring and thinking and experiencing. How do you wrap it all up neatly, the way Miss Andrews taught us, Roman Numeral I, an introduction with a good topic sentence; Roman Numeral II, the body of the story with A's and B's and C's; and Roman Numeral III, the conclusion? What is the topic sentence?

On Friday, March 7, 1980, which was the Friday before I left the Madeira School for good, I had expelled four seniors, who had been caught with marijuana in their rooms. The reasons are long since unimportant, because the Madeira board of directors' first worldly act, after I left, was to tell these students they could come back to graduate. The chairman of the board had told me, "I support your decision completely." One can only forgive, I suppose. It must be very nerve-wracking to be on the board when the headmistress is indicted for murder. If it occurred to any of them that I was innocent they didn't bother to tell me.

There were mixed emotions among the girls about the expulsion. Some stopped by in groups of three or four and said they were sorry, but they supported the decision because it was the right thing to do if we really cared about the school's honor code. Other girls were incensed. One of them called an all-school meeting, read a poignant message, and then screamed "you fucking hypocrites" at the members of the faculty. The academic dean felt I was too hard on the girl when I called her in and laced her out. The dean followed her out of my house, spoke with her for a few minutes and then bounced cheerfully back. "I told her it would have been all right if she had screamed 'you fucking assholes,'" she said. "It was the word 'hypocrite' that made you mad." I have become so accustomed to that kind of language in prison, I tend to forget it was used at Madeira too.

The dean was partially right. The word "hypocrite" was a soul-searing word for me. Had anyone asked during most of my life, "Will the people of integrity please stand up," I would have stood up tall and straight without an instant's hesitation. As a young woman, I was so sure of my values and of what the right answers were. Now I was struggling to be sure. I had given a speech on the subject of integrity the summer before Hy's death at my alma mater, Laurel, a school for girls in Cleveland. The faculty and administration had asked me to give a "keynote address" at the seminar they were having. I spent two months thinking about integrity, and, as with so many things, the more I thought about it the more complicated it became.

Here, in part, is what I said:

The hard part today is not how you respond to values so much as deciding what the values will be. While I was growing up values were easy to list. Definitions were simple then, and patterns of behavior were so proscribed that soul-searching about integrity seemed an unnecessary activity. Today we can't even define who is dead, let alone who is behaving well. Sophistry and relativism didn't mar that wonderful, comfortable, platonic approach I grew up with. We were told, and we believed, that there is objective truth, and the highest truth has ethical value. We were told that the pursuit of truth and knowledge is an intrinsically good activity . . .

I think the best definition I have found of integrity is "unflinching adherence to high standards." The unflinching part is key, since you can only imagine a person of integrity constantly assailed from every corner, yet mature, responsible, and courageous enough to hang tough. To some there are rather prim, stern connotations about the word, something that smacks a bit of blue stockings. This is a stereotype we must rid ourselves of if we are going to teach integrity to young people in today's world. Unfortunately—or fortunately, whichever the case may be—the lonely cry in all of us not to be nothing, to make some sign upon the universe is not answered by proprieties. If you at Laurel, and the parents who send their daughters here, truly subscribe to the concept that "the individual is most productive in a climate of freedom of the intellect and of the spirit," we need to think deeply about the implications of that in today's world. A young woman of integrity has high standards, but they are not necessarily your standards or mine, and she is not necessarily your idea of "a good little girl." She is strong, imaginative, courageous, and she can give you a lot of grief.

Hy, in his considerable wisdom, never pondered on a subject as long as I. "God! You're like a dog with a bone," he said sometimes when I wouldn't let go. I read a quotation in *Harper's* recently that reminded me of Hy: "The powerful know that complexity is the province of underlings." It makes me smile.

I had written my Laurel School lecture as though only the young were struggling for answers. I had made the same mistake Dr. Buffy Miles, Madeira's consultant psychiatrist, made after Hy was dead. "Madeira students," she said, "are still in the process of forming and becoming, so they may be more seriously damaged by the indictment of their headmistress than grown-ups who are not in as vulnerable a stage of life as the girls."

It is a popular myth, but a myth nonetheless. We are "forming and becoming" all of our lives. As adults we are vulnerable too; in fact, the more we know and the more we understand, the more life will touch us. Children enjoy the circus; adults marvel at it. There is never a moment in our lives, in our society at least, when we "grow up." There is nothing simple like a lion to kill, or six months in the Outback to survive, and I say "simple" not disrespectfully but in the sense that these challenges have a specific beginning and ending. If you are a thoughtful person you spend your whole life asking "Why?" and "How?" and "Is this what I wanted?" or "Is this what they meant?"

Of all the myths that I grew up with (they seemed pleasant and safe and agreeable for the most part; in fact, it often saddened me that so many had been shattered and not replaced with equally agreeable ones) the most destructive, the one that left me most vulnerable, was the one that said, "Because you grow older—or when you grow older—you grow up." Not so. You appreciate more, you wonder more at the beauty and sadness of life, and you become familiar with some of the odds so you can avoid—or teach your children to avoid—things that usually turn out badly, like running in front of cars, or playing with matches, or engaging in sex before you know what love is.

But if you are a thoughtful person, and a reasonably brave person, wanting to live life fully, you will always be tempted to touch new kinds of fire, and then have to make peace with the person you were before. Having learned the rules—those absolutes right and wrong— you soon discover that as humans we seldom have the luxury of absolute choice between the two.

After Hy died, a dear friend, Gladys Rusk, wife of Dr. Howard Rusk, wrote me many warm, hopeful, heartfelt letters. She was dying of cancer at the time, one of those long, terrible, painful deaths. But she rarely mentioned herself. After her death Howard sent me some of the notes and quotes and favorite poems that she had collected in a special notebook over the years. Among them was this quotation from John Middleton Murry:

> *For the good man to realize*
> *that it is better to be whole*
> *than to be good*
> *is to enter on a straight and*
> *narrow path compared to which*
> *his previous rectitude was*
> *flowery license.*

More than anything I could put into words, this describes what I believed and what I lived by after I met Hy. Whether it is reason or rationalizing, wisdom or wishful thinking, for me it was true.

I had been proud of my relationship with Herman Tarnower for many years. We were two useful people, stimulating one another, sharing the pleasures of learning new things together, but living quite separate lives too. There had been many women in Hy's life. He was a bachelor, interesting, rich, with an ego that needed attention. He led a merry life, but that was something I carefully closed my eyes to or joked about. When his relationship with another woman began to rub off on my life in ugly, dirty ways, my personal struggle over integrity became increasingly complicated. It was a relationship that had gone on for years, and even when I moved as far away as Virginia it did not come to a halt. Should I walk away without flinching or stay without flinching? And how could I be objective enough to figure out the answer? It was one of many things troubling me deeply that bleak Monday in March, when I left the campus.

2.

The headline in *The Madeira Spectator*, the school newspaper, read "Dr. Buffy Miles Aids Madeira in Trying Times." The doctor is quoted as saying the girls "would have a hard time understanding the circumstances of the relationship between Mrs. Harris and Dr. Herman Tarnower." As far as I know she didn't question why Mrs. Harris wanted to die. At bottom, the circumstances of the relationship revolved around my need for strength, and my vain efforts to stop being a bleeding heart and be more like Dr. Tarnower.

Hy's strength came from caring first and foremost about himself, doing what he wanted to do, and doing it well. This is not a criticism. Quite the contrary. I believe, without a trace of rancor or cynicism, that the need to like and to love oneself is the first, most positive and productive rule of life. The absence of self-love in the women I live among today is probably their outstanding quality and their first tragedy.

For most of my life "self-love" had a selfish, pejorative ring to it. It wasn't "nice." I spent years looking for my self-esteem in others. But self-love doesn't preclude manners or systems or rules or laws or whatever name we choose to give the parameters within which each society lives. It says "Love yourself first, for good and positive reasons, and then reach out to love others." Don't spend a lifetime expecting to find your identity in mommy or daddy or husband or lover or children. It's an unfair burden to lay upon them, and it's a fool's errand right from the start because your identity can only be found where it is—in you.

People are constantly asking me whether I have changed in prison. Learning is by definition change, and, circumscribed as my life is today, it has opened up avenues of learning and understanding that my former life could never have made possible. I have learned much, about myself, and about others. Much to my surprise, I have learned that I am a survivor, something I never intended or even wanted to be.

The woman who stood by Hy's bed that night, raised a gun to her temple, took a deep breath, and pulled the trigger, is still alive, still functioning. Though there should have been a bullet in that chamber, and wasn't, I don't, as some people tell me, think God was saving me for something special. I think it was, as so much of life is, as Hy's death was, a roll of the dice, something without a plan or a sensible reason, something that shouldn't have been but was.

For several years I thought that Hy had taken most of me with him. For both our sakes I'm happy to discover that it isn't so. Who then is this media creature, this "convicted murderer" who put down the chalk one afternoon, after thirty-six years in a classroom, and walked out to a battery of flashbulbs and headlines and hype? Does anyone care who she is? I finally do, so something useful must have happened in these six impossible years.

But where do all the children who were a big part of the reason for writing this book come in? Where indeed? They are the children of inmates. They fill my life here at Bedford; they motivate me; they make me laugh; they break my heart. They teach me about a world I never knew. They frighten me about its future. I have learned from them, for the first time, how truly underprivileged many of America's children are, and I would like to shout it from the housetops. Children have been the center of my life almost since I stopped being one myself, but not the same children in the same way. The child I was and the children I raised were not average American children, however average and run-of-the-mill we may have seemed to ourselves.

For me there were summer homes and servants, private schools, and a family of six that ate every breakfast and dinner together, lunch too on Saturdays and Sundays and holidays, even if you came in late the night before. Whatever package it may have come in, there was security, total security, a world in which we never doubted that bad things only happened to bad people.

For my own children, the servants were missing, but the rest was there, and I soon learned to double in brass as laundress, plumber, cook, school teacher, as well as wife, mother, and hostess. After my divorce I even bought a round dining-room table so it wouldn't look as though someone were missing. Unfortunately, geometry notwithstanding, no matter where you put the placemats there are four sides to a circle. It took me a while to be convinced, but my children knew it right away.

My lessons here in this large and foreign world began on February 28, 1981, the day I was convicted of "murdering Dr. Herman Tarnower." Since that day those lessons have taken me from the prison kitchen in the medical building, where I scrubbed and cleaned and observed the advanced art of stealing food, to a high school equivalency class where I was called a "Teacher's Aide," to the prison nursery, to a program called South Forty, and finally to the Children's Center where most of my work is presently done. With the opportunity to be with young mothers and children I began to feel alive again, after almost two years of wandering through a deep fog. The more I saw, the more I wanted to learn and to share.

With a young friend, another inmate named Dolores Donovan, I began working on a book of children's letters to their mothers in prison. Dolores did most of the collecting, and I did most of the writing—that is, an introduction and a conclusion to tie all the letters together. It would be small, we thought, a simple little book. But nothing that touches human life is simple. By now I should have remembered that. Moreover, letters from children whose mothers are in prison are rarely cute or funny, the kind the public enjoys reading, those nifty little books we use as stocking stuffers.

Even the few pictures they draw are often sad. The subjects are sad and the lack of creative vitality and self-assurance that they reflect are sad as well. Here's a picture of a child crying, "Why did it have to be you, Mama?" The tears are almost as large as the child. Here's a child imagining the day mother will get out. "Free at last, Ma, free at last."

Here's a picture of mother, stick figure, no neck, arms protruding from the head, an average drawing for a three-year-old but not for the seven-year-old who drew it.

And here's a cheerful note under a better picture of mother, "You may be twenty-six, Mama, but you still got your looks." Encouragement like that means a lot.

But there were some who found the letters "boring" and "too much alike." I found them heart wrenching. When Dolores was granted clemency, I put them aside. "The public will only sneer at them anyway," I thought. "These letters could never mean to those outside what they mean to me. I *know* these children." One tends to grow egocentric in prison. "Nobody knows the trouble I've seen. Nobody but Jesus."

Happily it is not my nature to indulge in that kind of misery indefinitely. Too many things outside of myself are interesting and important to me, and with age, perhaps even a modicum of wisdom, things that once seemed separate and disconnected have begun to come together in my mind as a living whole. Things I had thought of as the "right thing to do," or "the kind thing to do," or "the intelligent and obvious thing to do" have begun to acquire a broad new relevance. And I realize now that the children's letters are only part of the story to be told.

It would be hard to find a woman who had lived out her life more totally steeped in all the comfortable mythology about America and Americans than I. But observing from a new place, experiencing, listening, searching, reading widely, and questioning have dispelled many of the myths. I finally know how true it is that ignorance is bliss, but only for the ignorant, and not forever, even for them.

The purpose of this book is not to make you cry, and certainly not to romanticize or sentimentalize crime, but to make you care enough to become actively concerned and curious, to unload a few myths of your own, and prepare yourself to make some hard decisions in the years ahead about the role of children in America's future. Is it possible to build a moral society for them based on little more than the constraints of punishment, inflicted quite often by wrongdoers?

If anything that follows sounds like a blow to feminism, that isn't my intent either. To all the ladies who have become president of the bank or a partner in the firm, I say, "Right on! And bully for you!" I also say someone with a good education, the ability to think logically, who knows what it means to have a good parent and be one too, better be having a few babies along the way. And, some feminists notwithstanding, once those babies are born, someone must raise them, someone knowledgeable and caring about the needs of children—which doesn't mean the first warm body you can hire to cuddle them in front of the soaps all day. I wish I knew how to arouse the same concern for children that so many Americans express today for fetuses. While people march on Washington, and throw bombs at Planned Parenthood offices, ostensibly for the unborn, I know of few marches in behalf of prenatal care for mothers or postnatal care for infants. If Simone Weil is correct, and "indignation is the purest form of love," I'm afraid we use up our indignation too early in the life cycle, and children spend the rest of their lives paying the piper. It was not just for the right to life that our much revered Mr. Jefferson thumped the drum. He added "liberty and the pursuit of happiness."

What follows is not, I repeat vehemently, not a feminine whimper from "the belly of the beast." I have not been there, and had I been there I would have little to offer that would serve ordinary people like you and me. This is a voice that once lived in the world you live in, the world which by your daily acts or failures to act, you help to create. What happens here reflects the values of your world. The women you meet here could be you. Their children could be yours.

Part
I

Cleveland Heights:

The Early Years

*Human language is a cracked kettle on
which we beat out tunes for bears to dance
to, when all the while we want to move the
stars to pity.*

Flaubert

1.

I am a stranger to you, all the more a stranger because you may have
read about me. Notoriety, painful as it is, is a most effective way to
become anonymous, lost and buried in verbal garbage. It may give
some validity to what follows if I describe to you as best I can, the
person I am, and how I came to see this piece of the world as I do.

It smacks of relativism, though relativism has a pejorative ring to it
in my ears, to suggest, as I will, that anyone in prison deserves more
than the back of one's hand. Perhaps I am an echo of my mother and
grandmother who lived out their lives believing that love conquers
all, not romantic love, but love for one's fellow man.

I don't remember either of them ever saying an unkind word
about another human being. Granted, they never experienced the
no-man's land of prison, but that doesn't screen one completely from
reality. Most of the wicked never go to prison. Less than 10 percent of reported violent crimes result in incarceration; of that 10
percent, 5 percent of the incarcerated are innocent. Even today
with over 500,000 people in prison, and more than ten million in
and out of jail during the course of a year, the beat goes on; someone
just committed perjury; someone is about to be hurt; someone just

1

rented a woman's body; someone just sold a quantity of drugs, and someone, perhaps an acquaintance or relative of yours, just bought it.

My own first brush with "those less fortunate than we are," our comfortable middle-class euphemism for the poor and the black, came many years ago, and I remember it vividly. I was a junior at Laurel School, a girls' college preparatory school in Cleveland, Ohio, a school like Madeira which the media always mistakenly refers to as "a finishing school." On Thursday afternoons Laurel juniors climbed into station wagons—they were new then and the sides were wood, not metal painted to look like wood—and drove to a Settlement House to do volunteer work. I had a music and story-telling group, and I went that first day feeling grown-up and secretly suspecting that it was terribly nice of me to be going at all. There was a certain drama about it. I was going to spread happiness all over the place for "those less fortunate than we."

The children in my group at the settlement house were eight to ten years old; there were more than twenty of them. They didn't want to hear a story, and they raised hell all afternoon. I think, looking back to my childhood, I had decided that if you were poor you were lacking something more than money and you owed it to society to compensate for your inadequacy. Many people still think the same way. I told my mother about what had happened, adding, "You'd think poor children could at least be polite." I've remembered her answer all my life, naive perhaps, but laced with deep truth. She said, "You know, Jean, most of these little children have mothers who go out to work, and when they get home they're just too tired to say 'No.'"

It isn't true of all tired working mothers all of the time; I know because I was one for many years, but it's true of some, and it's the beginning of tragedy, of not knowing what the boundaries are, floundering in space. "No," I learned early, can be a loving thing to say. One rarely convinces one's children of it until they begin to say it to their own children. But loving, I have discovered, is something many of the women I live among have had little of, while I, I realize late, have had much, or at least something that was meant to be love.

Indeed there has been much happiness in my life, so much to be grateful for—two fine healthy sons, a deep love, health, laughter, music, interesting work, good books, armfuls of zinnias, and dogs that wagged their tails in greeting when I came home, I wonder how my story could have such a sad ending. If I had to give only one reason I would blame it on physical weakness, the inability to keep slogging along anymore and a genetic whim that has touched more than one member of my family, the same thing that destroyed my father's life and caused an uncle to commit suicide. The psychiatrist would probably start with "your relationship with your father."

The forensic psychologist who tested me for hours after Hy's death said, "I believe from the beginning of your relationship with Dr. Tarnower you experienced what could only be called 'partial death.' You permitted part of yourself to be consumed by the relationship." My husband said once, "You'll never be happy because you don't know what you want." Maybe he was closest to the target, though certainly for a long time I thought all I wanted was to do "the right thing," to be sugar and spice and everything nice with a star in the middle of my forehead, a paragon of someone else's devising.

It never occurred to me that life is something you plan for, with your own list of priorities, not society's. The result, as I look at myself, was an earnest but wimpy character, running all the way, tripping along behind the world, trying to do all the things that were expected, or that I thought were expected, and finally giving up.

I was the last kid on the block to stop believing in Santa Claus; I cried when my doll was broken; I cried when my feelings were hurt; I was at college before I cared enough or dared enough to figure out what a virgin is. My trousseau was picked out by my mother, with a hat to match every dress. And I still have no sense of direction, so when the man at the gas station says, "Turn left, three more blocks and it's on your left, you can't miss it," I always miss it. I either know exactly where I am or I'm hopelessly lost, or I feel hopelessly lost. There were many times when Hy didn't know how to get where we were going, but he was always relaxed about it. If it isn't this street it's probably the next one. I always wanted to stop and ask.

As I think about it, the getting lost thing is important. When I made a wrong turn it wasn't annoyance I felt, it was sheer, stark terror. I once called Hy in tears from a gas station in White Plains and asked him to come and lead me home. I was sure from where I was that I was going to wind up on the Bronx River Parkway. Hy was kind, arrived shaking his head, and led me home.

Over the years when I was silly enough to say which way I thought we should turn, he would pat me on the knee, shake his head and say, "Well, there's one thing to be said for you, Jean. You're consistent. You're always wrong."

I don't try to be wrong, but it's been a long time since I was afraid to be. I made my way through most of my life like the man who broke the bank at Monte Carlo, with an independent air, but always aching for someone to hold me and assure me, "everything's going to be all right."

From the time I was a little girl I was told in a hundred different ways that there was "right" and there was "wrong" and "good" people do "the right thing" and "bad" people do "the wrong thing." It made sense, and it's a great timesaver. Any decision making was lifted from my hands leaving me ample time to do the things I enjoyed doing, like reading and writing, singing, swimming, and playing with the dog.

Hy played a key role in uninhibiting me, and he was not forever after glad. I stopped presuming to tell the world what the rules should be, but having discovered what they were, I didn't pretend it wasn't so. Hy, like most of his friends, was perfectly comfortable with immorality as long as nobody mentioned it, and everybody was nicely dressed. I always called a whore a whore. It isn't an endearing quality.

Feelings were something never discussed as I was growing up. The subject was treated a little like where babies come from. They were just something you kept to yourself. Hy preferred it that way too. My feelings were vented on the beach in Canada, where I spent my first forty summers, and later along the ocean in Palm Beach. I breathed them out to the wind and the waves and the hot summer sun. I swung my arms wide and breathed deep, and dove into the water and swam out far and swam for hours without a qualm or a fear.

The closest thing to the facts of life I learned in my parent's home was the message on a picture that hung down in the "recreation room." It was a picture of an old man and underneath it read, "My only regrets are the temptations I have successfully resisted." I thought it was funny and rather wicked, but I didn't know exactly why. Temptation, as any fool knew, was something "good people" didn't yield to, so he must be bad, and bad was sort of funny.

I was eighteen before I heard the word "divorce," at least heard it in a way I remember. Mother called my older sister and me into the library and told us in hushed tones that Mr. and Mrs. X, old family friends, were getting a divorce. Mr. X had met "a woman from Chicago." None of the scarlet ladies of history past or present could have aroused in my imagination a more despicable creature than "the woman from Chicago." I never even felt quite the same about Chicago again.

I pictured Mr. X eating solitary lunches at the University Club for the rest of his life. Certainly "nice" people would never have anything to do with him again. But of course they soon did. And Mrs. X? She started teaching school, and after her friends had all taken her to the movies a few times she went about the business of growing old— alone. But everyone always admired her tremendously.

The things you've been told often have little to do with the things you observe and experience. A healthy distrust of idealism is much to be desired and admired, but I didn't have it. I'm not sure you can always recognize the difference between high standards and flaccid, sentimental idealism, even in yourself, even when you're trying to recognize it. Sincerity itself is a much overrated virtue.

I was constantly telling someone that any good idea carried to its logical conclusion becomes an absurdity, but I didn't spend much time applying that statement to morality. It too, pushed past a certain point, can become moral fanaticism and quite incompatible with individual freedom and diversity. I think of myself as a very logical person, but a literal person, too, though the two are often mutually exclusive. I need clarity and definite answers. Hy relished detachment and ambiguity. He was quite comfortable in the moral penumbra that had settled over our world. I have talked glibly for years about how the young must be taught to be comfortable with life's ambiguities, but the truth is I have never been very comfortable with many of them myself.

For the first forty-two years of my life I boxed myself into a world of moral absolutes, and like Santayana's *Last Puritan* I hardly got so far as to feel at home in this absurd world. I was slow to realize that reason and goodness are sometimes secondary and incidental.

My "absolutist conscience" remained for years "a pretender, asserting in exile its divine right to the crown." "You can't tell Jean anything. She thinks she knows everything" was a familiar refrain as I grew up. My mother called me "Miss Infallible" when I was being too self-righteous to bear. When self-righteousness spilled over into overt rudeness she washed my mouth out with Lifebuoy, or even worse, wouldn't let me play with my doll house.

I never pinpointed anything I wanted of life until I had two sons, and wanted zealously for them to have healthy minds and bodies, and the strength and self-confidence I feigned but lacked; and then when I had met Hy to know he would always be there, to love and to run to, however far the run might be. All my life my prayer for each day was the same, "Watch over the family, and give me the strength to do what I must, and get through the day."

Freud said, "The unanswerable riddle of the ages is 'What does a woman want?'" Maggie Scarf in her book *Unfinished Business* asked, "What do women at various stages of their lives require in order to live?" I don't know the answer for others, but I suspect it is primarily a feeling of security, a knowing that somewhere reachable there is safe ground where for a little while at least the hurting stops, someone touches you or talks to you, or really listens to you, and the hurting stops. When that place is too far away, and one seldom gets there, and the pounding never lets up, sometimes a person gives up. One's inward life and outward life come together in an ill-timed, indigestible stew and throwing it all up isn't insanity, it's the only thing the brain and the body can do.

The brutal truth of this I found out on a Monday afternoon, March 10, 1980, sometime after 3:00 P.M. I left my office where I had served for three years as headmistress of the Madeira School, stopped at my secretary's office to say, "I'm leaving, Carol. I've had enough," and went home to write my will, a few personal notes, and gather together insurance papers that the boys would need. It was the culmination of ten years of a growing depression.

Whether it was a lifetime of feeling inadequate, or the mysterious chemistry of my brain that had led me to that point, I do not know for certain, but I will always believe it was the latter, an explosion of anguish over which I no longer had control, which I only knew had to end.

I hate the knowledge that I gave up, but given the same combination of pressures and traumas and hurts, I might do it again. Only might. I'm stronger now. And ten years of prescribed drugs about which I knew nothing, and Hy knew too little, are behind me as well. It wasn't fear of hard work or seven-day work weeks that did me in. The one true blessing until that day had been to be perpetually busy.

Yet in all the soul-searing, soul-searching months and years since Hy's death the one regret I have not felt is walking away from Madeira, and from a job that many people, both men and women, aspire to. I see that glorious view of the Potomac River stretched out as my front yard, and for me it is a picture of loneliness and impotence too deep to explore. It wasn't cowardice or self-pity or ineptness or jealousy that brought me down. It was simple unvarnished exhaustion from caring too much and trying too hard, and feeling utterly alone in the process. Intellectually I believe I know some of the answers to life's problems, but I couldn't seem to apply them to my own life anymore. I was a good teacher and an ineffectual self.

Perhaps it went way back to my growing up a priggish little girl and woman to the onlooker, but filled to the bottom of my soul with that immortal longing to love and be loved. If any character of the Bible had left his indelible mark on me it was wise old Noah. Two by two he welcomed them to the ark, and I don't think for a moment he'd have wasted time building it for any other reason. We are all needed by each other, without sharing there is only emptiness. I am not totally unrealistic. I know perfectly well that sooner or later someone has to empty the garbage and pay the grocer, but I'm still tempted, given the choice, to take one daffodil for ten shares of IBM.

Whatever it was that my father did to mold me into the kind of woman I became, I'm not sure; but most of the molding was done by default, never by sitting down and talking or sharing ideas. He was a difficult man. He was more than a difficult man. I'm afraid, he was a tortured man. His inner doubts came out in striving all his life to be very good at what he did, which he was—but in a deep, cancerous bitterness as well.

He really didn't like anyone. He died shortly after Hy did. I think the tragedy and turmoil of Hy's death hastened the death of both my parents. Dad's was a quiet and peaceful death and for that all of his children were grateful. It was the kind of death one would wish for all of us. Perhaps for him it was only fair. His life was not peaceful, and I do not believe it was happy. He avoided happiness almost as one would avoid a situation he knew he couldn't handle.

The only thing he really loved was his work. I grew up believing that nothing in the world was more important than "what Daddy did." He designed steel plants and oil refineries, some of the largest all over the world, from Magnitogorsk in the Urals to Brasília in the jungles of Brazil, from the panhandle of Texas to Oil City, Pennsylvania, from Trinidad to India and back. I loved hearing him talk about all the places he had been.

My summer in Russia several years before I met Hy was prompted by the bits and snatches of information about that great enigma that I had heard from my father. But it wasn't easy to get him to talk about anything but the job itself, Aramco, Bechtel, Standard Oil, Petróleo Mexicano—these were what peopled his world—not people themselves. I didn't understand all the reasons "Daddy" traveled so much, or what he did "at the office," but whatever it was I never questioned that it helped keep the world's wheels turning.

It was so important that no one, not even my mother, was ever permitted to call him at the office. It was all just too important ever to be interrupted. I remember the first time I called Hy at the clinic, hesitantly and apologetically, and was amazed that he didn't sound angry, or too busy to talk.

My father's professional life was colorful and successful. His home life was not. He seemed to need what I still feel was an inordinate amount of praise and thanks. I don't think I visited him for thirty-five years that I didn't some time early in the visit find my-self thanking him for sending me to college. There was never a mo-ment when he seemed to realize that his children were now doing all those same things—even paying taxes, something he never stopped believing was a very personal affront that Congress had meted out to him.

I don't remember my father ever hugging me, or holding me on his lap—or hugging any of us. I don't remember a special joke, or his saying something funny or silly. I know he loved Christmas and he wanted it to be special and wonderful for us. He was very generous, but somehow before the tree was up and it was time to enjoy, his temper over the lights, and where the pliers were, had frightened too much of the joy away. His anger terrified me. I can remember running to my room and wrapping a blue satin comforter over my head to drown out the sounds of it. Like Hy he was a bright, talented man. Unlike Hy he rarely took the time to enjoy. I don't remember his ever exclaiming over a full moon, or a beautiful fall day, or an armful of flowers.

From the time I was a little girl I was forever bringing flowers into the house, starting, I suppose, with dandelions and burdocks. Years later the first graders in my classes always loved Edna St. Vincent Millay's poem that ends "She said, 'Oh what a fine bouquet,' but later on I heard her say 'She's always bringing in those weeds.' " By the time I could drive at the cottage up in Canada I knew for twenty miles around where the fields of wild sweet pea or black-eyed Susan or tiger lilies or Queen Anne's lace and thistle were.

And all the farmer's wives would sow a row or two of zinnias and asters and calendulas in with the beets and carrots and lettuce. At least once a week I would gather buckets of flowers and then spend a happy part of a day arranging them. My son David now has the handsome blue mixing bowl that always spent August in the middle of the long dining-room table ablaze with every color of zinnia. How I wish my father might have enjoyed at least one such simple pleasure.

Hy found the same pleasure in trees that I found in flowers. I loved walking with him any time of the day, any time of the year while he exclaimed over a cut leaf maple, or worried about the way the three birches near the pond looked, and especially when he just breathed deeply and said, "God! Aren't we lucky." It was balm for all of life's wounds—whatever had hurt or ached ceased to exist. And sometimes when we stood there on a rainy day or a moonlit night or a cold, snowy morning and he put his arms around me I felt as though the whole world could fall down on me and I would walk away unscathed. I knew moments of peace and happiness and a blessed feeling of "safeness" with Hy that were beyond anything I could have read about or imagined.

When Dad was traveling, which was most of the time, I remember my childhood as peaceful and pleasant. The moments that come most quickly to mind are moments spent alone, lying on a large blue sofa with my feet up over the back of it, looking out the window at a huge flowering almond tree; walking along the road that led to the cottage, the elm tree that grew beside the gate, and a picture-book maple tree that grew in the wheat field just to the right of our gateway. It was too beautiful to cut down so Mr. Hill plowed and planted around it for years, until it was struck by lightning. I never stopped missing it after it was gone. The field always seemed eerie and empty.

Playing with my doll house was a favorite activity, rearranging furniture, giving names and personalities to the family of dolls that lived there, and often just lying on my stomach, peeking through the curtains at the dolls and the coziness of the house where they lived.

I enjoyed all kinds of make-believe—playing "school" and "office" were favorites. I can still see my dolls propped up on small chairs while I taught them the alphabet, or read them a story. To my parent's despair I was constantly retrieving old bills, and important-looking papers from the waste basket, carrying them around in an old pocket-book of my mother's, or sitting at my desk and making marks on them with red pencil. I remember a stack of old ledgers that my grandfather gave me as one of the great gifts of my life. They were from the little tobacco business that he owned and ran in Baltimore.

I played with them all the way home to Cleveland in the back of the car and stashed them in drawers all over the house. My mother called them "trash" and I said they were "important," so Jean's "important trash" became a familiar name and a familiar nuisance to the whole family. I think it took mother about three years, disposing of them a few sheets at a time, to get rid of the whole collection. But by then I was taking dancing lessons and singing lessons and piano lessons so it didn't matter. Mother loved music and theater as much as I did.

It was my mother that I telephoned for the first two years that I was in prison. I was permitted two five-minute telephone calls per month, scheduled at the convenience of the prison, not the prisoner. A guard dialed the number, and when Mother answered, a kitchen timer was set at five minutes. When the bell went off the conversation ended abruptly. The first of three shrieking, screaming, howling scenes that I have given way to in prison was over one of those calls. The C.O. (Correction Officer) found my mother's name, Mrs. Struven, too inconvenient to learn how to pronounce. He called her by her given name, "Mildred."

"This is Jean calling Mildred." It was bad enough to have this unsavory little man call me "Jean" when by directive he is required to call me by my last name, but to have him call Mother "Mildred" was like a knife in the heart. I howled with pain and trembled for hours afterward. It proved to be, of course, an open invitation to most of the C.O.s in the phone room thereafter to call Mother "Mildred" as disrespectfully as they dared.

Deliberate unkindness is something totally foreign to my nature. I am never prepared for it. It always shocks me, it always hurts me, and I usually respond to it in a way that makes the perpetrator want to do it over again. "You're just as big as the things that make you angry, Jean," was one of my mother's favorite remonstrances to me whenever she thought I was overreacting. I'm sure she'd have said the same thing if she had known about the telephone scene. It seemed a very large thing to me at the time.

Our conversations, Mother's and mine, were about everything except where I was: music, the theater, old friends, how the boys were. She always asked how I was and said I sounded fine, but she never once mentioned the word "prison." Her modus vivendi and mine were the same. We simply did not discuss what was unspeakable. It may not be wise but it's one way to survive. I would have sworn I was the last person in the family who would have done anything to hurt her, and I was the one who ended up hurting her the most. I asked her once if she intended to watch a much publicized television program about "the trial." She answered, "Why would I, dear? It has absolutely nothing to do with you."

By the time my father died they had been married for sixty-two years. How much of the woman she had been was left I'm not quite sure. There were sparks of the old humor, and always the love of music. The last time we spoke was on the hundredth anniversary of the Metropolitan, and we shared our pleasure over the televising of the celebration. Two days later, she died in her sleep. The last thing my sister heard her say was, "I've just had a nice talk with Dad." I didn't ask to go to her funeral. A prisoner goes to her mother's funeral in handcuffs and chains, with an armed guard beside her. I had brought her enough sadness. I would never have added more.

Because of the nature of some of my reading, and because I am the daughter of Mildred Witte Struven, I have thought a good deal about religion—thought about it more than I practiced it. I am a thoughtful person, but whether or not I am in any true sense a religious person I cannot say. I am forever taking the Lord's name in vain which is a poor beginning, and it was also a source of sorrow to my deeply religious mother. She, when pushed almost beyond human endurance, would say "doggone it" and then look a little embarrassed by her outburst. I think of Hy and my mother as archetypical survivors, one with an abiding faith and one with an abiding ego. Take your pick. Trying to think your way down the middle is idiot's delight.

I was brought up in the Episcopal church, but then where else for the "socialite headmistress of the exclusive Madeira School"? My sons were both confirmed in the Episcopal church, and we all attended church together regularly for years. I began to be a little disillusioned with the whole thing when I needed help and felt the church had turned its back, too consumed with its social life.

But maybe that isn't fair. Rewriting the service in the vernacular spoiled the lovely old familiarity, the feeling of "going home" I once had on Sunday mornings. Before Hy's death I went to church occasionally, but by then I never knew what page we were on. Considering what society was doing to all the other familiar things I had once found comforting and supportive, I think the church might have left the communion service alone for a little while longer—at least until the class of '45 "passed on."

I believe in God and in the very deep-seated human need for ritual, for doing a certain thing in a certain way repeatedly—not to make God happy but to make humans feel safe. You shouldn't have to decide about everything all the time. Although he was an atheist, H. L. Mencken's definition of religion in his *Treatise on the Gods* was one I found reasonable and understandable for years. I haven't the book with me but in essence he said, "Whether it's the hocus-pocus of a dancing Hottentot or the high incantations of a Catholic archbishop, religion is every man's effort to discover the power that controls his destiny, and to persuade that power to be kind." I think there's still a great deal of truth in that.

I realize, as I put myself through the agonizing paces of trying to look at myself objectively, that I am an unfortunate combination of my parents' two most sensitive qualities: my father's volatile drive to over-achieve, and my mother's infinite capacity to love and forgive. It's a self-flagellating combination. And yet I will always think of my life as essentially happy.

I don't even remember adolescence as a painful time, though over the years I've certainly read enough books assuring me it is supposed to be painful. Perhaps that is because I was more adolescent at forty than at fourteen. I have always loved reading, responded with plea-sure and excitement to new ideas, and enjoyed the peace and quiet of being alone. That triumvirate of traits removed a great deal of the pain of growing up, but it also slowed down the process.

I can still remember with great clarity some of the significant steps in my learning, and I can see now how each played a small role in developing the attitude that permeates my responses here at Bedford.

Mother was, as mothers are, my first teacher and her familiar homi-lies have stuck through a lifetime. "Judge people from the neck up, Jean"—that was an early admonition. It disturbed her that I had as a little girl been beguiled by curtsies and felt put out because she didn't require me to curtsy as my friends' mothers did.

"Look people in the eye and say 'How do you do.' A curtsy tells you nothing. Judge people from the neck up, Jean." I may have learned the lesson too well. One can be beguiled by talk as well as by curtsies.

I must have been about 2½ years old when my sister, Mary Mar-garet, read to me my first favorite story. It was about the old woman whose pig wouldn't jump over the stile, so she couldn't get home that night. Fire wouldn't burn stick, stick wouldn't beat dog, dog wouldn't bite pig, and the pig wouldn't jump over the stile. The logic of all that cause and effect was somehow very satisfying and orderly to my mind. Moreover you could make up endless variations of it on your own. I never tired of it.

2.

I don't remember learning to read, though for me it was much like being born. My first big remembered learning plateau was reached in second grade. I wrote some spelling words on the side of a painted green table, and my teacher saw it. It was my introduction to the word "cheating," and it was my first awareness that spelling was something difficult for me. I didn't know at the time that spelling would dog me all my life. I live with a dictionary on my lap and still send out letters that would horrify some of the good English teachers I have had. I don't know whether I'm forgetful or dyslexic. It doesn't much matter now. The results are the same.

In the third grade I helped to build a papier-mâché castle, complete with moat and turrets and drawbridge and portcullis. Miss Vincent was the lady who let us build it, and I thought of her often when my own classroom was awash with fingerpaints and torn strips of paper and pans full of paste made from flour and water. The castle, which I remember as a splendid castle, taught me there is a thing called history and that history is about people and how they live. It made history a tangible reality.

I cheated again during a fifth grade English test when the question was "What is Deuteronomy?" I copied from somebody else, but she didn't know the right answer either. "Two heads," I have often assured students when I saw them copying, "are not always better than one." After the fifth grade I made my own mistakes. The first question on the history college board I took in 1940 was "How was Delcassé the nemesis of Bismarck?" I had never heard of Delcassé and I didn't know what nemesis meant. Fortunately, it was before Smith was hard to get into.

I haven't been afraid to say, "I don't know" ever since, as student or teacher. I don't enjoy saying it, though, and many of the times that I have had to are still fresh in my memory. Knowing right answers was my security blanket as a student. When I didn't know them I stood naked. Later, when I was the only woman in the room who wasn't married, when I went places because I was "the headmistress" or "Dr. Tarnower's girl" not because I was me, clothes became my security blanket. Whatever they all thought, at least I looked as good as they did.

In seventh grade I learned the word ethnic and made an ethnographic map of the city of Cleveland. I was struck by the fact that when Hungarians came to Cleveland they settled where other Hungarians lived, and Chinese sought out other Chinese, and so with Italians and Swedes and all the others. Up to that time I had belonged to the Great American Melting Pot School, but something about those pinks and greens and blues made it very clear to me that people reach out for what is familiar, what makes them feel safe. People need people who understand them and share their values. The melting pot myth was one of my first to bite the dust. Millions of Americans still believe in it, which is one of the reasons, I suppose, that running for political office in America is such a chancy, difficult, frustrating thing.

Mr. Purvis was my civics teacher that year. I must have liked him very much because he was the only teacher I ever asked to "please write in my pink autograph book." He wrote, "To the spirit of the Phoenix with great good wishes." I had to look up what the Phoenix was and I have absolutely no idea why he wrote it. Perhaps even then the round-bottomed doll that you beat on, but it always bounces back, was taking shape.

I learned to write a proper research paper at Laurel School: outlining, footnoting, bibliographies, all the useful proper stuff. The first substantial independent research paper I wrote was in my senior year at Laurel and was on the Federalist Papers. I had the good fortune to go to Washington that spring, and was allowed to walk into the Rare Books Room in the Library of Congress, without fanfare or special privilege, and hold in my hands, and read from Hamilton's and Madison's and Jay's own copies of the papers, complete with their notes jotted in the margins. The experience was another leg up for my sense of the reality of history, and my personal understanding that the men pictured in Muzzey (our history text) had actually touched my life. It was 1940, and on that same trip we sat in the Senate one night late and watched the Lend-Lease Bill be passed.

I went to Smith College because I heard that Smith didn't have sororities. I knew little or nothing about sororities, but I imagined them as something that would make me extremely uncomfortable. They invoked my two least favorite words: "boyfriend" and "girl-friend." (That was before I fell over "mistress" and "lover.") I have never been much of a joiner, and I pick friends slowly, not in packs, and not because they know the secret handshake. I couldn't picture myself standing around in a dark room, wearing a long robe, carrying a candle and swearing to do or die for Beta Theta Pi. It wasn't snobbery. It was simply a matter of knowing my own limitations.

My years at Smith were not what one would call "normal." Pearl Harbor was bombed that first December, and the war in Europe ended just before the class of '45 graduated four years later. "The bomb" was still to be dropped. When I read about the war now, years later as an adult, not in *The New York Times* as it happened, it shocks me to think how little it touched me, how appallingly unaware I was of the enormity of what was happening. I have often reminded myself of that when I found the self-absorption of the young particularly galling. For the most part, I dug into an unused storage room in the basement of the Smith library and read for four years.

"Prudish" would probably be a kind description of what I was at Smith, still afraid to take a very honest look at life, still not tempted by the secrets on the other side of childhood. My senior year I took a seminar on international cartels with Mr. Orton, a delightful, tweedy, pipe-smoking Englishman who had been a member of the British Labour Party. There were five of us in the course, and we met at Mr. Orton's house, not far from campus.

The girls stopped one day on the way there to buy a bottle of wine, a daring act in those days. Mr. Orton brought out wine glasses and started to pour. I stopped him at my glass with, "Oh, no thank you. I don't drink." He smiled pleasantly and said, "Well far be it from me, my dear, to lead you down the primrose path," and poured a little extra wine into his own glass. It was one of those uncomfortable moments when I finally realized I was out of place and rather silly.

Mr. Orton has another special place in my memory. The last lecture he gave in one of his courses began like this: "Well I hope by now you are all thoroughly confused." I suppose others may know instinctively that the first step to real learning is figuring out what the questions are. The answers come much later, and perhaps never. But hearing it said out loud made a difference to me. His whole lecture that day seemed wonderfully relevant to me. I sat there listening and enjoying, and trying to write down every word. I still have the notes.

My major was economics, which happily was still a philosophy course in those days. A young man named Keynes was just beginning to be heard from, and a philosophy was about to be renamed or at least finally taken seriously as a science. I think today there are many who might suggest putting it back into the philosophy department. The two college courses that have meant most to me over the years, enriched my life by making me far more aware of the world around me, had nothing to do with economics. One was geology, the other was the history of art. Marshall Schalk, the young instructor of geology who taught me, has been professor emeritus for twelve years now, and writes occasionally to tell me about his grandchildren, and to wish me well. It pleases me that he remembers me. Over the years I have encouraged hundreds of young people to take at least one course in geology and one in art history.

I may have learned a little more about how to think at Smith. A remarkable woman named Esther Cloudman Dunn certainly did her best to make me think, and so did Mr. Orton, and Esther Lowenthal, and others. But I don't remember having much courage in that area until years later. My teachers, right back to the first grade, would say I always thought for myself, but it wasn't so.

I asked a lot of questions, but for all practical purposes, I was monolithically establishment for more than forty years, sure that if the textbook said it, or *The New York Times* said it, or the teacher or the bishop or the Junior League said it, it must be the straight stuff. I clung tenaciously to safe "right" answers. Probably for that reason I graduated Phi Beta Kappa and magna cum laude. The satisfaction that being elected a Phi Beta gave me was contained in the few minutes it took me to race back to my dormitory to call and tell my father before he left for the office.

Twenty years later when I earned my master's degree I could no longer avoid the fact that my thoughts were as valid as the teacher's, even if they weren't the same, even if they were wrong. When I finished an M.Ed. I thought seriously of earning a Ph.D. in philosophy. I wrote a long, earnest paper for my philosophy professor and handed it in feeling that it was very wise and very significant. The professor gave me a B— on it, and his only comment was, "You're a hopeless idealist." The Ph.D. was forgotten. Later I told Hy, "I've earned my doctorate in you." Since his death, I have learned to my sorrow, that I was no better versed in Hy than in philosophy. Another B—.

Grosse Pointe:

Mrs. Harris

I was married in 1946, the year after I graduated from college. I fell into wifehood, and motherhood, and Junior Leaguehood because that's what girls did, not because I thought it through, listed the options, and made a choice. That's not to say I think it's a poor choice. Quite the contrary. I often said to the girls at school, when we were talking about their wonderful plans for the future, "Remember, the best thing there is is a happy marriage." A senior said to me one day, "I can't believe you said that, Mrs. Harris. I really can't believe you would say anything that dumb." A freshman whose mother had been married five times said, "God! If I thought that I wouldn't want to go on living." I was always delighted to find some happy traditionalists in the group who looked forward to marriage and motherhood. Indeed, they are almost the new breed of nonconformists.

I was married to James Scholes Harris and divorced nineteen years later. He was a very nice man. But then this is almost a very nice story. I had known Jim since I was seven years old and he was ten. His family owned a summer cottage near ours in Canada. He was born and brought up in Grosse Pointe, Michigan, the son of Albert and Helen Harris. His mother was a handsome woman, and a very decent scout, though her first question about anyone was invariably, "Who was her mother?" and out would come the Social Register. My own mother's approach was, "I don't care who she is, I expect her to behave."

In spite of obvious differences in their list of priorities, our mothers

got along very well. Our fathers were something else. Mr. Harris—
everyone called him "Butts"—was a great favorite of mine from the
time I was a little girl. He was short and funny and had a most
congenial smile. If he ever got terribly angry, it wasn't when I was
around. Even the day Jim threw a firecracker and it exploded on the
canvas top of his father's new convertible, he showed great restraint.
On weekends he used to sit with me out on the cliff overlooking the
lake and watch the cranes fly by.

He had a wonderful library of hundreds and hundreds of books, and
he had read them all. I can see him now in the middle of a conversation about almost anything, get up, take down a particular book, flip
through it a minute, chuckle and say triumphantly, "Here! Read this.
Read this, you'll love it." And I always did. H. L. Mencken was a
particular favorite of his and mine—in spite of the things he said
about Roosevelt—but then so were Conrad, and William James, and
Trollope, and dozens more. He didn't make you analyze them, he just
used them to make the subject of the moment mean more. I was given
most of his books when he died, and I have packed and unpacked and
carried them about for years, reading them, treasuring them, but
finally having to give most of them away for want of space.

My fondness for Butts made him a particular target of my father's
criticisms, but his unforgivable sin was political. Butts voted for
Roosevelt four times! His devotion to Roosevelt was deep. The
Harrises lived for years on a little lane called Roosevelt Place. In 1936
the staunch Republicans on the block tried to have the name changed
to Theodore Roosevelt Place. Butts fought them and won, but old
friendships were strained beyond repair in the process. I'm not sure it
was worth the price, but I admired the man very much. He was kind
to me and I wish he had lived long enough for my sons to know him.
He would have filled a very large void in their lives.

Jim, like his father, was an attractive man, more easy-going, not
intellectual. I can't think of any enemies he ever had. He had a kind
word for just about everyone, and usually took the time to say it. He
went to the University of Michigan, became a Deke, drank beer and
schlepped around until the university and his father agreed that the
navy was a better place for him.

The Second World War had just begun. He ended up as a lieutenant in the Naval Air Corps and spent several years in places like Ottumwa, Iowa, and several years in places like Green Island, in the South Pacific. He was a navigator on a PBY, picked up pilots out of the ocean, and won the Bronze Star and the Navy Cross. Like many men of his generation he remembered the war years with nostalgia and real affection.

We were married in May 1946 and divorced in 1965. He was a good husband by lots of standards and definitions: no heavy drinking, no extra-curricular women; he cut the grass every weekend and edged the garden, and played baseball with the boys, and thoughtfully asked, "Where do you want to go to dinner?" On weekends we played bridge with old friends, or went to a country club dance. In the summer we chartered a boat with friends, and sailed up into Georgian Bay, or had friends visit us at the cottage in Canada which my father had given us. In winter we took the boys skiing from the time they could barely walk, and usually stayed with friends in an old school-house they had converted to a ski chalet.

What sense does it make to divorce a nice man and a nice life like that? I don't think even he knew the answer and I could never quite explain it myself. When the divorce was final he had said, "All right. You've gotten that out of your system, now let's grow up and get married."

That I write little of Jim does not in any sense diminish him as a very decent man, or reduce him to an irrelevancy. Given his choice were he alive to be asked I'm sure he would say, "Include me out." He wanted to be a good father, and I know his sons remember him with true affection. I find it hard sometimes to remember him. Our life together was a period of marking time, of doing what nice young couples do—or did.

The two things I can remember arguing about with him he was right about, though I certainly didn't think so at the time. He read the newspaper with a proper amount of worldly wariness. I was sure it must be so "because the paper said so." And I was always so smugly positive when I thought I was right. He said people ultimately acted out of self-interest; they did what they did because they wanted to. Not so, said I. Many people acted as they did "for a higher reason. What about the mother who plunges into the sea to save her drowning child?" I asked, sure that the example settled the question. "She does it because she loves the baby and wants it safe—not for the baby but for herself," he answered.

I thought most of us were "nobler" than that. Why I thought it I don't know. It was the accepted mythology of the day, I guess. It sounded so "un-nice" to do something just because you wanted to do it. I didn't leave Jim because he did something "wrong," or I did something "wrong." I wasn't suddenly seized with a burning desire to kick over the traces, do something wild and irresponsible. I simply needed to fill the void that I was finally aware my life consisted of. And it didn't even occur to me that not loving was part of the void.

Years ago *Life* magazine had an article on different kinds of music, and how musical tastes reflected whether you were "upper class, upper middle class, lower middle class, or lower class." My favorites, the golden oldies, were "lower middle class" right across the board. I was in good company though. Cole Porter, Rodgers and Hart, and Noel Coward were there too. Music speaks to me in special ways. The way the aroma of a bakery or a special garden can evoke a whole part of someone's life in one delicious deep breath, a song can bring back moments in my life or express something I can't say in any other way. There were songs, lower middle-class songs if you will, that said to me there is more to life than this.

I used to try to get Jim to talk about the future—some of the things we'd do together, as a family or later when the boys were grown up and on their own. The furthest ahead he ever got was "when the boys get ready for college we can remortgage the house." "Is that all there is? Is that all there is—if that's all there is my friend then let's keep dancing." Right now, right this minute what is an ordinary person like me doing on the other side of the world? What is she thinking, what makes her happy, will she have to gather twigs to make the fire for dinner? Will the parameters of my world always be Jefferson and Lake Shore and Mack Avenue?

I remember one night after we'd been out for the evening, Jim was asleep and I put on my coat, a good black one with a pretty mink collar that is still tacked on a suit or something. I went out to the boys' play yard and swung on a swing and then stretched out on the sand and looked up at the sky and felt a kind of inexpressible longing and frustration. It consumed me. I was part of the sand and part of the trees and part of the earth and I felt not yet born, but maybe, just maybe about to be.

A few nights later the boys were in bed, I had tucked them in and done all the right stuff, I thought, and now my schoolwork was spread on the living room floor and I was planning lessons for tomorrow. But Jimmy kept turning his light on and not going to sleep and Jim went up and put him back to bed and on the way checked the toothbrushes in the boys' bathroom, a favorite activity of his. They were bone dry. I hadn't seen them perform the rites of the toothbrush.

Jim was very cross, and suddenly as he stood there in the living room reviewing my misdemeanors and oversights, I knew it was the end of the marriage. There wasn't an ugly scene or even much of an argument. I simply said, "Jim, it's 10:30 and starting right now I'm not your wife anymore." It was all very civilized and painless for me, not for David and Jim. When they were finally told, they couldn't understand what it meant. They had liked our life the way it was.

It all smacked of Dick and Jane. If the house on Hillcrest had had a white picket fence around it, and the Kerry Blue Terrier named Bonnie had been a brown-and-white thing named Spot, you could package it and sell it to Scott Foresman.

It had never occurred to me that I would become a "working woman." My job-hunting was prompted in large part, I think, by my fear of women. I enjoy housecleaning, fussing to make the guest room look pretty, and arranging flowers and such. I do not enjoy women's card parties and luncheons. I am afraid of women. I have spent my entire life, whenever I found myself in a roomful of them, feeling totally out of it, suspecting everybody there knows something I don't know. Secrets! I haven't a single recipe anyone would want; I hated having another woman come into my kitchen, and I was devoutly grateful that they didn't come into the bedroom.

Cute names are my nemesis—Pinky, Punkey, Petey, Suki, Ceci, Kiki—my life has been punctuated by them, each with a tennis racquet slung casually over the shoulder, and a needlepoint cover that zips into place and matches the rick-rack on the tennis dress. A group like that can intimidate the hell out of me, even if I'm thinner, or soberer, or even ostensibly in charge.

Job hunting was a convenient escape hatch. And the closest thing to where I lived that hired women was a private school. It isn't an inspiring beginning to what was to become a happy and successful lifetime career as a teacher, but that's the way it began.

Teaching wasn't the last thing I wanted to do, but if I had ever made a list it would probably have come somewhere near the end. My interest in it grew in spurts as bit by bit I discovered ways to share my own pleasure in learning, and as I discovered the books of great educators. Alfred North Whitehead was a name I had never heard when I found a copy of his *Aims of Education* with nothing more to speak for it than that it was lying on a table of old paperbacks and marked 10¢. I read it. I devoured it, and was never quite the same again.

Jerome Bruner's *The Process of Education* confirmed what I had already discovered in a first grade classroom—any subject, at some level of understanding, can be taught to children of all ages. When an infant learns that the ball is round he has begun the study of geometry.

A. J. Nok's book *Memoirs of a Superfluous Man* had a healthy irreverence about many things, learning among them. He helped me lay to rest the notion that "the right answer" is always the most important thing. He also had a kind word for educational elitism, an important fact of life that Americans persist in feeling squeamish about.

My "cause" became helping young people to discover the adventure of learning, and the sheer pleasure of it. It was always that for me; it still is, and my modus operandi as a teacher was always with that in mind. I have taught every age group from nursery school to senior American history, but first grade was always my favorite. For the youngsters I worked with the love of learning was still so spontaneous, so untarnished, there was virtually nothing that didn't pique their curiosity. They weren't afraid to be wrong, and they didn't learn in little boxes—everything was relevant. This is where the line is drawn, the terrible difference between rich and poor. The children of suburbia can be just as full of hell, and just as devious as any other children—in spite of all the good stuff Mom has told them. But they are excited by life. They have been praised, and urged to walk a few steps farther. They believe if they get involved they can make something happen, and they can't wait to see what the something may be.

Reading is a pleasure that has enriched my life, and it was one that I shared with Hy from the very beginning. His first gift to me was a book. We didn't have the same favorite books, but then we were two such different people. I reread *The Brothers Karamazov*, and everything by Loren Eiseley and Edna St. Vincent Millay. He reread Gibbons and everything by Churchill.

Dostoevsky's passage from *The Brothers Karamazov* about the Grand Inquisitor I have read and reread many times, sometimes as the Grand Inquisitor, bearing the truth alone and keeping the masses content; sometimes as the masses, wishing someone on high would toss me a comforting lie. I used to say to my husband, "What will it be like ten years from now, Jim? Where will we be? How will we grow? Lie to me a little. Let's pretend."

But my very honest, very logical, very pedantic husband wouldn't do it. Couldn't do it. Now, I live in a world of perjury, lies and dissembling, where truth is often ignored or sneered at, where it is actually despised by some. "You'll never be happy, Jean, because you don't know what you want." Ah, those moments that come home to roost.

As for Edna St. Vincent Millay, every woman must find herself somewhere in those poems. And every man would find someone he has loved there if he bothered to look. I don't think she is read much in English classes today. She isn't abstruse. You don't have to read the footnotes to figure out what she means. I have wiped my tears on the corner of my apron, and thought of Penelope, "Penelope who really cried." I sat on the side of my bed holding a bouquet of flowers that last night, while Hy hugged his pillow and said he wouldn't talk, and remembered:

> *Love in the open hand, no thing but that,*
> *Ungemmed, unbidden, wishing not to hurt,*
> *As one should bring you cowslips in a hat*
> *Swung from the hand, or apples in her skirt*
>
> *I bring, you calling out as children do,*
> *Look what I have—And these are all for you.*

It was the last line I had always loved especially. I didn't know until Hy had died it was from a collection of her poems called "Fatal Interview."

I love humorous books and I laugh readily. I am told that a true sense of humor means seeing ourselves as others see us. I am not able to do that, although there are people who find me "funny." My humor, for want of a better word, usually consists of saying something ridiculous about myself before someone else beats me to it. I have no conception at all of how others see me. When from time to time I am forced to hear, it often leaves me shaken, or puzzled, or hurt, and always eager to avoid hearing more. And for reasons that I don't pretend to understand, kindness or praise leaves me far more shaken than unkindness.

Both Hy and I had wonderfully eclectic collections of books. Neither of us read many novels, though I enjoyed some of them more than Hy did. I think he felt his reading time was wasted if he didn't finish a book knowing something specific he hadn't known before; the difference between the Sunni and Shiite Moslems; the history of guerrilla warfare; the history of China; the origin of the Jewish tribes. This sort of thing excited his interest. Character development in a novel was something he didn't have the patience to think about, and too much stuff about inter-personal relations was "silly as hell." The one magazine he always read and enjoyed was *Encounter*, a British monthly. He used to mark things for me to be sure to read and finally he just gave me a subscription.

After Hy had died and his house was sold, my lawyer and I were permitted to go back to examine his room. Everything was changed. Everything was gone—except his books! The big coffee-table-things he never read were gone. Someone took the Harvard classics, but the others, the ones he loved and read and reread had all been left behind.

The books that sat for years right over his bed because he reached for them so often are still sitting there. It made me realize in the starkest possible way that the man I had known and loved, and the man others had known and professed to love, were two quite different people. His books would have been the first thing I'd have packed. It was heart wrenching, standing there in his bedroom, answering a lawyer's questions, trying to be helpful, trying not to see how much of him was still there in the room. I wanted to take the books over his bed and sweep them up in my arms and run away with them. But they belong to strangers now.

New York:

The Fateful Year

1.

The last significant learning epiphany of my intellectual life, if it can be called that, before I sat in a court room, that is, and learned about justice, came in 1966, a watershed year for me—the end of one life and the beginning of another.

I was divorced after almost twenty years of marriage, and left Grosse Pointe, Michigan, where I had lived those years, and with my sons David and Jim, moved to Philadelphia. I stopped being a full-time teacher and became a school administrator, unable to turn down the head-turning salary of $10,000 a year. I began to investigate a new course called "Man: A Course of Study," and on December 9th of that fateful year, I met Dr. Herman Tarnower. It was knowing and loving Hy that ultimately brought me to prison. It was that long ago course that has helped me to survive in prison, and to see with a certain amount of clarity what is going on around me.

"Epiphany," Webster's tells me, is an "intuitive grasp of reality through something simple and striking." My reaction to the course was exactly that. The course had begun to take shape in 1963 when a group of teachers and social scientists from all over the country met to consider ways to improve the teaching of "social studies"—a junk term that meant a little of anything. Units like "My Friend the Policeman," or "My Friend the Grocer," were boringly predictable, and they didn't get to the heart of the matter, which is humanness. "What is human about a human being? How did he get that way? How can he become more so?" were the questions around which the course was built. With the help of anthropologists like Donald Oliver, Irven deVore, Niko Tinbergen, Konrad Lorenz, the course took shape. Jerome Bruner took a year's leave of absence from his position as head of the Center for Cognitive Studies at Harvard to head the project.

To create the course, which was directed at children in the fifth grade, but is appropriate for all ages, meant giving children access to materials about animal groups and simple human societies, studies that were just then giving birth to the new science of ethology. Ten years later Tinbergen and Lorenz shared the Nobel prize for science with Karl von Frisch. It was the first time that ethology had been so recognized.

There are many themes woven through the course: What is learned and what is innate behavior? How does the structure of our bodies determine our behavior? Why are human babies born so helpless? What role does our dependency upon our parents play in shaping the creatures we become? What are some of the patterns of behavior in the relationship between children and adults? What are cultural behavior patterns and what are individual behavior patterns? Why is learning the human imperative? How does learning increase our range of options and adaptive behavior? What is "acceptable behavior" and how do we decide?

It is difficult to explain how deeply this course affected my thinking and my teaching and my living. It certainly made living more interesting to me, and enriched all my travels. I was much more tolerant of other cultural values and behavior after I had taught the course, and I finally understood W. H. Auden's line, "You shall love your crooked neighbor with your crooked love."

The teacher's manual observes, "We hope the students will gain a new perspective on themselves and the culture they share through an understanding of another way of life, and that they will develop a vocabulary for thinking about the human condition in ways that will assist them in coping with the immense cultural distances that divide the modern world."

What better preparation could one have for going to prison?

I met Hy at a dinner party that Marge and Leslie Jacobson gave. Marge had called me and said, "Jean, there's someone I want you to meet. He's a bright, interesting man, you'd be great together. You like the same things." I was living in Philadelphia by then. David and Jim were at Chestnut Hill Academy and I was working right next door as director of the Middle School at Springside. My father always called it "Springdale or whatever." A trip to New York, even including Marge and Leslie's hospitality was a big budget item, and I gave it some thought. Should I go all the way to New York for a dinner party? Before it began, that dinner party was a "special occasion," and almost from the moment it ended, my life became "a special occasion."

I don't know who else came to the party, but I remember Hy and me sitting on a sofa talking the evening away, interested, enjoying one another, showing off about our recent trips to Russia, trying to be clever and laughing at ourselves as we were to do so many times again. At 11:00 P.M. sharp with the party in full swing, a bell rang: Henri van der Vreken, Hy's chauffeur, had arrived for Dr. Tarnower. Hy rose, said his goodbyes, and like Cinderella, bid a hasty retreat. I hadn't yet learned that leaving the party early was Hy's custom, and nothing and nobody would ever change it.

I was disappointed to see him go: I thought he had been enjoying the evening as much as I, and I went to bed thinking I would probably never see him again. A few weeks later he sent me a copy of Yaguel Yadin's book *Masada* with a card that read, "It's time you learned more about the Jews, Hy Tarnower." His Christmas note was more traditional and read, "You were a delight to be with. I kept wondering if you could keep up the pace."

I wrote and thanked him for the book and said it had arrived at a perfect time because I was in the hospital for minor surgery. He responded at once with a dozen red roses. For the next two years he must have supported a florist in Germantown who delivered dozens and dozens of roses. They were there waiting for me when I came back from New York; they were there when I couldn't get to New York; they were there cheering me, warming me, wooing me, watching me fall completely in love with the sender. And it wasn't the sound of one hand clapping, for Hy was falling in love too.

He hardly overwhelmed me with attention after the Christmas card. Hy moved, as he would always move, in his own good time. He was always on time for everything, but he never rushed. He walked slowly, "the cardiac shuffle" he called it. He planned his next move well ahead of time, and when it suited his purpose he had the patience of Job. Finally he wrote. He had planned a safari in Kenya that February and would be back the first week in March. Was there any chance I might be in New York that week? There was. I would be attending meetings of the National Association of Independent Schools.

I left the Friday afternoon meetings early to buy a pair of black shoes at I. Miller—splurging. I still have the damned shoes—they've worn better than I did. Hy picked me up at the Barbizon Plaza at 7:00 P.M., Henri driving the big blue Cadillac which looked to me, seven Cadillacs later, like the one he was driving the day he died. His explanation: "You know what people think of Jewish doctors who drive big Cadillacs. I enjoy a new car but I don't enjoy advertising the fact that I have one."

We had dinner at one of those little New York restaurants where you order something special, ahead of time, and the chef comes out and tells you he hopes you enjoyed it. Hy beamed happily. He was like a kid with a new girl. The months before we met had been lonely ones for him. His constant companion had grown weary of waiting for a wedding ring and had left him to marry someone else. Other women had done the same thing over the years, but this one had upset him deeply. He was fifty-six years old, approaching the point of no return. He still believed that the complete social acceptance he ached for required marriage, and he still couldn't bring himself to make that commitment.

You might say Mrs. Harris dropped by while the doctor was nursing a broken heart—cracked anyway. But his powers of recovery were splendid. I didn't know until after Hy died that as soon as her marriage failed the old friend was back on his doorstep—the door to his bedroom that is, furious to find that I had entered the picture. Apparently the anger has never subsided. She is one of the few people who has vented her wrath through the media, making outrageous statements about me, a woman whom she has never even met and one who for many years felt a kinship and concern for her.

After I was convicted of murdering Hy and had been sent to prison, I received this letter:

I was Dr. Tarnower's lover before he met you. He couldn't possibly have hurt you any more than he hurt me, but I wouldn't have murdered the man.

His friends and I are glad that you are in prison, and we hope you die there.

I don't know who the author is, or where she came in the pecking order of Herman's playmates, but she isn't one of my favorites, whoever she is. I realize now, as I take the time to think about it, that the question is not why I fell in love with Hy, but what in the name of God he saw in me. What needs did I fill in the world he aspired to live in?

We left the restaurant and headed for the bar at the Pierre, a favorite place of mine ever since. Hy had two Manhattans, almost unheard of for him; I had two whiskey sours, almost unheard of for me. We talked about politics. I had met Richard Nixon a few weeks before at a dinner party in Philadelphia, and remember predicting that they certainly couldn't seriously consider running him for president. But most of the time we danced. Hy was a marvelous dancer, "The sine qua non of bachelorhood" he laughed. He was graceful and full of rhythm. The stuffy side of him, and there was a very stuffy side, was left behind when he danced. The stuffy side of me, and there is a very stuffy side, was left behind when I danced with Hy.

Years later when we were dancing at the Century Country Club one night, and I felt as I always did when I danced with Hy—sailing two feet off the floor—he said, "You know, you're a helluva good dancer. But you sure were stiff as a board when I first met you." This didn't come as a surprise. My husband had always said in a half teasing, half serious way, "Okay sweetie pie. Let's have the duty dance."

Two weeks after our first date was spring vacation, and the boys and I went to New York for the weekend. Friday night I took them to see *Mame*, their first New York play. Saturday night old friends of Hy's gave a dinner party for his fifty-seventh birthday. It was the first of thirteen birthdays I would celebrate with him. We celebrated it in Nepal, in Hong Kong, in Hawaii, the Bahamas, Purchase, all over the world. It wasn't until eight years later that Hy discovered when my birthday was—quite by accident. He never asked and I never told him.

That Sunday the boys and I drove to Hy's house for lunch. I still remember the curried shrimp. It was my first glimpse of the house on Purchase Street, a place that was like home to me for many years.

I visited Hy three or four times in the next two months. He came to

Philadelphia, he called every evening at 6:30, he wrote and sent flowers. I stayed at Hy's friends Arthur and Vivian Schulte's house in Armonk when I came. The largest problem was seldom being alone with him.

Hy loved to give and go to dinner parties. I didn't. One weekend when he had promised we wouldn't go to any, I arrived to find Saturday night booked with a dinner party so fancy he hadn't been able to bring himself to refuse. We took a long walk that afternoon, sat on a hilltop where we could look out over Long Island Sound, and later, as he drove off to dinner, I drove back to Philadelphia.

I learned very early on that dinner with the Wasps in Grosse Pointe and dinner with "Our Crowd" in New York involved very different rituals. The two groups worshiped different idols. In Grosse Pointe it was the martinis. In New York it was the food. Dinner was later in Grosse Pointe because of the martinis—but mercifully people drank them instead of talking about them. In New York they talked about the food. In my entire life I had never heard food and the preparation of it so thoroughly and so constantly discussed. "Was the cook good? Was the cook hopeless? Wasn't it ghastly trying to find a new one? Did you ever have better bird's nest soup? Is the bouillabaisse as good as it was in the darling little restaurant down in Rio?"

I'm not a bad cook. At least I was once not a bad cook. My stuffed peppers, pot roast, egg dishes, shepherd's pie, and blueberry pie were darned good. I don't think I could rustle them up today. Every single time for fourteen years that we sat down to eat with Hy's closest friends, Arthur and Vivian Schulte, the subject was always whether Vivian liked the food, and whether it was half as good as she could have prepared it herself. She even tasted the food on your plate that you ordered in a restaurant and told you if that had been properly prepared too. Since the Schultes were hosts to me many times, or hosts to Hy, with me the broad-he-brought, I sound ungrateful and I don't mean to. But those meals left a lasting scar.

Vivian and Arthur came to my house for a meal only once. They came to Philadelphia to visit old friends and I invited them for Sunday brunch. Having done so I then proceeded to wish I hadn't because I realized that I was terrified. Vivian was a food expert, and Arthur had a long list of stuff he absolutely had to have or absolutely couldn't have and I hadn't mastered the list. I asked Mary, one of the maids who worked at Springside, if she would come and help and she graciously agreed.

The guests arrived, the Schultes and their friends, and some of us had Bloody Mary's and Arthur had his usual Scotch and water. We nibbled some good smoked salmon with our drinks. Lunch started with soup because Arthur likes soup. It was gazpacho as I recall because the boys liked my gazpacho. I hadn't told Mary anything about pouring wine because I intended to do that myself. But in between courses, while I was talking instead of listening, Mary came in looking like something out of a William Powell movie, with a white linen napkin wrapped around what I assumed was the wine. She proceeded to pour and I continued to talk.

Suddenly there was a rather awkward silence and Arthur said, "Jean, did you really mean for all of us to have a glassful of Scotch with lunch?" If there had been any ice, that pretty well took care of it, and I relaxed and enjoyed the rest of the meal. Vivian was kind and never gave me a run-down on how it could have been improved, though she probably had a long run-down tucked away.

Over the years I have developed such a deep-seated feeling of inadequacy about cooking that I quake at the threshold of the kitchen. I baked thousands of cookies for the girls at Madeira—but usually late at night when no one was looking. And to kids at boarding school a chocolate chip cookie is a chocolate chip cookie. I not only never prepared bird's nest soup, in my heart of hearts I have never even harbored a desire to prepare it. I can miss a meal without missing it, and by and large I like to be able to identify what's on my plate instead of guessing or having someone tell me. Right from the start I was something of a misfit in old Herm's life, and he was certainly a misfit in mine, but that was part of the attraction.

"Well he can certainly do without her," I heard the hostess say with feeling to one of the other dinner guests. I was the "her." It was the first time I had been there for dinner, though there were many other dinners to follow. The conversation had centered for quite some time on the problems of giving your children their inheritance while you were still alive, or waiting for the will. One concerned father said his daughter was spending it so fast she'd have it all used up by the time he died. Didn't this possibility worry the hostess? "No way, darling," she said. "There is no way they can spend it all in my lifetime."

Brooke Astor was one of the guests that night, a charming lady as I recall. "She's richer than Croesus, darling, and believe me she earned every bit of it the hard way. He was a perfect bastard." It was a Noel Coward play and my part hadn't quite jelled in the author's mind—or I had come in before my cue. I wasn't intimidated. Human attitudes and poses fascinate me. I was a deeply appreciative audience, but my natural candor was showing, and the lines I made up for myself had the ring of an outsider, someone who didn't take the problems under discussion seriously enough. "I don't know where he found her but he can certainly do without her."

Hy wrote his script very well on these occasions. That little Jewish boy from Brooklyn could wing it with "Our Crowd" and leave them begging for more. And he loved being there, rubbing elbows with people who had lived with big money for generations. None of this "well-to-do" garbage—rich, really rich, that's what he loved. It was the ultimate redeeming feature as far as Hy was concerned. If you were going to be rude, if you weren't very bright, if you came late to one of his dinner parties, you better damned well be rich.

My friends never said it within my hearing, but the message of their polite silence after they had met Hy came through loud and clear. "What on earth does she see in him? Jean, of all people, giving up hearth and home for that." My mother was never judgmental or unkind about something she at best would never understand, but she did say finally, "Dear, when you write to Dad and me please, don't mention Hy's name." To each his own. Who can say what attracts people to one another? I guess you have to know and understand their needs first. Love, like happiness, doesn't come ready-made. It has to be made to order.

Within the next two months after I met him, Hy had asked me to marry him and had given me a beautiful ring, a four-carat diamond.

I told Springside that I would be leaving to get married, and since the timing was poor they were annoyed: A member of the Springside administration had met Hy at lunch once and said, "He'll never marry you. I know his type, and I know Jews."

That was pretty much the end of any rapport that she and I had. Later, Hy broke the engagement and I stayed on at Springside. The following year, the same woman turned to me over her third bourbon one night and said, "They'll never make you headmistress now.

34

Everyone knows you've been living with a Jew." Nothing I experienced in those fourteen years brought me closer to Hy than that, though it was an experience I never shared with him. When I told a member of the board what had been said his answer was classic. "Oh, I'm sure you must be mistaken. Why some of my best friends are Jews."

After Hy had died, several of his friends and relatives suggested to the press that Mrs. Harris had probably gotten her job at Madeira through "the doctor's influence" or "one of his friends." How wonderfully naive. How positively American. Loving a Jewish doctor is not the royal road to the headship of a private school. But there was never a job I wouldn't happily have bypassed if the alternative had been not seeing Hy.

2.

We went to Jamaica that first winter for a week, and then out West the following September. In between we saw little of each other and went about our own particular lives. Mine consisted of being mother, housekeeper, and a very hard-working teacher and administrator. Hy's consisted of being a very conscientious doctor and having one helluva good time. We had thought that summer would be marrying time.

The day that Hy called to tell me he couldn't go through with the marriage wins handily as the second worst day in my life. I had rented a wonderful old house in Philadelphia for the boys and me. It was very old; it had seven fireplaces, lots of atmosphere, and squirrels in the attic and funny sounds in the walls. I woke that fateful morning in my full-of-atmosphere bedroom and saw something gray moving up the wall; I watched, fascinated. It could have been a shadow. Then suddenly I looked down and noticed another gray shadow moving across the floor where the dog always slept. I got out of bed to investigate and the gray shadow was tiny ticks, hundreds and hundreds of ticks, moving slowly across the room and up the wall!

The sight of one tick disgusts me. It is only love of a dog that gives me the courage to touch one. This was a Hitchcock movie "The Ticks!" I rushed to the Yellow Pages to find an exterminator, dialed, and a friendly voice assured me I had come to the right place and he would be there today. He told me ticks can lay eggs in woodwork and the eggs can lie dormant for years. Then when a new host dog appears, overnight they can burst into bloom. He added, very discreetly, that his truck had no lettering on it so the neighbors wouldn't know the exterminators were there. I assured him he could come with signs and sirens, just get there.

While I waited I swept up ticks with broom and dustpan. Then, as I stooped over to pick up a wastebasket, my back, which hadn't gone out for years, suddenly snapped and a sharp pain tore through my whole body. I managed to crawl to my bed and drag myself up on it. It was while I lay there, tears streaming down my cheeks because of the pain, heaps of unswept ticks still crawling past the broom and dustpan, that Hy called to have a heart-to-heart talk about how he thought it was late in the day for him to play the role of husband and father, and he didn't think he could go through with it. I felt like Job in drag.

"Now I don't know which part of me hurts the most," I cried—and burst into tears all over again. Hy's roses arrived that afternoon just before the exterminator. With Jimmy clutching the dog's leash and everyone's toothbrush, and me clutching the roses, and David carrying the houseplants I managed to crawl into a friend's car and she took us home with her for the night while the exterminator did in the ticks and whatever was making noise in the walls. I wrapped up the ring that night and sent it back to Hy with a caustic suggestion that he give it to Suzanne van der Vreken, his cook, since she was the only woman he really needed or wanted to hang on to. The next day I was fitted with a special corset that I had to wear part of the time for the next five years. And Hy did what he always did, went about the business of living his life pretty much as he wanted to, and I went about the business of doing what I would always do, loving him.

In less than a week the ring was back with a note that said, "It's yours forever, darling. If you won't wear it, save it for David." And with it came a bottle of Percobarb, ostensibly for the pain in my back. At first Hy said, "We can't see each other anymore. You're a wonderful woman, Jean, and you ought to be married. What I have to offer isn't for you." He could have carried it off. I couldn't.

After I had come to terms with the reality of his inability to marry, it was I who wrote the reassuring letter. In some ways Hy was more concerned about it than I was. It indicated a weakness in him that he found hard to come to terms with. Later on, about five years later, he was comfortable with, "Well, I married my profession." But at age fifty-seven he knew that wasn't the only reason and it troubled him. He still cherished all the middle-class values—I'm glad I knew him then—and felt that full respectability and social acceptance required marriage. He also harbored the frightening suspicion, which he voiced from time to time, that people might think he was a homosexual because he hadn't married.

By the time Hy and I met, I was forty-two and Hy was fifty-six. The sociological reasons for marriage, nesting and raising the young, were past. The reason now was to enjoy the companionship of someone you loved. Enjoying the "social security" a woman feels when the man at her side is her husband is pleasant too, but not reason enough to walk away from love and "get married." My friendship with Hy was a monument to my conviction that a very true love is more important than loneliness, and certainly more important than "what people think" when no pledges or commitments are being broken, and no one else is being hurt.

Hy's friends, some who grew fond of me over the years, used to take me aside at dinner parties and say, "Jean, why don't you give up. You ought to be married, and he's never going to get married." I think many of them thought I was hanging on, just in case. I never for a moment thought he would change his mind—he couldn't—and I never felt any loss of integrity because we didn't marry.

It was sometime in early 1970 that Hy called to tell me he thought he was going to marry a woman with four children. I was standing at the phone in the kitchen when he called, and I can remember saying to him, "Herman Tarnower, I know and you *should* know that you aren't going to marry anyone. So why don't you stop hurting so many women, and just concentrate on hurting me." He seemed to enjoy that line. I loved his hearty laugh.

From that moment on we saw more and more of one another, and when I finally moved to Connecticut in 1971 we spent almost every weekend together until I moved to Virginia in 1977. Before I reached Connecticut, however, there was a second lady with another four children that he took a careful look at too. I've never quite figured out how he worked in both of them in that short space of time, but he did. To misuse a metaphor, there was never any grass growing under Herman's feet.

Without the opportunity to get completely away from Hy's social life our relationship, whatever it was, however one chooses to label it, would never have happened. It was only when we were alone, at home or away, that Hy was the very special person I fell in love with. There was a beautiful little pond in front of his house with a small island in the middle. I loved walking around the pond with him. He was proud of having created it out of a swamp. He knew every forget-me-not, buttercup, iris, waterlily, cattail that grew beside it. He had planted many of them himself, and he smiled at each one as we walked arm in arm beside them. My last birthday gift to Hy for his seventieth, which he didn't live to enjoy, was some lily bulbs for beside the pond. He had orange and yellow ones. I had added ten more colors.

If I could relive only one time in our lives together it would be a Sunday afternoon, one of two: a Sunday walking slowly around the pond and then up the hill to check the old peach tree and the wild raspberries in the back of the property—or it would be a Sunday afternoon at a small dacha about twenty miles outside of Warsaw, where we went for lunch at the home of a Polish surgeon whom Dr. Howard Rusk had introduced us to. The dining room had French doors opening on to a late September garden. I remember sitting there listening as our host talked about Poland in the years since the war. His daughter and I took turns making occasional trips to the kitchen, and the conversation went on for several hours.

The late afternoon sun came through the lacy old curtains at the windows in such a special way that time stood still for a while, and I knew that for some hard to explain reason I would remember the moment all my life. I was far away from home, but Hy was there, and the light through the window reminded me of a scene from a Pasternak story, or of home when I was a little girl. I loved Hy for being part of the moment and for giving the moment to me. It was nine years ago and I can feel it and hear it and see it and smell it still. It is a physical part of me. What difference do the why's make? It just is.

3.

Our first trip to Palm Springs was short and happy, and memorable for another reason. I walked into Saks looking for some black-and-white shoes while we were there and found exactly what I was looking for. Hy was there with me and when I went to give the saleswoman my charge plate Hy had already paid for them. I was traveling with a man who wasn't my husband without even the slightest tinge of guilt or feeling of impropriety, but having him pay for a pair of my shoes embarrassed me. I never wore them without remembering and feeling self-conscious.

The lines between etiquette, morality, respectability and manners are dimly drawn, though each is quite different. We each choose our own particular niceties to give priority to, always trying to separate the specious from the real thing. Over the years Hy gave me some lovely gifts, expensive gifts I suppose, but having him buy my clothes smacked to me of being "kept," something I did not wish to be, and never was. Except for a Liberty scarf, and a cotton skirt he insisted upon giving me because he bought a similar one for our hostess in St. Martin, Hy did not ever buy my clothes.

I discovered, years later, during the trial, that his friends and family apparently thought that he had paid many of my bills. He didn't. And that was the way we both wanted it. From the moment I fell in love with Hy the only thing that mattered was seeing him, when I reasonably could. Never seeing him was the price I couldn't pay. I picked up all the other tabs, social, professional, and some rather steep financial ones with no regret.

That one of Hy's friends should suggest to the newspapers that he had probably helped pay for my sons' education enraged me. I would never have permitted it, the boys wouldn't have wanted it, and Hy would never have suggested it. Besides, I was very proud that I did it myself. It wasn't easy. That anyone would suggest it is an indication of how little he had tried to know me. Hy did offer to send Jim to a camp in Europe one summer. I thanked him and declined. When Jim finally went abroad he worked his way over on a freighter.

It was when we put New York behind us and traveled that Hy was at his best, a best many people never saw. He was a perfect traveling companion, bright, funny, never tired, well informed about what he was going to see, never complaining, determined not to let the normal annoyances of travel make a difference. The happiness, the exhilaration of our trips together are something I could not exaggerate.

Hy would arrive at the airport smiling and taking charge, and I became the happy follower, a role quite foreign to me in my day to day life, but one I played most willingly with him. There was friendship and companionship and sharing the sheer joy of touching another part of the world, shaking ourselves free of the small boxes we all seem to live in most of our lives. We read, we reached out to one another and to new experiences, and we learned. When we returned we were never quite the same people again. Maybe it's presumptuous to speak for Hy. I know I wasn't the same again. We understood a little more, cared a little more. Places we had hardly heard of before became important to us, and so did the people who lived there.

There was one drawback, but I learned to live with it. It never seemed "wrong" to me for us to be together. I felt no need for moral false faces. Hy wasn't as open and honest as I, but then his life was much more complicated than mine. He could seem open and ingenuous when he was being most secretive. He wrote many "dear all" letters as he traveled around the world with me beside him, but he never mentioned my name. I don't know whether that was to protect my privacy or his, but I imagine it was the latter.

That way he could send letters to all the ladies on the "dear all" list without any deletions or complications. I couldn't have written about those trips without mentioning him. It was sharing the pleasure of them with him that made them so special. He acted as though he felt the same way, but when he wrote the letters he could lift me out of the picture with no effort at all. I was shifted from person to nonperson very quickly. As with so many unpleasantries I was hurt for a moment, and then forgot about it in the rush of new adventures.

We ran the gamut from a suite at the Ritz in Paris to a crowded, buggy little room in Varna, a Bulgarian town on the Black Sea coast; from the American Embassy in New Delhi to a tiny ranch house in Montana; from a splendid room overlooking the bay in Hong Kong to a place in Khartoum where we sprayed everything with Lysol and sat out on a terrace until late at night, sipping tea and putting off the moment when we went inside; from sipping champagne in first class on Pan Am to wrapping ourselves in sweaters and jackets on the deck of a dangerously overcrowded ferry between Iraklion and Piraeus, sharing two oranges, a package of biscuits, and a bottle of Manhattans for dinner and breakfast.

We bought wine and bread and cheese and sat in the sun and the wind at Knossos, reading the guide book and then winding our way through the labyrinth. There was a wind from the Sahara, you could feel the sand from all those miles away, but the sun was warm. It was early spring. Early March was usually when spring vacation came, and that meant we were often lucky enough to arrive before the spring flowers had been trampled. Indeed, in many instances we visited places before tourists had taken much notice of them: Bali, Nepal, Burma, Afghanistan, Bahrain, Jiddah, N'Gor, and many, many others.

We wakened at daybreak in Kandy in central Ceylon, to the beating of the drums at the Temple of the Tooth; we watched from the terrace of a small rest house in Ratnapura, while hundreds of monkeys swung from the trees and finally settled down for the night and returned to our room where netting covered the beds and a large lazy fan in the ceiling provided more noise than air. We flew into Kabul, that city in the land of Cain, with snow on the mountains and almond trees in bloom, and savagery just below the surface. It was more than a different place; it was a different moment in time, a scene from the Middle Ages.

Trips with Hy, or just visits with Hy, were the times I breathed free for a little while and thought about something more than my next move, or how to placate the next irate constituent. I became a thinking, feeling person again with horizons broader than the walls of an office. The very word "mankind" became something more than statistics on a page or a sound made by teachers. Thanks to Hy, the word "mankind" has become a kaleidoscope of pictures for me.

It's the women in Afghanistan picking up twigs along a dusty road where a stick five or six inches long is a treasure—and they do it every day for firewood and cooking! It is the women of Senegal standing tall and stylishly decked out in bright gowns and headdresses, balancing large bundles on their heads. It is the women of Kenya who carry heavy bundles on their backs with the help of a strap that goes across their foreheads; the young woman with a deep indentation across the forehead is considered very marriageable; it is a badge of honor, proof positive that she is a good beast of burden. It's the man with a Ph.D. in geology from the University of New Mexico who married a Nepalese woman from a small mountain village where men go down into the valley twice a year for salt and cloth. It's an old gentleman in Kenya, late of Her Majesty's Indian Army "till they closed India down"; complete with khaki shorts and monocle, reminiscing "Mahvelous duty, that. Everything so cheap, you know, whiskey, tennis balls."

It is the hundreds of children in Ceylon, spilling out of little thatched cottages in spotless white dresses and shirts, on their way to school. It's the hundreds of young men in Ceylon, Kenya, Senegal, and so many other places, who have just enough education to feel disdainful of their old ways of life, and are quite incapable of making a living in a new way of life; it is the young Burmese doctors who will graduate this year from medical schools into an economy that can support only a handful of them. The rest will join cadres of workers out in the country, working for food and shelter, struggling through the years of red tape that may in time bring them to America.

It is gypsies making their way through the Khyber Pass in bright painted wagons like the pictures in my fifth grade geography book. It's the jovial Franciscan monk who showed us through the archaeological digs on the island of Bahrain, and the sheik who governs that rich, strategic island, he of the Salukis and Persian carpets and falcons and private beaches for his "girls." I don't think it's called a harem any more.

It's the women who threw their babies away with the trash in the unmercifully crowded refugee camps in Saigon, or the boy on the streets of that city who pulled an old sleight-of-hand trick while exchanging dollars for piastres and left Hy with a package of folded newspapers. Hy laughed and said, "Well, he outsmarted me." Later he added; "Don't you tell Arthur." I thought of the two of them that day at Madeira when I discovered that many of the girls had been using a stranger's charge card to make phone calls all over the world. "There's no such thing as a free lunch, my friends," I told them, "but all your life someone will offer you one."

Only once in all our travels did Hy ever get angry with me, at least so that I knew, and the anger was strange and deep, and left me cowering like a wounded rabbit for twenty-four miserable hours. It was in Rome. The concierge had told him he couldn't get us reservations for dinner at the place Hy had named. He looked disappointed, and I wanted him to know that anywhere we went was splendid with me. "Oh, well, let's try . . ." and I named another restaurant. "Goddammit!" he shouted. "Are you running this, or am I? If you want to run things, just let me know, and I'll turn it all over to you. Just take over or shut up!"

He sulked and was angry that night and all the next day. I was accustomed to that behavior in my father. He never took a trip that wasn't four parts yelling to one part enjoyment, but I was spoiled now by Hy's good spirits and kindness. Jolly thing, kindness. One is never happier than when other people are good. I wouldn't have angered him for the world, but I did, and it terrified me. I was like a child wanting to put things right again, and probably annoying him all the more because I cared so much.

Only once in all our travels did I ever get angry with him. It wasn't until we reached the Ritz in Paris in 1976 that I realized the letters that had followed us around the world for years were from Lynne Tryforos. I had said to him in Hawaii in 1972 when we picked up the mail and he fumbled around awkwardly trying to hide what became very familiar handwriting, "Hy, why would you travel with me if you give your itinerary to another woman?" He did not enjoy being asked for explanations, and he answered with obvious annoyance. "Look, dear, they have it at the office. There's nothing I can do. It's just a little note from one of the girls at the office."

In Paris the letter had been slipped under the door of our room, and was waiting for us when we arrived. It was my first trip to Paris, and laden with all the old stereotypes; I had even bought that first black nightgown for the occasion. We had been gone almost three weeks, through eastern Europe, and were ending the trip in Paris. It had been an exceptionally interesting and happy time. Now the first thing that greeted us was Lynne's letter. It looked like a twenty-page term paper. Again it was quickly and awkwardly whisked away. I said nothing. A few moments later, while Hy was dressing for dinner, I walked over to the mantle and started to put my pearls and earrings down where Hy had laid some cuff links. They were ones he had had for several years, "From a grateful patient."

He had put them face down, and there staring at me, engraved in gold, was all Lynne's love. The pleasure of Paris was pretty well laid to rest, and I was angry enough to slam a closet door very hard. As I did, the floor to ceiling mirror on it shattered all over the room. I hadn't expected that, but I wasn't sorry.

Hy reacted as if nothing had happened. He simply ignored it. He apologized for the letter and for bringing the cuff links, asked me if I was ready for dinner, and we headed for the Crazy Horse Saloon—a terrible place! By the time we returned, the mirror had been replaced, and there wasn't the smallest chip of glass on the floor to indicate anything had been amiss. Two years later, when friends who had just returned from Paris were moaning about how expensive breakfast was at the Ritz, Hy smiled at me and said very quietly, "Their mirrors are damned expensive, too." That's the only reference he ever made to it.

I used to say to him, especially when he was beginning to talk about another trip and ask me where I'd like to go, "You know, Herm, we don't have to go far. I could be very happy with you on the Staten Island Ferry." Hy didn't respond to the Staten Island comment at the time; but years later, when the sun was just going down and the lights of Hong Kong were beginning to sparkle in a hundred different colors on the water, we stood on the deck of the ferry to Kowloon and he said, "It's taken a long time, but I finally got you on the Staten Island Ferry."

Brooklyn:
Hy

1.

For fourteen years Hy had been "there," filling my life, being bright, being difficult, being thoughtful, being selfish, letting the world think he was being any damned thing he chose to be, but carrying burdens and scars I have only now begun to acknowledge. He was the kind of man you were attracted to, or you probably couldn't stand—no middle ground, and he felt the same way about you. If he found you interesting, or useful, he was a good friend, or useful in return. If he didn't like you, you could go to hell.

It would be difficult to describe the nature of our relationship. I'm not sure what it was myself, what made him so important to me, what attracted me to him. The forensic psychologist who tested me for more than nineteen hours after Hy's death wrote:

I feel that this patient in the years since 1966 seemed to live what Dr. Menninger would describe as "a partial death and substitute for suicide." She had truncated her life through her subjection to Dr. Tarnower in such a manner as to kill part of herself in masochistic surrender. She had recurring bouts of depression as she realized that she could not free herself from the man . . . who denied her status, sadistically teased her, and was a figure of complicity in her long standing, self-destructive vulnerability.

If true, and I'm still not the best judge, it was certainly something neither Hy nor I planned or wanted, Hy least of all.

My own strong conviction is that I would have resorted to suicide long before if Hy hadn't been there saying, "Welcome home, darling," and teaching me how to enjoy life, or at least letting me watch him enjoy it. Saul Bellow, in a short story called "A Silver Dish," wrote, "It's usually the selfish people who are loved the most. They do what you deny yourself, and you love them for it."

Like all of us, Hy was a mixture of good and bad, a distillation of his heritage, his different environments and his own unique self. The story of his life is a success story for men, and a cautionary tale for women. He was not an introspective man. Life is not conducive to reflection today, and that suited Hy just fine. Reflecting was not what he usually enjoyed. Doing, seeing, learning, experiencing now was for him. He worked much harder at enjoying than understanding.

Digging too deep was a bore, or a threat, I'm not sure which. He didn't clutter up his life with peripheral considerations. He got to the main point very quickly, and then had a tendency to oversimplify by making that the only point. Perhaps by trial and error, perhaps by instinct he had found the straightest line between survival and the good life. People who tarried too long over all the possibilities he dismissed as fools. "You're wacky," he was constantly telling me in a smiling, affable way. It was what I expected to hear when I arrived in his bedroom that night in March.

When I think of Hy now (he could never quite remember how he got that nickname), I hear the sound of his footsteps first, on the stairway coming up from the garage. His head appears, and then the rest of him. He's smiling and he says, "Hello" with the accent on the O. "Welcome home." I was usually in the living room reading when he came home, and I would stop my reading and go to kiss him.

I have read descriptions of Hy that sound nothing at all like him to me. People emphasize his nose, and make him sound very severe. I picture beautiful deep brown eyes, a bald head, and a big, broad smile, or a warm private one, with his eyes smiling too. He was just under six feet tall, he kept his weight between 175 and 180, and he was proud of his very flat stomach. My favorite picture of Hy is one Audrey Topping took of him in China in 1973 . . . tie open, carryall in hand, and a smile that said, "I am doing exactly what I want most to do, and I'm loving it." It is Hy at his most ingenuous, something he wasn't always good at being.

The carryall in the picture probably held his shaving kit, his passport and traveler's checks, a few small gifts he had picked up, a sweater, and three good books. If he had lost all his other baggage it wouldn't have dampened his spirits a bit. It usually took him twenty minutes to pack for a world tour, and in the fourteen years that I knew him he always took the same things: three pair of tired khakis, a few drip-dry shirts, sweaters, two pair of the ubiquitous blue pajamas, undershorts, two good shirts, two ties and a suit. He wouldn't have made the best dressed list even in China, but he was comfortable. He wore the clothes. They never wore him.

At home his clothes were very conservative, very good, and they lasted forever. Many of the jackets hanging in Hy's closet had been there for more than fourteen years. He never liked wide lapels or wide ties so he wasn't inconvenienced by passing fads. Suzanne, his cook, asked me every year to make him buy himself a new topcoat but he had the old one relined and some magic performed on the cuffs and wore the same one. Besides, Suzanne knew very well nobody made him do anything.

The last few years of his life he began to get a bit more daring sartorially, especially after friends gave him a bright green sweater when we celebrated one of his birthdays in Palm Springs. His first reaction was that it would have to go back. Then he decided he liked it. He even graduated to a yellow Izod and a pink Izod for golf, and a few handsome striped shirts instead of whites for the office. I always thought he looked wonderful on his way to the office, partly because I liked his tweeds and choice of ties, and partly because he always looked refreshed and eager for whatever the new day would bring. He couldn't wait to get started.

Six days a week for almost forty years he was up and on his way to the hospital and then the office by 7:15. I've known him to make three house calls in the middle of the night and still be up and out by 7:15 the next morning. I think he had discovered the fountain of youth . . . good health, work that he loved, and the capacity to play as hard as he worked.

Hy loved being rich, but he was a liberal by nature. He found it hard to be a bigot or to deny something his intellect found obvious. The solution was not to think about troublesome things too long.

Hy was a moral man where his medical practice was concerned. He was amoral where women were concerned. I think he was comfortable with the arrangement because he had divided the world into givers and takers, first class and second class, and men were the former and women were the latter.

He simply never questioned that God designed the sexes to occupy different spheres. He wasn't interested in a woman filling the benign roles of wife and mother. On the other hand, if you worked as hard as he did, and I did, it still didn't buy you more than a second-class ticket to life. His behavior swung from the side of grace to the side of hubris, an anomaly I was never equipped to understand fully or cope with intelligently. Instead, I simply endured it, remembering the good parts, loving enough to forgive the bad parts.

As a happy and contented friend he was the most agreeable companion imaginable. As a practicing physician he was bright, intuitive and courageous, always willing and ready to consult, as well as to be consulted. As a member of the profession he was a one-man band, not a member of a committee, not a joiner, not a political animal. There we had something in common. Hy was one of the founders of the Westchester Heart Association, the first chairman of its board and later honorary chairman, but while he never stopped caring about the Association and working for it, he needed to be given a specific job, do it, and be done with it.

He was not a patient member of any meeting. To be so meant to suffer an occasional fool, and this he never did—not unless there was something much more in it for him than chairmanship of a committee. A year or so before he died he was asked to help find new board members for the Association. I was sitting beside him when he called Oscar Dystel and asked him if he would consider serving. "Hy," Mr. Dystel answered, "I am already a member of the board of the Westchester Heart Association." It was a gaffe that would have shaken and certainly embarrassed anyone else. Hy looked sheepish for a moment—but only a moment.

Hy's tolerance for anything or anyone he didn't like was largely used up on the wives of his two closest friends. He cordially loathed them both. "Jesus! She is impossible" was his constant refrain. They are two intelligent, independent women and very devoted wives. Hy saw them only as women who talked too much. He said one night as we drove home from an evening with both of them, "You know, they are probably the only two people in the world who would have invited

Einstein for dinner and corrected him when he started explaining relativity!" By and large he was charming and uncharacteristically long-suffering with them both, because he was devoted to their husbands.

There isn't much to tell about the early history of Hy because for him his history began when he became a doctor. He isn't an easy person to imagine as a child. I loved to hear him reminisce but he didn't do it often, and he rarely went back further than college. I've forgotten some of the particulars; I listened with interest and affection, but always with the comfortable feeling that I'd hear him tell it again. I particularly loved to hear him use an occasional Yiddish word. It was almost always in a light, warm moment, and it gave him roots, whether he wanted them or not.

He didn't seem to remember much that would fall under the heading of "fun" as a youngster. There are few carefree children in Yiddish literature. Maybe he was part of a tradition. He grew up in Brooklyn with his mother and father, and three sisters, Billie, Edith, and Jean. He played the usual street games—stickball, stoop ball, punch ball, handball—all, I imagine, with a ferocious will to win. He fought with his sister Jean—she must have been the one most like him, and played pool whenever he could. On a number of occasions his mother came and pulled him out of a local pool hall. It's a picture I can't quite imagine. "Because it was late or because of the company?" I asked. He smiled, "A little of both, I guess." He never got over loving to gamble, but he never gambled recklessly, and over the long haul I think he was a winner. Framed in his dining room was a royal flush in clubs—trophy of a big night. "It helped to build this house."

Hy's family had very little money. I thought it was wonderful that he had started from nothing and "made it" on his own. His father was in the hat business and made a respectable lower middle-class living until the depression, when people stopped buying hats. Then "we barely scraped by." He always spoke of his father with affection and respect. He was a quiet man while Mama did the talking. "He didn't have much money, but whatever he did have he was generous with. He paid for my college—how the hell he did it, I don't know. He even bought me a little secondhand roadster after I'd been hitchhiking for years."

Hitchhiking? Dr. Tarnower? My son Jim was incredulous when I

49

told him how Hy hitchhiked across the country one summer during his college years. I think in Jim's mind Hy had slipped out of the womb with the umbilical cord wrapped around a new blue Cadillac. It was just part of the package that was Dr. Tarnower. Herman, without a ticket to Kenya and a handful of graphite fishing poles? Nonsense. No hundred-foot swimming pool? No tennis court? You're thinking of another Dr. Tarnower.

2.

I don't think there was ever a moment in his life when he didn't want all that good stuff—when he wasn't figuring out how to get them. I picture Herman always on the make. When he was feeling particularly satisfied with his life, which he did more and more the last few years, he would get a thoughtful expression on his face and say, "It's funny, isn't it, what motivates a kid. My parents never talked to me about college. They didn't give a damn if I went or not but they paid the bill." He always thought I made too much of a production of taking and picking up the boys, at boarding school or college—station wagon filled with squash racquets and stereo. He was right.

"Hell," he said, "I just threw a few things in a bag, said 'Goodbye,' and hitchhiked to college. It wouldn't have occurred to anyone to take me, and it wouldn't have occurred to me to expect it. They didn't even come to my graduation." There was a funny mixture of love, resentment at what had been missing, and pride that he "did it anyway." I know that after he established a successful practice nothing would have made him happier than to do things for his father, but by then his father had died.

It *is* funny what motivates a kid. Hy grew up in a cultural Sahara. He was the only one in his immediate family who went to college. He never mentioned a home that had books or music in it, but he tried to teach himself to understand and appreciate culture in all its forms. He had an extensive record collection of symphonies, some with the seals still unbroken. He would sit himself down sometimes, like an earnest schoolboy and listen purposefully, trying to like it.

But he never did. Later he repeated the lessons on tape, but with no more success. He was very sensitive to some art forms, especially Oriental art. We spent an unplanned and hurried day in Bangkok once and arrived at Jim Thompson's beautiful house on the Klong just at closing time. A kindhearted guide let us wander through by ourselves for an hour. Hy was almost reverential in his appreciation of some of the Buddhas. We both loved stopping at Mona Kaia on our way home from a trip partly because of the beautiful Oriental art that is there. We especially loved the large Buddha that sat at the top of the stairs leading to our room.

Music in any form was not particularly Hy's thing. He never recognized any of the big band songs when I'd say, "Oh, gee. Remember that one?" And he didn't remember ever having danced to one of them—which made me realize he was working hard, getting started, and cutting fiscal corners during those prewar dancing years. He did a lot of dancing later on—even took dancing lessons—but that isn't the same.

His growing up was not family fun and games. He often mentioned that his family never celebrated birthdays—never even acknowledged them. Imagine, no paper hats or snappers that you pulled on, that made a noise and told your fortune. I didn't really believe him until we went to dinner at his sister Billie's house on his sixtieth birthday. I thought it was going to be a party, but I was the only one there who knew it was his birthday.

His attitude toward his mother was a little like Portnoy's: loyalty, and a grudging respect because she was his mother. He heard me admonishing one of my sons to clean his plate once and said, "Oh God, leave him alone. My mother said it to me so often I still eat stuff I don't want."

He was on a year's fellowship abroad, having just graduated with honors from the University of Syracuse Medical School when his father died at age fifty-four. Hy finished out what was a broadening and unforgettable experience for him in Europe, still not knowing. When he returned he found his mother a widow with a $5,000 life insurance policy and nothing else. She gave him most of the $5,000 to set himself up in practice, and he supported her for the next forty years, in a manner to which a good Jewish mama soon grew accustomed. He made a deal with his sister Billie, "You listen to her, and I'll pay the bills." It worked out satisfactorily for all. Hy visited his mother often, but they were quick stops—five minutes to say hello and see that she had whatever she needed.

He never suggested to me that she had been in any way a burden to him or that he resented all those years of running two households. He showed his hand only once, when I made a facetious remark about my son David being "the crutch of my old age." He stopped me short and his voice was stern, "Don't ever say a thing like that again. It's a damn poor joke. It's no joke at all." It fascinated me that she never worked in all those years, or apparently even considered it.

I met Mrs. Tarnower only once. She was blind by then and came with her sister for sunning and swimming while I was visiting Hy. The family talk at that time was "I guess they're going to get married." I was wearing the beautiful ring Hy had given me. Her sister said, "It's Mrs. Harris, she's very pretty." "Harris. Harris?" Momma asked. "Is that the Jewish Harrises?" Never mind what she looks like, let's make sure she isn't goyim! Hy always found that an amusing story.

Hy had mixed feelings about being a Jew. One moment he resented it and thought of it as an infirmity, the next moment he was reading another book about where the ancient Hebrew tribes came from, and who they really were. "You know," he said to me one evening in a particularly expansive mood, "I'm an agnostic. Now if you were an agnostic, you'd just be an agnostic. But I'm a Jewish agnostic. You never stop being Jewish." And then, as though he had exposed too much, he laughed and said, "What the hell. If I hadn't been Jewish it would have been too easy!" I loved that line.

Socially, and perhaps even intellectually, Hy might have preferred the upper middle-class wealthy Wasps of Scarsdale to the rich, rich, rich Jews of Manhattan, but it wasn't an option he ever really had. It wasn't until the late 1970s that he was asked to be a member of the Westchester Country Club.

"*Now* they ask me," he said, with a rueful smile and some honest bitterness in his voice. "It would have meant so much to me to be asked thirty years ago. What do I want with the Westchester Country Club today? I was the personal physician of four presidents of that club, but not good enough to be a member." I remember touching his arm and saying, "Herm, when you told them 'no thank you' I hope you were polite."

Every spring some of Hy's old Wasp friends and patients in Scarsdale gave a series of lovely dinners, and parties, usually crowded around Memorial Day weekend. Hy and I went to them together and enjoyed them for fourteen years. He was proud to be invited because, as he put it, "I think I'm the only Jew they ask." (Actually, there were one or two others.) They were the comfortably wealthy, old shoe type of people I had grown up with, not the rich, rich, rich, and of Hy's friends, certainly the ones I started out feeling most at home with. They were also the ones who liked me least.

The anti-Semitism I had lived with so long in Grosse Pointe, Michigan, was present at those parties but they were genuinely fond of Hy, and I never really thought about the other until one of them said after Hy was dead, "Oh yes. We often went to Hy's to dinner. The food and wine were beautiful, but he always invited us with Jews." Since Hy was a Jew, and his family was Jewish, and most of his friends were Jews, it stood to reason one would rub elbows with them at his home. The only "goyim" things about Hy were "those Scarsdale parties" each spring, and the women he slept with. As for the latter, maybe that was happenstance—or personal preference; or maybe it was Herman's way of saying, "Screw the Gentiles."

I know that for me those years of loving Hy were a lesson in anti-Semitism, something that is still rampant in our country today. And so much of it came from the mouths of decent people who simply don't hear themselves, and who would be genuinely upset if you pointed it out to them. "We looked at a new house in Darien, Jean. You should have seen the bathrooms—hideous pink—so Jewish looking." "His wife is pretty nice, but her hair—terribly Jewish looking." I'm glad I was brought up by a mother who was incapable of bigotry in any of its forms.

If there was any in me it didn't last very long. I know I was anxious that Hy not wear a particular blue and beige and brown summer jacket of his when he met some of my Grosse Pointe friends for the first time. But that was because I knew how establishment we all were and I didn't want anything to get in the way of their seeing what an interesting man he was. A few months later I loved him so completely it didn't matter to me what he wore or what anyone else might think of him. I wanted people to like him but if they didn't it didn't change anything for me.

Mr. and Mrs. Tarnower came from Poland. Hy was unsure about the family's true origin. We went to Poland together in 1976. He wanted to visit the ghetto in Warsaw, and the basement of the Gestapo Headquarters that is now a shrine to the countless Jews who died there. It was very important to him to go, but having seen it he said little and didn't seem deeply moved. But by then he worked at not being deeply moved, or not appearing to be. At first he said the family had probably come from the Polish town of Tarnow—sounds reasonable. But later, in Bulgaria, we met a woman who said there was a small town not far from where she had grown up with a name that sounded like Tarnow too. She wrote the name of the town on a match clip I still have.

What makes you keep things like that—and why does it still matter to me where they came from? Until we left Bulgaria, Hy spent an inordinate amount of time studying Bulgarian faces. He decided his nose and his father's nose were "definitely Bulgarian." I loved Hy's face, his beautiful dark brown eyes and what I thought was a fascinating profile. It reminded me of some of the Egyptian heads at the Metropolitan and I used to tease him, "I will always believe there was a little hanky panky at the palace, Herm, before Moses got the family out of town." I think he rather liked the idea.

Hy went through college and medical school in four years. I imagine he was a very cocky young man. He looked like one in a college picture that I saw—with a great shock of hair he was hardly recognizable. A man who had known him during his college years introduced himself to me during the trial. I asked what he was like then. He smiled and said, "Full of hell!"

Hy told me, a number of times, that he never took notes in class, and was inclined to look out the window during lectures. It didn't mean he wasn't listening though, so if the professor commented on what looked like inattentiveness he could always repeat what had been said. He did the same thing in the army—which, with his hat pushed back, and his cocky manner, must have annoyed more than one superior officer.

54

I was one of those earnest characters who wrote down every word—and then underlined it in red, and studied the notes assiduously.

We both had taken history courses from Professor Hans Kohn, I at Smith, Hy later as an adult at New York University. He was a brilliant lecturer, and he and Hy became friends. Hy's fertile brain required an occasional evening with the Kafka and casserole set, although over the long haul, to be with "the right people" he could endure mind-bending boredom.

The Kohns and Hy and I spent an interesting weekend together in Purchase years ago. Hans was not happy with quite so much conspicuous consumption, but he did enjoy Hy's gift for asking good questions and being a good listener.

I read in a newspaper description of Hy that he never listened, just talked. Quite the contrary. Until the last few years, he listened much, much more than he talked—socially at least. I can't speak for the office. He may have acquired the habit at Syracuse where he was kidded about his "Brooklyn accent," and was called "Brooklyn" for the first year he was there. Freshman year, with characteristic Tarnower grit and determination, he took a speech course and began practicing in front of the mirror.

Slowly the sounds that screamed "Brooklyn" began to recede. He worked at it for four years. Henry Higgins might have spotted the vestiges of those sounds thirty-five years later when I met him, but I didn't. It was a "Tarnower" accent by then, obviously New York, but all the r's were in the right places, and the general effect was pleasant as far as I was concerned. The last six or seven years he began saying "vawze" instead of "vase," which seemed a little more gilding than the lily needed, but if that was self-improvement, too, so be it.

Hy learned to dance, to play golf, to play tennis, to shoot, to cast for salmon the same way—practice, practice, practice.

He could lose gracefully, at least to all outward and visible signs, but all his life he played everything to win. He would never start a golf match without at least a half-hour's warm-up on the practice tee. I have seen him practice casting for four hours nonstop, in the rain, and then after lunch and a nap give it a go for four hours more. He would watch a gin game or a bridge game, observing "tactics" as he called them, and find a significant lesson in something that had no meaning to me at all.

If he were going to do something he worked very hard to do it well. And he worked hardest at being a good doctor. He enjoyed his years at Syracuse and kept in close touch with classmates all over the country, and all over the world. He even went back to his forty-fifth reunion, which didn't seem like something he would do. We visited one of his classmates in Teheran years ago. He was obstetrician to the Empress by then, and had delivered that much wanted heir to the Peacock Throne.

The year after medical school, Hy won a scholarship abroad and while he traveled and studied he made other lifetime friends; very special ones were a young Dutch doctor and his wife, who over the years were to have nine children, and six of them became doctors too. They visited often on Purchase Street. Hy's fellowship grant was for $1,500, a large amount in the early 1930s. It was to cover all travel and living expenses. He studied part of the year in England and then moved over to Paris. He showed me the house on the Left Bank where he lived for five months in an attic room.

"You could see the river if you leaned way out the window!" It was there in Paris that he saw his first pink chestnut tree, and decided on the spot to have his own some day. He had several of them there in Purchase, and he welcomed their blossoms each spring with great pleasure and always remembered again that spring in Paris. Hy's gift for appreciation of the things he liked and understood was boundless. It gave me vicarious pleasure just watching him enjoy—breathing deep and smelling the viburnum on a summer night, looking out over the pond he had built, listening to the ridiculous sound of the frogs at night, checking to see how the two small tulip trees were, "volunteers" that had suddenly appeared at the end of the driveway.

Hy took his internship at Bellevue. He was proud of having served there. We drove by from time to time and he always pointed out the old red building where interns slept—when they had a few minutes—which wasn't often. It usually reminded him that later the club for doctors who had served their internship at Bellevue was closed to him because he was a Jew. I can't believe that it's still true—hard to believe that it was then, but he went to a meeting once, assuming he was a member, and was told he wasn't, and couldn't be. As for cardiology, it wasn't a particular choice of his. It was hardly a field of practice then, "so they opened it to a Jew!" He went on to take his boards in internal medicine as well, and then, though cardiology was always his special field, he really practiced as a general practitioner for the next forty years—"just a country doctor" he liked to say, with something less than a modest smile.

His years at Bellevue, and maybe the growing-up process in Brooklyn as well, convinced him early on that he wanted no part of New York City practice. While riding the ambulance, picking up kids who'd been bitten by rats, Bowery drunks mutilated in accidents, people hurt who would be mended only to go back and be hurt the same way again, he told himself he wanted to go where he could make more of a difference. And anyway, always the pragmatist, he wanted no long lines of traffic to get to the office and home again. He lived his life right from the start in a way to gladden the heart of Adam Smith— or Ayn Rand. Enlightened self-interest illuminated the path. He was never a do-gooder—but he did a lot of good. Not I. I was born to be Don Quixote, never consciously looking for windmills, but constantly finding them. I don't know whether it was being a teacher or a rather complex woman that made it inevitable.

It took Hy two years to find a suitable place in Scarsdale to live and to work. Same old problem. He was Jewish. Then, finally, having settled into an apartment where he could both live and work, he waited for patients. "I didn't go to a movie for years for fear a patient would call while I was out." I can hear him saying it. "I went to the synagogue one day, thinking that I could meet people that way. But when I got there I felt guilty about using it when I didn't believe what it taught—so I left. I've always been embarrassed that I did it."

He took on all comers, and since it was the depression there were some who couldn't pay. Not to worry. There was Tony who brought fresh flowers and vegetables to Hy's house every Thursday until the day Hy died, in gratitude for all the doctoring he had done for Tony and his large family all through the depression and right up to the time he went off to war. There was Joe who would stop work on anyone else's car to fix Hy's because Hy had cared for Joe and his family through some hard years. There were Margaret and Willy and Tubby and others.

Hy never talked about them, but over the years it was hard to miss how many there were. It made me very proud of him. His house, and later his wine cellar, was filled with gifts from grateful patients—an eclectic collection at best, but obvious expressions of gratitude and affection. The "valuable art collection" the papers talked about at his death was largely a collection of "loving hands at home," therapy paintings that nobody but Hy would have hung. The paintings he had bought himself were in the $100–$200 range—a wax resist from Kenya—a delightful watercolor called "The Gamblers" from Yugoslavia.

His Buddhas, large and small, some handsome bronzes, and the stone carving over his mantle were the closest Hy himself came to buying "art." He loved the ostrich egg he found in Tanzania. He loved the anka he bought for $10 from the elephant driver in Nepal, and his favorite piece was simply a small rock he picked up on the island of Cos, where Hippocrates had taught. He kept it on his dresser with a small ivory figure sitting on it.

3.

By the time World War II came Hy had a fine practice established, and had invested heavily in expensive equipment for his office. As a bachelor he knew he would be gone "for the duration," and as a man who was always thinking ahead, he knew there would be a doctor shortage back home. He looked around for a good doctor with wife and kids and a high draft number, and made a deal.

If the doctor would move into Hy's office, and keep the expensive equipment paying for itself, he would guarantee the doctor $500 per month. That was a lot of money in 1941, more than the young doctor had made, and Hy was prepared to pay the difference out of his army pay if the practice didn't live up to his expectations. The deal was made and both doctors prospered. I guess in a way this was the beginning of the Scarsdale Medical Group. The young man who held down the medical home front for four years has just recently retired from the group.

Hy thrived playing his role in the war. He became a colonel and enjoyed the privileges of rank for the first time in his life. True to army tradition for snafus, though he was a cardiologist and internist his longest tour of duty was in a psychiatric hospital. It must have been a rather trying time for everyone because Hy had almost no use or respect for psychiatry. He used to say, "There are exactly three psychiatrists in the City of New York I'd send a patient to. The rest aren't worth a damn." The hospital was in Kentucky, and Hy used what time off he could wangle to hunt, birds and broads. He became very good at both.

When he finally knew he was going overseas, his last worldly act was to race out and buy a portable deck chair. He enjoyed crossing the Pacific much more than those who sat on the hard deck and leaned against smoke stacks. That chair became rather famous during the crossing and was probably won and lost in a number of poker games. I would be very surprised if Old Herm didn't finally sell it at a profit.

The high point of his army career was being chosen a member of the Atomic Bomb Commission to go into Nagasaki on the first plane to enter the city after the dropping of "the bomb." He was proud that he had been chosen for the mission, and for the little piece of history that it made of him, but he never talked about what it was like or how he had felt walking through the devastation and horror. I asked him direct questions about it a number of times but the answers invariably cut off the next question. He lectured at Williams College directly after the war, but after that he had little or nothing to say about it.

A year and a half before the war was over, feeling his usual farsighted and optimistic self, Hy wrote his sister Billie and asked her to order him a Cadillac "with everything on it." He didn't want "everything on it" but he figured that kind of an order wouldn't be lost or put on the bottom of the pile. Obviously there would be a long waiting line for cars when the war ended, and he wanted to be at the head of it. A doctor needs a car. Billie didn't put in the order and Hy never completely forgave her. I must have heard about that unordered Cadillac at least a dozen times. And it was thirty-five years later!

He was like an elephant when it came to things you had done to displease him. He brought them up repeatedly. It always surprised me that he did. At the risk of sounding sexist I think of it as a female characteristic. I finally said to him when he was bemoaning one of my old transgressions, "Hy, that was eight years ago! If my sins are so few that you have to dredge them up from eight years ago, I think I have a pretty good track record. From now on let's make anything older than a year off limits." He laughed and said he would, but he didn't remember.

His first few months back in Scarsdale after four years away at war taught him a lesson that changed his life-style for the rest of his life. "I had glued myself to the office for years for fear I'd lose patients if I weren't always there. Then I took four years off and nobody seemed to know I'd been gone. I figured what the hell was all the sitting home for. From then, on, when I wanted to take a two, or four, or six week vacation, I took it. It never affected my practice."

In the years right after the war he moved several times, always expanding his office. When he moved into a new private apartment his first worldly act was to have the gas disconnected so that none of the women in his life would insist on cooking for him, and fixing little intimate dinners at home. For more than *twelve* years he ate every meal out, breakfast, lunch, and dinner. No wonder he enjoyed dinner at home so much, after he had bought a house, and Henri and Suzanne had taken up residence with him.

Hy drove around Westchester for years looking for a piece of property "with a view." When he discovered the Pforzheimer property he loved it at once. He spent hours sitting on the old brick wall to the left of the deck he built—looking out at Long Island Sound in the distance. It was several years before he persuaded the family to sell him a little over five acres with the pool, the pool house, and the tennis court.

The pool house consisted of a large living room, dining room with an old stone fireplace at one end, a tiny kitchen, two dressing rooms and baths, and a terrace room between—also with a large open fireplace. Hy added a large living room to the right of the pool house, with a bedroom, dressing room, and two baths above, and a garage down below. A swamp area he turned into a lovely pond with an island in the middle. He never stopped planting perennials around it and it grew lovelier every spring. Later, after I knew him, and he had asked me to marry him he added two bedrooms and two baths on the other side of the house. I didn't know until years later that while I was picturing where the children's books and toys would go, the carpeting, draperies, and bedspreads, all very good goods were a gift from his last paramour. She was then married to someone else, but Herman never looked a gift horse in the mouth. Gold watches, gold cuff links, gold fountain pens, gold tie pins, gold belt buckles, needle-pointed vests and slippers. It was quite a collection.

I said to him the first year we met, "Someday, Herman, if I'm ever very rich, I'm going to buy you a Steuben hunting bowl and collect all the dates so lovingly inscribed, engraved, needlepointed, and hemstitched all over this house—and have them all etched on the bowl . . . the true Tarnower hunting trophy—certainly better than those elephant tusks. And who knows, Herm, if you give it your best shot you may be able to fill the whole damned calendar."

It amazes me as I reread that that I could have said anything that callous without really knowing what I was saying—or to whom I was saying it. Too much of it was like a play. I made fun of the truth instead of facing it. Hy told me all of the gifts came from "grateful patients." It was years before that term had a pejorative ring to it for me. I simply never put two and two together. Not even one and one. That "grateful patient" was Hy's euphemism for the newest woman in his life simply didn't occur to me. When a new pair of gold cuff links appeared on the dresser they were always from a "grateful patient."

I'm afraid Herman left a number of grateful patients around West-chester who didn't get the treatment at the office. And they weren't exclusively in Westchester either. He met a woman on the long flight to Kenya once, the wife of a prominent American. By the time I met him in Kenya a week later she was already a "grateful patient." She didn't even know his right name. The note slipped under our bed-room door was addressed to Dr. Hyman Tarnower. He had a rather sticky two or three days explaining all the phone calls to the room, and why he had to keep running downstairs to "check reservations" and "check traveler's checks." And I didn't suspect a thing because I didn't want to and I didn't want others to. It seems to me an unnatural, cynical, most unloving way to live. But Hy loved his life and I didn't love mine, so what does it all mean? What is the code?

I hasten to add that Hy gave most generously too, often more generously than he received. He loved buying cases of champagne for special friends, invariably those who already had a cellar full of it. He was quicker than anyone at any table to pick up the check, and he certainly returned in kind the favor of all those golden baubles. The last thing he wanted was to be beholden to anyone. It made him feel vulnerable. Unfortunately, the deep sentiment with which many gifts were given to him he soon forgot. Just before Hy died, my son Jim lost the watch that his father had left to him. Hy immediately volunteered to give him a very grand gold watch to replace it. When I recognized it as one a woman had given him I told him he really ought to be ashamed, and wouldn't let Jim have it.

There seemed to be different levels of giving for Hy, not necessarily classified by cost so much as by caring. We were waiting in the airport in Denpasar at the end of a trip to Bali one day, I reading, Hy looking in the little airport shops. Suddenly an attractive woman sitting near me turned to her husband and said, "My God, did you see that man over there? He's buying jewelry as though it were prizes for popcorn boxes!" It was Herman, filling up the General Fund. He did the same in Ceylon, and in one of the bazaars in Khartoum. I've seen some gold earrings and a large topaz ring I watched him pick out in Colombo, Ceylon, being worn by one of his "grateful patients" in Scarsdale.

Years ago, when he went to China he asked, "What do you want me to bring you?" I said, "Anything at all Hy, but please just buy one." Later, before he handed me a very beautiful jade ring I said, "Hy, whatever it is, please keep it if you bought it by the pound." He said, "Dammit, this was expensive. I couldn't have bought more than one." He saw me wearing a pair of costume earrings I had bought at Saks once, and said, "Where did you get those? I'm supposed to buy your earrings." Over the years he gave me some handsome pieces of gold jewelry, most of it, I'm happy to say, bought thoughtfully, and lovingly for me. Some of it came from the General Fund.

Hy's timing, when he bought his house and the clinic, was fortuitous to say the least. The price was right and both of them gave him many years of pleasure and deep personal satisfaction. The city of Scarsdale was not especially happy to have a clinic built right in the middle of a very posh suburban area, but it was tastefully done, quite unobtrusive, and over the years has proved a great asset and convenience to the community. Every step of the planning and building entailed a fight, council meetings, irate property owners of Heathcote, articles in the Scarsdale papers—the whole bit. It took vision, determination, courage, and a very thick skin to see the thing through to completion.

Hy had them all. He was sure all the fuss was just another manifestation of "the Jewish thing" but it probably wasn't. He was trying to get more parking space for the clinic when I came into the picture. He had the acreage but the community didn't want to run the risk of "more traffic." He regaled me with stories of the fight and I pictured myself, little Wasp wife, dressed in my most respectable suburban costume, standing beside my man in battle. Unfortunately—or fortunately perhaps—it wasn't to be. Hy wouldn't let me go with him to any council meetings. They finally compromised and some of the land was made parking space and some of the land was left park.

The house gave him as much pleasure as the clinic gave him satisfaction. It was a bright, cool, open house, with lovely large rooms except for the kitchen. That remained butler pantry size in spite of the glamorous meals that were constantly being prepared in it. There was never a woman in the house whose opinion and convenience were a priority item—not even Suzanne, the cook, though she probably came closer to it than any other woman.

Dinner at Hy's was very fancy—and grew fancier as his celebrity grew. He had learned about wines from Alfred Knopf, a true oenophile. Alfred and Blanche Knopf, and Hy and heaven knows who, drove through the French wine country together more than twenty years ago. During that trip Hy ordered many cases of wine shipped to him, most of them recommended by Alfred, and that began his wine cellar.

By the time he died, his wine was probably the most valuable thing he owned. He was a generous host, and he loved giving small dinner parties of six or eight. Like Melville he knew "Who has but once dined his friends has tasted whatever it is to be Caesar." I think he felt a little like Caesar at the head of the table.

Suzanne did him proud every time. Game birds and chicken were most often the main dish. He loved the "Oohs" and "Aahs." He loved someone trying to guess the vintage of the wine. And he loved good conversation. He was very conscious of the interests and talents of a particular guest, and always threw out a few provocative questions, and then sat back and enjoyed the answers—that is, after he had asked every man in the room, "Are you buying or selling?"

Hy's love of good conversation and his earnest efforts to encourage such conversation, sometimes against mighty odds, were one of his outstanding qualities. He hungered to learn and to know. He had great respect for the expertise of others. And it drove him wild to have to sit and listen to somebody's small talk when something of interest was being said on the other side of the table. He kept his dinner parties small and then tried gamely to have one conversation at a time. If someone in the room, or at the table, started a second conversation he was quite uninhibited about saying in a very authoritative way, "Let's have just one conversation going at a time."

An old friend of ours was reminiscing with me about Hy recently and remembered the time he was sitting at her dinner table. She turned to say something to him and he shushed her with the "just one conversation" line. When he suddenly remembered it was her house he added, "Please." Some people resented this in Hy. Others made fun of it. I found it an imminently logical and acceptable modus operandi. If you stop to notice at your next party you will probably find that almost everyone is talking and almost no one is listening. In many ways Hy was a very civilized man, and more sensitive than many supposed. He said to me one night, after the guests had gone, and almost like a hurt child, "Have you ever noticed I'm always asking other people what they think, but they never ask me what I think?"

What he had as a conversationalist he lacked as an interior decorator. I didn't like any of the furniture in Hy's house, or what passed for decorating. On my shoestring budget I thought I did much better. But somehow that didn't matter. It would never have occurred to me to try to redecorate. Early and late Second Avenue "antique" shop or early and late bachelor was the general period and style—but there were always fresh flowers and somehow the total effect was generally pleasant and bright.

The living room was getting very crowded—nothing was removed as stuff was added. Where there should have been leather Hy settled for plastic. The webbing in the bamboo chairs was perilously thin, and once, nicely aged wrought iron pieces were painted shiny black by Mrs. Tryforos when Hy and I were away on a trip. Does anyone find that bizarre besides me?

I liked the way the house was only because it satisfied Hy. Every piece of furniture, every piece of bric-a-brac had a story to it, a small piece of his life. That was good enough for me. Far more open and honest than a nifty packaged deal from an interior decorator whom he could easily have afforded. Each time I bought something for the house, and that was almost constantly, it was done in an effort to improve slightly while maintaining the status quo—to keep it the way he liked it, but keep it fresh.

The only time the rugs and carpets were cleaned in fourteen years I paid the bill. When a lamp shade fell apart I replaced it. When a chair needed reupholstering or recaning, I had it done. Many things Hy didn't even know had been done, and I didn't stand around saying, "What a good girl am I!" New living room curtains, water glasses, dishes, sheets, towels, irons, all the unsexy stuff you couldn't have engraved were my domain. And that's the way I wanted it.

Hy often said to me, "I've never asked anything of you," and since it seemed to make him happy to believe it, I spent fourteen years letting him believe it. He never understood that the hardest thing he could ask of me was "nothing." There were nights on trips when I waited until he was asleep to wash one of those three pairs of tired khakis he traveled with for fourteen years. He always insisted that he didn't want me to "bother" and sooner or later in our wanderings through Asia and Africa we'd reach a place with room service. I didn't want him ever to feel "obligated." I didn't want to be part of "the cuff link collection" either—and I never was.

Scarsdale:

The Diet

The story of Hy's book is a chapter in itself. It was a watershed in his life, and nothing, most of all Hy, was ever quite the same again. I was in Virginia by then but each trip back was less the same, and each trip back made me happy to see him someplace besides home—Palm Beach, Nassau, Washington—somewhere that the change wasn't so stark. Suzanne said it to me one day. "It isn't the same here now. There's a bad feeling. I don't know what it is. It isn't the same."

Hy was becoming a little like a child who'd been struggling to win the game, "Mother, May I?" and suddenly and deliberately took a giant step backward. Demur if you wish, and tell me I am still impressed by a curtsy, but I found something sad about a man who had stood in front of a mirror at Syracuse University for four years practicing diction ending up with an entourage of hangers-on, and a woman who called him "Ma Chair" and "Super Doctor."

What was the whole exercise for—to get so rich you could revert to type? And all the time I had filed it under "c" for "character" and "w" for wonderful. He stopped being that marvelous, bright man getting "ahead" by some reasonably acceptable set of rules. He had always made some of his own rules, but now he could write them all. Wherever he was standing was the head of the line, so screw saying, "May I?"

Hy's book made him rich (richer) and famous, and those are things I'm sure were fun to be. Imagine trying to save a man from all that. Imagine believing he was too good for it. I did everything I could to persuade Hy from writing the book, but when the contract was signed and there was no turning back I did everything I could to help make it a little better than it otherwise would have been.

We were sitting in the living room on Purchase Street one Sunday in April 1978, *The New York Times* spread around us as usual, when someone called Hy and said, "Say, you're famous! There's a mention of your diet in the *Times Sunday Magazine*." We quickly turned to the right page, and sure enough, in an article about diets, Hy's was mentioned. We both thought that was quite exciting. Diet had always played a key role in Hy's ministering to the sick, especially his heart patients.

He had said, "No fatty meats, no butter, no bread, no liquor, no rich desserts" so many times he finally sat in his office one morning, wrote out what he considered a sensible diet, the diet he essentially followed most of his adult life, and had his secretary type it up and run it off on the mimeo machine. It took him "about an hour." He gave out those mimeographed sheets for nineteen years before the book was born.

Many of his patients were the well-heeled and well-traveled and they took the diet with them all over the country and all over the world. As word of it spread—or as Samm Sinclair Baker put it, "As word of mouth expanded," there were so many demands for it that Hy's mailing costs finally hit more than two thousand dollars a year. Some people sent self-addressed envelopes but most of the expense Hy paid out of his own pocket. He didn't know it at the time but he was casting bread upon the waters, and those sheets were making his book famous before it was even written. Seymour Topping, managing editor of *The New York Times*, was an old friend of Hy's, knew of the diet, and I think it was he who started the ball rolling.

By early that Sunday afternoon Oscar Dystel, an acquaintance of Hy's and then head of Bantam Books, had called to see if Hy was interested in writing a book. By that evening three other publishers had called. Each time Hy came away from the phone laughing and shaking his head, saying, "This is silly as hell. How could you make a book out of a one page diet?" A week or so later so many people had approached him on the subject of a book he was having second thoughts. Maybe he would combine the diet with some good common sense observations and medical practices that forty years of experience had proven sound and valuable. He had some things worth saying. Maybe this was the time.

He made a brief outline of what might conceivably be included in such a book, and took the outline to his old friend Alfred Knopf for advice. Alfred simply wouldn't give the subject the time of day, and kept turning the conversation to things of greater interest to him. Helen, Alfred's second wife, was kind and encouraging right from the start, but Alfred gave him nothing. Hy was deeply hurt by this and never really forgave Alfred. "I've spent a lot of hours ministering to that man, going to him at all hours of the day and night, listening to his problems and he wouldn't give me ten minutes of his time." I knew just how he felt that Monday night in March.

Hy thought that Alfred could at least have told him more about Samm Sinclair Baker, and advised him about contracts. In all fairness to Alfred, maybe he felt as others of us did who loved Hy, that a diet book would not reflect well on him, and he shouldn't go ahead with it. After the book was finally out Alfred praised it highly. I'm afraid I was never courteous enough to do the same.

Hy's next approach was to Random House through Tony Schulte. Tony is Arthur's son, an old friend of Hy's, and an executive at Random House. Like Alfred, Tony thought Hy's outline was thin. Tony's step-mother, Vivian, thought Hy was in way over his head since nutrition was certainly not his field, and Tony wrote what I thought was a decent letter saying in the nicest possible way for Hy to think about it some more before he went ahead with the book.

It impressed me as a letter that Tony had spent a good deal of time composing. Hy was angry when he showed it to me. He never asked favors, never. Now, for the first time in those two close relationships he was asking for something and he didn't get it. Or he didn't get it in the form he wanted it. He didn't want them to publish a book for him, but he did want their expertise on how to go about it.

My feeling was that Tony was putting friendship ahead of making an easy buck, but maybe I'm wrong. Certainly Hy didn't see it that way and he plunged ahead completely on his own. If his friends weren't going to help him there were plenty of people around who would, hucksters who knew that the timing was right and the advance publicity was red hot.

Samm Sinclair Baker, who had co-authored *Dr. Stillman's Fourteen*

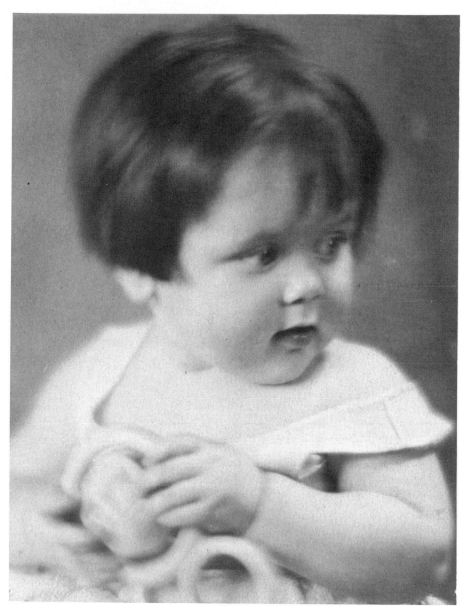

Jean, age one

Mildred Witte Struven, Jean's
mother, 1916

Albert Struven, Jean's father, 1918

(Left to right) Virginia, Mary Margaret, Jean and Bob Struven

Jean at summerhouse in Canada, 1942

Jean at Smith, 1942

Jean and the boys with Jim, 1960

Jean at Thomas School, 1974

Jean at Aspen Executive
Institute, 1973

75th Anniversary of Thomas School, with Dan Lufkin

Jean in her room at Thomas School

Graduation in the garden at Thomas School, 1973

Jean at Madeira, 1980

Jean at Madeira, 1977

Day Weight Loss Program, called and said he would be happy to write the book, and in a short time he had a contract and 50 percent of all monies. Later, when Hy began to realize how much that 50 percent was going to be, and how little he thought of Samm's writing, it gnawed at him. But he always said, "Well, Samm thought of the title, which was very important, and I never could have written it without him, so I guess it wasn't a bad deal." Samm wrote him about writing another book together but Hy made it clear that if there were a second book it wouldn't be with Mr. Baker.

By August of 1978 Samm was busily grinding out chapters of the book and Suzanne van der Vreken was spending every spare moment at her typewriter doing the recipes. Mrs. Baker later changed some of them, but the lion's share of them were the work of Suzanne. Samm's contribution to the recipes were some catchy little names, "Breast of Chicken Herman" and "Spinach Delight A La Lynn." I said, "My God! You actually saw this ahead of time and let him print it?" Hy said, "Well, Samm thought it was cute." It's adorable! I had tried a little cuteness too but Samm red penciled it. We were working on the table of contents, and since the diet, which is why you buy the book, doesn't come until Chapter IV, I suggested as its title "Enough of This Lovemaking, Off with the Calories!" I guess Samm found it too risqué. But you can't beat "Breast of Chicken Herman" for cute.

I had planned all summer to spend the last two weeks of August and Labor Day with Hy. When I arrived he was in a state I had never seen him in before. Samm had written the first few chapters of the book and Hy thought they were awful. He had made his own efforts to edit them, changing a word here or a tense there, but he wasn't satisfied with that either. He was genuinely upset. "I've signed a contract to publish this damned thing and look at it! Jesus!"

It was something he couldn't walk away from. It was also the first time in all the years I had known him that I was conscious of his profanity. And it was the first time in all those years that he needed a kind of help I could try to give. I knew that I wasn't a writer, but I knew that I could improve upon what he had.

I sat down at the table just outside the kitchen and started crossing out and rewriting. I sat there working for two entire weeks, day and night. It was my summer vacation. One of those nights Hy took Lynne Tryforos to a dinner party that their dentist gave. I was served a quick hamburger by Henri and went back to writing the book.

Hy's concession to "good manners" was to be home by 9:30. It wasn't the first time he had done it. The first time I had been sad that he was capable of doing it. That night I was too caught up in the work on the book to be concerned one way or the other. Disillusion had already set in, but then love and friendship are for better or for worse. Aren't they?

Hy's spirits began to rise as changes in the book were made. We had many favorite lines from Samm's original version but our first favorite was in his question and answer chapter. "Q: I want to lose five pounds. How long should I stay on the diet? A: Stay on the diet just long enough to lose the five or six pounds." I found more knee-slappers than Hy did, and after two weeks of my caustic remarks I'm not sure whether he was more teed off at me or Samm.

The last day of my writing holiday was a lovely sunny Labor Day and we took a leisurely drive up to Greenwich. In the course of the drive I told Hy it had been one of my happiest holidays with him because for once I knew I had done something helpful for him when so often it had been the other way. I didn't mention that it was happy in spite of his flagrant extra-curricular activities. Suddenly he turned to me and said, "Look, I'm going to give you $2,000 because it's convenient for me this way—I don't have to tell you why—and maybe next year I'll give you $2,000 more, but that's at my discretion. I don't have to if I don't want to." So much for a loving gift.

I left the next morning and wrote him a rather anguished letter about his callousness, but I don't believe I ever mailed it. He called several times as though nothing had happened and mentioned that he was having "a helluva fight" with some of the doctors at the clinic who were now claiming part of the book's potential returns . . . which by then were looking sizable. He said, "I'll just stop practicing medicine for a year if I have to—or maybe I'll move the office to the house, but by God they're not going to take this book away from me."

A few days later I saw an article about the Scarsdale Diet in one of the newspapers they sell at the grocery store checkout counter. The headline of the story was: "The Magic and Mysterious Chemical Formula of the Scarsdale Diet." It worried me because there wasn't any "chemical formula" and I didn't want anyone to think Hy had claimed it. I wrote him:

Sept. 10, 1978

Dear Hy,

I'm glad that E. Rawson is doing a good job for you. I know it's a great relief and helps alleviate some of the mounting pressures in your life. Certainly, they're only temporary ones, but obviously too they're pretty onerous at the moment.

I hope the "knock-down fight" you mentioned has helped clear the air. I really don't see how you can avoid taking some time off after the book comes out. The demands on your time will be tremendous, whatever your contract with Dystel says. You'll have a "public" then and the public is probably more of a demanding task-master than publishers are. It might be a very handy tax break to take the house off for a year as your place of business anyway. Even though you talked about it with a certain amount of equanimity I think it is really dreadful for any of the doctors to expect to be paid proceeds from the book. It seems to me they're the only real losers if you take a year off. I think it's more a matter of wanting to hurt you than wanting the money. You are widely respected and admired, Hy, but you don't always bring out the best in people, because, as you've been told before, I'm sure, you often hurt them deeply. The only time I even think of your money is when I want to match you—hurt for hurt—and I know there are some hard times to come with the doctors—maybe you read my letter and resented it—but Monday when you offered me $2,000 "because it's convenient for me this way—I don't have to tell you why—and next year maybe I'll give you $2,000 more—but that's at my discretion, I don't have to if I don't want to. I don't owe it to you," your voice sounded as though you were offering a little tip to a $2,000 whore. It was cold and utterly contemptuous.

I don't want a pound of flesh, Hy. I was quite happy to settle for "thank you" and I still am. If the book's successful I hope you may decide on another trip, somewhere, anywhere, together. If I were an acquisitive woman you may be sure that at the age of 55 I wouldn't be in the position I'm in.

You have said to me a hundred times "I never ask anything of you . . . I never ask anything of anyone." But my dear it isn't true. For starters, you ask every woman to be as incapable of love as you are. That's like asking her to be a paramecium, or a woodcock, or some damn thing she isn't. I spent a good deal of time this summer thinking about the qualities a woman should have to survive in today's world—men and women as a matter of fact. Then I wondered how a woman like me, who lacks many of these qualities, could presume to teach them to the young. My opening address to the girls was on this subject, and I'm told it was a very good talk. In fact I've been asked to give it again in Richmond in Oct. and in Washington in Nov. What it lacks in brilliance it makes up for in "down-home" sincerity. There'll be violins in the background! At any rate, my dear, I wish I had been born a door-mat or a man, instead of the miserable half-breed I've turned out to be. I want very much to feel like your equal—but love is no equalizer.

71

One of the female characteristics they call the "Anointment Syndrome" at Wharton School of Business, Univ. of Pa., is still strong in me even though I can talk quite objectively about it in others. In her heart of hearts most women think that sooner or later hands will be placed gently on her head and a voice will say, "You have been a good girl. You have done what you were told and done it well, and now I am going to promote you"—or reward you— or whatever.

I guess on Monday, I was expecting anointment—not a tip—and my idea of anointment from you, my dear, is just a pleasant drive in the country. That's all I bargained for. That's all I wanted.

This crazy article that really prompted me to write at all upset me at first. I thought it might mean lawsuits, etc. But the more I think about it the more useful to you it seems to be. It is a classic example of how people misread, misquote, mix-up, cash-in-on, or just plain prostitute a reputable thing. The "chemistry" myth is abroad in the land whether you encourage it or not. As long as you cover it in the chapter of Questions and Answers, no one can lay it at your feet. The fact is people want it to be a chemical miracle and they're pretty well disposed to believe it no matter what you tell them. It will, I'm afraid, sell books without any push from you. There are big months ahead Hy—please know I'm in the cheering section—not lined up for a piece of the action.

Love,
Jean

A week or so after my letter Hy sent me a check for $4,000 and this note:

MEMO FROM HERMAN TARNOWER

Wednesday

Dear Jean,
For reasons that I cannot explain, it is imperative that I make all book disbursements at this time.

I am enclosing a check for $4,000 that I hope you will accept.

Love,
Hy

I told him that I wouldn't cash it. He interpreted this to mean, poor troubled man, that I might be holding out for more, and offered to double it again. I cashed the check for $4,000, and admitted to myself that Hy had become quite a different man than the one I had imagined him to be, or the one he had once been.

I still don't know what possessed Hy in the best of spirits to intrude on an otherwise beautiful afternoon drive to make his $2,000 offer, but in retrospect I think it was either because there were so many people hovering around the till, or because for the first time in all our years of friendship he wasn't the giver, he was the taker or receiver, and it wasn't a role he was comfortable with. He didn't want to be beholden to anyone. He had long since entered his "I don't love anyone, I don't need anyone" period and he wanted to be sure that I didn't leave with any illusions of grandeur.

After Hy's death Samm Sinclair Baker did a great deal of talking to the press about Mrs. Harris having absolutely nothing to do with *The Complete Scarsdale Medical Diet*. One of Hy's old friends was quoted as saying, "Mrs. Harris's name in the book's dedication was gratuitous kindness on the doctor's part" part of "his letting her down easy." Another said, "Mrs. Harris was jealous of the doctor's book."

Gratuitous kindness to a woman was something Hy was never guilty of. The remarks were made by people who didn't know either of us well or anything about our relationship.

We were down in Lyford Cay in Nassau visiting the John Loebs, sitting in bed as a matter of fact, when Hy handed me the first copy of the book, with the kind of expression on his face that David and Jimmy had when they gave me the bookends they had made in manual training. "Look at the acknowledgment," he said, beaming. It took a great deal of tongue biting to keep from saying "Oh, Hy. How could you?" There, at the top of a long list of women who had served him in various capacities while the magnum opus took shape were the words:

We are grateful to Jean Harris for her splendid assistance in the research and writing of this book

There had never been anything that public about my friendship with Hy and I certainly didn't want it now. And the word "research" troubled me. My "research" had consisted of spending an hour in the White Plains Hospital library looking up definitions of "ketosis." I had more than enough of my own "research" to do and I certainly wouldn't have presumed to do it for a doctor. As for whether I did an appreciable amount of writing for the book, I did, and a number of people, including Henri and Suzanne van der Vreken, Samm Baker and Lynne Tryforos are quite aware of the fact.

Henri and Suzanne watched me writing, and rewriting for those two weeks, told me where to go in Rye to get Xerox copies made, saw the crumpled sheets of paper accumulate around me and heard the occasional obscenities as I exploded, "How in the hell did a man with his brains get involved in this creepy thing?" I went with Hy to deliver some of the rewrites to Samm's house, and by then Samm was getting a little testy about all the changes, and Hy was trying to be diplomatic but firm. Hy said himself, on a number of occasions, "Jean wrote the book." He said it to a woman who interviewed him for *The Washington Star* and I protested and walked away for fear the "socialite headmistress of the Madeira School" might get some publicity she certainly didn't want.

Sitting in my lawyer's office today are the chapters of the book as Samm wrote them and my handwritten corrections and rewritings. It was a large piece of work lovingly done to the best of my ability because I never stopped wanting the world to know Hy was as good as I thought he was. I didn't want him to look like a second string "diet doc" when he was a first string cardiologist and internist.

Later, of the almost four hundred potential jurors that were questioned in the process of picking a jury for the case of the People of New York State vs. Jean Harris there were probably fewer than thirty who didn't refer to a splendid physician named Dr. Herman Tarnower as "that diet doc." Ironically enough it was Assistant District Attorney George Bolen who rose and requested that the judge himself stop using the term. Judge Leggett answered, "That's the way he's known, and I'll use the term if I choose."

Philadelphia:
Springside School

I was a teacher for thirty-six years. The last twelve of them I combined administration and teaching. I had thought at first I would write about them another time, and maybe never. It would be easier that way. There is so much, it's hard to know what to put in and what to leave out. But if it is beyond the ability of some of Hy's closest friends to imagine that anything could have troubled me that March night except one of the doctor's girlfriends, then how could a stranger know what filled my life, moved me, motivated me, frustrated and exhausted me? How could he know unless I told him, and how could I write about myself leaving anyone with the thought that my life was so empty it held nothing but Hy?

There's a good deal of folklore about "headmistresses," remembered with a mixture of fun, fondness, and fear by those of us who matriculated at their various seats of learning. The place you had to sit when you were called before her "presence" for corrective purposes had different names at different schools, but meant the same thing. At Miss Hall's School it was called "the little green chair." At Laurel it was "the bench." At Springside it was "Miss Potter's hot seat."

There is still a hot seat in every headmistress's office, but today the headmistress is sitting in it. Today, before degrees from the proper halls of ivy, one would have to list as minimal requirements for a successful school head, the hide of an iguana, need for a maximum of four hours sleep per night, a law degree, and a wife. Just about anyone on the campus grounds, or anyone within earshot of the campus grounds, would be happy to tell you how to run the place. The constituency is much wider than the school's size would suggest, and since every private school worth its salt has an annual deficit to cover each year, one's main occupation is often raising money instead of raising the intellectual level of the young.

On the other hand, teaching in a private school can still be quite agreeable, especially if you have a sizable family trust fund to pay your bills. It's harder than it used to be, but it can still be enjoyable.

By and large, a teacher in a good private school enjoys the privilege of teaching—not collecting the milk money, filling things out in triplicate, or patrolling the halls, but teaching. The state governments are doing their best to change this and spread the misery around, but one still can teach in a private school, or "independent" school as they prefer to be called.

You also enjoy in these schools reasonably competent students, probably as well motivated to work as any group of people in our country. That could be damning them with faint praise, but newspapers do love to refer to private school students as "preppies," the consummate country club set, and the coddled rich, when the truth is, if everyone on the Detroit assembly lines had been putting in the hours of honest-to-God-hard-labor that the average Exeter, Madeira, Farmington, Andover student does there would be more Chevies and fewer Toyotas on American highways.

Best of all, a private school teacher has the intellectual freedom, given certain agreed upon goals, to achieve those goals in ways that make sense to her. She can use a new book, spend a little extra time giving a play one week and make up any lost time another week. I have been in public schools where posted in the front office is the *exact* page every third grade reading class is to be on for that day—an educational travesty that doesn't seem to embarrass the administrator who posts it.

For the privilege of enjoying these intellectual freedoms, however, private school teachers pay in cold, hard cash. There is a popular and comforting myth beloved by many private school parents that private school teachers teach "for the sheer joy of it"—so they go through their professional lives paying their students' tuitions, motivated by all that unbridled joy. That is an honest observation, not a complaint on my part, since as a parent I was the recipient of much private school generosity.

The median salary of private school teachers is anywhere from $3,000 to $10,000 less per year than that of the public school teacher around the corner. Most boarding schools make up the difference by providing campus homes and meals for faculty, adding, of course, some of the necessary parental responsibilities in return.

Some of us weighed the intellectual pluses, and the very practical plus that to teach in a private school in most states you didn't have to be state certified, which required countless tedious hours of "education courses," and opted for a lower salary. Required standards of proficiency in order to teach are very much needed, but, as presently written by some states, they permit seriously unqualified people to teach, and keep out others.

I was told when I looked into a public school teaching job in Michigan, "Lady, Albert Einstein couldn't teach physics in a Detroit school if he didn't have a certificate." I was told by an accrediting official in the state of Virginia, "I could cry when I read the ungrammatical letters we receive from English teachers asking to renew their certification." That doesn't mean that there aren't outstanding teachers and scholars in the public schools, but it means there is a sizable amount of deadwood too.

Today, scores of students who list teaching as the profession they aspire to when they take their SAT exams, now rank below those of students checking fourteen other listed professions. In other words, if you aren't much of a scholar today, you are more apt to go into teaching than into fourteen other fields.

I was fortunate enough to begin my teaching in a splendid country day school in Grosse Pointe, Michigan—now known as University-Liggett School. I taught there for nineteen years. Both of my sons started school there in three-year nursery school. Jimmy went through seventh grade, David through tenth, both tuition free, before we moved to Philadelphia. A small salary was of little concern to me and the teaching was pure pleasure. Today, fewer schools give this important plus because of IRS complications.

In spite of the fact that it sounds much more liberated and impressive to be a female doctor or lawyer, you can't beat the combination of a gratifying profession and the knowledge that your children won't find the key under the mat—and you can vacation together. It was a lovely luxury for all of us. For those teachers who didn't have children there were no compensating salary increases, however, so I was one of the parents who enjoyed what I consider the only truly unforgivable thing about private schools. The faculty pays a large slice of the tuition. The answer certainly doesn't lie in unionizing—that would close most private schools. It lies in educating alumnae and businesses to a better understanding of what a well-educated citizenry is worth.

I enjoyed the experience of teaching. My first two years of teaching were in American history to the seniors, civics to the ninth grade, and current events to the seventh grade. I taught thirty-two classes per week and was paid $1,800 per year and could hardly believe my good fortune. The year was 1946, and there was a serious teacher shortage.

After two years of watching me work until long after midnight to prepare classes, my husband Jim made me resign. The school said, "Would you consider working half a day? We need a kindergarten teacher and the children go home at noon." For the next two years I was a kindergarten teacher. After David was born I stayed home for two years except for trouping in Junior League plays in the public schools. I played Pinocchio and a mean sister in Cinderella.

One August, when Jimmy, my younger son, was three months old, my old school called to say their first grade teacher had been in an accident and it might be a month before they could replace her. Would I fill in? "Well, I'm not sure—what do they do in first grade?" "They learn to read—you'll love it." I hurried to the library to take out every book on reading I could find—and eleven years later I was still teaching first grade, one of the most intellectually exciting jobs a teacher can have.

It pleased me to have the opportunity to help children start really thinking long before I had. I had an inquiring mind in the classroom, but I was more concerned about "the right answer" than anyone with an original idea can afford to be. I always coughed up what the teacher wanted—a coward's way out—and I missed a lot along the way as a result.

As a teacher, I am happy to say, I never made the same mistake. Nothing delighted me more than an offbeat answer or even "the wrong answer" from a student with a thoughtful reason and the courage to defend his idea or maybe just a lovely sense of humor. I guess I say "his" because as I look back and remember some of those splendid wrong answers they usually came from a little boy. I learned as a first grade teacher that a really bright child will often miss "simple" questions on a standardized test because his fertile brain has taken the question a step beyond the adult who made up the question.

We spent a lot of time painting in my classroom. I tried to get little girls in clean white pinafores to use their arms and elbows and even their feet for the fingerpaints—not just the top of the pinkie. We spent a whole year trying to figure out what color water is, and the class collected a grand portfolio of pictures showing every possible color of the sea, from pure gold to jet black. A mother of one of my students wrote me in prison that the seascape her then six-year-old daughter painted that year is still framed and hanging in her dining room.

We came to terms with the fact that there isn't a big empty space between the sea and the sky, and flower stems don't always stand ramrod straight, and we drew flowers the way they probably look to a ladybug. We listened to the songs of whales; we learned some poems by e. e. cummings, and we wrote our own endings to the story of Stuart Little. In a ninth grade civics class we spent some time trying to rewrite the Constitution in our own words and discovered it would be pretty hard to improve upon it. And I spent some uncomfortable moments with a family lawyer who was very angry because I had given him a C on the work he had done for his client's child. We tried to define "civilization" in an eighth grade class, and some first graders tried to figure out the difference between work and play, a job so complicated we never did agree on anything definitive.

My first graders wrote a lot of plays, taking as characters the dolls and puppets the children brought for show and tell—or the masks they made for Halloween, or the people they thought might gather in a certain place at a certain time. They would make up their list of characters, each would choose the person or creature he or she wanted to be. Then I'd say, "Okay. Your part in this play is as good as you make it. Figure out whom you want to talk to, what you want to say, and write it down." They knew their letters and the sounds they made, and they would set to with a will.

That night I would take all their writing home, spread it all over the living-room floor and begin to put the pieces together like the parts of a puzzle. Somehow, they always came together and became part of a logical whole. I always encouraged them to "write their own script," a privilege Hy would later remind me I didn't have.

"You can't write the script, Jean," he'd say. "You can't write the script."

My master's thesis was built around a history of Detroit which I wrote one year for a particularly bright group of six-year-olds: There were no holds barred on the vocabulary. I would write a chapter every week or two, read it to them, and within a day or two if not on the spot, they could all read it too. They loved watching the book grow and taking it home to read something to the family that they knew had substance to it.

They became totally immersed in old Fort Pontchartrain, made a model of it in their spare time (it ended up on display in the Detroit Public Library), made visits to the Historical Society, on their own time, and by spring, when I had had more than my fill of Fort Pontchartrain, the children insisted upon writing a play about it, completely on their own. They started, as we always did, by listing who was probably there in the spring, what they might be doing, and then choosing their characters and writing the parts. While I have worked with every age group from nursery school to high school, I will always believe that teachers who have never worked with first graders have missed a special part of the joy of teaching and learning.

Why does a reasonably happy teacher become a school administrator? Very easy. She needs the money. Much has been written about Mrs. Harris's need for "power," "need to be in control," written by friend and foe alike, but the fact is even in 1966 it was rather difficult to support yourself and two children on $8,500 a year (before taxes!).

It is also true that while I like to talk about ideas I am an impatient person who likes to see the idea become a reality. I don't see myself "needing to be in control" but everyone else does so I bow to their ability to be more objective. I can only say in my behalf I was a cooperative Indian for more years than I was the chief. I thought the control I sought was control of me. Moves up the ladder paid the bills.

Because you have been a good teacher it does not necessarily follow that you will be a good head of a school. As everywhere else in life, one is dogged by Parkinson's Law that we rise to our level of incompetence. Along with an intelligent concern and affection for the young, and a long list of other things, one must also take a kind of humility into that nifty, neatly slip-covered office, an ability to say "mea culpa." I think that I did, though "humility" would hardly be listed as my strong point by either friend or foe.

My first administrative job was at Springside School in Philadelphia, as director of the Middle School. The boys and I lived there for five years and whatever W. C. Fields said about Philadelphia I second the motion. In five years I was quite literally never once introduced anywhere to anyone, by anyone as "Jean Harris." It was always "This is Mrs. Harris. Mrs. Harris is the director of the Middle School at Springside."

I never got a run down on how everyone else in the room made a living, but "director of the Middle School at Springside" was part of my name for those five years. My sons loved, and still love, Philadelphia, a very important plus, and Springside was a splendid school and a fine place to begin my administrative experience, so what's to complain? I remember it as the place and time when I began to be a nonperson.

My years at Springside, 1966 to 1971, as director of the Middle School were those very disruptive years nationally when young people were breaking out of the cocoons of the fifties and early sixties, protesting against the Vietnam War, protesting about what we were doing to the environment, and, most frightening of all for parents, beginning to use drugs. It was a whole new experience for suburban parents and teachers and it marks the time, on my calendar certainly, when parents began turning more and more to the schools and saying "do something."

From those years on, teachers and administrators in what are still our "better" schools began to play roles they had not bargained for and still aren't really prepared for. There were many times as I sat in my office and parents poured out their fears and frustrations about their children and ended with "What shall we do?" that I was tempted to cry "How in the hell should I know!" I often said, "If I had all the answers I suppose I'd have two perfect children. In the long run the answer depends upon love, common sense, and the energy it takes to say 'no.' "

I don't think we've grown one bit wiser in the last fifteen years about how to raise children. Instead, we've kept backing down and learning to accept what they want—before we've taught them what all the options are. Worst of all, we've taught them that "love" means lying for them and making excuses for them. It's something many parents do today. My notes from parent conferences read like the parent-conference notes of every school administrator along the East Coast during those years:

"One mother came in to tell me she 'knows for a fact that some of our eighth grade girls are smoking pot.' She said her daughter had seen them 'on several occasions.' She refused to give any names because 'One of the families involved have been friends for years. I know them well enough to know they wouldn't do much about it anyway, and I don't want to spoil the friendship. I think you ought to do something about it, Mrs. Harris.' I assured her I couldn't react to anything that vague and therefore on behalf of the school I couldn't help." In one three-month period there were eleven different parents who came for conferences that ended with "But I can't say anymore because of what the other girls will do to Ethel—or Mary," or whatever the daughter's name was "and anyway I just don't want to get involved."

Another mother rushed into my office one day, very upset, having just come from a town meeting where drugs were being discussed. She had asked the speaker what a responsible citizen should do if he knew a person was selling pot. The speaker had said, "Report that person at once to the police."

The mother had been told by her daughter of a boy in the neighborhood who sold pot. Mother gave me the boy's name and urged me to call the police. "If I called them myself it would destroy my daughter's confidence in me. I promised her I wouldn't tell." The school became a dumping ground for everyone's nasty little secrets, or worse, nasty little rumors, and then Mother went home feeling cleansed.

We scurried around to find good films and convincing speakers about drugs but there weren't many to be found. Most of them simply served to widen the credibility gap, and one of our speakers, a doctor and parent of one of the students, gave them the "I'd rather see them use pot than alcohol" line, which didn't help very much.

In a memo to Miss Potter, headmistress of Springside, dated April 1969, I wrote, "This is my last parent conference on the subject of pot. If anyone else brings it up I will refer them to you. I don't know in my own mind what the answers to the pot questions are, and I have played the go-between, detective, and villain for the eighth grade to a very tiresome degree this year. Next year I'm going to try to be an educator again." I noted at the end of the memo that while I was writing it three disgruntled eighth graders had come into my office and prefaced their conversation with, "Why does the school always have to get involved in everything we do?"

Why indeed! I've asked myself the same question many times. The answer I think is that adults and children are both frightened: There aren't many social rules anymore to make them feel safe. They all want someone to blame for their discomfort, and someone to make them feel more secure. They often ask the school and the school administrator to play both roles. It wasn't without reason that I often talked to the girls about our "schizophrenic world."

Eleven years later I had apparently changed my definition of what an "educator" is, or is supposed to do. The last letter I dictated on Monday, March 10, 1980, was to an old and dear friend of Madeira's who had written me a lovely, rambling, philosophical letter about integrity and had asked me for more copies of my speech on the subject. I told him briefly of the sadness of having to expel four seniors just two months before graduation and added:

I like to believe that morality on this campus has now bottomed out, and there is no place to go but up. It is the top item on my agenda for the rest of the time I am here. A Merit Scholar without a conscience is no scholar at all.

In a tragedy where irony has run rampant this is perhaps the greatest irony of all. Within hours after she wrote that, the earnest lady who wrote it was indicted for second degree murder! I keep thinking, with a sad smile, of the old Russian peasant saying "When the fox preaches the passion, farmer watch out for your sheep." I wonder how many people since that March night, standing with a drink in the hand, have said, "Who the hell was she . . ."

I keep on preaching, knowing that I am not the fox, but forgetting sometimes that many people now think that I am.

Twice in my naiveté have I told parents, without couching it in "maybes" or "possiblys," that I thought their daughter was using drugs. In each case I believed there was no doubt, but in each case I couldn't have proved it in court.

The first mother already knew about it and wasn't worried. "Everybody talks about it because the drab, square little people around here have always been jealous of me, and their daughters are jealous of Jackie. They're ratting on her because they're jealous and I think it's absolutely shitty of them!"

She added, "Of course I can't make Jackie do anything she doesn't want to do. The only approach is to make the children know it isn't chic to smoke pot anymore—people aren't doing it." These were her exact words. Unfortunately, the only reason it isn't "chic" today is because it's so commonplace.

The second time, at another school, one of the seniors slipped out of her chair onto the floor and lay there, sound asleep, in the middle of an assembly, practically under the nose of the speaker. At the end of the assembly her friends nudged her and woke her and she did her best to leave the auditorium before I could say "Please go to my office." She stayed there until her mother arrived. Mother listened to what the girl had done and said, "She was bored."

In the course of relating what had happened I had used the term "spaced out." Mother's second sentence was "I'll see you in court. And you better be able to prove that in court." The case never materialized because I think it must finally have become evident to the family how very deeply involved in drugs the girl was.

One of the country's most prestigious boarding schools was sued by the parents of a student expelled for using pot. The parents' case was "if the school had been doing its job properly, and instilling the right values, the student wouldn't have used pot." In the last fifteen years private schools have spent thousands and thousands of dollars on litigation of drug related offenses. The young haven't been served, the use of marijuana hasn't abated, tuitions have gone up, and untold hours of teaching and administrative time have been wasted.

Since 1968 I have read virtually every article and book on the subject of marijuana that I could find, and have read or given many of them to students. Hy, who had very strong convictions about the danger of pot, sent me anything of value on the subject that came to his attention. In fact, he always sent extra copies so that I would send one to each of my sons. I have talked with doctors, policemen, and psychiatrists on the subject, and had them talk to students. I have expelled students for selling, using, or possessing pot on campus because it was against not only federal or state laws, but against the clearly stated and written rules of all the schools I have worked in.

What I have done many educators and parents all over the country have done. Today the TV program "60 Minutes" tells me that marijuana is the largest cash crop in the states of Hawaii and California. A number of (more than five) Madeira students have told me, quite openly and ingenuously, that parents of their friends in some of America's poshest neighborhoods "sell pot." "But they're really very nice people, Mrs. Harris. They'd never sell bad stuff." What will happen is what has always happened. When enough people do "the wrong thing" it becomes "the right thing." The words "progress" and "evolution" both carry with them the mythology of "getting better."

We look at the apes in the zoo or picture a Neanderthal man dragging his mate by the hair, and we look at ourselves in the mirror and think, "Fantastic! It all came out so well!" Since change is the one thing you can bank on perhaps it's a good myth to cling to; far wiser though to accept Lewis Thomas's article of faith "that we humans are a profoundly immature species, only now beginning the process of learning how to learn. . . . Young and old, we are always students in an introductory class."

At the three schools where I have served as an administrator there was a building that could have been used for a small day-care center. Each was a good building, homey, attractive, a place where I would have let my own children attend nursery school. In each case I was willing to do the work required to start a nursery, to find the money, and to make it part of the curriculum for students to staff it. In each case there were working mothers nearby who needed such a facility. In each case the building did not meet federal OSHA standards about how many square feet and how many toilets go to make a good day-care center, so the potential came to nothing. The more we talk about individuality the more standardized we become. To too many people individuality means "anything you get, I get," whether it's floor space or toilets or a college diploma.

Private schools are especially big on "individuality," "individual attention," "the importance of the individual," and "helping the individual to achieve her full potential." The very difficult part, the part that most students and parents and board members everywhere can't accept, is that consistency is the first casualty when you're a firm believer in individuality.

"Mrs. Harris is too emotional and she isn't consistent," were the two complaints brought to me by the president and vice-president of the board at Madeira when they gave me my new contract and a large raise. I told them the first criticism was certainly deserved and I would work on it, and I did, very hard. To the second criticism I could only promise they would hear more of the same as I continued to make as honest an evaluation of each student and each situation as I could.

The same thing never happened twice. It was only on the surface that things looked the same. Decisions that sounded "inconsistent" were not made precipitously, and some may have been wrong, but the school's philosophy was to have high moral standards for all students and to value and honor and encourage individuality, and that's what was done. It is not an easy combination of goals to achieve, again because the lines are not clearly drawn between what we want and what we think we want.

Of the four schools where I have worked, one gave grades and had an academic honor roll, one gave grades but had never had an academic honor roll, one gave grades and was about to give up its honor roll last I heard, and one gave no grades at all, only written comments. The stated philosophical goals of all four schools were almost identical. "Equality" and "individuality" were the educational passwords in the middle sixties, and all through the seventies, private as well as public schools rode off in every direction pursuing them.

Madeira, for philosophical reasons I have never heard explained, gives elaborate silver bowls and endless ribbons for riding but awards no prizes or recognition of any kind for academic achievement. It won't even allow Yale or Harvard to award a book to an outstanding student. If one is simply motivated to do one's best academically, why not the same motivation on a horse? There is a splendid, illogical smugness about the old riders of Madeira that refuses to be confused by logic. I was reminded many times that "the riders give more money." I'm afraid it will always be so. It was a "riding" member of the board who said to me with venom in her voice, "It is obscene to suggest selling one inch of these four hundred acres for endowment." She never suggested that it was obscene to ask a good teacher and father of three to live on $10,000 a year.

By the time I reached the Thomas School I could defend, even though it still wasn't my first choice, the school's recently adopted system of no grades at all, only comments. Grades had become so inflated that "average" had squeezed out the Cs and become a B on almost every campus in the country. The old bell-shaped curve, for good or for ill, had disappeared with the whooping crane.

Rowayton, Connecticut: Farewell to Thomas

I moved to Connecticut in the fall of 1971 to take over as head of the Thomas School. The school had just been refused accreditation by the New England Association of Schools and Colleges for a long list of reasons.

Among others, the budget indicated that there would be a $78,000 deficit that year and no one had any idea how it would be covered. The alumnae were all mad at someone or something; the cocktail party circuit said the school wouldn't open another year. Many of the school's old records and reports had no dates on them and grades were often noted on the back of an old envelope in Miss Thomas's careful script, so preparing a transcript was sometimes an all-day affair. Renaissance history was being taught in the seventh, eighth, and tenth grades because some of the alumnae remembered what fun it had been to dress up in thirteenth century costumes and have splendid pageants on the shores of Long Island Sound, and the American history classes were still reading Muzzey, virtually unchanged since I had used it thirty years before! Fortunately it went out of print the second year I was there.

All those things notwithstanding, there was a sense of community about the place, some fine girls, a few master teachers, and a beautiful plant to work with. (Besides being beautiful the plant had a very large demand mortgage whose interest rate jumped from 5½ to 8 percent one day in 1973!) The board consisted of some very decent people who were willing to give the place one more good try at survival against rough odds. They were completely honest with me about the school's problems—to the extent that they knew them. No one can ever predict what various members of the alumnae will do at any school, but especially a school that had been founded fifty years before "for the exceptional child," meaning, from what I saw, exceptionally bright, exceptionally dull, exceptionally talented, and exceptionally trying— some of each. I too was willing to take the gamble because the experience would be valuable, it would be wonderfully gratifying if we succeeded, and Philadelphia was a dead end. I could stay and become the grand old lady of the Middle School if I lived long enough, but that didn't sound like an appealing option.

Many splendid things happened at Thomas. The school was small enough so that we could do things together, mixing ages from twelve to eighteen, moving school to the Delaware Water Gap for a beautiful week in October with a wonderfully enthusiastic faculty happy to cooperate, enjoying almost a family closeness. Unfortunately, it was too small to pay its bills and ultimately the board with my strong recommendation voted to close the school and give its assets to another girls' school, the Low-Heywood School in Stamford. The schools' last year and its closing were remarkably orderly and productive, especially in view of the difficulties thrown in its path by a small but very vocal and emotional group of alumnae.

I had no sooner arrived at Thomas than letters arrived threatening no support until a teacher who had been fired the year before was reinstated. That another teacher was now under contract to teach the man's classes, that the man had been introduced to me once and been unconscionably rude was of no matter. One woman assured me the school would never get "another dime" until it rehired four of her favorite teachers who, over a period of seven years, had bit the dust. One had left because of poor health, one now lived in Florida, another was working happily in New York—details—get them back. Fortunately, "another dime" was about all she had ever given so the next one wasn't missed. One alumna whose daughter was a senior when I arrived hadn't paid her tuition bills for two years. Other alumnae thought it was "absolutely rotten" of me to make an issue of money with a nice old graduate of Thomas. "Give her a scholarship." There are many alumnae—not just at Thomas—who can't see why it "costs anything" to have a couple more students around, as long as "the teachers and things are there anyway." How the teachers will get paid simply doesn't concern them. The alumna in question finally gave us a lien on her house for the $6,900 she owed us when her daughter graduated. When her house was sold we were sixth on the list of lien holders and got nothing. Later, when a very emotional group of alumnae and neighbors were holding public meetings to "save Thomas," the lady in question very publicly signed a pledge of $1,500 for the school if we stayed open another year. If you are going to help save a private institution you profess to love, something in addition to your heart has to be in the right place!

In the early spring of 1972 I asked the seniors what preferences they had for a commencement speaker and what subjects they might like to hear about. The replies tell much about what was happening in schools that year. There were mixed returns on preferences, though "poetry reading" was first. One girl summed up for all of them the subjects they didn't want. "I don't want to hear about drugs, war, pollution, apathy in students, the generation gap, women's lib, college, or sex!" I was a little tired of that list too, but while you could pick the graduation speaker you couldn't pick each day's traumas and crises. Enrollment in private schools was falling in 1972–1973 and admissions policies in a school like Thomas were very elastic. We ran the gamut from happy, well-adjusted, varsity hockey type Merit Scholars to some pretty troubled young ladies who brought a lot of their trouble with them. There were some all-American types with sad problems too, like the one who left to have a baby, gave it up for adoption, and then didn't go to her senior prom because "I don't know anyone to ask."

The everyday problems of running a school were no different those four years at Thomas than at most schools. There was constant agitation for a smoking room. Just at the moment when there was proof positive that smoking was harmful, school after school knuckled under and gave the kids their way. The principal of a large public high school in Connecticut said, "We know it's crazy, but at least this way they don't lock themselves in the lavatories and rip the fixtures off the wall." My firm "No" remained a firm "No" at Thomas and the students came back with their favorite argument, "You're a hypocrite if you don't let us smoke because you know we're going to do it anyway."

Clothing was a big item which you tried to downplay because there were always eager candidates for martyrdom if you made it too much of an issue, ready to fight for their God-given right to be dirty, sloppy and inappropriate. At Springside the girls wore uniforms but the imaginative young could think of hundreds of ways to sidestep the intent of the dress code and still be "legally" within bounds.

At Thomas I tried by example and gentle persuasion to upgrade appearances and finally had to resort to a written plea to parents because the message was coming back "Mrs. X brought her daughter to look at the school but wouldn't consider sending little Sally where students looks so ghastly." Harvard can get away with it, but a struggling little day school had to dress up for company. We were on the road to respectable compromise by the time it closed.

Thomas's last graduation was a beautiful one, out in the garden with the rhododendron in full bloom. The students were all accepted at other schools for the next year; most of the teachers, not all, had new jobs. Two retiring teachers who would have been virtually destitute were given generous retirement settlements from the sale of the school property. All teachers were given severance pay based on years of service to the school; Miss Darling, in her late eighties, who had lived at the school since she had retired years before as the music teacher, went to a retirement home run by her church, with her rent paid by the school; and $250,000 was given to Low-Heywood-Thomas. Mildred Dunnock, an old friend of the school, read from T. S. Eliot's "East Coker."

There were tears, but it ended in an orderly, dignified way, not in chaos and tragedy as it might have.

Virginia:
Headmistress

1.

It is hard to be the head of a boarding school, and it's particularly hard if you don't have a wife. You have to be twice as energetic—and hug the dog when you feel hurt. Better still you should be very tough and not feel hurt. Ask any good headmistress, and there are some fine ones, what she was like as a child and she'll tell you, "I was a tomboy, climbed trees, and played center field for the neighborhood team." Today she can down two double martinis at lunch and still go back to the meeting and remember what anyone said. While they were climbing trees I was playing house, and while they're ordering the second martini I'm still on my first whiskey sour. Maybe I should have admitted to myself after that first meeting of the Headmistresses Association of the East that I was no match for them. But I loved the challenge and I tackled the job with a will.

A headmistress is thought to be a "role model," and so she can be sometimes. I think I was willing to be one, but I wanted the role to be that of a woman first—a woman who happened to be a headmistress. I'm afraid that wasn't the model the Madeira board had agreed upon. At best the board was ambivalent.

I had said to the search committee before I came to Madeira, "Please know that I will work very hard for the girls and for the school. But I will not marry Madeira. I will have a private life away from the school, a life that will refuel me. I will not live my life vicariously through the girls and their kind letters. I want to live life as fully as I hope each of them will." I'm sure no one was listening.

I have probably been told a hundred times, "You sure don't look like a headmistress." A child said it to me once and added most ingenuously, "You just look like somebody's mother." I would be willing to bet that no one ever told Ted Sizer of Andover, or Charlie Lord of St. Timothy's, or Emmet Wright of Woodberry Forest, "You sure don't look like a headmaster."

Headmasters come in all sizes, shapes, and ages—though the truth is they are often very attractive, gray, if at all, in just the right places, with leather elbow patches on the tweed jacket, a pretty wife from one of the Seven Sisters, and two adorable, apple-cheeked children— once in pinafores, now in hip-hugger jeans. If old dad lasts long enough at the job the apple-cheeked children can become very troubled, or very troublesome from being reminded so many times they are the headmaster's children, and a healthy number of the nifty wives are finally saying, "I'll be glad to run the bazaar, and have eighty for coffee, twenty-five for dinner, teach Latin, and proctor the library—as soon as I'm on the payroll. No tickee, no washee!" But whatever his other problems, and they are considerable by the very nature of his job, he is not expected to be physically unattractive.

Headmistresses still are. Bifocals, short cropped gray hair, big feet, short and waistless, or uncommonly tall and gangly, someone who kept rising on the educational ladder because she didn't get a better offer. It's terribly outdated and it was always inappropriate but it's still pervasive. Even grandparents who now tell you casually about the "nice boy" their granddaughter is living with still expect a Mrs. Chipsy type, safely married or safely unwanted, sitting in the headmistress's chair. And heaven knows, whatever the life-style of the students, their parents, and the board members may be it mustn't be hers. Hers is but to do or die.

I haven't any statistics, but as I think of the headmistresses I know today most are happily married, to what must be a very special fellow who puts up with the intrusions on their privacy and gives her the support that keeps her going. I don't know any bachelor headmasters.

I was not a stranger to the traumas and pressures of running a school or to family pressures when I arrived at Madeira, but by March 1980 I was growing less and less resilient. I fell harder and bounced back slower. There was never anyone there to catch the fall. I had been told by the board of directors of Madeira that I was their unanimous choice as head of the school. They had rung my bell, not I theirs, and they had pondered about their choice for over six months after their first interview with me, and they had checked into every corner of my life. They arranged a large reception for me where I was introduced to the school's constituency.

What I did not know until two years later was that they were still having a cat fight over the selection five minutes before the first guests arrived. I don't know if Hy played any part in their deliberations, or not. He certainly did two years later after his ill-timed but well meant acknowledgment of me in his book. Shortly after it came out I was told by a board member, "You have no right *ever* during the school year to leave this campus on a weekend unless it is on school business."

It was spring 1979, the junior and senior students had unlimited weekends but the woman who worked seven days and nights a week to run the school was actually told by a popular member of the board that from September 5 to June 8 the parameters of her life were to be the Madeira campus. This from a woman who had professed friendship and support until the day she made this senseless pronouncement, right after her announcement in a board meeting that, "As far as I'm concerned you're on probation." Not one board member raised a voice in my behalf.

Not one board member protested. Not one board member asked the reason for her statement. Not one board member called later and said "Forget it—she's an idiot." The woman herself never responded to two letters from me, nor returned three phone calls. And another member of the board said, "Oh heavens, of course you aren't on probation." She refused three requests of mine to put that statement in writing. A student treated in the same arbitrary way would have brought suit. I was given a $5,000 raise and another year's contract but no civility and no apology.

In February 1980 I was given my fourth one-year contract and another $5,000 raise. I had gone to be headmistress of the Thomas School in Connecticut in the fall of 1971 knowing that it was a calculated risk as to whether the school could be salvaged. The board was well informed about the condition of the school—late in becoming so, but certainly honest with me. I went to Madeira believing I would have the active cooperation and support of the board and believing it was in a much stronger position than it was. In that respect the board hadn't been dishonest. They had simply been totally uninformed about what condition the school was in. And I was the messenger who brought the bad news.

Among other things, heads of private schools are mendicants, always shaking the tambourine, always in need of money, the reason being, by and large, that they charge what the traffic will bear, not what services rendered actually cost. If competitive schools can pay their bills charging $9,500 per year for tuition, room and board because they have invested endowment to cover at least part of their deficit, then Madeira had to keep its tuition within that ball park figure and spend the rest of the year in an annual fund drive. Half a million dollar deficits per year are not unusual in many secondary schools today—and that just pays the bills and and adds nothing to endowment.

One member said, at my first board meeting in October 1977, in a half annoyed, half defensive tone, "Whadda ya mean Madeira needs money? I thought we had plenty of money." This was in response to my observation that Madeira was ten years behind comparable schools in building an endowment. Madeira's endowment in 1966 was $1,600,000. Eleven years later, after the halcyon days of fund raising had passed, it was $2,300,000. Nothing had been done to protect the school against tomorrow, and tomorrow was now bearing down upon it with a vengeance. The reaction of the then chairman of the board when I said we must start immediately to organize long-range planning was "If you start any long-range planning around here you'll tear the place apart." He was wrong. It only tore me apart.

When I expressed my strong conviction that we needed faculty housing an earnest old friend of the school said, "What about those houses we built eight years ago?" There were three houses built then, making a total of eight houses and one decent apartment on a campus with 215 boarding students and another hundred day students. Two of those eight houses were lived in by maintenance people, one by the business manager who had no contact with the students, one by the headmistress, one by the assistant headmistress, one by the daughter of the school nurse, and two by full-time teachers. One of the two teachers was in the process of divorcing his wife in order to marry one of the Madeira seniors. There was no guidance counselor, no chaplain, and no adult living in four of the six dormitories.

In short, not one normal family situation was available to the girls on the entire four-hundred acre campus. From 4:30 P.M. until 8:00 A.M. the girls were virtually on their own. This does not mean there was chaos in the dorms. Miss Keyser, the retiring headmistress, was a strong taskmaster and a very hard worker and there was a very good system of student housemothers—but there was not a touch of the warmth of family life or close contact between generations, and little opportunity for faculty to come across as humans as well as pedagogues.

Ted Sizer, before he retired as headmaster of Andover, wrote in a thirty-three page report to the board of Andover (I doubt there were many members of the board at Madeira who would *read* a thirty-three page report!):

House counseling is the most sophisticated, demanding academic job on this campus. Unless a student is "together" in the dormitory his or her French, or algebra, or history, or field hockey will suffer. . . . House counseling isn't merely supervision: it's education . . . it is a central part of the fabric of this institution. . . . Accessibility, caring, sensitivity, genuine interest, the courage to be condemnatory, to be the taskmaster or mistress as well as the readiness to be a friend: these qualities can't be categorized by "hours on duty" or items on a list to be checked off. But they are the heart of a good residential education.

Mr. Sizer is 100 percent correct. His statement is simple common sense to anyone who has taken the time to spend a single day and night on a boarding school campus, especially a day in the past ten years. I had said essentially the same thing to Madeira's board for almost three years. The reality of the message is expensive, however, and Madeira's board simply chose over the years to ignore it. I am told they have recently completed housing I urged eight years ago.

I immediately set up a system of faculty advisors for each student and an Adult-on-Duty who used my office from 3:30 Friday until 10:00 P.M. Sunday so that every girl leaving or returning to campus checked into a warm, living-room like atmosphere (the Madeira dorms have no living rooms), often with a fire in the fireplace and always proctored by a member of the faculty or Mrs. Harris. It was one of many new burdens I placed upon the faculty, since it meant a long drive back to campus for most of them—and sitter problems for their children.

In time they began to bring their children, which was an important plus for the campus, and the girls began to enjoy seeing the math teacher doing her needlepoint, or reading to her children, or watching a football game, and that office became a popular gathering place on weekends. They even came down in their pajamas and did their homework in front of the fire.

I told the school nurse that I wanted always to be told of any injuries the girls sustained; and, if they needed to be taken to the hospital any time at night, I wanted to take them. I watched a number of bones be set, a thumb sewed back, and heard a girl be told in the gentlest and saddest conversation I have ever heard in my life that she was indeed an alcoholic. In a very weary, little-girl voice she responded, "I wasn't sure but I was beginning to be afraid so . . ." And I heard a doctor, whose license to practice should at least have been temporarily withdrawn, say in the most callous possible way to a terrified youngster who had been burned on the face, "Get her to a plastic surgeon—it's too late for me to help"—and he turned on his heels and walked away.

Picture yourself on a campus seven days and seven nights a week with a small group of adults—maybe five on a good night and two or three other nights—and 215 teenagers you care very much about, every one of whom has some kind of a problem, from a mother dying of cancer, to a playboy father, to a dad out of work or a beau who never called, or a D − on a paper she worked her heart out for, and tell me where you begin. I know where you end.

My first year at Madeira I gave diplomas to girls I barely knew. From then on I taught a weekly class to freshmen and I made every effort to spend time with the seniors—first in half-hour conferences in my office, then when time interfered I began to invite groups of day students to lunch in fours or fives—and ask the boarders to come by in groups of three, four, or five about 9:00 P.M. for cocoa and cookies. The conversation began rather awkwardly. They were mixed groups of girls, some "in" members and some "out" members, but in a very short time they found a subject they cared about and the conversation often went until 11:00 or 11:30, with me walking the girls back to their dorms. It was obvious that they hungered for conversations with adults, and while most of the people on campus, especially a splendid dean of students and the young head of publications, did yeoman duty all hours of the day and night, there simply weren't enough adults to go around.

I urged the board to borrow $250,000 at once (at 8½ percent) and make room for trained adults and families to live near the girls. I had, and still have, great respect for the student housemother system, and for the right of boarding school faculty to a modicum of privacy and normal living. Many boarding schools have too much "togetherness." We had simply gone the other extreme. I even had plans drawn up that would have put space in three existing buildings to far better use and in the process would have added four excellent, well-placed faculty apartments. Unfortunately, by the time I arrived, the school's much touted solar-heated science building was about to fall apart and the next three years of the board's attention were spent trying unsuccessfully to put Humpty Dumpty together again.

I did not lack courage when I went to Madeira. I was quite willing to put my neck on the block and make whatever decisions needed to be made. And I knew what many of those decisions were—but no one can run a school (or a business either unless you own it) without a board with the courage and integrity to back the person to whom they hand the responsibility.

When I arrived at Madeira it had never, to the best of my ability to find out, been evaluated by an outside group of its peers and equals. There was a provincialism, a smugness about it that made it feel wonderfully safe about its superiority and very closeminded about "the real world."

State accreditation requires 180 days of school. Madeira juniors, because of a unique program, a six-week Christmas holiday and a two-week period on Capitol Hill, had less than 130 days of classes my first year at Madeira. The library was seriously inadequate and often used as a big recreation room. A once fine riding program was beginning to deteriorate but the male members of the board were too intimidated by a few wealthy riders to do anything about it; and as a final note there had never been a funded maintenance program set up so the beautiful fifty-year-old buildings had very leaky basements, tile roofs that could go at any time, and furniture and equipment that was falling apart and uninventoried.

At the end of my first three months at Madeira I felt a kind of urgency to get moving that bordered on the frantic. By the end of the first year I had cut Christmas vacation in half, brought Latin back into the curriculum, brought mid-year and final exams back into being, increased already taxed faculty responsibility by setting up an advisor-advisee system for every student, changed the administration of the school to include a dean of students and an academic dean, written a faculty handbook, rewritten the student handbook, begun to organize board committees for long-range planning, and begun to pull school files and records together.

My first year with the seniors was a nightmare. They had come to terms with Miss Keyser's style and wanted no part of mine. A favorite "Madeira tradition" as they called it was an arrangement whereby each class chose a "class hymn" and the assistant headmistress led them in contests to see which class could shriek its hymn the loudest. This was called chapel.

When one of the student singing groups sang some original lyrics at a Mothers' Day luncheon—lyrics that were tasteless and offensive in the extreme—and the singing itself had been unrehearsed and sloppy at best, I met with the girls and told them I hoped they would continue to sing but with two caveats: (1) that they practice before giving a performance, and (2) that they not use words that were inappropriate for them and an embarrassment to their audience.

Various versions of our conversation quickly spread across the country and all hell broke loose. One very feisty and thoroughly uninformed young lady wrote, "Maybe your priorities for the school and the students are misplaced. In my opinion the headmistress should deal with major issues and leave the harmless issues to the discretion of the students. You should not restrict all aspects of the students' lives. Songs represent a release and a form of entertainment for the students."

I was constantly being told that shrieking and screaming in chapel and in the dining room were "our only release—you can't take it away from us . . . it's a Madeira tradition." The four hundred glorious acres they could walk, ride, and scream their heads off in were rarely traveled by any except the horseback riders.

It took three years and a lot of strength and determination, but I brought music back to Madeira while I was there—the joy of it and the beauty of it—something totally missing when I arrived. It isn't the sort of thing I had expected to have to fight for.

It also took three years of unpleasantness and overt rudeness from students and parents alike, even several board members, to turn what had been called "Mothers' Day" and "Fathers' Day" (there was no parents' association at Madeira) into school weekends where faculty, students, and parents were *on* campus getting to know one another and sharing their school experiences.

When I arrived in 1977 the day consisted of a quick run-through of morning classes, a box lunch, a quick cocktail party with the faculty, and then two days of partying and shopping with old Dad or Mom in Georgetown. My recommendation that everyone stay on campus for a father-daughter dinner was met with howls of protest and open hostility. I was destroying "another Madeira tradition." I was simply introducing a little common sense.

But in April 1980, after I was gone and Hy was gone, Fathers' Day had become Fathers' Weekend and it went off as I had spent three years struggling to have it. One kind father wrote and thanked me.

2.

There was not one single move I made at Madeira that did not have an unpleasant backlash. When I wrote the students late in August and asked them all to bring a few dozen daffodil bulbs back with them, to start what I hope may now be a tradition to fill the campus with spring flowers, I received one letter. It didn't say "What a nice idea." It said:

September 8

Dear Jean,
The epistle of the daffodils was not well received in this household and I have heard of similar reaction in a couple of other households. Though the gals sometimes act like second graders, I suspect they react better to pleas couched in adult terms. Withal, I cannot quibble with a Lady Bird Johnson effort and will send Audrey some bulbs when they come on the market in these environs.

I sent a good-natured reply to the effect that I wasn't "talking down" to anyone, it was just my way of expressing myself, and signed it "Rebecca of Sunnybrook Farm." She wrote back, "Dear Rebecca, You're a neat gal—loved your letter, thanks, . . ." But everything, every move, had to be explained, however simple and innocent it seemed to me when I made it.

Even Christmas became something to fight about. For four years the girls had left school the day before Thanksgiving and returned in January, having had a six-week "Christmas break." In 1978 I changed the calendar back to a three-week Christmas break, and then I set about trying to resurrect the Christmas traditions, as Madeira had once celebrated them. I was reminded almost immediately that not everyone at Madeira was a Christian and wasn't I being anti-Semitic. I have probably told more little WASPs about the beautiful festival of Hanukah than any other Episcopalian could, without her own televised talk show, so my conscience was very clear on that score.

I was open to all suggestions and the deans and I spent many hours figuring out a calendar of events, trying not to step on any academic toes, trying to keep the Glee Club happy (that was *very* important to me), find time to gather greens and teach the girls to make wreaths, decide when to light the big tree (and should it be *required* for the day girls) and how to serve a turkey dinner to four hundred people in the gym without lines that were unmanageable, etc.

No two people remembered the "traditions" in quite the same way except for the traditional Christmas story that *everyone* remembered Miss Madeira reading to the girls each year. And they remembered it with great affection. I was given Miss Madeira's own copy of it by a dear and generous lady who handed it to me as though she were turning over the Holy Grail.

It was called "How Come Christmas," charming in its day perhaps—if you were white—but written in an "all dem chilluns is gwine wait fo dat old Sandy Claws." At one time I would have read it with the same good will and innocence that Miss Madeira read it and her girls enjoyed it. It made me realize in the starkest possible way how smug what we called "innocence" could be and was. Today it would be unthinkable to read, an affront not only to the black girls but to all of us. Needless to say, by omitting it from our celebration I lost brownie points I sorely needed. At the last minute I searched for a Christmas story that might be new to the girls and read them Damon Runyon's "Dancing Dan's Christmas." They didn't like it, so the next year I read them "Gift of the Magi" and they were quite content.

How do you figure out a generation of young women who play "Why Don't We Do It in the Road" on their stereos and still sit enchanted by "Gift of the Magi"? I think for some of them it was the first hearing. One of the girls asked who Noah was, so anything is possible.

By the second year everyone seemed more relaxed about my intentions toward Madeira's traditions, a madrigal group had been formed, the girls who really loved music had been enticed back into the Glee Club, the "Wums" and "Humditties" and "Agonies" were better than ever, and the wonderful, spontaneous humor and warmth of the girls were reflected in their delightful decorations in each dormitory.

It was Christmas again at Madeira, even if the headmistress was still suspect in the eyes of many. I baked cookies for the entire school when we lit the tree in Main, and the bigger one at the Chapel was decorated with toys for youngsters at Children's Hospital. Some of the girls gave a party for children from the Alley Library.

Giving, as I knew but relearned at Madeira, is not a God-given instinct. It is learned. And we have to be reminded of it from time to time—in fact, educated in the ways of it—in order to be thoughtful about it. My first fall at Madeira the girls (all of them) contributed a total of $27 to the United Fund. If they didn't know any better than this, we had short-changed them. There are legitimate reasons for not giving to the United Fund or to anything else if you aren't so inclined, but this was a thoughtless, uninformed kind of not giving, unacceptable behavior in my opinion in young women being educated to be productive and aware of their world.

There were weeks when they cashed as much as $5,000 to $6,000 in personal checks at the school bank. They thought nothing of calling a cab to deliver $150 worth of ice cream from Baskin-Robbins.

Working through the student council and especially the senior class, we talked a good deal about values and needs and self-indulgence. I added a strong suggestion in the student handbook that $40 to $50 per month was a very generous allowance at boarding school. Some parents appreciated the suggestion, a predictable group said, "Who the hell are you . . ." We investigated community needs, saw where United Fund monies were used, and in two years the girls' contributions had hit five figures. I believe that is so, though I haven't the statistics with me. I think the figure that first year was a clear reflection of how much the girls needed adults in their lives.

My last school year at Madeira started sadly because of a careless accident, one I could have avoided had I had the strength and courage to banish another "old Madeira tradition" from the campus when I wanted to. In spite of all the extenuating circumstances I never considered myself less than fully responsible, because, as Mr. Truman was fond of saying, "The buck stops here."

A number of years ago a group called the BHs was founded at Madeira. BH stood for "Brazen Hussies." I happen to know the decent woman who founded it. I met her later, and I know the group was started for fun and high-jinks, to add a little life and humor to the boredom of campus life at a time when students had only two weekends off campus per semester, and time must have hung heavy for active teenagers. Members' names were supposed to be secret, but by the time I arrived they seemed to be widely known, at least by the seniors. To be a BH was considered the "in" thing to be.

Depending upon the year, and the members, the pranks played by the BHs ranged from totally innocent, to annoying, to downright destructive. A few years before I arrived they had "rearranged" the curtain pulleys in the school theater so that $1,500 was needed to put them right again. The BHs paid the bill. While I was there they collected all the toothbrushes on campus and strung them from trees, moved every piece of furniture out of my office and set it up in the quad with a sign that read, "Just Airing Out the Administration," hung silly signs out to welcome parents to the campus, wrapped my house in foil and tied it with a big red ribbon, all foolish stuff that everyone seemed to enjoy. Quite harmless.

I entered into the spirit of fun wholeheartedly, and even won a prize for the best Halloween costume one year without anyone knowing who I was. Part of the costume was black net stockings, and though the rest of it was a weird combination of anything I could find to cover up in, they agreed, "She's got good legs whoever she is." I had written one of the faculty follies we put on while I was there. The faculty needed rehearsals and another night at school like a hole in

the head, but they were good sports and we brightened up two Feb-
ruaries with them.

On one of the follies nights it was snowing so hard the faculty all
had to spend the night on campus filling the infirmary and any faculty
house with a spare bed. We let the girls stay out of their dorms until
11:00 that night to enjoy it. I will always remember one of the girls
lying in the snow in front of Main, making angel wings with her arms
in the snow, watching the snow come down through the branches of
one of the big elm trees, with light from the buildings making it all
sparkle, and saying, "Oh, Mrs. Harris. Isn't it wonderful!"

Somewhere in its history the BHs activities had become involved in
Red and White Day, a day in early fall when all the new girls were
accepted into the Red or White Teams. Special freshmen were picked
to be initiated. BHs were assigned a new girl, made her a costume
based on some theme, and then late in the afternoon there was a
cookout for all freshmen and seniors at the cabin. The BHs made a list
of any freshman who walked across the oval, or went in the senior's
special entrance to the dining room, or committed any other faux pas
that would bring them to senior attention. Freshmen hoped to get on
the list. It was an early foot in the door to be one of the "in" group.

Red and White Day that last year began with the BHs waking at the
crack of dawn, waking the freshmen on their list, taking them over
near the swimming pool, blindfolding them, smearing them with
something sticky, like shampoo or vaseline, or even peanut butter,
then hosing them down and sending them shrieking and squealing
back to their dorms. They had in years past even been made to climb
the fence into the pool area where they were thrown into the pool in
the dark. Some had even been tied to trees.

Miss Keyser, the retiring headmistress, had told me something
about the BHs, mentioned the damage done to the theater, but said,
on the whole they were a harmless "vent" and an accepted part of
Madeira. Jean Gisriel (Giz) whom I had made the dean of students
told me about their activities in greater detail and together we made
up a list of rules the girls must follow if the BHs were to continue.

It was an awkward thing for me to do, because, as a freshman, I
would have found no pleasure in being part of it and would happily
have been left out. I wonder if that isn't true of many of the girls, but
we make being "included" so important. The first rule was that the

BHs must inform the night guard when they were going to be out of their dorms after 10:00 P.M. Secondly they could never climb into the pool area. Third, if their pranks became destructive they would not only pay the damages but risk suspension, and under no condition were they ever to tie one another to trees.

Giz didn't tell them; but it was also arranged that when the guard was informed, she would be told by him so two adults would be up and in the area while the BHs went into action. Giz got up at 2:00 or 3:00 in the morning enough times to say to me, "If the guard and I go on meeting this way, I'm going to have to buy some new nightgowns." It was, in my opinion, the ultimate indulgence of the young, without their knowing it. The only thing I could say in its favor is that it was safer than it had been before. Or so I thought.

The night before Red and White Day, Giz reviewed the rules with the girls and was assured no one would get hurt. The next morning at about 4:00 A.M. as the BHs gathered to wake the new girls, one of them remembered she hadn't brought any shampoo or vaseline with her so she ran back to her bathroom to get it. Her roommate was senior class president and they shared a connecting bathroom with two other seniors.

So as not to wake anyone she went in the dark and grabbed the shampoo, only it turned out not to be shampoo. It was Vanisol, a plastic bottle of a liquid used to sanitize the toilets. It was 14 percent hydrochloric acid. By the time she caught up with the others all the new girls had been blindfolded, thank God, and were so smeared with shampoo and vaseline that the Vanisol barely touched them.

When a few girls began to complain, "Hey, this smells funny, and it burns," the seniors took off the blindfolds, hosed the girls down, and sent them back to their dorms to take showers.

Two girls were cold and didn't want to be hosed so they ran ahead and jumped in the shower. One of them didn't realize at the time that she had been badly burned on the face. She came out of the shower rubbing her face and saying, "I can't get this sticky stuff off." She wasn't in any pain, but she was rubbing off her own skin. When the other girls saw her they rushed her to the infirmary, the nurse called me and I took her at once to the hospital.

And this is when the doctor had his one sentence for the child's mother, who met us there, "Get her to a plastic surgeon." He is near the top of my list of people who should not be permitted to practice their chosen trades.

Both mother and child were wonderfully brave and wonderfully calm, and last I knew, except for one small spot, her face has healed and is fine, but that terrible morning we didn't know that it would.

When mother had left with her daughter I did what I had done for fourteen years and ran to the phone to call Hy. His calmness and reassurance was catching and helped me to get through the two long weeks that followed with television cameras all over the campus, and irate parents saying, "What are you going to do to the girls who did it?" Hy told me exactly what would and did happen.

"Jean, she's young and the young body has wonderful recuperative powers. It will probably heal itself largely. She'll have tender skin, and have to stay out of the sun, maybe for the rest of her life, but you will probably see most of it heal itself."

There were, as I have explained, several people on campus who wanted the headmistress's job, and her head as well. I'm told it was one of them who alerted the press immediately. I can remember saying to one of the press people who kept calling and trying to get some kind of inside information that didn't exist, "The girls in this school give just over 100,000 hours a year of volunteer service to the city of Washington and environs. As far as I know this has never brought you running to Madeira for pictures. Now suddenly there is a tragic accident, nothing more, and we're red hot news. Come and see the good things that happen on purpose, not the sad thing that happened by accident."

The child who grabbed the Vanisol was from El Salvador. Her family had been moved to Florida for safety but her father still lived between El Salvador and the United States. It was a shaky time for him personally, and what should be done about his daughter became more complicated than it might otherwise have been. Lawyers quickly got into the act, as lawyers do. I met with the school lawyer, the family, and the family's lawyer and before we could make any suggestions the family said they were taking her out and putting her in another school.

I'm happy to say she had a successful senior year in her new school. I think the girl who was hurt recovered as well as she did certainly in large part because her family was so calm, and so supportive, and put its energy into making her better instead of heading right to the courts. It was a sobering experience for the entire school. Had I stayed another year I'm not sure what I would have done about the BHs, but initiations would have been out. They are good-hearted girls, and would not hurt someone deliberately.

The day the girl from El Salvador left was one of the longest days I spent at Madeira. All her things were packed and down in the front hall, stereo, tennis racquets, radio, books, clothes, a large collection of boxes, and suitcases. Mother and father had flown in to get her and rented a car at the airport to come and pick her up.

The only problem was that where the child lived in El Salvador, mother and father had always driven her to the airport in a tiny sports car convertible, while her suitcases followed in a servant-driven station wagon. Her parents had no idea how much was packed to go with her. They arrived at Madeira in another tiny sports car convertible and had to return to the airport and rent a station wagon. The girls sat in the front hall and wept with her until mother and father came back for the second time. Why on earth I didn't put her in my car and follow them I don't know. It didn't occur to me until just now.

To the students I was often much too strict and hardnosed. One of them eagerly told reporters how I banished oranges and crackers from their diet for several weeks because after many reminders and warnings they still threw orange peels and cracker wrappers around the campus. I tried to explain that wasn't "discipline": it was "training," like making the puppy use newspaper instead of the carpet—training, I would like to add in a very loud voice, "that should have been taken care of at home."

To some parents who believed any casual remark their daughter made, especially if it were critical or derogatory, I was much too casual about discipline. An alumna wrote a few weeks before I left Madeira, "I have it on good authority that Mrs. Harris is lax and disinterested in discipline."

I had spent thirty-five years of my life disciplining children, but more especially trusting children and helping to teach them the responsibility that trust means—helping to teach them to make good decisions instead of scaring them to death. It is a long, tedious process, not greatly enhanced by critics who have made no effort to understand or to observe at firsthand.

Almost invariably the people who can't play it straight make life very unpleasant for all of us. The sad thing is there are more and more such people. Stealing is a problem in boarding schools, increasingly so. It is a problem in day schools too, and private clubs and churches and business offices—law offices too, I'm told, and heaven knows in stores and on the streets. Lying, cheating, stealing, drinking are not new to any campus. They were not invented by this generation of students. What is new is the growing comfortable conviction of parents and students alike that lying, cheating, and stealing are just a normal stage in the adolescent growth process. "So what's the big deal?"

A mother whose fifteen-year-old daughter I suspended for two weeks for leaving her hotel room late at night during a school-sponsored trip and going down to the bar for a drink said, "You're making such a big deal of it. Frankly, I'm rather pleased. I didn't think she had the guts." A father who wrote, "Right on! I support you completely," in answer to a letter I had sent to parents about liquor and drugs behaved unspeakably less than three weeks later when his daughter was expelled for a drug related offense.

On one of the nights, when the students and I sat around munching cookies and chatting, we discussed whether or not a student council member who had broken a major rule should automatically go off the council. To me the answer was quite obvious, but the girls themselves expressed grave reservations. A very popular member of the council had just broken a major rule and I had insisted that she step down immediately. Now they were wrestling with writing this into a charter. They disapproved of my action because the student in question was a fine girl who happened to make a hasty and very bad decision and knew beyond a shadow of a doubt that she had done so.

The question arose, "Should student council members, given as they are a great deal of responsibility at Madeira, be asked to take a simple oath to uphold the school's rules?" We talked until late that night and the girls left with no decision made, still asking why a student council member should get any more punishment than any other student—that is, the regular punishment, plus dismissal from the council. There were three more meetings about it before they could honestly see the equity of it.

There was a bad storm during one of our meetings and one of the mothers who didn't want to drive back home in the rain had been invited by me to stay and have dinner and spend the night at my house, called "The Hill." She sat there listening to the girls that evening and said after they had left, "If I hadn't heard that conversation I wouldn't believe it ever took place. They really seem to have no convictions about right and wrong. It's all relative."

It was true. But it's true of our whole society and we criticize it most in the young—the ones who learned it from us. Less than a month before I left Madeira for good, the daughter of that woman did something seriously dangerous, to her own safety and to that of others as well. Her mother was on the phone until after 1:00 A.M. protesting vehemently and angrily about the punishment she was about to receive—a few days' suspension.

Hardest of all—I guess it's everyone's problem today—was finding time to think, and people who wanted to think with me. I wanted to think about education and the needs of students and how both can best be served. I wanted to evaluate what we were doing and how we could do it better, especially in the light of swiftly changing times. In almost three years at Madeira I had exactly one quiet, pleasant discussion with one of the twenty board members about education and its place in the lives, the unspeakably complicated lives, of young women today. The word came back so often that "board meetings are boring!" It came to seem almost a waste of time to write a report for them.

In a report written for the school by Russell Browning Associates, a board member was quoted as saying, "Mrs. Harris thinks with her mouth." I was hurt and shocked by the rudeness, but a case can be made for doing just that. Useful thoughts do occur to intelligent people as they share ideas.

Browning's report, requested at great expense by the board of directors to evaluate the school's position before embarking on a large fund-raising drive, turned out to be a long mishmash of rumors and quotes with none of the sources named. In it, both the board and the headmistress were labeled inadequate.

One director expressed serious doubts about Mrs. Harris and felt the headmistress was "irrational, at least she acts as if she is." Another member felt the board should admit they had made a mistake in hiring Mrs. Harris and see that she leave Madeira "quickly and as nicely as possible." The board was then advised to hire an interim head and form a new search committee which would be more "thoughtful."

Rarely had the head of a school become such a controversial figure in such a short time, and never had the head been less aware of it. I knew that the board should be helping me more than it was, and I knew that many of its members were obviously bored during board meetings, but I kept plunging ahead, eager beaver that I was.

On seeing the report, I was devastated, yet I appreciated the chairman's decency in showing it to me. I had worked very hard and the good results were beginning to show. There had been not one suggestion made to me in two years that the board had any questions about my competency, or that they questioned the efficacy of my efforts in the school's behalf. They just sat around at parties and discussed it. Fewer than a third of them had ever called and asked to help me in any way. I had entertained all of them at my own expense. About half of them had invited me to their homes, or bothered to take me out to lunch.

The total contribution of one of the male members of the board was to drop by occasionally and tell us how important he was, and whatever our problems might be he had connections that would set them all right again. As it turned out, he was one of the main causes of the biggest problem.

I showed Hy the report, and discussed briefly with him whether or not I should stay or leave Madeira. His comment didn't make me feel any better: "Hell, they won't fire you. They don't want the trouble of looking for someone else."

When it was released, the report caused an instant furor, and it left me totally sick at heart. Nothing had prepared me for anything so casually, irresponsibly cruel. An immediate vote was taken, unbeknownst to me, by telephone, to decide whether I stayed or went. One board member told me, "There was just one vote against you." Later, another member of the board smiled a nasty little smile and said, "Congratulations. You won by one vote." To this day I have no idea which one was telling the truth. By not knowing it drew the iron curtain down all the more firmly between me and Madeira. There was now no one to trust.

<h1 style="text-align:center">3.</h1>

The classic symptoms of depression that I had felt and fought for a long time were finally overwhelming me. That exhaustion is a symptom of depression hadn't occurred to me and certainly Hy didn't suggest it. I thought it was just long hours and seven day work weeks. Hy reminded me a little of my mother—a good, practicing Christian Scientist who saw all four of her children through everything from mumps and measles to whooping cough and scarlet fever with a big smile, a bowl of barley soup, and the warm assurance that, "You'll be fine tomorrow, honey."

Hy would say, "God, you've got it all. You're so lucky. Stop complaining. You ought to spend a few days doing rounds with me, and you'd count your blessings."

A few months before his death he said, "I'm going to make you spend a day in a nursing home some time and you'd stop complaining about how you feel."

I liked having him talk to me that way. I thought it was just what I needed. Toughen up, lady, and count your blessings. The formula worked for fifty-six years.

I had been checked for thyroid deficiency a number of times, even for ulcers, and told I was in tip-top condition. I was taking vitamin B shots, lots of vitamins, and eating candy bars by the dozen because I thought they made me feel peppier. I had started taking Desoxyn in small quantities years before. Hy prescribed it. I had said to him so many times, "I know how to do it, Hy. I know what is needed but I'm afraid I'll run out of strength."

The challenge of the job, the pleasure of working with bright people and new ideas, the driving desire to help young women grow up better prepared for life than I was, thinking ahead, growing strong without so many scars—these kept me motivated and moving. And occasional weekends with Hy helped me refuel when I had given all of me there was. Unfortunately, the more of me I gave the less I could get away to see Hy.

There were Fridays when I arrived at Purchase just about able to crawl over the threshold on my hands and knees, totally spent. By Sunday I was alive again. Much of the weekend I spent alone, reading, sunning, working my way through a briefcase of letters and reports, but doing it in an unhurried way, not running in to defrost the refrigerator, answer the phone, be Adult-on-Duty, or polish silver for another mothers' coffee. Hy would be at the office in the morning and, depending on the time of year, go hunting, play golf, or get into a gin game in the afternoon. My being there didn't change his pattern in any way, but it did mine. I was at peace there.

It says something sad about all of our society that the moment Hy died so many people were comfortable with the "murder of passion" explanation for his death . . . the jealous woman scorned, and we all know what "hell hath no fury like." The fact that I had moved to Virginia three years before, that Dr. Tarnower's affair with "the other woman" was at least ten years old, and that during that ten years and before, there had been a number of other women, including two he thought he would marry, are all simple facts they don't want to confuse their prejudices with. The fact that Mrs. Harris was exhausted and depressed, holding down a back-breaking job while her relationship with the people who were meant to help and support her, the Madeira board of directors, was shaky at best and openly hostile in some cases, did not appear in any newspaper. It isn't sexy or lurid, or even simple.

Suicide was not a new idea to me. It had been somewhere in the back of my mind for many years, the final steam valve, the final option. I don't fully understand why, but I had spent many years contemplating death, not in a morbid way, but as the final place to run to when I wasn't competent enough to go on living.

I have felt for many years that my depression was a chemical thing in my brain, something over which I had no control, the same thing that had destroyed my father's life, and caused an uncle to commit suicide. How the medication that Hy had given me for ten years affected the final explosion in my brain I cannot say.

The day I bought a gun in Virginia was not the first time I had tried to buy one. The first time was down in Florida in 1974, when Hy and I were in Palm Beach. Hy was playing golf and I spent a day driving around trying to find a gun. When I finally found one small enough for my hands they wouldn't sell it to me because I didn't have a Florida driver's license. Then, when I tried to find my way back to LaCoquille Club I was hopelessly lost. I got back just as Hy returned from eighteen holes of golf. He never knew, or had any idea how I had spent the day. There was so much we didn't know about one another. Perhaps it was inevitable that we would spend that last tragic night together as total strangers.

My own strong conviction is that I would have resorted to suicide long before if Hy hadn't been there saying "Welcome home, darling," and teaching me how to enjoy life, or at least letting me watch him enjoy it. Being put down was old stuff to me. My father's idea of the lowliest of human endeavors was teaching, and he rarely missed an opportunity to say so. Then he would stop short and look as though it had just slipped his mind that I had been teaching for twenty or thirty years.

Hy seemed to respect what I did, and what I was. He is the only man who ever made me realize that being a woman can be a good thing to be. Alone with him I felt elevated for many years to the dignity of being a person. At parties I usually slipped back into feeling like a faceless "girl friend." At parties, away from Hy, I was simply the extra woman, the headmistress, the extension of a desk that walked and talked.

Part of my depression over the years had grown from the constant reminders that for all the honest to God giving of myself that I did, I was a nonperson in large parts of my private and professional life. To the faculty and students I was real as long as school was in session. To the members of the board I was a little like "the sad nervous boys in a Strindberg book—well fed, well groomed, well cared for but unacknowledged as a fellow human being." To Hy's friends, the four closest whom we saw constantly, I was a warm body, an interchangeable part, taking up space at the table. When Arthur Schulte, Hy's closest friend, wanted a gin game, which was all the time, he didn't care if the woman sitting quietly in the background was the "socialite headmistress of the Madeira School" or the madame of a local whorehouse. His wife Vivian did, but not Arthur.

The newspapers referred to me as "Dr. Tarnower's girlfriend," an

opprobrium I despise. Oddly enough Dr. Tarnower was never referred to as "Mrs. Harris's boyfriend" or even "Her aging lover." The
feminists still have their work cut out for them.

In the end, I had become a nonperson to Hy too, or perhaps I now
had to admit what had always been true. From 1971 on, Mrs.
Tryforos's letters, phone calls, telegrams, cute little gifts had never
stopped following us around the world in our travels. Just before Hy
died we spent Christmas together down in Palm Beach. We were
there for two very happy weeks. Mrs. Tryforos outdid herself this
time. In addition to phone calls and telegrams, she placed an ad on
the front page of *The New York Times* to tell the doctor, long distance,
that she loved him forever. It was something that might be considered
"cute" if you could spare the $250 that it cost, if you were in your
teens, and if the person you addressed it to wasn't a sixty-nine-year-
old man spending a two week vacation with another woman. Under
the circumstances it would be hard to imagine anything more tasteless and deliberately mean.

Hy looked at it in horror. "Jesus!" he said. "I hope none of my
friends see it."

I should have said. "I'm your friend, Hy, and I see it." But the habit
to laugh off hurt was too ingrown by then. "Why don't you have her
try the Goodyear blimp next time, Herm?" I asked.

A woman simply wasn't a man's friend in Hy's world, no matter how
she had been tested, and God knows I had been tested. She was
something men had on the side—in addition to friends.

I believe the sad truth is that Hy was incapable of loving a woman,
though he wanted desperately to be able to. He worked at it assiduously, and he was never happier than during those brief periods when
he thought he had succeeded. How very sad that I know him better
now than I did while he was alive.

Hy was never a complainer, but far more than his back and his
stomach hurt him from time to time, and one enduring hurt lasted all
his life. Hy prized money and social respectability as perhaps only a
bright, ambitious, poor Jewish boy can. But social acceptance in his
lifetime, and in spite of all the protests, even now, require men to
make love to women, not to other men. Hy worked at it overtime, a
girl here, a woman there, a chippie here, a rich widow there, a whole
goyim beanery of them. He made a lifetime job of trying to prove to

himself and others that he was in every sense of the word eminently male, and therefore eminently respectable.

But treating women badly, putting them down, was a physical necessity for him. He disliked them. He spent a lifetime collecting them and throwing them away. He said to me many times, with deep feeling, "There is no way you can know another person's suffering, Jean." And each time I thought he was talking about his patients.

Hy was a master of the game of one-upmanship. If the rules of the game said a bachelor was supposed to have women, then by God he'd have them. He fought what I think God made him every step of the way. But the closest he came to honest-to-God love was in his relationship with other men. I have no way of knowing whether those relationships were sexual. He often talked around the subject with me, how the ancient Greeks and Romans were considered quite respectable if they had young boys as companions. The only reason Hy ever gave me for breaking our engagement was, "I'm afraid, Jean. I'm afraid of the boys." I thought he meant they might be too noisy. Maybe he did. If I had had daughters he'd have found another reason.

At least one of Hy's closest friends felt as he did, used women but loved men. I rather imagine their relationship from beginning to end could have been photographed for family time on TV, but they loved one another more than they loved women. Two bright, rich, ambitious old men, yet burdened with loving one another, burdened and comforted.

It was probably harder for men Hy's age to face this in themselves, but easier to pass socially, since women, in their generational myths, were not too bright, not too able, not even too stable, but merely decorative and functional. You could sneer at them more easily and still be socially attractive.

One of Hy's closest friends said to me once, "Hy loves to put you down. Why do you stand for it?"

It really didn't matter to me. I had always found putdowns a much more endearing sign of friendship than flattery. There were so many strengths in Hy to love. For his sake I was sorry about the weaknesses, but they weren't important to me in any other way.

Hy was the only man I ever loved. I respected the many good things about him, and was proud of his competence. He gave me more solace than I gave him because I obviously needed more—or I couldn't find it in as many places as he could. But I led a very full life away from him, full of family and hard work with few illusions about him sitting alone for months at a time when I couldn't see him.

One summer an old friend of Hy's greeted me on the terrace of his club with, "How grand to see you. I thought Hy was just seeing that Lynne person now." It had come out too fast and she looked embarrassed.

"Oh, Margaret," I said, "Hy has always had other women. It's nothing new."

Later I told Hy about it. He laughed heartily. "Is that what you told her? Good for you! It was just the right thing to say."

In 1977 before I moved to Virginia we were reaching a fork in the road. I would be working, and working hard for another ten years. Hy was slowing down, professionally. I don't think he would ever have retired, but vacations were becoming more and more frequent, "and I won't travel alone, Jean." He even talked about buying a home in Florida. Happy accidents of geography and timing had made it possible for us to pursue our professional lives to the fullest and still see one another often. It would never be possible again. I wrote him a long, earnest letter about our friendship, and we both vowed we would always touch base when we could.

The word "earnest" makes me smile and think of a satire about "earnest" women that Nora Ephron wrote recently. We should always be done in satire.

I wrote him that summer about my busy life at Madeira and my hopes for the school and ended:

Since the moment I met you I have made my own life. I go on making my own life and by and large it's as interesting as the next, more so I suppose— but that doesn't replace the knowledge that somewhere at the other end of a phone, or a plane ride, or a damned long drive you are sitting there alive, well, self-contained, bright, interesting, quite smug about how well you have planned your life, aggravating, remarkably cruel at times, unbelievably kind at others. And nothing and no one can replace the gladness I feel that you are there.

In spite of all my brave plans for Madeira I was obviously lonely— loneliness is something most of us live with, and I'm sure people die of it too. But it was the belief, one I still hold, that I no longer had the strength to perform my life's work, that made me finally truly suicidal.

Where the strength had gone, whether it had been honestly used to the last full measure, or dissipated in unproductive ways, is of little consequence now. I only know it was gone.

I had spent a long weekend with Hy three weeks before he died. He gave the rehearsal dinner for my son David's wedding. He was funny and kind and warm and passionate, the closest thing to loving he knew how to be. We sat on his bed that Sunday morning before I left. I thanked him for all he had done and said to him, "You don't act like a man who's in love with another woman. But then you never have."

"You of all people should know better than that," he said. "I don't love anyone, and I don't need anyone."

It isn't a message to gladden the heart—quite the opposite—but it was old news to me by now.

I knew Hy as well as anyone could know him. I told him I was appalled to hear that he was thinking of taking someone else to a dinner given by the Westchester Heart Association in his honor. It was the culmination of his medical career and I expected to be there to honor him.

He said the predictable, "Look—it isn't that important," and then added, "She's done a lot of work for the Association."

"She should, Herm. She's a paid employee of yours."

He smiled, uncomfortably. "I know. I guess you're right."

I told him I would be in New York anyway on April 18 to be part of a seminar at Columbia University.

"Fine," he said.

We would make it a weekend in Purchase. He kissed me goodbye and I headed back to Virginia.

Besides the memory of a lovely weekend I carried with me his rough draft of what was to be the first chapter of his new book. He asked me to write into it some changes and suggestions I had made that weekend. His version and mine were both terrible, but he thanked me enthusiastically when I returned it rewritten a few days later. Assistant District Attorney George Bolen was to tell the jury, "She stole it. He didn't give it to her."

As I left the house and headed up Purchase Street I remembered that I wanted to call Dan Comfort, a friend of Hy's who was instrumental in planning the dinner, and tell him all was well for the nineteenth. I had called him a few weeks before because Hy had been ambivalent about that weekend. I had said my goodbyes and didn't want to go back to Hy's house, so I stopped at the public phone at the old post office. It was the same place I would head three weeks later seeking help for Hy when his phone was dead.

I was deeply hurt that Hy would play games about something as important as the dinner, that he could be so insensitive to an old friend. Our relationship was different now, but I was, what I would always be, a loving friend, and I expected to be treated as one. My overreaction to everything Dan had said three weeks before should have been a signal to both Dan and me that I was cracking up. Dan had invited me to sit at his table, which was kind of him, though he obviously wished I were burdening someone else with the call. Now I called him from the post office phone, told him what a great weekend we had just had, and assured him I would see him on the nineteenth.

I had long since had every reason to be disillusioned with Hy, his obsession with self, his insensitivity. I knew that distance had changed our life together and that his new life-style, with quite different people now kowtowing to a "bestseller," required someone on call, someone able to pick up and travel whenever he whistled. He was another man now, and it was well that I didn't see him too often—that way I could cling more easily to the memory of the old one. I knew that I would never love anyone else.

Too many lovely memories had woven a knot that no one would ever unravel. I knew that I would always be alone and that over the long haul hard work would be the only "lasting relationship" for me. Perhaps that's why it went on being important to me that someone strong, whatever the source of his strength, be there to touch base with. I didn't admire Hy's morality, once I discovered what it was, but I admired his strength and I wished that I had it. I thought the buffeting I took from him was the best thing in the world for me. For some perverse reason I never stopped feeling safe with Hy. Away from him I was more vulnerable. In the end, if he had lived in California I would have made my way to see him before I died.

I had started that Monday morning by mailing a letter to him, feeling deeply depressed. Vacations were particularly onerous. I dreaded them. Suddenly the campus was so quiet and empty. The reason for being there left when the girls left, and I hated the loneliness of three weeks on those four hundred acres and the terrifying prospect of time to think about me. The letter was a long, confused, bitter polemic written that weekend in response to a phone conversation I had had with him on Thursday at the height of the hand-wringing and soul-searching about expulsion of four of the seniors. I sent the letter by registered mail because so many things I had sent him in the past three years had mysteriously never arrived—not even a telegram that Western Union records show was delivered, not even the invitation to David's wedding.

As soon as I had mailed it I was sorry. It would make him cross because it wasn't the usual happy, funny stuff I usually ground out. It was an anguished wail, held back for many years. A few moments later my own mail arrived with a letter from one of the students about the recent expulsion. It was that one rotten, extra straw—the coup de grace, the culmination of almost three years of hard work, loneliness, and trauma. My reaction to the letter was out of proportion to the letter itself, but not for me at the moment. It was annihilating. I sat through the day's appointments trying to listen and respond. At 3:30 P.M. I said to my secretary, "Please cancel the next appointment. I've had enough, Carol. I'm going home."

I walked back to The Hill, the house I lived in on the Madeira campus, and rewrote my will. I had it witnessed by three ladies in the office, and wrote notes to my sister Mary Margaret, my secretary Carol, and to the chairman of the board. No one questioned the will. I was distraught but somehow no one knew. My mind was a shambles but my house was in order. There was only one thing I wanted to do— see Hy for a few moments, just chat with him one more time, and then go down to the pond, to the right of it where the weeping willow used to be and so many daffodils bloom in the spring, and kill myself. I began to feel as anxious for death as I had once felt anxious to see Hy, that feeling of urgency and exhilaration each time I turned in the driveway at Purchase.

I called Hy about 4:15 P.M. to say I was coming—not why. Henri, Hy's chauffeur, answered the phone. He said Hy was out and was going out to dinner. I said I'd call back. I had called Hy off and on all weekend as I had felt myself crumbling away. But he was always out and Henri or Suzanne, Henri's wife and Hy's housekeeper, answered instead. Suzanne had heard the anguish in my voice and said, "Are you all right, madame?" and I had said, "Oh no, Suzanne, I'm not. I'm not all right at all." But it wasn't her problem.

At 5:15 P.M. I called again and Hy answered. I said, "Darling, I'd like to come and talk with you for a little while tonight."

He said, "Well, Debby's coming for dinner." Debby was Hy's favorite niece. Even at that point he couldn't say "Debby and Lynne."

"That doesn't matter. She always leaves early and it will be almost 11:00 before I get there," I replied.

"It's more convenient if you come tomorrow."

"I can't talk with you tomorrow, Hy. Please just this once, let me say when."

"Suit yourself," he answered. I told him I would leave right away and we hung up.

What a sad little line that was, "Please, just this once let me say when." It sounded like Lynne Tryforos years before when she kept coming to the house while I was there, never venturing inside but spending many hours outside.

I had said to her finally, "Lynne, does it not seem bizarre to you that you are here when I am here?"

She looked puzzled.

"Lynne," I repeated, "why are you here?"

"I'm here because I'm allowed to be," she answered in a pouty, little girl voice.

It seemed a pathetic, sad answer to me then. It seems the more so to me today as I finally accept the reality that that was why anyone was there, including me. I thought for years it was a sign of his total disrespect and disregard for the woman that he would permit her to come to the house while I was there as long as she didn't come inside. Imagine such hubris and worse such naiveté in a grown woman. It is only since Hy's death, since I have started writing, that I have faced all these simple truths.

> *Pity me that the heart is slow to learn*
> *What the swift mind beholds at every turn.*
>
> "The Harp Weaver"
> *Edna St. Vincent Millay*

I took the gun out of the closet and out onto the terrace and shot it into the air. I had put two bullets in the gun, pulled the trigger, expecting the relief of an explosion, but it had only clicked and clicked again. Finally it fired. "Dear God," I thought, "I don't want that to happen tonight. This is suicide, not Russian roulette."

I took out a small handful of bullets and put them in my pocket while I tried to pry out the empty shells. (I didn't know until months later, when my lawyer Joel Aurnou showed me, that a simple press of a rod in the cartridge would have emptied it. Had I known that much about the gun I would have died before Hy did.) The shells wouldn't budge. I took the gun into the kitchen, opened the drawer where the ice pick was, and poked out the shells. I was hurrying now. I filled the cartridge with bullets, or thought I did. It was five months after Hy's death before I learned that I had put only five bullets in. One space in the cartridge was empty.

I put the gun in my handbag, propped the three notes and an envelope filled with all the papers David and Jim would need on a chair in the hall, hugged Cider, the big golden retriever the Madeira girls had given me, and Liza, the little springer spaniel David and Jim's gave to me, and went out to the car.

As I opened the car door I saw a bouquet of flowers on the front seat. A teacher who had seen me read the student's letter that morning, and who had watched the mounting trauma all week, had brought them to me with a note that read:

Monday, March 10

I believe in mythic renewal—the resurrection of the spirit—yours, mine, and that of the unpredictable young!

Love,
Ruth

Not wanting to disturb me by ringing the bell, she left them on the seat of the car. I wish she had rung the bell. I wonder if I would have run a comb quickly through my hair and answered the door as though nothing were wrong, or thrown myself into her arms and wept.

I had been screaming for help for years but somehow whatever came out never rang true, or never sounded important enough to take seriously. I had said to Miss Florence, my history teacher at Laurel, that I had doubts about myself heading off to college. "You—doubting yourself? You'll thrive there. You always do." That was the stock answer. Years later, after my divorce, when life was proving more than I could understand or cope with, I cried "Help" in earnest.

I turned to the minister at Christ Church—or tried to. I called him three different times, told him a little and asked to see him. I guess I picked bad times—he had more trauma than he could handle then. He never called back, and he never came to call. Finally, one night after the boys were in bed I stood on the landing of the stairway and quietly and deliberately tore off my skirt and blouse and ripped them into a hundred small pieces. It was like lancing a boil. It helped. Then, having humiliated myself with this mindless self-indulgence, I picked up the pieces, threw them away and set about the business of being a conscientious mother and teacher again.

In Philadelphia we lived three blocks from church. The boys and I went every Sunday; Jimmy was confirmed there—Hy was there that day. One Sunday afternoon when the accumulation of exhaustion and despair had me wondering if I should be in a hospital I called the minister and asked him if I could come see him. It wasn't convenient, but I begged and he said, "Very well—come along." I stayed for two hours sobbing out my sad little sadnesses. He gave me a cup of tea, patted my shoulder sympathetically, and sent me home. We stayed in Philadelphia another year after that visit. The minister didn't call, but he smiled warmly on Sunday mornings. The day the moving van was moving us to Connecticut he walked by the house and waved, and asked where I was going.

While we lived in Connecticut and New York, from 1971 to August 1977, Hy was my sounding board, my oasis, my warm and reassuring friend. That's not to say I was constantly wringing my hands, weeping, and saying, "Help me." Quite the contrary. I was jovial, happy company. Touching base with Hy gave me a feeling of safety and stability so I could cope with whatever traumas life tossed my way. It was after I had been at Madeira for several months and was visiting Hy that I called a young psychiatrist in Connecticut. He had worked wonders for several students at the Thomas School and I was ready for a small wonder myself. I cared deeply about Madeira and about doing a good job there. It is a fine school and nothing I write should ever give the impression that I doubt or question that. But I assumed too much about it when I took the position and the board was never honest with me, so a job which under the best of circumstances is tough became backbreaking and heartbreaking.

The young psychiatrist was warm and friendly on the phone but I couldn't bring myself to say why I had called. I didn't really know what to say—and anyway when I talked about myself I always wept, which disgusted me, so I said a friendly "Hi and goodbye." I had heard so much from Hy about female patients with nameless symptoms who thought they were sick when they were just bored or lonely or self-indulgent, and I didn't want to be one of them.

"To hell with it," I decided. "There's nothing wrong with me I can't handle myself." I sublimated; I made a joke of it; I bought a mink hat; I told myself I was lucky and whatever it was that hurt didn't matter— and a few months later I bought my security blanket, a .32-caliber gun, and I comforted myself with the knowledge that if the pain of living grew unbearable I could use the gun—on me. That is the only use it was ever meant for.

I have spent a lifetime trying to make myself believe that I mattered enough to go on living. I think I did believe it when I decided on suicide, but I had run out of energy by then and I knew I no longer had the heart or the physical strength to go on functioning in a useful way.

Did I say "decided"? It's the wrong word. You don't sit down and list the pros and cons. It becomes your only option—even more, it becomes a physical need. The plug was pulled and the only thing I wanted more than a quick, clean ending was to see Hy one more time before I went, and to die there by the pond at the place I loved, a place that had been home for me for almost nine years.

I had no thought of hurting Hy or telling him that I intended suicide. I had no intention of letting him see the gun. He was my last stop: I wouldn't keep him long. I didn't for a moment think it was an unfair or unreasonable request. It would be a nuisance getting rid of the body the next morning, but doctors are used to things like that. And Hy had said it himself many times, "I don't love anyone. I don't need anyone." He would have been sorry. But it wouldn't have ruined his day.

Harrison, New York:
The End of the Line

It began to rain about an hour after I had left Madeira. The last thing I saw as I drove out the long, lovely drive was the bright smiling face of Kathleen Kavanaugh out walking her little dog, "Killer." How ugly innocent things sound now. "I could kill that boy for leaving his room like this!" I must have said it many many times. "People who dump their beer and liquor bottles around this beautiful pond should be shot." I said it one day months after Hy died and then froze. "My God—what if Jim Ferron—heard me. He walks by the same pond and writes for *The New York Times*. Proof positive—I heard it. She's a killer!"

The drive was a strangely peaceful and mindless one. The decision to kill myself was so firmly made it was comforting. No more endless sleepless nights, no more ugly phone calls in the night, no more fighting each step of the way, usually about things you shouldn't have to mention twice; no more ugly conversations with my father about my children, my two very decent sons; no more watching grown men and women on a board of directors making poor decisions to mollify other members of the board who cared more about their memory of Madeira, than Madeira as it should be today. No more imposing on Hy for comfort, when turning seventy depressed and frightened him and he was settling into his own kind of comfort.

I walked into the house on Purchase Street that night as I had for fourteen years, full of love and happy to be there. I expected to be dead within the hour. Hy hadn't left a light on though he knew I was coming. It was pitch black and raining, and I stumbled on the stair. But I was relieved to be there. I felt safer than I had all day.

The story of what happened in Hy's bedroom on the night of March 10, 1980, is one I have told again and again to the very best of my ability. I have told it to doctors, lawyers, and family and friends. Had I been given another trial I would have told the same story again. The truth doesn't change.

What follows is taken directly from the public record of my trial. It never for a moment occurred to me that I should not take the stand. I am the only person alive who knows what happened that night. I had a moral obligation to Hy and to myself to take the stand and tell it. I believed it was the right thing to do then. I still believe it, although there were many who wrote later, "Mrs. Harris convicted herself. The jury didn't think she proved her innocence."

I took the stand on January 27, 1981, the thirty-eighth day of the trial, and was questioned for the next nine days. Having first identified myself I was asked to identify the papers I had left propped up on chairs in the front hall at Madeira: my will, insurance papers, and letters to the chairman of the board, my secretary, and my sister Mary Margaret. The letter to the chairman had been prompted by the Browning report, and by a letter I had received that morning saying I shouldn't have expelled four girls because "lots of other girls are doing the same thing. You don't know what is going on."

Joel Aurnou read my letter to the board chairman to the jury.

Dear Alice,

I'm sorry. Please for Christ's sake don't open again until you have adults and policemen and keepers on every floor. God knows what they're doing. And next time, choose a head the board wants and supports. Don't let some poor fool work like hell for two years before she knows she wasn't wanted in the first place.

At this point Assistant District Attorney Bolen objected and said, "Can we establish when these comments were made, if at all, in relation to March 10, 1980, especially when this document was purportedly written?"

The letter had already been turned over by the chairman of the board and sworn to by her as having been found in the front hall of the house I lived in at Madeira early in the morning of March 11, and was in evidence. But what did he care? The game of justice turns truth upside down.

The letter continued, "There are so many enemies, and so few friends. I was a person and no one ever knew." It took nine pages of testimony to get those six sentences out, with Bolen's constant objections, and the judge's repeated "Sustained." Finally, Joel asked:

Aurnou: On March 10, 1980—Jean, look at me please. When you wrote the words "I was a person and no one ever knew," tell the jury what you meant.

Harris: I don't know. I think it had something to do with being a woman who had worked a long time and had done the things a man does to support a family, but still a woman, and I always felt that when I was in Westchester I was a woman in a pretty dress and went to a dinner party with Dr. Tarnower, and in Washington I was a woman in a pretty dress and the headmistress, but I wasn't sure who I was, and it didn't seem to matter.

Aurnou: It mattered to you, didn't it?

Harris: I was a person sitting in an empty chair, Joel. I can't describe it anymore.

There was a brief recess and then the questioning went on.

Aurnou: When you went to Hy's, that trip took several hours?

Harris: Five hours.

Aurnou: Tell the jury, please, exactly how you felt, what you were thinking about during that trip, what emotional state you were in.

Harris: I can really only remember thinking two things. For about the first hour I felt as though I should call friends and tell them I wouldn't be there for dinner. They were having the first big dinner party since their marriage and I had been looking forward to it sort of, but I couldn't think of anything to say to them. I was afraid if I called them I'd burst into tears. So I kept thinking about it and it was on my conscience, but I didn't stop to call them to say I wouldn't be there. Then after it was late enough, it didn't make any difference. They already knew I wasn't going to be there. I really had a very peaceful, mindless kind of a trip after that.

I felt at peace with the knowledge that I had finally come to the end of the road and dying didn't frighten me. Then, just as I came across the George Washington Bridge, I thought if I stayed too long—what if Hy said something that spoiled my resolve to die, and I brushed that aside very quickly, thinking I won't stay that long, I just want to see him for a little while and feel safe one more time, and I won't let him—I won't let him know what I am going to do and I won't let it spoil my resolve, and after that I just drove until I drove into his driveway.

Aurnou: And when you got to his driveway and drove up the driveway, will you tell us what you saw?

Harris: I saw a house that was very dark, and I felt just as good as I always did when I drove in that driveway.

Aurnou: But there were no lights on?

Harris: No, not a light. Not that I saw. . . .

Aurnou: What did you do after you stopped the car?

Harris: I stopped right in front of the front steps and I was sort of surprised not to see a light on, but I thought, well, maybe he left the door ajar and didn't want to leave a light on. So I got out of the car and started up the steps, and then I remembered the flowers and I thought it would be nice to take him the flowers. So I went back and opened up the other side of the car and I reached in for the flowers and I had put them on top of my pocketbook and I picked up my pocketbook, too, and the flowers, and I closed the door and walked up the steps to the front door and it was locked.

Aurnou: When you went back and got the flowers, you also got your pocketbook at that time?

Harris: Yes. I just picked it up the way you would pick up your pocketbook. I hadn't left the driver's side with anything in my hand, but I did go back for the flowers and took my pocketbook, too.

Aurnou: When you picked up the flowers and picked up the pocketbook, where was the gun?

Harris: It was in the pocketbook.

Aurnou: What happened next?

Harris: I walked up the stairs and tried the door and it was locked. So I just walked back downstairs and went in the way we usually went in, anyway, which was through the garage. I opened the garage door on the right-hand side, the one where Henri and Suzanne had their car, and then I walked around in back of Hy's car and I pushed the button for his door in order to make the light go on, so I could see what I was doing, and then I walked up to the first floor, and it was all dark there and quiet, and I called to Hy from the bottom of the stairs and then walked upstairs.

Aurnou: What did you say when you called to Hy?

Harris: I just called, "Hy, Hy," and I walked upstairs and he was just beginning to stir when I got to the top of the stairs, and I walked over and sat—

Aurnou: Wait a minute. You got to the top of the stairs.

Harris: The first floor.

Aurnou: Now you got to the top of the stairs at some point on the second floor, did you not?

Harris: Yes.

Aurnou: What did you have in your hands?

Harris: I had the flowers and my pocketbook.

Aurnou: What did you do?

Harris: I heard Hy just stirring and I walked over and sat on the edge of my bed and reached over and turned on the light, and the light over his bed went on.

Aurnou: First of all, Mrs. Harris, is that a dimmer switch?

Harris: No, it is not. It's just a switch that turns lights on or off.

Aurnou: Could you tell us how it works? Is it anything more than a click switch?

Harris: Yes. It's a nuisance. I think there are two parts to it and there are several different lights on the same connection. I have never seen anything quite like it, as a matter of fact. You turn this knob and push the switch and the light over Hy's bed would go on, and then you turn it again and push the switch again and the light over the table would go on and you turn it again and push the switch and the light over my bed would go on. But they were either on or off. They couldn't make them darker, dimmer, or brighter.

Aurnou: In other words, whatever position the switch was in would control which lights went on?

Harris: That's right.

Aurnou: But whichever lights went on went on in one intensity; it was not a matter of a dimmer switch?

Harris: That's right.

Aurnou: When you actually pressed it that night when you came in and sat down on your bed, which light or lights was it that went on?

Harris: I didn't turn the switch. I just pushed the thing and I guess the last thing to go off was the light over Hy's bed, so that's what went back on again.

Aurnou: What did you do next?

Harris: Well Hy was just waking up and rubbing his eyes and I said, "Hi. I thought you would leave a lamp in the window, it's black as pitch out there," and he was not enthralled to see me and he said, "Jesus, it's the middle of the night," waking up (indicating), and I said, "It's not really that late and I'm not going to stay very long. I just came for a while to talk with you," and he said, "Well, I'm not going to talk to anybody in the middle of the night," and he turned toward me.

He always had two pillows on his bed and he was lying on one and hugging the other one and he said, "I don't feel like talking in the middle of the night," and he closed his eyes. So I sat for a minute thinking he would wake up. He usually woke up very quickly, because he was used to phone calls in the middle of the night and getting up and getting dressed and racing out to a patient very fast, but he didn't seem inclined to wake up fast that night, and I finally said, "I brought you some flowers."

He didn't answer. And I said, after I waited a little while, "Have you written any more on the book?" and he said, "Jesus, Jean, shut up and go to bed," and I said, "I can't go to bed, dear, I'm not going to stay that long, I'm just going to be a little while," and I sat a while longer and he lay there hugging the pillow with his eyes closed, and I finally said, "Won't you really talk to me for just a little while?" and he didn't answer, and I sat some more, and finally I said—I didn't want to leave yet.

I was sure he would wake up and stick the other pillow in back of his head and say, "You're some kind of a nut to drive five hours in the middle of the night to talk, but what do you want to talk about?" So I was just kind of waiting.

And finally I said, "There is a shawl here, I want to be sure Kathleen has it, I'll just get it." I had given her a white shawl that she seemed very pleased with and I had a pretty black shawl somewhere in the drawer where I kept things.

Aurnou: Where was the shawl?

Harris: It was in the drawer in Hy's dresser that he had given to me where I would keep things over the years.

Aurnou: What if anything did you do then?

Harris: I got up and went around and opened up the drawer and I saw the shawl. It was on the bottom of a lot of other things.

Aurnou: Someone has described a drawer back in the dressing room area as being open in this area. Was the drawer to which you went for the shawl in that general area?

Harris: Yes. It was that drawer. It wasn't open when I went there. I opened it.

Aurnou: Before you opened it, did you do anything in that area?

Harris: Yes. I turned on the light so I could see. There is a light switch almost above where the cross is that was supposed to be where the drawer was. That was the one switch I used the most because it didn't have one of those turning dials on. It was just an ordinary switch. So a lot of time when I went up there in the dark I went around and turned on the dressing room light instead of fussing with the one in between the beds. Anyway, I turned that on so I could see what I was doing.

Aurnou: When you were doing that, where were the flowers?

Harris: On the bed where I had put them.

Aurnou: Which bed?

Harris: On my bed. I sat down. My pocketbook went to the left of me and the flowers went to the right of me. Hy was not enthralled by the gift of flowers. He wanted sleep.

Aurnou: Where was your pocketbook when you went back to get the shawl?

Harris: Right where it had been, on the side of—should I show you there?

Aurnou: No. Just tell us which location it was in.

Harris: If you were sitting facing Hy on my bed, it was on my left, near the foot of the bed, and the flowers were near the pillow. I think they were on the pillow.

Aurnou: And you went back to get the shawl and what happened?

Harris: I pulled out the shawl and I think I pulled out a couple of other things with it. I am not really sure. I don't remember what I brought with it. . . . I walked around and put them on the bed and looked at Hy and he still had his eyes closed, though I think by then he was wide awake, and then I turned back and went into the bathroom. I turned on the bathroom light.

Aurnou: Which bathroom did you turn the light on?

Harris: The one on the—

Aurnou: The one with the bathtub or the one with the shower?

Harris: The one I always used, nearest the bed. The one on the right-hand side.

The Court: Is that the one with the tub or the shower?

Harris: The tub. That's the one with the tub. And I turned on the light and I saw a number of things in the bathroom, one of them a negligee, a greenish blue satin negligee.

Aurnou: Was it yours?

Harris: No. And I looked at it, and having believed for a year that some things of mine had been destroyed by the owner of the negligee, I picked it up—I didn't pick it up. I took it off—

Bolen: Your honor, I ask that be stricken.

Harris: That was my reason.

The Court: I will sustain an objection. The last portion of the answer will be stricken, as to what somebody else may have done to her garment in the past. That item will be disregarded, ladies and gentlemen. You can go to the point where you picked up the negligee that you saw.

Harris: I took it off the hook where it was hanging and I walked into Hy's room and threw it on the floor. And Hy was still paying no attention. I thought I saw the negligee land on the floor. I don't know. I went back in the bathroom. By this time I felt hurt and frustrated, because the script wasn't working out the way I expected it to. I had looked forward to a few more quiet minutes with Hy and I guess I wanted to feel safe one more time and I thought it was a reasonable request, but it wasn't happening, and I walked back into the bathroom and I picked up a box of curlers and threw them. I didn't really know where they landed. I just threw them in the bathroom, I thought, but I guess they went out into the dressing room, and I heard the noise. They apparently broke a window, though I didn't know until many months later that they had broken a window, and as I walked out of the bathroom Hy was standing at the door and his arm swung out and he hit me across the face.

Aurnou: Just a minute, Mrs. Harris. You were in the bathroom when you threw the curlers?

Harris: Yes.

Aurnou: Where was the doctor at that time?

Harris: He was in his bed.

Aurnou: Did you actually see him get out of bed?

Harris: No, I didn't see him until I walked out. I didn't really see him even, I just felt him. . . .

Aurnou: You said that you came out of the bathroom, your bathroom, and the doctor was there and he swung and he struck you. Where?

Harris: Just across the face (indicating).

Aurnou: Had he ever done that before?

Harris: No, indeed, he never had. But then I had never come to his house and thrown something before, either.

Aurnou: Well, let's talk about that. When you drove from Virginia to Purchase, did you ever intend anywhere along that trip before or during or right up to the moment you got there for Hy to kill you?

Harris: No, I certainly did not, and I am happy to finally be able to say it. It wouldn't have made any sense to get in a car and think I would drive there and hand a man like Hy a gun and ask him to kill me with it. He spent his life saving people's lives, besides which, I wouldn't have done that to him. I didn't want him to know what I was going to do. I had no intention of his ever seeing the gun or knowing anything about how desperate I was that night. I hoped it would be a quiet, pleasant, last few minutes.

Aurnou: And while we are back, was there anything unusual about the way you entered the house that night? Had you ever done that before?

Harris: That was the way we went in most of the time. The front door had no outside lock on it. If it was closed from the inside, the only way you could get it open was to ring the doorbell. The only time I ever rang the doorbell was when I saw Suzanne in the kitchen and knew she didn't have a long way to walk. Otherwise I always went down through the garage.

Aurnou: Now you are outside the bathroom and Hy has smacked you. What did you do?

Harris: My first reaction was to throw something else. So I turned around and went back in the bathroom and picked up something. I didn't know until I was told in this courtroom what it was. But I picked up a box and threw that, too. I threw that and it went into a cosmetic mirror of mine and smashed that and then scattered around on the floor.

Aurnou: Let me ask you this. After the second thing that you threw and the cosmetic mirror belonging to you shattered, where was Hy and what did Hy do?

Harris: He was standing right where I left him and I walked back out and he did the same thing over again, exactly the same way, exactly the same spot. I made him very angry.

Aurnou: You told us originally that you went there because you felt safe and you wanted to have a quiet few minutes.

Harris: Yes.

Aurnou: What had you planned to do after that?

Harris: I had planned to leave and go down near the pond and shoot myself.

Aurnou: And here was the doctor, he smacked you twice in the face—

Harris: But he didn't know what I was going to do, Joel.

Aurnou: But what did you do then?

Harris: I didn't have any desire to throw any more things. It just hadn't turned out the way I thought it would, and I simply wanted to get dying over with. The pleasant talk was not to be. So I calmed down and I walked in and I sat on the edge of my bed facing away from his and I put my hair behind my ears and I raised my face to him and I closed my eyes and said, "Hit me again, Hy, make it hard enough to kill," which I guess I told the policeman something about, and that's what started the stupid story that I had gone to Westchester to ask Hy to kill me. It was the furthest thing from my mind.

Aurnou: But you did say it, then?

Harris: Yes, I did say it.

Aurnou: And what if anything did Hy say or do?

Harris: He didn't say anything. He stopped in front of me for an instant, I guess. It was long enough, so I wondered how much it would hurt if he did it, but he didn't touch me again. He walked away, and it probably took a great deal of self-control, because I am sure he was very mad by then. But he didn't hit me again. He didn't say anything. He just walked away around my bed and over to somewhere near his bed. I never really saw exactly where he was standing right at the moment, and it was very quiet, and I got up, I think to go, and I walked around the foot of the bed and I picked up my pocketbook and I felt the gun and I unzipped the bag and took out the gun and I said, "Never mind, I'll do it myself," and I raised it to my head and pulled the trigger at the instant that Hy came at me and grabbed the gun and pushed my hand away from my head and pushed it down, and I heard the gun explode. It was very loud. It seemed very loud, because I didn't think I'd hear it, and Hy jumped back and I jumped back and he held up his hand and it was bleeding and I could see the bullet hole in it and he said, "Jesus Christ, look what you did," and we both just stood there and looked at it. I think he was as appalled as I was. I wasn't aiming the gun at Hy and I didn't even know he was looking at me, but he moved very fast and he was the one who was shot, and he stood and looked at it—

Aurnou: Just a minute, Mrs. Harris. When that happened, did you intend to shoot or harm the doctor?

Harris: No. I didn't even know he was nearby. I didn't even know he was looking at me. But I know I was the one who fired the gun.

Aurnou: Was that the first shot fired in that room that night while you were there?

Harris: Yes, it was.

Aurnou: Do you have any doubt about that at all?

Harris: No, there isn't any doubt about that. I know that beyond a shadow of a doubt. That's where I was standing and that's what he did.

Aurnou: After he looked at his hand and said, "Jesus Christ, look what you've done," what did he do next?

Harris: He sort of stared at the hand for a minute and then he turned and went into the bathroom, and I stood there for a little while. I didn't have, I don't think, exactly a normal reaction to it, because I couldn't believe it had happened. Ordinarily if he sounded hoarse, I was upset if he didn't take a pill, but I didn't feel—I didn't rush to help him. I stood there and stared at him, and then I followed him into the bathroom, or I started following him into the bathroom.

Aurnou: What stopped you, if anything?

Harris: I got about halfway around Hy's bed and I suddenly realized that the gun was still in here, and if I went back and got it fast enough, I could shoot myself before Hy—I could hear the water running and I thought I could get it over with before he even came back into the room. So I didn't go all the way into the bathroom with him. I turned around and went back and I looked at the foot of the bed and I didn't see the gun and I looked in between the beds and I didn't see it, and I got down on my knees and looked under my bed and it was there, and I reached under to get it. I was on my knees, down low, and I pulled it out, and as I pulled it out, Hy came out of the bathroom—I didn't actually see him at that moment. I didn't realize what he was doing until I could feel him, and I think he just flew over the bottom of the bed and he grabbed my left arm and he held it very, very tightly, and it hurt, and it made me drop the gun.

Aurnou: I would like you to look at Exhibits C, D, and F in evidence.

Harris: Yes.

Aurnou: What part or portion of your body that Hy touched at that time is visible, if any, in those pictures?

Harris: The upper part of my arm, from the elbow on up, is visible.

Aurnou: Did you at any time that night have occasion to suffer any other injury to that portion of your arm, other than the time that he grabbed it and squeezed it tightly while you were holding the gun?

Harris: No. He wasn't trying to hurt me. He was trying to make me drop the gun.

Aurnou: Did you?

Harris: Yes, I did.

Aurnou: What happened then?

Harris: He picked up the gun. He held on to my arm for a while and he picked up the gun and then he got up and walked over and sat on the edge of his bed next to the little ledge where the telephone was and the buzzer, and I was on my knees and I looked at him and he looked at me and I came over in front of him—I don't think I got all the way up. I was kneeling in front of him and he buzzed the buzzer. He buzzed it several times.

Aurnou: Which buzzer are you talking about now?

Harris: The buzzer that would ring in the kitchen to make Suzanne and Henri come.

Aurnou: When he did that, where if anywhere do you recall the gun being?

Harris: Hy had it in his hand.

Aurnou: Which hand?

Harris: In his right hand, because he was buzzing with his left hand. He was sitting—should I show?

Aurnou: You can.

(Harris leaves the stand.)

Harris: He was sitting on the edge of the bed here.

Aurnou: Talk a little louder while you are away from the mike.

Harris: He was sitting on the edge here (indicating) and his left hand was pushing the buzzer and his right hand had the gun and he put it down on the bed and put his hand on the bed.

(Harris returns to stand.)

And I came over to him and I was on my knees. From the time he first buzzed the buzzer I was panicked, because I was afraid Henri and Suzanne would come running up the steps any minute, and I said, "Hy, please give me the gun, please give me the gun, or shoot me yourself, but for Christ's sake let me die," and he looked at me and said, "Jesus, you're crazy, get out of here," and he pushed me aside and he reached for the phone, because once you buzz the buzzer you have to pick up the phone and talk to someone on one of the other phones.

Aurnou: Why were you afraid that Henri and Suzanne might come up?

Harris: Because he buzzed for them.

Aurnou: But what if they did come up?

Harris: Well, then I didn't have a chance of getting the gun again. I didn't think I did, anyway, because Hy even with his injured hand was stronger than I was.

Aurnou: What was it you thought they would prevent you from doing?

Harris: I wanted to shoot myself, Joel, and I was doing it in the wrong place.

Aurnou: After Hy buzzed the buzzer for the servant and picked up the phone with his left hand while you were kneeling in front of him, what happened next?

Harris: I pulled myself up on his knees, as a matter of fact, just holding onto them, and I was just about straight and the gun was there. He wasn't holding it then. I think he put it on his lap by then. That's where I remember reaching for it, and as I got up, I grabbed for the gun and Hy dropped the phone and he grabbed my wrist and I pulled back and he let go and I went back on the other bed. I fell back the way you would in a tug-of-war and Hy lunged forward at me, as though he were going to tackle me, and his hands came out like that, around my waist, and there was an instant when I felt the muzzle of the gun in my stomach. I thought it was the muzzle of the gun, and I had the gun in my hand and I pulled the trigger and it exploded again, with such a loud sound, and my first thought was: My God, that didn't hurt at all, I should have done it a long time ago. And then Hy fell back and I got up and ran.

Aurnou: Why did you run?

Harris: Because I wanted to get far enough away from him to shoot myself before he caught me again.

Aurnou: Where did you run to?

Harris: I ran from where we were between the beds around his bed, and I got almost up near the end of his bed, I thought right near that closet. Near the edge of the closet between the bathroom and the closet is where I thought I was. I stopped right about there.

Aurnou: Where was Hy then?

Harris: He was down—he was on his knees, actually, between the beds, and that he wasn't chasing me was what was important to me.

Aurnou: What did you do?

Harris: I stopped there at the head of the bed near the closet and I put the gun to my head and I took a very deep breath and I pulled the trigger and the gun clicked.

Aurnou: You mean it fired?

Harris: No, it didn't fire, and I had gone to great pains to see that that couldn't happen, and I tried to think of an adjective for that too.

Aurnou: What did you do next?

Harris: I heard the gun and I looked at it, because I couldn't see—I was sure I loaded it, Joel, with six bullets, and I thought there were a lot of bullets left, and I looked at it and I pulled the trigger and it exploded, and I thought it had gone possibly back into the rug. I found out months later, as you know, that it had gone into the cupboard right next to the headboard. And I put it back up to my head and I shot and I shot and I shot and I shot and I shot and it just clicked, and Suzanne and Henri hadn't been heard from, but part of the panic was thinking, "God, they'll be here any minute," and the gun was either not working or it was empty, or I had to find some more bullets for it, because I wanted to get more bullets in it and be dead before Suzanne and Henri got up there, and I know I had put some bullets in my pocket when I filled the gun. I haven't any idea how many I put in, and I looked for my coat and I couldn't find it. I ran around the room, and finally I found it on the floor next to the television set. I don't remember taking it off or putting it there, but that's where I found it, and I took it into the bathroom and I emptied the pocket on the floor and there were some bullets in it.

Aurnou: Was there anything else in your pocket that emptied out on the floor?

Harris: I didn't know, at that time. I saw some change in the picture, but I don't remember that. And I pulled out the cylinder and again tried to pull out the shells and they didn't move. So I banged the gun on the tub and they didn't move. So I banged it on the tub again and they didn't move, and I think I banged it a third time and I banged it very hard and it flew out of my hand and went into the bathtub, and I leaned over and picked it up and it was broken. When it fell into the bathtub, the cylinder part wasn't part of the gun anymore. It had broken. It was the crane. I heard the word. I don't know. It broke the thing that attached to the rest of the gun.

So I spent a frantic—I don't know how long. I suppose a minute or seconds, minutes, and tried to put the cylinder back into the gun, and I got it part way and almost all the way in, but I couldn't really line it up, and finally I walked back into Hy's room and I saw him just dropping the phone—not the whole phone, the receiver, and he turned and he was pulling himself up on my bed and he obviously hadn't gotten an outside line yet, and I went over and I picked up the phone and I listened and heard nothing. There wasn't a buzz, there wasn't anything. And I pushed the thing and nothing happened, and I put it back down on the hook and I said, "Hy, it's broken. I think it's gone dead," and Hy said, "You're probably right." That was the only civil thing he said all night, and that was the last thing I heard him say. And he pulled himself up and he leaned on me and he went back over toward his bed and I helped him back on to the bed, and when I left Hy, he was lying on a blue velour blanket near the head of the—near the foot of the bed, and when he went back, his hands both went out, and he looked exhausted, but he didn't look dying. His color looked—I looked at his face and he looked at me and I guess we were both in a state of shock, wondering how something could—how something that ugly and sad could have happened between two people who didn't argue, even, except over the use of the subjunctive, and I ran downstairs and I ran to the front door, and when I got there, the light was on in the dining room, and the door that Henri and Suzanne usually had closed in the dining room was open, and I could hear Suzanne's voice. She was in the dining room, but I didn't see her.

She was talking to someone and I got to the door and it was all dark in the foyer and on the steps, and it has another one of those turn switches, and I saw it and I said, "Somebody turn on the goddamn lights, I'm going for help," and I pushed something and the light went on. I'm not sure which one it was, but I could see my way down the steps and I ran down, leaving the door wide open, and I got in the car, and I headed toward the Community Center where I knew there was a phone.

Aurnou: How far away was that?

Harris: I don't know how far. I know it's exactly one mile to Anderson Hill Road, because Hy wrote that on the first instructions he wrote me on how to get there, but I don't know—I guess it's about half a mile to the Community Center. I don't know.

Aurnou: As you got into the Community Center parking lot, what if anything happened?

Harris: I turned in and drove up toward the phone booth. You can see it easily. It has a light on it. And I looked up and I could see off to the right the Anderson Hill light and I saw a police car coming with flashing lights, and when I saw it, I didn't get out of the car, I backed around and I turned back and headed back to Hy's house. I got almost to his driveway and I thought, "My God, maybe they are not coming to his house, maybe they are going to the airport or something." But I went into the driveway, and by the time I got to the toolshed, I could see the lights following behind me.

Aurnou: Had the policeman given you any sign or any signal of any kind indicating that you were to stop or follow him or do any particular thing?

Harris: No. He didn't know where he was when he followed me into the driveway. I think he followed me in because he was going to ask me how to get to where he was supposed to go. I got out of my car, and the policeman, whom I now know to be McKenna, didn't get out of his. He was listening, I guess, to his radio, he said. I ran over to his car and I can remember shouting, "Hurry up, hurry up." I don't know whether I said, "Hurry, he's been shot, please, hurry up, hurry up," and I ran up the steps with McKenna behind me, and Henri was standing at the top of the steps silhouetted against the front door. He was outside of the front door and he was screaming hysterically, "She's the one, she did it, she's the one," and I ran into the house and Suzanne was somewhere inside the foyer and we ran upstairs. I believe Suzanne ran up first. I ran next. I know McKenna came up last. And I got to Hy's bedroom—

Aurnou: Did Henri come up at that time at all?

Harris: No. He didn't come up until another policeman came. And Hy was on the floor lying on his back between the two beds.

Aurnou: When you first got back there, Hy was on the floor on his back lying between the two beds?

Harris: Yes. He was right exactly where McKenna described him in his police report that night, though it's not what he said to the jury when he came here.

Aurnou: Who was in that room first when you got back to the house, you or McKenna?

Harris: I was there before McKenna.

Aurnou: Did anyone get in that room before you did?

Harris: Suzanne says that she ran up before we got there. I don't know. She may have been up there before.

Aurnou: When you came back to the house with McKenna, in what order did anyone go upstairs?

Harris: Suzanne and I went upstairs and McKenna came up in back of us.

Aurnou: How long did McKenna stay?

Harris: He just looked at Hy and ran back down for his oxygen equipment.

Aurnou: Was Henri there then?

Harris: No. Suzanne and Hy and I were in the room for at least a moment alone. At least as long as it took for McKenna to run down and get his oxygen.

Aurnou: What did Suzanne do?

Harris: Suzanne went over and knelt on the floor beside him and took his hand and spoke to him very gently, and I lay across the bed and leaned over and caressed his face and talked to him, too.

Aurnou: What did you say?

Harris: I said, "Oh, Hy, why didn't you kill me?" I couldn't figure out why he was on the floor when I left him on the bed, and then I looked up and saw the receiver from the phone dangling down. Everybody else had said it was on the floor, but I remember very clearly it being up on the shelf and the receiver hanging down and covered with blood, and I realized Hy had gotten up and gone over and tried to phone again, and then fallen back. He was trying to talk to us then, too, but he couldn't speak, and not three minutes before he spoke perfectly clearly.

Aurnou: Mrs. Harris, when you left the house to go to the telephone to get help, did you know how many bullets, or how many bullets did you think had actually been fired in that room?

Harris: Well, I knew that I had now shot all the way around it. They must have all been shot. I knew of three shots. I knew of the one in his hand, I knew of the one when I thought I shot myself in the stomach, and I knew of the one that I shot into space or the floor or wherever it landed, but it wasn't anywhere near Hy.

Aurnou: Have you thought since then of when the other two shots were fired?

Bolen: Objection. I object.

The Court: I am sustaining the objection as to the form. You can ask her whether she knows now.

Aurnou: Have you made any effort in your mind since March 10 to recall the events of that night?

Harris: I spent eleven months thinking about it, Joel. I know when the first shot was fired and I know when the last shot was fired and I know that I shot at myself, I thought, when we were there between the beds, and I know the only time Hy and I were close together struggling for the gun was in that minute or so between the beds when I grabbed for the gun and he grabbed for my arm, and it had to be in that period of time. I don't know—when he grabbed my hand, it's possible it went off then. I believe when I fell back, it went off then, but I did not know when I left Hy that night the first time or the second time when the police made me go downstairs, I did not know that he had been shot any place except in the hand, and that was the only place I saw bleeding ever, and he was not, as Mr. McKenna changed his mind, and as Henri changed his mind for this jury, on his knees with blood pouring out his back. There was very little blood near Hy. The only thing that really bled was his hand, and he was lying on his back. McKenna saw a chest wound. I didn't see that. But I really only remember looking at his face and touching his face when I came back.

Aurnou: Mrs. Harris, after you lay across the bed, stroked the doctor's face, talked to him, what happened then?

Harris: Well, McKenna came back up first with some oxygen and put it over Hy's face, and very shortly thereafter another policeman came up and that was when Henri came up, too, and the other policeman told me I had to come downstairs, and I asked him to please let me stay with Hy and he said, "You can't, you have to come down," and I got up and went downstairs with him, and I believe Henri and Suzanne came down then, too.

Aurnou: At any time that night did you intend to harm Hy?

Harris: No, I did not, ever, ever, not for one instant.

Aurnou: Did you ever that night intend to shoot or kill Dr. Tarnower?

Harris: No, I didn't. The most violent thing I did was throw a box of curlers, and I didn't throw them at him. I never for a moment wanted to hurt Hy, never in fourteen years, and certainly not that night.

2.

Hy was taken to the hospital and died there at 11:58 P.M., March 10, 1980. Shortly thereafter I was arrested and brought to the Harrison police station. I spent the rest of that night in the Harrison jail, in a small cage, guarded by a kind woman who did what she could to make it easier for me. I remember it as a long night when I didn't feel anything at all, no concern about me, little awareness of Hy's death. The next day I was moved to the jail in Valhalla, and the following morning my sisters, Mary Margaret Lynch and Virginia McLaughlin, and my brother Robert Struven flew in from all over the country and bailed me out.

From Valhalla I was taken to the mental ward of the United Hospital in Portchester, where I stayed for ten days. I had always had a good feeling about Portchester, without knowing anything about it. In the years that I drove from Philadelphia to see Hy, Portchester meant I was almost there. I will always remember the kindness of the women on the mental ward floor. I welcomed the idea of going there. I wanted a world with women in crisp white uniforms and sheets pulled tight. It sounded safe. Instead, I arrived to find everyone in slacks and tee shirts, nurses as well as patients. It was all very informal, the way, I'm told, most mental patients respond the best. Not I.

"My God," I cried, "I don't know which are the nurses and which are the patients. Get me out of here." I had been told that I wasn't being "committed," that I could leave if I wanted to, but by the time I realized that I wanted to leave, the doors were locked and no one was quite sure who had the key. Finally, they quieted me with a shot of something, and I slept for twenty-four hours.

When I awoke, the volunteer on the floor came in to talk with me. She was out of slacks and wearing a suit. Five days later she said to me most kindly, "Mrs. Harris, I know you were upset by all the people in slacks when you came in, but slacks are what I usually live and work in. I'm running out of skirts. Would it upset you now if I went back to slacks?" In every possible way, both staff and volunteers did what they could to help a desperately sad and shaken woman. For ten days the media banged on doors trying to find out where I was, and no one told them.

I was allowed to use the public phone there on the floor, and I used it only once, to call Hy. White Plains nine, eight, three, eight, nine had been my lifeline for a very long time. I felt a physical need to dial it. Suzanne van der Vreken answered the phone. She cried and so did I. Then she said, "Oh madame, it is so sad. They say I cannot speak with you again." That was the last time I heard the woman I had known as Hy's cook and housekeeper for fourteen years, the one who had given me one of her paintings when I left for Virginia, and which Henri had framed for me. When I saw her again on the witness stand at my trial, she had become a total stranger, describing a woman I never was.

143

Using all the physical and mental powers at my disposal during those ten days in the hospital I managed to play solitaire, stare into space, sleep, and weep. I couldn't read or write for many weeks. Suicide was still much the best, much the most logical choice. Part of that ten days was spent taking psychological tests. I found it difficult to take them. I didn't want to have to talk that much or think that much. The tests were administered then and later by Dr. Eileen Bloomingdale, a forensic psychologist, and, I believe, a very wise woman. The first test she gave me was a Wechsler Intelligence Test, a basic IQ.

The hardest part for me was forgetting words, simple words and simple facts. I couldn't remember who wrote Faust and that bothered me. At the time it seemed terribly important to me that I remember it. I tried playing games with the doctor, "I'll tell you how the story in the picture ends if you'll just tell me who wrote Faust." She wrote a great deal later about my "need to be in control." I thought then, and I think now that it was control of me I wanted, not of others. Finding answers that made sense to me and satisfied me has used a lot of ergs of my energy over a lifetime.

I'm afraid the thing that frightened me most about the tests was the very real threat that they would discover I wasn't intelligent and then everyone would know. I could imagine my IQ in a *New York Post* headline. I had functioned as a reasonably intelligent person for a long time, but maybe it was just something I had gotten the hang of, a part I had played, and right down at rock bottom the truth was I didn't have too many marbles.

There are two parts to a Wechsler Intelligence Test, one verbal, one performance. One thing I was absolutely sure of was that my verbal score would be higher than my performance (putting puzzles together, matching, this is to this as that is to what). The other thing I was sure of from long years of studying student IQs was that a twenty point difference between verbal and performance scores usually meant something was amiss and the student in question could profit from some psychological counseling, because a gap that wide did signify some lack of balance.

As it turned out my performance score was twenty-three points higher than my verbal. I could put the puzzle together like nobody's business, but I couldn't remember words. As for my IQ, it turned out to be high enough so that the *New York Post* wouldn't have any fun printing it.

The Wechsler Intelligence Test was followed by the Rorschach Ink-blot Test, the Bender Gestalt drawing of shapes, Benton Visual Recall, Minnesota Multiphasic Personality Inventory, and Thematic Apperception Tests. Later, when two EEGs indicated "dysfunction of the brain when not in resting position," "definite abnormalities when hyperventilating," I went back for more tests; the Goldstein-Scherer Sorting Test, Halstead-Deiton Trailmaking Test, Lurea Nebraska Neuro Psychology Test. They didn't explain the EEG, and I was assured by the neurologist who poked and prodded me that all my reflexes are normal, that the brain is a mystery, and they will probably never explain my EEG.

When I left the hospital, there was still a houseful of my worldly possessions sitting in the headmistress' house down in McLean, Virginia. David, my son, drove me there the next day, and in nineteen hours we had packed everything and were gone. Not one member of the Board came to see me. One called. The School motto, "Function in disaster, finish in style" is for the students—and the headmistress.

The months between Hy's death in March of 1980 and the beginning of the pre-trial in October still have a quality of unreality about them. They were quiet and lonely and private and sad. I walked the dog and went to the psychiatrist, and read and wrote, and sat alone in a bedroom in a kind friend's house. Within a few hours after Hy's death, and the public announcement that Joel Aurnou would be my lawyer, Frances Baxton called his office and left the message that if I were not allowed to leave Westchester, I was welcome to stay with her.

Frances's husband, Carter Braxton, had only recently had a stroke. He was still in the hospital. Hy was his doctor. In fact, the last professional visit of his life was to Carter in White Plains Hospital.

We were a strange household: Frances with her cats, I with Cider, my golden retriever, and poor desperately ill Carter. When he came home from the hospital there were nurses for him almost around the clock, but not from 5:00 in the evening to 11:00. Nights when Frances went out were the only times I did anything remotely useful. I fed Carter and bathed him, and brought him whatever I could figure out he might want. I never knew exactly how much he understood about what I was doing there. Sometimes when I tried to explain, he held my hand very tight. Other times he just stared into space.

Other than those evenings alone, my only contact with Carter was bringing him flowers from the garden. I picked them for him and arranged them in his room. I picked them for Hy too, and brought them to his grave. And then finally, it was October, and while I moved into the courtroom to live, Cider moved into Carter's room to keep him company. I think Carter became fond of her.

My only real connection to the outside world during those long months were the letters I received, hundreds and hundreds of them from old friends, classmates, students, students' parents, fellow teachers, people for whom I had worked, and people who had worked for me. Before the trial began almost four hundred people had written offering to be character witnesses for me. I didn't know until later that character is of no consequence in a courtroom. The kindness of the letters reduced me to deep, wracking sobs. It was often hours after they had arrived before I could finish reading them.

Many of the girls at Madeira wrote wonderful letters, kind and remarkably sensitive in what was an unthinkable situation for them as well as for me. The seniors dedicated their yearbook to me. They had voted to do it long before, but they took another vote after Hy's death, and they still dedicated it to me. They could have changed it but they didn't. This note came with the yearbook when it arrived. How could I ever tell them what it meant?

Dear Mrs. Harris,

On behalf of the Senior Class, the *Epilogue*, and the rest of the Madeira community we would like to present you with this year's annual. We have worked long and hard on the book and we hope that you like it. We have carefully chosen to dedicate the book to a very special lady we respect, admire, and love very much. We feel strongly that she is quite worthy of this honor. This year's *Epilogue* is proudly dedicated to you. Unfortunately it is only a small recognition of an appreciation of you and all you have done for Madeira. The dedication comes from the bottom of our hearts. We truly miss you and hope the very best for you. Thank you for all your support of the *Epilogue* this past school year. We hope that you enjoy the book.

Sincerely,

The very first letter to arrive followed a telegram to Joel saying, "If there's anything I can do I will come at once." It was from a young woman who lives in Denver and whom I hadn't seen or heard from since she graduated from the Thomas school five years before. She wrote, "I'm not sure you ever really knew what kind of influence you had on me. You changed my life at Thomas, from being a wandering minstrel to being a responsible, productive human being. I knew what you expected just by the air you had about you, and I think by graduation day I had begun to prove to you, my family and myself what I had to offer the world." At the end she wrote, "I hope you will be able to find a new dimension in your life and receive some profit from what you have invested in other people's lives."

Some well meaning friends believed what they had read in the papers and wrote, "Whatever you did I forgive you." That is not a sentence to gladden the heart, whether it comes from a child, a friend, or a stranger. Two of the girls from Madeira, in all innocence and kindness wrote, "No matter what you did I love you and forgive you." I was deeply troubled by these and answered them with long philosophical treatises on how I hoped they had faith in my innocence, but if they thought I had murdered someone they hadn't the right to forgive me.

One old classmate of forty years ago wrote what I am sure she meant in all kindness. She remembered that I used to swing my leg nervously in Miss Andrew's English class and was relegated to a back seat for it. She remembered that I was always "taut as a wire" and that I always had "very high standards for yourself and for others." From that she had deduced that now, forty years later, I must be capable of murder—and anyway she almost did her husband in when he walked off with his secretary, so the whole thing would be logical and forgivable.

What she didn't seem to know, and indeed what the media didn't acknowledge and the District Attorney forgot, is that loving an old bachelor is always a no-win situation, and you come to terms with that early on, or you go away. It may be a shock when you find that love letter or motel key in a husband's pocket, but you don't go through pockets to find a bachelor's other women. He brings them all home. A little scarf, a little earring, a little curler, even with his trusty "house manager" hiding it all as best she could. It's always there. If you are honest with yourself you never indulge in the luxury of thinking that you're needed. I wrote to Hy years ago, "I wish I had been a doormat or a man instead of the miserable half-breed I've turned out to be. I want very much to feel like your equal, but love is no equalizer."

There were letters from women, most of them friends, some strangers, all of them wishing me well and then bursting into the story of their own sad lives. Letters from men usually came later. It was harder for men to write than for women. Women are less self-conscious about tragedy, more at home with it. I loved the letter that came in September from one of the men I had worked with in New York at Allied Maintenance:

"My thoughts and opinion of you are the same as when we worked together. I admired your honesty, competence, dedication, and sharp humor. You always seemed to be on the "up" side of things, and could see the day and the work through, this in spite of everybody else. I am hesitant to ask How are you?, but, well, How are you? Are you going to see the day through with your high standards of respect and competency? I hope so."

Old friends wrote very personal and loving notes:

"Remember when I was so sick and I couldn't stand anyone near me but you, and you sat and sang to me?"

"Remember when Carl was dying and you came and cut the front lawn and edged the garden?"

"Remember the shake-down cruise of the *Galetea* and you and Dee Dee and Liz insisted it was a put-down to be called "the girls" so from then on we called you "the former girls?" Remember? Remember, Remember?

Teachers wrote:

"The campus is beautiful and each time I stop as I walk across the campus I think of every flower you have caused to be planted. A daffodil in bloom anywhere this spring has reminded me of you."

"I've thought of your pain. Yes, I've thought of that quite a lot. I can't imagine that you have room in your personal structure for sympathy, and the inherent limitations on presuming to empathize. . . . I don't know the word, if there is one that expresses my awareness of you, my belief in you as a person, and my belief in those qualities of living which you have instilled in so many of the girls and the faculty."

Heads of schools wrote:

"I know that you have the strength to get through this rough time. I remember how strong you were in the Thomas School situation, and I prize your years at Madeira. That superb Harris intelligence and humor brought a refreshingly open atmosphere to an old and solid school."

"Because I, like many of your colleagues, have known and admired you as a capable and delightful person, we have come to love and admire you. . . . Life certainly can take matters out of what we consider our capable and decisive hands."

Students, bless them, wrote:

"I want you to do as you once told me, rest, eat well, and keep your spirits up. We've both worked hard this year and we're going to make it."

"I remember when you helped me through a very difficult time in my life . . . you always seemed to have a moment to talk and ask me how things were going."

"I've written you two letters before but I was too embarrassed to send them. One was about a beautiful speech you gave at chapel about a month ago. You talked about getting to know people, giving them a chance, even if they live in a different 'box.' That hit home. I realized how many doors I had closed to myself. I'm enjoying getting to know people I thought were 'nice' but a little strange."

"Much love to a dear lady. Don't worry about us. We'll make it. We love you."

Westchester:
The People of New York
State *vs.*
Jean Harris

On October 15, 1980, the first contingent of potential jurors gathered in the large auditorium at the Westchester courthouse. Ordinarily a pool of four hundred citizens are notified to report for jury duty. For the Harris trial one thousand people were notified. Judge Russell Leggett who was to preside over the case introduced himself, the lawyers—Joel Aurnou for the defense, Assistant District Attorney George Bolen for the prosecution—and the defendant Jean Harris. He read the three charges for which I was indicted: count one, murder in the second degree, count two, criminal possession of a weapon, in the state of New York, second degree, and count three, criminal possession of a weapon in a place not the defendant's home or place of business, third degree.

The judge then gave a dignified pep talk about the American system of justice. "You will be," he charged them, "judges of the fact. You are the sole and exclusive judges of what the truth is. You will bring with you here your common sense. Without your common sense you defeat the purpose of your being here. You are fact finders, and as such you decide credibility. Your verdict will be 'Guilty' or 'Not Guilty.' Your job is not to find innocence." I still don't fully understand that.

Judge Legget continued. "This case comes here by way of an indictment in Westchester. An indictment is of no evidential value—it simply lists charges—you cannot decide guilt because of an indictment—the defendant is presumed innocent until proven guilty. Our jury system is the greatest bastion for justice that has ever been devised by the minds of men. You must come in with a fair and impartial mind—no prejudice or sympathy—sympathy has no place here. The burden of proof is upon the people. They must convince you, beyond a reasonable doubt of the defendant's guilt, or you are obliged to find her not guilty. You do not need to be given proof beyond all possible doubt, only beyond 'reasonable' doubt." What is a reasonable doubt was to become the best kept secret of the trial.

"Reasonable doubt," the judge explained, "really gets down to common sense and your own home-grown intuition. What you happen to think because of your interpretation of the facts as you see them."

When the Harris trial is mentioned, even today, the first question is usually "Why didn't she plead extreme emotional disturbance, EED?" The answer is simple. My lawyers didn't recommend it, and their explanation of it was such that I wouldn't have wanted to.

That I was extremely emotionally disturbed is obvious, but the explanation of EED given to me, during the trial and the three years after the trial was always, "If you want to plead EED you have to first say that you murdered Hy, but you did it under extreme emotional disturbance."

Again and again I protested the same way. "But that's Catch 22. It doesn't make any sense. You're telling me that the way to be acquitted of murder is to say that I murdered a man. I didn't murder Hy, and nothing and no one will ever induce me to say that I did." It was always the same conversation, with the same advice, and the same frustrated answer from me. Joel said it was probably a lucky break that I was indicted for murder because there was "No way in hell anyone could find you guilty of murder." He worked very hard to make that be true, but it didn't happen.

Picking a jury is a complicated, frightening business—so much is at stake. At the initial screening all the questions were put by the judge. Some people were excused "for cause," some were asked to return November 1, by which time Judge Leggett thought the formal voir dire would begin. If there were no obvious "cause" for dismissal and the two lawyers disagreed about a candidate, Judge Leggett decided whether to dismiss or ask the person to return. What caused one or the other lawyers to object to something was sometimes obvious, sometimes not. It could be a gut feeling, or merely the other lawyer's enthusiasm. Good poker players have an edge here.

I had no idea how long and how grim the screening of jurors could be. Each session seemed interminable. Next to Suzanne van der Vreken's testimony and Bolen's summation, screening of jurors was for me the most traumatic part of the whole endless ordeal. I was unprepared for the ugliness, still believing as I did that my life spoke well of me. "Everyone knows she's a murderer. Why should I give my time to serve on a jury for her?" "This whole trial is a farce. It's just a big expensive game to promote legal careers." On the third day of screening I passed this note to Joel.

"Joel, is it required by law that I sit through this? If it is not, I wish to leave."

Joel wrote, "Why?"

I answered, "I am totally disinterested in who gets on the jury. I consider the trial over."

He looked annoyed, and wrote, "That is nonsense. Please allow me to concentrate on the proceedings."

There were lighter moments, though not very many. My presence inhibited many people who felt obliged to search for appropriate euphemisms to describe what they thought was my relationship to Dr. Tarnower. "I know there was something between them that went beyond the normal course of friendship." "They had a, you know, an adult relationship." "Well of course I understand. My son is divorced now, so he's just a consenting adult too." "I read that they had been— that they had a relationship." "I only know she was supposed to be with him—you know—with him." When a brash young woman breezed in and was asked if she could be impartial in judging Mrs. Harris, she replied, "After the life she's led, I certainly couldn't."

Judge Leggett, feeling that perhaps the girl was going too far in judging my morality or lack of it, made some comment to that effect. "Oh," she said, "I don't think she's immoral. I think she's an idiot!" I wrote Joel a hasty note: "I can make a case for that. Let's take her." But she was dismissed for cause.

An elderly candidate had the story confused, but no qualms at all about speaking his mind. "I have a personal reason that keeps me from being impartial," he said. "My niece took up with a married man. I have strong moral feelings." Leggett asked, "Would moral disagreement make it hard for you to be impartial? Could you decide on the facts?" He answered, "I would try, except I feel deeply it led to this situation."

Knowing of the long Tryforos affair with Dr. Tarnower, George Bolen turned to his assistant Tom Lalla and said, a little too loud, "I'm not sure which way he's going. I think he should go for cause." Having never "taken up with a married man," I shared the man's strong moral convictions. I wanted to keep him. He too was excused for cause.

Another candidate said, "I read in two papers quite a bit. I'm very much in favor of the poor guy who got killed. I'm in favor of the death penalty." After this Leggett asked, "But would you have trouble being fair to both sides?" It's in the record!

Because of the notoriety of the case some people were obviously torn between their personal obligations and thinking it might be "fun" to get involved. The more eager they seemed, the less eager either lawyer was to have them. One woman, obviously a detective story buff, said she would be "enchanted" to serve, but first she had to clear up one question. Leaning over toward the judge because she felt embarrassed that I might hear her, she stage whispered, "Where did they actually find the gun? If I know that, I think I've solved the whole thing."

The overwhelming influence of the press on the jury and the eventual outcome of the trial was immediately obvious. Potential jurors walked into the courtroom carrying under their arms newspapers that screamed, "Officer Testifies Mrs. H. Said She was Slayer." "She Told Me Harris Shot Dr." "Diet Doc's Girl Hopes to Die with Her Lover." "Police allege she had written certain notes indicating she was going to commit this murder." Not one single paper reported that there was no confession of murder. Of almost four-hundred people finally screened by Judge Leggett, there were fewer than ten who had not heard about the case through the media.

Prospective jurors went on interminably about what they read in the press:

"I read about the case in the papers. The doctor was alone. I think everything was pretty obvious."

"Have you made up your mind if the defendant is guilty?"

"Yes."

"Based on what you've read in the papers?"

"Yes."

"I'd have trouble separating what I've read and what I hear in court."

"I've read about the case and formed an opinion."

"I've read everything in the paper. I've half formed an opinion. It would be a little hard to forget what I've learned. I think I would be confused."

"I have definite feelings about the case. This woman came up and shot the man . . . let her . . . why should we take all that time being on a jury?"

"I've read about it. I really don't know if I could be impartial about it. She shot him in a rage."

Page after page after page of such comments accumulated as the screening went on. By October 27 Judge Leggett had asked 106 women and 81 men to return for the formal voir dire. "I am convinced," he said, "that all those who have been asked back are able to be impartial." A number of those asked back had even questioned their own ability to be impartial. Four of Hy's acquaintances were asked to return, as was a woman whose family was, in her words, "best friends with his sister, Mrs. Pearl ("Billie") Schwartz."

Joel Aurnou thought long and hard about a change of venue out of Westchester for the trial. But by October, there were in his office three large volumes of national newspaper and magazine clippings covering the case. There was no place to move to in New York State, or even any other state if that had been an option, where the story of the "Diet Doc and the aging mistress" had not been headlined and reported in the most lurid terms. The trial remained in Westchester. On November 5, 1980, the formal voir dire began, and on November

21, with twelve jurors and four alternates finally chosen, the trial began.

Both lawyers can challenge as many potential jurors as they wish "for cause," that is, for some legitimate reason that they cannot serve impartially. Each lawyer was also given twenty "peremptory" challenges, to remove a candidate for no other reason than that his instinct told him there might be a problem. When the jury had been chosen, Joel still had twice as many peremptory challenges unused as Bolen did. There was always the chance that if you took out this one, the next candidate would be worse.

The trial of the People of New York State *vs.* Jean Harris lasted from November 21, 1980, until February 28, 1981—fourteen weeks. More than twelve-thousand pages of testimony were taken. Ninety-two witnesses were called. The crux of the trial was intent. The indictment was for premeditated, deliberate murder. Did Mrs. Harris intend, and therefore deliberately kill Dr. Tarnower? The simple, unvarnished truth is that never at any time ever did the defendant express orally or in writing a desire to kill Dr. Tarnower, or indeed to harm hin in any way. In fourteen weeks of testimony, with nine months to prepare his case, with total control over the evidence, Assistant District Attorney George Bolen produced no evidence, of any kind, that could be interpreted as proof of such intent. It does not exist; it never existed.

On November 18, when twelve jurors and four alternates had been chosen, and not one minute sooner, Mr. Bolen, as he was required by law to do, released several hundred pages of Rosario material to the defense. Rosario material is any written reports, letters, statements, notes about some facet of the case made by a potential witness. The material was handed over at about 7:00 P.M. on the evening of November 18. At midnight the defense team and Jean Harris were still trying to get them in some semblance of order, making copies, and indexing them by subject, and by witness, everything written by and about Detective Siciliano in one place; everything by or about Suzanne van der Vreken in one place; extra copies of sheets that dealt with more than one person, and so on, until fifty-five folders took shape.

It left one torn between loving and hating the copy machine. In the state of California all this material would have been given to the defense attorneys at the very beginning—back in March. In New

York State it is part of the legal game to keep it all hidden away up to the very last minute. Police reports written about the defendant on March 10, 11, and 12, 1980, could not be seen by the defendant until November 18, 1980. Even my arrest report was zealously guarded for nine months for fear the person most directly involved would see it.

The prosecution is legally obliged at the start of the voir dire to list names of prosecution witnesses that will be called. It is not, however, obliged to tell the order in which they will be called. This meant that Joel Aurnou had to be prepared each day to cross-examine any one of fifty-five people listed by Bolen, some of whom he couldn't even identify at first.

When the defense presented its case, all the same courtesies were returned. No part of it is designed to advance the search for truth, but then, as the prosecution's case unfolded, it was soon quite apparent to me that the truth had barely a walk-on part in George Bolen's drama.

Some Rosario material was so badly copied it was unreadable. Sheets of paper that were related, perhaps part of the same report, were not necessarily together or even numbered consecutively. Some pictures were handed over along with Rosario material, but not all of them.

In December, when Judge Leggett ordered that well over a hundred pictures that had not previously been made available to the defense be turned over, I had to pay to have the county photographer and a member of the defense staff flown to Corning, New York, for Professor MacDonell to examine the negatives. By then there wasn't time to mail things back and forth. And two defense witnesses, one from Maine and one from Pittsburgh, had to be rescheduled, and flown back and forth twice to Westchester at the defendant's expense, too, although the reason for delay in their testifying was due solely to the prosecution.

The Rosario material gave me my first glimpse of the many police reports written between March 10 and March 12. Information noted the night Hy died should have been very inconvenient for prosecution witnesses nine months later. But it wasn't. All they had to do was say, "I was wrong when I wrote that." "It isn't true what I wrote there." "I remember better now." "I just mixed up the two." And the jury believed them. Officer McKenna, Detective Siciliano, Henri and Suzanne van der Vreken, and deputy medical examiner of Westchester, Dr. Louis Roh among others, were all to testify in contradiction to their original written reports, basic contradictions which in themselves should have provided "reasonable doubt" as to the defendant's guilt.

The official arrest report of Jean Harris reads:

Arrest made 11:05 P.M., March 10, 1980
Crime committed 11:08 P.M., March 13, 1980
Arrestee's rights given 11:08 P.M., March 11, 1980

As a matter of fact, I didn't see a Miranda card until after Hy was taken to the hospital.

The affidavit for a search warrant, written and signed by Officer Gary Holt of the Fairfax County Police Department in Virginia states, "At 0349 hours, on March 11, 1980 I received a call from a person identifying himself as Sergeant Carney of the Harrison Police Department, Harrison, New York. He indicated that Dr. Herman Tonover had been murdered in their jurisdiction. They had arrested a suspect Jean S. Harris and charged her with second degree murder. . . . He also indicated that the murder had been premeditated, and that there were certain writings in her office at Madeira School to indicate that she was leaving town to kill Mr. Tonover."

Sergeant Carney, witness at both the pre-trial and the trial, was desk officer at the Harrison police station the night of March 10, 1980. He was going to law school at the time, and may be a lawyer by now for all I know. His statements, as recorded by the Fairfax police, were soon in the hands of the press and widely quoted. They formed the basis of the much publicized "confession" which all the potential jurors had read about, and which Joel Aurnou was never permitted to question Carney about in the presence of the jury. At the pre-trial, without a jury, Joel asked him:

Aurnou: Did you give them (the Fairfax police) any information regarding the subject of premeditation?

Carney: If I recall, I may have inferred that it was, or implied that it was, or implied that it was inferred that it was, whichever is the correct grammar.

Aurnou: Would you tell us what you mean by that?

Carney: Well I believe, that is I recall, information was given to me alleging the possibility that the crime committed may have been premeditated.

Aurnou: Is that what you told the Virginia authorities?

Bolen: Objection.

Leggett: Sustained. . . .

Carney: I told them that there had been a . . . I believe there had been . . . I believe I told them that there had been a shooting and that the victim had expired.

Aurnou: Did you tell them a shooting or a murder?

Carney: Possibly a murder.

Aurnou: And that was kind of a rush to judgement on your part, was it not?

Bolen: Objection.

Court: Sustained. . . .

Aurnou: Sergeant, when you talked with Detective Siciliano that evening about the case, did he tell you that the defendant had made any statement whatsoever indicating premeditation?

Carney: I can say he did not. . . .

Aurnou: Did you tell Sergeant Holt in Virginia that "It seems that this apparently was premeditated?"

Carney: Yes.

Aurnou: And you had never been told that by Detective Siciliano?

Bolen: Objection. Told what?

Court: Sustained. . . .

Aurnou: Sergeant, did you ever tell them in Virginia in words or substance that there were certain writings in Mrs. Harris' office at the Madeira School that indicated that she was leaving town to kill Dr. Tarnower?

Carney: I don't believe I said that Mr. Aurnou, no.

Carney was shown the affadavit and the search warrant to re-read. Having re-read it, he was asked:

Aurnou: Does that document refresh your recollection, Sergeant, as to whether you made the statement I just inquired about?

Carney: I can't swear to that Mr. Aurnou. I really don't believe I said that. . . . I can say as I re-read this that it is absolutely positively not my statement, without any hesitation, now that I re-read it.

As the questioning continued, it became apparent to me that Carney was putting himself in the position of calling Officer Holt a liar. Presumably, he didn't want to have to defend such a position. So, despite his earlier testimony, when Mr. Aurnou asked, in conclusion, whether the statements that the Virginia police wrote down and used to obtain a search warrant were accurate or inaccurate, Sergeant Carney responded "They were accurate, I assume. Accurate."

When the jury trial began, Joel was not permitted to go into any of this as a means of demonstrating Carney's prejudice against the defendant. Bolen didn't want the jury to hear that Carney "implied an inference" to get a search warrant, and most of all, he didn't want the jury to hear any suggestion that Mrs. Harris was not a confessed murderer.

Up until the point at which Carney called Fairfax, the only person who had questioned me was Detective Siciliano. It was on the basis of what he learned from Siciliano that Carney called Fairfax. In October, under cross examination by Aurnou, Siciliano testified:

Aurnou: Did she ever indicate that she had come to Harrison, New York with the intention of committing a murder?

Siciliano: No sir.

Aurnou: Did she ever indicate to you in words or substance that she intended in any way to harm the doctor?

Siciliano: Not to my knowledge.

Aurnou: Is it fair for me to suggest from what you have just said, Detective, that she certainly never told you that whatever happened was premeditated, insofar as the doctor's injury? Do you understand my question, sir?

Siciliano: I do perfectly.

Aurnou: And she never did tell you premeditation, did she?

Siciliano: That's a fair assumption.

Aurnou: I have trouble with the last word, Detective. Is it a fair statement?

Siciliano: Yes.

Aurnou: I just want to be sure that it's clear on the record that I am not assuming it, but that what you are telling me is that as a matter of fact she never said that to you or any words equaling that—Correct?

Siciliano: Can you rephrase that?

Aurnou: Certainly. What I am saying to you is she never told you she intended to harm or kill the doctor. Is that correct?

Siciliano: Yes.

Aurnou: She never told you she intended to commit a murder, and so she never told you she intended to harm or kill the Doctor. Is that correct?

Siciliano: Yes.

Aurnou: Yes she did not?

Siciliano: She did not.

Aurnou: In the course of your investigation . . . you asked her specifically who had control of the gun . . . is that right sir?

Siciliano: Yes sir.

Aurnou: What was her response to that?

Siciliano: "I remember holding the gun."

Aurnou: Did she say something before that? Did she say the words "I don't know?"

Siciliano: Yes.

Aurnou: Then would you continue please.

Siciliano: She told me she was—she had possession of the gun, she had the gun in her hand and she remembers shooting him in the hand . . . I asked her who owned the gun.

Aurnou: And she told you it was hers?

Siciliano: Yes, sir. . . .

Aurnou: And you asked her in words or substance who did the shooting?

Siciliano: Yes sir.

Aurnou: Is that the point that she answered you sincerely?

Siciliano: She answered me sincerely.

Aurnou: And what did she say, sir?

Siciliano: After she said the gun was hers, I asked her who did the shooting. She says, "I remember holding the gun and shot him in the hand."

Aurnou: And what did she say right after that?

Siciliano: "He wanted to live," to the best of my recollection, "and I wanted to die."

Aurnou: "He wanted to live and I wanted to die?"

Siciliano: Yes, sir.

Aurnou: Did she say that sincerely?

Siciliano: She said it.

That there was never a confession of murder, that any suggestion that there had been was nothing more than an "implied inference" of

Sergeant Carney's, was a well kept secret at the trial that Joel was not permitted to reveal.

The fact is, the information used by the Virginia police to obtain the search warrant for my campus house—and which formed the basis for the so-called "confession"—was made up out of thin air. Unfortunately, it colored all of the thousands of pages that were to be written about me and Hy's death. It played a role in the jury selection. It played a role in the rest of my life. It permitted the press and public to believe that letters seized in the defendant's house at Madeira proved Mrs. Harris's intention to commit murder.

The final irony was that, when I was finally allowed to see them, I tried to have the letters put in evidence, since every one reflected my deep, lasting, and very honest affection for Hy. Only part of one letter was permitted. The others were considered "self-serving and irrelevant." And because George Bolen announced that he was not going to use any of the papers seized, Judge Leggett did not have to make any decision as to the legality of the search warrant and the underlying (erroneous) facts on which it was issued.

A premonition of evil began to permeate the courtroom from the first day, and the cast of characters was beginning to gather.

For what seems like an endless number of hours, I have read and reread the testimony in the case of the People of New York State *vs.* Jean Harris. Thousands of pages. It is an ugly tapestry struck through with stains and slashes of untruths, a once clear picture that no amount of restoration will ever make clean and whole again. And worst of all is the knowledge that it doesn't matter much to anyone but my sons and me. I wish I could believe that it would still matter to Hy, but I can't. "Let it go," he'd say. "God, Jean. You're like a dog with a bone. Let it go."

The grimmest part is finally knowing and believing beyond a shadow of a doubt that Hy could have been saved that night. No single wound was mortal. Doctors, including the Harrison police surgeon, Dr. Harold Roth, testified that Hy could have been saved if he had been taken at once to the hospital. "Any minutes would have made a difference."

Hy rang for the servants from the moment his hand was shot through and he had gotten the gun away from me. Henri van der

Vreken, butler and chauffeur, who was sleeping, as he always did, in the guest room, was awakened by his wife who came to tell him Hy was ringing for them. Beside the bed in which he lay was a phone on which he could have answered Hy's ring. He didn't touch that phone. He didn't go upstairs. In fact, he didn't go near Hy until there were four policemen in the house. He helped call the police but he did not at any time lift a single finger to personally help the man he had worked for for sixteen years.

The police were not much more helpful than the van der Vrekens. According to their reports, Officer Tamilio and Officer McKenna, the first two policemen to get to Hy's room, both observed a chest wound after Tamilio opened the top buttons on Hy's pajamas. Such wounds can be treated, but they require hospitalization as fast as possible. Five members of the Harrison Police Department spent almost fifteen minutes trying to bring Hy down the narrow stairway that led to his room. They finally succeeded having first put him on a conventional stretcher, then switching him to a Reid stretcher of canvas, holding him upside down and bumping him from man to man down the stairs.

No one that I know of suggested the fireman's carry, which could have brought him down in seconds. By the time they passed me in the front hall, the sad burden they carried looked more like a sack of potatoes than a man. Only his right arm hung down outside the canvas. "Is that Hy?" I asked Siciliano, and fainted in his arms.

According to Siciliano's sworn testimony he may have arrived at the house on Purchase Street as early as 11:02 P.M. As the ranking officer there and according to his own sworn testimony, he did not ask how Hy was; he did not ask where Hy was; he did not ask if anyone was with him; he did not go or send anyone else to check on his condition; he did not ask if a doctor or an ambulance had been called.

The policemen in the house at that moment represented more than one hundred years of police experience, but not one of them was apparently adequately trained or equipped to deal with the situation. Plasma and fluid should have been administered. There was none. The police surgeon, Dr. Roth, who is not a trained policeman, wrote down the moment that he had been called, 11:12 P.M. This was thirteen minutes after the police had first been alerted and knew that shots had been fired and someone had been hit.

It seemed to me almost an afterthought that a doctor was called. Sergeant Carney, asked later if he had checked to see if the doctor had arrived, said: "No. I just assumed he did."

Put simply, with the same wounds, at another time and place, Hy could have been saved. Assistant District Attorney Bolen was later to excuse the fact that the police moved and handled virtually every piece of evidence in Hy's room by saying, "Of course they had to move things. Their only concern was for the doctor. They did everything humanly possible to save the doctor." He made similar statements again and again, but the facts simply did not corroborate the statements.

In his opening statement, Bolen said, "Evidence is very important in this case." In fact, he used the word "evidence" nine times in the first three pages of his speech. He knew as he spoke that much of the evidence in the case had long since been either thrown out, contaminated, given away, rearranged to have its picture taken, misrepresented, lost or never gathered in the first place.

The rug in Hy's bedroom and the glass door through which a bullet traveled were both thrown out without either of them ever being tested for blood and the defense never having seen them. They were absolutely essential to the defense case. Both mattresses and beds were given to the Salvation Army with no hope of tracing them. We tried.

Lynne Tryforos was permitted to come and take everything out of the room of hers that had any significance as evidence, and when it was needed I know the prosecution simply used other things instead of retrieving what I saw and what I am certain had been there that night. The bloody phone—Hy's hand was the one thing that bled copiously—had no sign of my prints or Hy's on it by the time the chief of police and the chief of detectives finished using it that night. The gun was thoroughly handled by at least five people before it was test-fired twice, fingerprinted, and then tested for the presence of blood, in that order. The report of Joseph Reich, Deputy Medical Examiner so states, though he too said the report was wrong. In spite of this, Hy's blood was still found on the hammer, the cylinder, and inside the frame—proof that he held it.

Pictures of a phone sitting on the floor with the receiver off the hook were taken after the chief of police and chief of detectives had made three phone calls on it. The blankets on Hy's bed disappeared by the time of the trial. The spread on his bed, which Bolen told the jury would be "very important" was never seen again, and it is not shown in a single picture.

The blood spatters on it would have confirmed where the first shot was fired, and in what direction, as could the rug and the glass from the door. Sheets and pillowcases from both beds, some with blood still damp on them, were thrown together in one pillowcase with no markings whatsoever as to what was the top or bottom, left or right of them.

The pictures taken at the scene are another matter. Unfortunately, at least for the defense, there were no records kept of what pictures were taken and when. Common sense, but apparently not police procedure, should *require* that police pictures to be used in a trial must be dated and numbered. A child can understand why. It is the only way there can be a clear understanding and a clear record of what was done first and what was done second.

Though Detective Siciliano was the one who took most of the heat for the Harrison police, Chief of Police Harris was at least equally deserving. Once he arrived at the Tarnower house, having first had to stop and call in to ask for further directions, he spent from 11:30 P.M. to 2:30 A.M. milling around in Hy's bedroom. He took no notes of any kind, wrote no report, and remembered nothing. At least he so testi-fied. He made no effort to maintain the integrity of the room, and was, in fact, the first to pick up a bloody phone and make at least two phone calls on it. He obviously made no intelligent effort to define and delegate authority, and seemingly content that I had blurted out a confession, he proceeded to serve as nothing more than a voyeur at the scene. If he didn't take notes, take pictures, or take charge, what was he doing there? We never found out.

Chief Harris responded to Joel's questioning:

Aurnou: How long did you remain in the room?

Harris: I don't recall.

Aurnou: Did you take time to examine the room or just go up and come right down?

Harris: I just superficially looked it over.

The rest of his testimony was more of the same.

"It's hard to place any specific person at a specific time."

"I don't recall."

"I don't believe so."

Chief of Detectives Della Rocco was no better than the others. He arrived at the house just after Chief Harris had arrived and just after Hy had been taken to the hospital. He went directly to the bedroom and found the chief making a phone call on a phone still damp with blood. He testified that he stood at the end of the two beds "for five or ten minutes" just looking around and waiting his turn at the phone.

Asked by Joel Aurnou whether it had occurred to him as chief of detectives that it might be unwise to handle a bloody phone in a room where a shooting had just occurred, he explained his actions by saying:

Della Rocco: I didn't know there were any other phones in the house, sir.

Aurnou: Did you trouble to ask?

Della Rocco: No, sir.

Della Rocco was in charge of physical evidence, and when asked whether any letters, papers, or notes were taken from the room answered:

Della Rocco: I don't recall.

Aurnou: Did anyone turn over any of them at headquarters?

Della Rocco: I am trying to recall. My mind on that is hazy. I don't want to say yes, and I don't want to say no. I just can't remember.

But it was Detective Arthur Siciliano who was given the hardest time at the trial. Nine months after Hy had died Siciliano still wasn't quite sure what his role in the tragedy was meant to be. The defense had been told that Detective Siciliano was in charge of the investigation, but apparently no one had told Siciliano.

Aurnou: You were the detective in charge of this case, were you not?

Siciliano: Possibly.

Aurnou: You aren't sure?

Siciliano: I was assigned to it. I had a lot to do with it, but there were many superiors other than me there.

Aurnou: Whose primary responsibility was this case?

Siciliano: Certain degrees and avenues were mine.

Aurnou: Was physical evidence one of these?

Siciliano: Possibly.
Aurnou: Are you sure? Do you know?
Siciliano: I'm not sure.

In spite of this unspeakable carelessness, there are, thank God, pictures of the rug and floor in Hy's room, taken that night and in the next two days. They are the one piece of physical evidence left which in and of themselves are proof that I was not trying to hurt Hy. They alone establish a reasonable doubt, even if nothing else did.

Had Hy been afraid of me he would still be alive. Had he been afraid of me he could easily have locked himself in his bathroom, or run downstairs. The stairs to Hy's room lead directly into his room. There is no hallway. Arterial bleeding leaves a unique trail of blood. The only artery struck was in his hand. His hand was wounded when he grabbed at the gun to keep it away from my head. Pictures, even the sloppy, inadequate ones taken by the Harrison police, show the trail of arterial bleeding into Hy's bathroom and back into his bedroom again.

Even George Bolen and his strange questions could not mask that trail of blood. Even Roger Sirlin, hired by the Tarnower family to represent Henri and Suzanne van der Vreken and Lynne Tryforos, and who allowed Henri to throw away the rug from Hy's bedroom, could not mask the trail of blood. Even Detective Joseph Reich, who tested the gun for blood in the inner workings of it, after the gun had spent an evening in someone's pocket, been taken out and examined by five different policemen at five different times during the night, then test-fired twice and fingerprinted, and only then tested for blood, could not undo the trail of blood. Even this Keystone group did not destroy the trail of arterial bleeding that led from the bedroom to Hy's bathroom and back into the bedroom again.

A man who loved life as Hy did, who had safely reached his bathroom, which had a stout lock on the door, who thought his life was in danger, would quickly have locked himself in. He would not, as the blood pattern clearly shows, have walked back into the bedroom and over to a person trying to kill him. He didn't even have to go as far as the bathroom to escape a murderer. The stairway was closer. He walked within three feet of it on his way to the bathroom.

There is no blood spatter to the top step. No one and nothing kept him from it, except concern for his hand which had just been accidentally shot through. Escape would have been the primary consideration if he had thought for one instant that I wanted to hurt him. He was very angry, but he knew he was safe from me. This is clearly confirmed by the blood pattern.

It became clear to me early on that some of the prosecution witnesses were quite ready to change their testimony on several subjects as long as it fit the prosecution's scheme of things, or as long as they thought it made them look better or me worse. Between March and December of 1980 two people changed their description of Hy's position when we found him, the wounds they observed, and the amount of blood they saw. And it was only the beginning.

Officer McKenna, the first policeman to arrive at Hy's house, wrote in his police report of that night, "I went upstairs and found Dr. Tarnower, age 69, lying on the floor between two beds. I observed a bullet wound in the upper chest area." Ten days later, McKenna told the grand jury he remembered the doctor kneeling dramatically against the headboard, his hand just out of reach of the telephone, and he observed two wounds, one in the chest and one in the arm. By the time of the trial in November, in front of a jury, he remembered three wounds, a wound in the chest, one in the arm, and one in the back. Furthermore, he now remembered that there was "an awful lot of blood."

"Where?"

"Just about all over, some on his back, front, pretty much all over. It was a lot of blood."

The place on the rug where Hy lay for at least twenty minutes shows no blood.

Henri van der Vreken, in a written statement prepared within hours after Hy died, wrote, "I run to the bedroom where I saw Dr. Tarnower shot and lying between the two beds." He also made the same statement to Siciliano who incorporated the statement into his notes of that night.

At the preliminary hearing, held on March 14 to determine whether Hy had made any exculpatory statements, Henri was asked when he first went upstairs to the doctor's room after the shooting. He answered, under oath, "When we have two officers there." Officer Tamilio was the second officer to enter Hy's room. He testified that when he entered the room he saw "the doctor lying on his back between the two beds, on the floor, head facing out, oxygen being administered." He noted in his report that he saw one wound, a chest wound. Henri, following Tamilio up the stairs, could only have seen what Tamilio saw. But his final description for the jury went like this:

Bolen: When you got to the bedroom what if anything did you see?

Henri: What I see there is Dr. Tarnower lying on his knees, blood coming from his back.

Officer Larkin, who put Hy on the stretcher, repeated five specific times under oath that he did not remember blood on Hy's pajamas.

Joel repeated the question: "You didn't notice a lot of blood on the pajamas?"

"No."

Best qualified to answer was Dr. Roth, the police surgeon who went with Hy in the ambulance and then into the hospital.

Aurnou: Doctor, I would like you to explain to the jury please, what you observed with regard to the external bleeding by Dr. Tarnower. Was it substantial, was it not very much at all, compared to a normal chest wound?

Roth: I don't believe it was very much at all.

Aurnou: So that the pajamas you were shown here have a great deal more blood on them than they did at the time you saw them?

Roth: I would think so sir.

Aurnou: In fact doctor, with no disrespect whatsoever, you know so because you removed, or under your direction, there was removed 1500 cc of blood from the interior of the right chest?

Roth: That is correct.

By the time Hy's pajamas were put into evidence they were indeed blood-soaked. He had still been wearing them when his chest was opened and 1500 cc of blood came forth. They didn't have buttons all the way down, and they had been ripped open as he lay on the examining table.

Is it any wonder the jury could never figure out what really happened? One thing I know for sure is that the picture of Hy on his knees, leaning against the headboard and bleeding copiously, is pure fabrication, designed to make a jury and the public believe that I had shot a helpless man while he was trying to make a desperate phone call, and then left him there on the floor. Needless to say, the blood-soaked pajamas were prominently featured throughout the trial.

Part way through the trial an old friend of Hy's, and one he admired very much for his business acumen, came up to me during a short break. He put his hands on my shoulders and said quietly, "Jean, you've got to make Hy the bad guy. I've been involved in litigation, and I've seen a lot of jury trials. A jury wants a good guy and a bad guy. That's what they can understand. If the bad guy isn't Hy, it will be you. He's gone now. It doesn't matter to him. If you're going to win this trial you have to make Hy the bad guy."

The last weekend I spent with Hy, just three weeks before his death, he had been wakened in the middle of the night, dressed quickly, and rushed to the bedside of this same man. It was only indigestion, but he had thought he was having a heart attack. Hy had been at his side within fifteen minutes. I was shocked by his words at first. I thought he was being disloyal. But he wasn't. I know now what a friend he was, perhaps to both of us, because a compounding of his tragic death was not what Hy would have wanted. I believe that.

Unlike his family and friends, I will always want to believe that Hy, knowing the truth of that night, would have far rather seen the truth prevail than vengeance. We were both "the good guy" and we were both "the bad guy." Hy was what he was, and I loved him in spite of it and because of it. He had always welcomed me back. But he had never begged me to come. What happened that night could easily have been avoided—by me if I had killed myself on the terrace at Madeira and not indulged myself in the need to see him one more time—by Hy if he had just once understood the depth of my anguish that night and given me ten minutes of his time, or just left me alone to kill myself when I finally tried. There was no way I could bring myself to tell the world I was the good guy and Hy the bad. It would have been easy, but it wouldn't have been true.

George Bolen had no such compunction about creating a bad guy, and I was it. It was important to him that the jury think I had crept upstairs in the dark, pumped four bullets into a sleeping man, and then proceeded to spend the next half hour in Hy's room throwing things.

To make me a little spookier still, Bolen added a black glove—a right-handed black glove—in a black room, on a black night, at the top of a steep, narrow, winding staircase. It was Nancy Drew stuff, and the media loved it and the jury remembered it.

A left-hand glove was never found, and I am left-handed, but that is the kind of detail jurors in a long trial will soon forget about. Had I been wearing black gloves, it would certainly, in my mind at least, suggest premeditation. The glove was not an unimportant issue. It was very soiled and the thumb looked as though something had chewed it. I personally believe that it belonged to my dear Cider, the golden retriever who went almost everywhere with me in the car. She had a large collection of mittens and gloves that she had picked up all over the campus, and carried them about with her wherever she went.

The dirt on the back of the glove looks to me as though it could be saliva. If it is Cider's, it could only have been found on the back seat or floor of my car. And according to Judge Leggett's decision, the search of my car was illegal and anything found in it except the gun could not be used as evidence in the case. But it was used, which without question should have made for a mistrial.

As carefully as I have studied the testimony of my trial, I still could not say exactly how many times the prosecution witnesses changed their sworn testimony. It is key points in the trial that catch my attention. George Bolen suggested repeatedly to the jury that if Jean Harris had wanted to kill herself she had ample opportunity to do so. She had a working gun and bullets. He made light of the fact that by the time Hy had stopped trying to get the gun from me and I was trying to remove the spent bullets, it was broken and I couldn't get it back together again, and I couldn't remove the bullets to replace them, though I tried very hard. Under questioning by Bolen, Detective Siciliano gave the following testimony:

Bolen: Before you got to headquarters, of your own knowledge, sir, where were the five spent shells?

Siciliano: In the cylinder.

Bolen: And where was the cylinder?

Siciliano: In my pocket.

Bolen: And where was the cylinder in relation to the frame?

Siciliano: In the frame, but not completely intact.

By the next day, however, under cross-examination by Joel Aurnou, Siciliano's testimony went like this:

Aurnou: I think you told us on direct examination that when you picked up the gun, the cylinder was in the frame but was not perfectly seated?

Siciliano: It was perfectly intact.

Aurnou: When it was on the seat and you picked it up, the gun was in one piece, or appeared to be in one piece?

Siciliano: Yes sir, intact.

Aurnou: Did you examine it at the time and see if the cylinder and frame were lined up?

Siciliano: I looked at it and it was intact, yes.

Aurnou: I didn't ask you about intact. I asked you about lined up.

Siciliano: I looked at it and it was in its proper position.

Aurnou: Completely lined up?

Siciliano: Yes sir.

Aurnou: And you are certain of that and have never said otherwise?

Siciliano: Positively.

One of the strongest points on which we would later appeal was the fact that I was not allowed to make a private call to my lawyer. There is no question about this. It is clearly indicated in the testimony. I was too far gone by the time Hy was carried out of the house to be concerned about myself or my own best interests. I never questioned the integrity and decency of the people milling around me.

After he had helped carry down Hy, Officer Tamilio returned to the front hall where I was standing, waiting to make a telephone call.

Bolen: Did she say who she wanted to call?

Tamilio: Originally, the first time, yes, her son.

Bolen: Her son?

Tamilio: Yes.

Bolen: Please continue.

Tamilio: The lieutenant said it was all right, and she walked to the kitchen telephone, and we didn't get a dial tone on the phone.

The lieutenant said that he would try to use Henri's phone—that was the housekeeper's husband—in his bedroom.

Mrs. Harris gave him a telephone book and she asked him to call a lawyer. That was the number that she gave him. The lieutenant and Henri walked back into Henri's bedroom and made the call from there.

Bolen: Where did you stay when Lieutenant Flick went with Henri?

Tamilio: I stood out at the table with Mrs. Harris.

Bolen: You mentioned this name Henri. Do you recall the last name of that person?

Tamilio: No, I don't.

Bolen: Please continue. What if anything then happened?

Tamilio: The lieutenant then came back and said he had the party on the telephone, and he asked me to assist Mrs. Harris back into the bedroom.

Bolen: And what if anything did you do with Mrs. Harris?

Tamilio: I walked her back into the bedroom.

Bolen: At that point, what if any personal knowledge did you have as to the identity of the person on the phone? Did you know who it was?

Tamilio: At the time?

Bolen: Yes.

Tamilio: No.

The Court: Excuse me. I want to see if I follow this. You said you didn't know the identity of the person on the phone. In other words, you didn't know his or her name. Is that what you are saying?

Tamilio: Right. I know originally I heard mention of a Mr. Jacobson, but I hadn't heard who was on the phone. I knew she had asked for her son and then later her lawyer. The lieutenant said he had the party on the phone.

The Court: If I understand you correctly, then, Officer, and I want to see if I am clear, you didn't know who was on the phone, is that correct, whether it was her son or an attorney, or some third person?

Tamilio: Right.

Under cross-examination by Joel Aurnou, Officer Tamilio was given his official police report of that night to read and refresh his memory.

Aurnou: Do you now recall that when Mrs. Harris spoke to Lieutenant Flick she said that the person she wanted to call was her lawyer, Mr. Jacobson?

Tamilio: Yes, sir.

Tamilio then repeated that Flick and Henri went back to Suzanne's room to make the call. In a few minutes the lieutenant returned to the front hall, where Mrs. Harris and Tamilio were standing.

Aurnou: What if anything did the lieutenant do or say?

Tamilio: That he had Mr. Jacobson on the phone . . . and I should assist Mrs. Harris back to the back bedroom.

Aurnou: What did you observe about her manner of motion, if anything?

Tamilio: Like I stated, she was walking very slowly.

Aurnou: You also told me she appeared to be unsteady. Is that right?

Tamilio: Yes, sir.

Aurnou: At that point was she making any sound?

Tamilio: No, sir. You mean speaking? No.

Aurnou: Or any other sound?

Tamilio: No, sir.

Aurnou: Did you pick the chair into which you sat her?

Tamilio: It was right next to the telephone.

Aurnou: Was that the reason you picked it?

Tamilio: Yes.

Aurnou: When she was seated in the chair, was she able to pick up the telephone?

Tamilio: Yes, sir.

Aurnou: At that point, before anything was said, you were aware, were you not, that the person on the other end of the telephone was Mr. Jacobson?

Tamilio: Yes, sir.

Aurnou: And that he was an attorney?

Tamilio: Yes, sir.

Aurnou: Did you nevertheless remain within earshot, within hearing?

Tamilio: Yes, sir.

Aurnou: Did you make any attempt of any kind to get out of earshot and give her privacy to speak with her attorney?

Tamilio: No, sir.

In denying our appeal, the judges wrote: "Mrs. Harris was allowed to go back in the kitchen and call her lawyer." How they could have read what Officer Tamilio said on the witness stand and deduced that I don't know.

Right from the start, Dr. Louis Roh, assistant county pathologist, and Suzanne van der Vreken were the main witnesses for the prosecution. It was their testimony before the grand jury that played a key role in my being indicted for second degree murder. It was their testimony that played key roles before the media and the jury. Roh told the grand jury categorically that what had happened could not have happened in a struggle. Judge Leggett was to observe later that a pathologist wasn't qualified to make such a determination, but obviously the Grand Jury wouldn't have agreed. Suzanne established a clear case of the jealous woman scorned. Before the grand jury, and under oath, she was asked by one of the prosecutors:

Abananti: Do you know of your direct knowledge why Mrs. Harris's visits became less frequent?

Suzanne: Well I think when Dr. Tarnower met Mrs. Tryforos he saw less of Mrs. Harris.

Abananti: Do you know a Mrs. Lynne Tryforos?

Suzanne: Yes.

Abananti: How long do you know her?

Suzanne: I know her about three, four years ago.

Abananti: How do you know her, other than—how did you come to meet her?

Suzanne: I met her in the Scarsdale Medical Center where Dr. Tarnower had his office. She was a nurse.

Abananti: You said she was an employee of Dr. Tarnower's?

Suzanne: She was a nurse.

Abananti: Did she ever come to the Tarnower residence?

Suzanne: Yes.

Abananti: Do you recall when she first came to the Tarnower residence?

Suzanne: She comes first about four years ago, but just to swim, you know.

This was said, under oath, to the grand jury by a woman who knew that Lynne Tryforos had worked as a receptionist for Dr. Tarnower for twenty years. She had started there after high school, four years before he met me. Suzanne herself had known the woman for sixteen years. She also had sixteen years of diaries which indicated Lynne Tryforos had been "sleeping over" for ten years. And since she knew everything that was up in the doctor's bedroom, she also knew that Mrs. Tryforos had given the doctor gold cuff links seven years before, and not for the use of his swimming pool.

At the trial, nine months later, she repeated the same erroneous statement, and corrected it only under cross-examination by Joel.

Aurnou: Let's start when you first met her. That was at the Scarsdale Medical Group?

Suzanne: Yes.

Aurnou: And that was not in 1976?

Suzanne: No. It was before.

Aurnou: Many years before?

Suzanne: Yes. I don't remember the year.

George Bolen had to know about Suzanne's sixteen years of diaries. She had brought them out the night Hy died and had given Siciliano information from them, which is written in his notes. But the defense was not told about them. Joel found out about them by accident. They proved to be a veritable fountain of knowledge about Hy's sex life.

As the loyal "house manager," a title she bestowed upon herself, and to which there was more truth than poetry, Suzanne had kept track in the diaries for sixteen years of every woman who had gone up that "steep, winding stairway" and not come down until breakfast. One can only wonder how this Boswell of the kitchen had meant to serve the best interests of a very private man, and how she might have hoped to serve the van der Vrekens.

If I make light of the diaries it is only from habit. It is almost an instinct with me to laugh about the things that hurt. What Mrs. van der Vreken's terrible little black books revealed I would like never to have heard:

February 14, 1974 Mrs. T sleep over.
February 15, 1974 Mrs. H for dinner.
November 5, 1974 David and Mrs. Harris for dinner
November 6, 1974 Mrs. Tryforos sleep over
September 15, 1976 Mrs. T. sleep over
September 16, 1976 Dr. Tarnower and Mrs. Harris leave for three weeks abroad.
January 5, 1978 Dr. return from trip to Florida with Mrs. Harris
January 6, 1978 Mrs. T. sleep over

November 5, 1978 Mrs. Harris leave for Virginia
November 6, 1978 Mrs. T sleep over

Page after page after page.

I sat there wondering whether it was Suzanne or Hy who always called to tell Lynne the coast was clear. It must have been Hy. Suzanne was kept busy changing sheets. And hiding clothes. It is ugly to learn something like this about someone you love under any circumstances. It is twice as ugly to learn it in a public place while a morbidly curious public stares, waiting to see what you'll do. You are stunned by the immensity of your own inadequacy. The tears they want don't come. It is kindness and beauty and compassion that reduce me to tears. Cruelty I can face standing tall. I guess it has always been true until that last day at Madeira. I didn't learn until later that the jury would find it unforgivable, and Bolen would say again and again, "She showed no remorse."

The role of Suzanne van der Vreken in Hy's life was a large one. Early in their relationship, Hy had promised both of the servants, Suzanne and Henri, $2,000 apiece per year for every year they had worked for him, if they were still working for him at his death. It was unquestionably a strong staying attraction after sixteen years. Still, Henri had been ready to leave for several years. It was Suzanne who insisted they stay. Suzanne was the brighter of the two, and always civil and usually very friendly. Henri was moody and unpredictable, sometimes quite funny, sometimes unspeakably rude, neither for any apparent reason.

I considered Suzanne a talented cook, and quite gifted artistically, from her flower arrangements and table settings, to her pâtes, and watercolors. I knew the two of them were important to Hy, and that made them important to me. They had unquestionably helped to make a home for Hy, one that he loved and enjoyed sharing with others, and I was grateful to both of them for that reason. It made Hy nervous from time to time when Suzanne suggested that he needed them more than they needed him, and he had finally given her the Old Tarnower fight song, "Look! I don't need anybody." It had become a refrain each time they asked for a raise, which was now almost all the time.

The district attorney's office had obviously realized early on that

Henri would be a difficult witness to handle. He did not testify before the grand jury, and his appearance at the pre-trial was just long enough for him to say, "I don't know, I don't remember" or "I don't recall" more times than I care to count.

Mr. Thomas Lalla, who assisted Bolen in the prosecution, confided to Victor Grossman, a young assistant of Joel's, that Bolen's first theory about the case was that Mrs. Harris would blame Henri and say he did the shooting while she left to make the phone call for help. One can only speculate as to what there was in Henri's demeanor that would give Bolen the idea. He must have heard early on that Henri hated Hy. Maybe the same fear that someone would say "The butler did it," prompted Henri to stand at the top of the steps screaming, "She's the one! She did it!" pointing to me as I ran up the steps, followed by Officer McKenna.

Nor had Henri remembered me standing at the front door calling out, "Somebody turn on the god-damned lights! I'm going for help!" Henri said he didn't remember answering my 4:15 call that afternoon and telling me Hy was going out to dinner. He didn't even remember Hy drinking a champagne toast to Suzanne's birthday that night. And he swore under oath he did not hear a word I said to my lawyer later that night, although he was sitting less than three feet from me, and looking directly at me as I spoke. Indeed, for Mr. Aurnou, there seemed hardly anything that Henri remembered while under Bolen's questioning, certain useful information seemed to return on cue. In October, Joel had asked him:

Aurnou: Did anybody indicate to Detective Siciliano either that a shot had been fired or that anybody had been wounded?

Henri: I don't remember.

Aurnou: And at that time did you hear Detective Siciliano ask anybody any question at all about who might have done it?

Henri: I don't remember.

Aurnou: Do you remember any other conversation before the Detective and Mrs. Harris sat down at the table?

Henri: No. . . .

Aurnou: Are you able as you sit here now, Mr. van der Vreken, to tell us who it was that told him what happened?

Henri: I just told you before I don't remember.

Aurnou: And aside from not remembering who it was, do you

remember what it was that was told Detective Siciliano before he sat down with Mrs. Harris?

Henri: No, I don't remember.

And again at the trial:

Aurnou: Did you see Lynne Tryforos in the house at any time on the eleventh, from midnight on?

Henri: No.

Aurnou: How about the twelfth?

Henri: I don't recall that.

Aurnou: The thirteenth?

Henri: I don't remember.

Aurnou: Could she have been there without your remembering?

Bolen objects and is sustained.

Aurnou: Let me ask it another way. Do you know whether any of Mrs. Tryforos's belongings were removed from that room during the week of your own personal knowledge?

Henri: No, no, no. No.

Aurnou: When you first went up to the room with the policeman, I want you to tell me what blankets, if any, were on Dr. Tarnower's bed.

Henri: Well, I don't know which type of blanket Dr. Tarnower used. I didn't notice anything, and I cannot describe anything.

This statement was made under oath after Henri had been helping to make Hy's bed, and turn it down in the evening for sixteen years.

Under Bolen's questioning at the trial, however, Henri remembered Mrs. Harris saying, "I did it," and then he heard Siciliano say, "Well, I will give you your rights." Under cross-examination, Joel reminded him, "Mr. van der Vreken, you testified yesterday that you heard Mrs. Harris say, 'I did it,' and six weeks ago you couldn't recall anything you heard." Henri replied, still under oath, "Yes. I had to refresh my memory, which is not easy by the way."

Henri had also remembered something else as well, and volunteered that the morning after the shooting, Hy's alarm clock went off, and because he couldn't go up into the room he went to the basement and shut off the power to the clock.

While it would be fascinating to see which switch in the basement would have turned off the clock in Hy's bedroom, the purpose for that particular flash of memory was presumably to establish for the jury how careful everyone had been to maintain the strict integrity of the bedroom. Since by Tuesday morning when the sun came up, fourteen people had already torn the place apart. Henri's story, even if true, was an empty gesture.

Mrs. "Billie" Schwartz, Hy's sister, beamed, hugged and kissed him as he left the courtroom.

The thing that puzzled me most about Suzanne's testimony were the erroneous statements she made not only about my relationship with Hy, but about things that had absolutely nothing to do with the way Hy had died. For example, the question about whose curlers I had thrown. At the pre-trial they belonged to Mrs. Tryforos.

At the trial they were Mrs. Tryforos's too, until Bolen nudged her and reminded her, "You had some curlers too, didn't you Mrs. van der Vreken?"

"Yes," she remembered. "They were mine. I lent them to her."

Suzanne also said under oath she had never seen me wear a four-carat diamond engagement ring that Hy had given me. In fact, she told me soon after I started wearing it that she and Henri would leave because she wouldn't work in a house with children. She swore under oath that she knew nothing about where I kept my furniture for three years, but the day I moved to Virginia, the moving van came first to Hy's house to pick up three rooms of furniture that had been in his basement for three years. In fact, by then, the van der Vrekens were using four of my chairs. I had given them permission to use three of them, and they were quite put out when I didn't tell them to keep them.

Mrs. van der Vreken referred to Lynne Tryforos for eight days on the stand as "that lady." She hated "that lady" and virtually every "scandalous" thing I knew about her I had learned from the van der Vrekens.

When I returned home from a trip with Hy to find many of my clothes hanging in a downstairs closet, ripped and destroyed, both van der Vrekens swore, "It had to be Lynne. She's the only one it could be. We saw her run into the house the morning before you came back. We didn't see her leave. We were in the garden."

When Hy's secretary of many years died, I said to Suzanne, "Maybe he'll make Lynne his secretary." "That one a secretary!" she said with scorn. She pointed a finger at her head and twirled it around. "How could that one be a secretary?" It was a van der Vreken refrain for years. "She's a terrible woman, madame, she shouldn't be allowed in the house."

At the pre-trial, Suzanne, describing me on the night of March 10 as I walked toward her room to phone a lawyer, said under oath, "Mrs. Harris look in the mirror and say, 'Oh, he hit me.' "
"And what else did she say?"
"That was all, nothing more."
At the trial she swore, under oath, that Mrs. Harris looked in the mirror and said, "Oh, he beat me. He used to beat me all the time."
She was questioned about this repeatedly by Bolen. "She used the word beat?"
"Yes."
"You're sure?"
"Yes."
Finally, under cross-examination by Joel, who confronted her with her own testimony of a few weeks before, Bolen agreed to stipulate that the word "beat" and the statement "used to beat me a lot" had never been used.

Because Bolen wanted the jury to believe that I had thrown many things that night, including a pair of slippers, he produced a picture for the jury showing one slipper in the bathroom. I didn't touch the slippers, and the slipper in the photograph wasn't in the bathroom that night anyway. It may have belonged to Suzanne or Mrs. Schwartz or Mrs. George Bolen, for all I know, but I do know it wasn't in the bathroom the night Hy died. Later, Joel discovered that the picture of one slipper was simply a cropped version of a picture with two slippers side by side. It had been cropped and then blown up again so the cropping would not be easily detected.

Telephones played an important role in Hy's death. By the time Hy realized that he wasn't going to get any help from the servants, he couldn't use his phone to call out. Suzanne, for reasons that she was never asked to explain, had removed the receiver from one of the three downstairs phones and left it lying on the kitchen counter. I didn't know that until the trial. Hy never knew it. The last thing I remember saying to him was something about the phone. "I think it's broken, Hy," or words to that effect. Hy said, "You're probably right," as I helped him over to his bed where he lay down, arms out-stretched.

For sixteen years the van der Vrekens had lived with and worked for Dr. Tarnower, and never had their own phone. Apparently Hy, as he grew older, had grown weary of answering their calls for them, and somewhere between six and nine months before Hy's death, they had their own phone installed. There was no way that I could have known about the phone, but if I had known then there would have been no reason for me to leave the house to call a doctor. Under Joel's questioning Suzanne said she thought the phone had been installed sometime in the fall of 1979. Since that time I had been in the house twice, in November and February. She had not discussed the phone with me, I had not been in her room, and the phone was unlisted. The only evidence that Assistant District Attorney Bolen was able to elicit from Mrs. van der Vreken as to whether there was any way I might have known about the phone was:

"Sometime in November '79 or February '80 . . . sometime when I was talking to Mrs. Harris, my phone rang and I said, 'Oh. I have to go pick up my phone. Excuse me.' "

Of all the dastardly deeds in that trial, and the word is rarely more appropriate than it is in this instance, the most egregious of Suzanne's "untruths" had to do with my feelings toward Hy, and whether or not he knew that I was coming to Purchase that night. Under oath, Suzanne told the jury she had heard me "threaten to sue the doctor, and make his life miserable." Yet in Detective Siciliano's notes, taken the evening of March 12, he wrote, "anger never directed against him."

Joel tried very hard to get this information put before the jury, but Bolen objected and the judge sustained. We were not permitted to say that "anger was never directed against him." But Suzanne was permitted to say that Mrs. Harris had "threatened to sue him and make his life miserable." This was the same woman who had said to me just months before Hy's death, "Oh, madame, you have put him on a pedestal. He is just an ordinary man."

Hy knew I was coming to see him that night. I think he told Mrs. Tryforos too, but that I can't prove. She had left her two young daughters at home for the past six nights in order to sleep with Hy. It's all there in the diaries.

But Monday night she came for dinner and "left by 8:30." Mother-hood was not one of the things for which Hy gave brownie points, but Lynne's custom over the years of leaving her children for days and nights on end was a test of his unconcern for children that no other woman had ever put him to. It is, I'm sure, one of the main reasons Bolen tried to keep her as far away from the jury as possible.

Having the lights out and the front door locked when I arrived was typical Tarnower. He didn't like someone else calling a play. I was out of line. He also knew that if he locked the door I would come in the same way we usually did, through the garage. It was unkind, but it wasn't out of character. The last thing in the world I would have done that night, or any night, was walk into Hy's house and bedroom unannounced. I wanted ten peaceful moments, not a confrontation.

I made three calls to Hy on March 10, 1980. They are clearly indicated on my phone bill for that month, complete, as always, with the length of the call. The first call was made at about ten minutes to ten in the morning from my office to Hy at his office. The call was six minutes long. I had just mailed him a long, anguished letter, and told him that I had mailed it and that it would upset him. It had certainly upset me. The contents of the call were not important and nobody's business until one of his patients, a Mrs. Edwards, who was in one of the examining rooms, "inadvertently" overheard the conversation. Hy had left the phone off the hook and gone to his office to talk.

Strangely, the woman testified that she had heard what Hy said, but didn't hear the person on the other end. Hy was not a screamer, or a shouter. I think if she heard Hy she also heard me, and could give a clearer and more complete report on the conversation than she did. She testified: "I heard him say in an angry tone, 'You lied and you cheated.' There was a pause and then I heard voices I couldn't make out, but could determine it was the voice of a woman at the other end. Then the doctor's voice said 'you know you are going to inherit $240,000.' I heard no more except that the phone clicked."

Who Hy was saying this to is something we will never know. He didn't say these last words to me, and he didn't leave me $240,000. Moreover, he knew that he had never discussed his will with me, and I wouldn't have known what was in it.

Oddly enough, the only person to whom he did leave $240,000, and who had obviously discussed the will in some detail with him, was Lynne Tryforos. The following morning, before Hy had been dead six hours, Lynne phoned one of his former lovers to tell her, "Hy left you $10,000 in his will." It is a bizarre thing for a grieving woman to do. Moreover, she had, not long before his death, signed a "palimony" agreement for Hy, written by Hy's friend and lawyer, Henry Neal, promising that "If our unique relationship should come to an end" she wouldn't try to sue him. The quid pro quo could have been $240,000.

The morning phone conversation ended with Hy saying he would see me the weekend of April 5. I felt a little better after the call and started on my day's appointments. But I was too far gone by this time to get through the day. Every person with whom I met that day testified as to my state of mind. "It was as though a curtain had come down between us." At 3:30 P.M. I left my office and went back to the house to write my will.

My second call to Hy was made at 4:15. By then I had finished writing my will and made up my mind I wanted to see Hy one more time. While Suzanne testified that she answered that phone call it was actually Henri who answered the phone. I asked Henri if Hy were there. Henri said no. He told me Hy would be out for dinner, but would be back before he went out. I said I would call back. The call was less than a minute long. Between that call and my third one, I rushed over to the school business office to have my will witnessed. I came back, washed, put on a skirt and blouse, and called Hy again. It was 5:16 and Hy answered the phone.

Five different times, between March 10, 1980, and March 23, 1980, Suzanne van der Vreken signed statements, or swore under oath, or reported to members of the district attorney's office that she received one call from Mrs. Harris on March 10. She wrote it out in longhand for Detective Siciliano the night Hy died. She swore it to the grand jury. She told it to inspectors, D. H. Raab and R. H. Donnelly, from the district attorney's office the night of March 12. She added her own version of the call since she hadn't heard what was actually said, but the important thing was that she swore there was only one call.

On November 26, nine months later, she took the stand, and under oath swore that she had received two calls from Mrs. Harris on March 10. The reason, as far as I'm concerned, was simple. In April, after all the reports had been written, the district attorney's office finally got a copy of my phone bill. It was poor timing, but better late than never. Suzanne swore that she had not seen my phone bill, but by some mysterious alchemy she now told us that one of the calls she had received had been five or six minutes long. My call to Hy's office had been six minutes long. She also apologized for forgetting the second call, but she began to remember it "right after the grand jury met." It was like something little children would do to cover their tracks, but there in a court of law, under a sign that reads "In God We Trust," it was played out by adults, and it worked.

The important thing is that Hy knew I was coming that night. In his summation, Bolen told the jury: "She starts walking up that spiral staircase, unannounced, unexpected." I wasn't announced, but I was expected.

George Bolen has been quoted by one of his fellow assistant district attorneys as saying, "I didn't win the case. Aurnou dropped it in my lap." He is too modest. Probably few juries have sat down to make a decision more misinformed than the jury in this trial. There were many contributing factors; the media had long since convicted me and insisted "there was a confession;" the trial was unnecessarily long and complicated and the jury was tired, bored, and confused; some jurors had slept through key testimony; witnesses, key witnesses, perjured themselves. I took the stand and offended the jury with my manner and my clothes.

Worse still was Bolen's handling of the search for truth. His questions often left the point he was trying to make out in left field. They did absolutely nothing to edify.

He asked me: "Now before you opened the drawer, was the drawer closed?"

"Did you know that the doctor was a doctor?"

He asked Detective Siciliano: "And what was the position of the door just before you opened it?"

"Closed," Siciliano answered, proud to know the right answer.

He asked Siciliano what Mrs. Harris was wearing that night. "She was wearing clothing at the time, was she not?" Later, he asked, "Was she wearing anything under her coat?"

He asked Dr. Bernard Ackerman, after the doctor had explained, "I did my undergraduate work at Princeton, my medical training at Columbia College of Physicians and Surgeons, and my residency at

Columbia, University of Pennsylvania, and Harvard."

"Now you did graduate from medical school, did you not?"

When Marjorie Jacobson told the jury Hy and I had met at a dinner party at her house back in 1966, he asked; "How many guests came to the party?" "Was it a New Year's Eve party?"

Finally he asked, clearing his throat, tapping his chin with one finger, and pausing to emphasize the importance of what was to follow: "Now did you introduce Mrs. Harris to Dr. Tarnower, or did you introduce Dr. Tarnower to Mrs. Harris?"

Are questions of this sort a trick one learns in law school? Are they something one does in spite of law school? Are they what Saul Bellow had in mind when he wrote of "the peculiar, gentlemanly, high-toned illiteracy of lawyers before the bench?" I only know that with fourteen weeks of this type of questioning under their belts the jury was, at best, confused. Sir Thomas More didn't permit any lawyers in Utopia. He described them as "a sort of people whose profession is to disguise matters." Wise man he.

Bolen's blatant rudeness to witnesses that were not his own left me appalled by his bad manners. Herbert MacDonell was a particular trial to him. MacDonell, widely acknowledged as an expert criminologist, was the only person involved in the case who knew how to measure points of impact and deflections in order to trace the path of a bullet. At least, he was the only one involved in the case who bothered to do it right.

He and Bolen started off on the wrong foot because Bolen had twice called him and asked him to work for the prosecution. MacDonell had told Bolen exactly what he told Joel Aurnou, "I will examine the evidence and my testimony will be whatever the evidence shows. I will not testify for or against anyone." In front of the jury, Bolen denied the nature of the call. MacDonell has a tape of each call.

MacDonell studied Hy's room in great detail, everything in it that hadn't been removed or destroyed. He made detailed diagrams to illustrate what had happened. The first bullet had gone through Hy's hand and then out through a glass door near where we were standing. The bullet hit a plank on the wooden deck outside of Hy's bedroom and then was deflected again, to the left and ended up with part of the bullet imbedded in a wooden post. The rest of the bullet was never found.

To discover if the indentation on the deck floor was indeed a bullet ricochet mark, MacDonell folded a piece of paper, held it firmly over the mark on the plank, and rubbed a pencil over it, as one does a tracing or rubbing of an indented or raised picture.

The rubbing showed clearly the shape of the bullet and confirmed MacDonell's conviction that this was indeed a deflection mark. Bolen didn't want it to be one. He wanted the shot through Hy's hand to be called a "defensive wound." That way, and only that way, he could prove, he thought, that the gun had been aimed deliberately at Hy.

Whether or not Bolen understood MacDonell's reasons for reaching his conclusions is hard to tell. His cross examination, pointing to the piece of paper on which MacDonell had made the rubbing, went like this:

Bolen: Is that particular piece of paper that you have before you drawn to scale?

MacDonell: It's not drawn. It's traced, one to one. It is a scale.

Bolen: So it's traced to scale, is that correct?

MacDonell: Yes.

Bolen: Is there a scale marking on that particular piece of paper?

MacDonell: Yes.

Bolen: Could you point that out to me please?

MacDonell: All of the lines are scales. Anyone can measure them and they are a scale.

Bolen: Is that in centimeters or inches? Usually the scale I'm talking about is an inch representing something. Is that on there?

MacDonell: No. It's one to one. One inch represents one inch. One centimeter represents one centimeter.

Bolen: Are you telling us the thing that is traced on that . . . is that tracing the actual size of the indentation or impression that you saw on the deck?

MacDonell: That's correct. It is.

Bolen: Your honor, I object. I object to that document coming in in its entirety, because all the witness has told us is it's just an impression of an indentation, nothing more.

The judge received it, in spite of Mr. Bolen's fascinating questions.

Detective Joseph Reich helped to buttress Bolen's theory by testifying that the shot through the window was "a direct hit" and couldn't have gone first through Hy's hand. He offered this useful opinion as "scientific fact" because he had done an experiment. He had bought a piece of glass, stood in front of it, and at three different distances had fired a .32 caliber bullet through it. In each case, the bullet went through the glass just fine, "direct hits." When questioned by Aurnou, it turned out that Reich had never measured the thickness of the glass in Hy's room, the space between the double pane, the tensile strength of the glass, the angle at which the gun had been fired, the angle at which the glass was hit, or the age of the bullet. His opinion, too, was based on thin air, and Judge Leggett instructed that Reich's conclusion be stricken.

The conclusion of MacDonell's report on his findings states: "All physical evidence that has been examined and evaluated thus far is completely consistent with the events and their sequences as reported to me by the defendant, Mrs. Harris."

MacDonell still shakes his head and says, "How a jury could have found you guilty of murder I don't understand." I don't either, but there are those who do.

In his summation to the jury, Bolen said of MacDonell:

His diagrams in no way account for the possible deflection of a bullet through not one but two panes of glass. . . . You must take into account that when a bullet passes through an object there is a certain amount of deflection. He doesn't account for that in his diagram.

Page after page the patient Mr. MacDonell had described and explained to Mr. Bolen and the court his findings and his diagrams. Page after page he tried to explain to him basic, elementary facts about the trajectories and deflections of bullets. There are more than fifty page references in which he discussed and explained the subject. He is an acknowledged expert in the field. He has testified on the subject all over the world. These facts didn't keep Bolen from telling the jury quite the opposite.

As it happened, George Bolen was made to take the stand and swear an oath, late on the Friday evening of January 9, 1981, after the press and jury had gone home. A mistrial hearing was held because Bolen had made three calls to a Henry Ryan in Maine, who was to be a defense witness. Bolen explained, under oath, that he had made the calls simply to thank Mr. Ryan for sending him a Christmas card, and in the course of conversation he, Bolen, just happened to mention the

Harris trial. Mr. Ryan was feeling very chatty and mentioned to Bolen, among other things, that the shot through the hand could not have been defensive, because had it been, there would have been spatter on the pajamas and probably on the face of Dr. Tarnower, and there would have been palm tissue in the chest wound.

Since there was no spatter on the pajamas or on Hy's body, the only way there could possibly have been a defensive gesture would be to find palm tissue in the chest wound. The thought apparently hadn't occurred to Bolen before or been suggested by any of the doctors who had studied the autopsy slides, because there was no palm tissue in the chest wound, and Jean Harris had described exactly what had happened when the hand was wounded.

It was now ten months after Hy's death, all medical reports had long since been written, slides had been examined and re-examined, and no one had suggested that there was any palm tissue in the chest wound, including Dr. Louis Roh who had spent the longest amount of time with the slides, and who had performed the autopsy.

But Ryan's words planted an idea in Bolen's brain. He hung up and called Dr. Roh and told him to get out the slides and see if he could find some palm tissue in the chest. With no trouble at all Dr. Roh obliged, and overnight he wrote a whole new report. Under oath Bolen swore that he had not known "for a fact" that Henry Ryan was a witness for the defense until he called and talked to Ryan on Wednesday, January 7.

Yet on the Monday before that, January 5, he had told Judge Leggett, and it's in the testimony, that he knew "for a fact" that Ryan was a defense witness; and he moved for the judge not to permit him to testify because he, Bolen, hadn't received a copy of Ryan's report. Joel told him again that Ryan hadn't written a report. His main point in coming was to refute Dr. Roh's irresponsible comment to the grand jury that what happened in Hy's room "couldn't have been an accident."

"It could well have been an accident," Ryan testified when he took the stand.

When the mistrial hearing was over, Judge Leggett essentially concluded that Bolen could telephone anyone he wanted to, and that Ryan was a big boy and should know better than to talk so much. Ryan later told Joel, "I feel as though I've been raped." He never bothered to ask how I felt.

As the defendant, I had a legal right to attend the mistrial hearing, but I don't recall even being informed that there was going to be one. Instead, I was kept sitting alone in a nearby courtroom for almost two hours while the whole thing was played out. Presumably, someone didn't want to embarrass Bolen with my presence. I believe, however, that Joel had an obligation to ask if I wanted to be there. There is nothing in the testimony which indicates that he bothered to ask. From that point on, the entire trial revolved around whether or not the first shot was a defensive one.

Dr. Bernard Ackerman, one of five pathologists who testified that there was no palm tissue in Hy's chest, has written extensively on the subject of the medical testimony in the Harris trial, and of the need for peer review of doctors, when they testify in court. (Excerpts from his report are in the Appendix of this book, and I hope every reader will take the time to study it. This could happen to you.)

Dr. Ackerman said to me recently, "Jean, that trial stands out as one of the most traumatic experiences of my life. A doctor's oath is sacred, and until I sat in that courtroom and listened and watched what was going on I thought it was sacred to the whole brotherhood of the medical profession. What I saw made me ashamed. It must be stopped."

There is so much else that should be known. There was Hy's prescription book which we needed in order to show that he had prescribed Desoxyn for me for almost ten years. It was Joel Aurnou who was to tell me, ten years too late, "Jean, do you realize what Desoxyn is? It's speed."

Shortly after I arrived at Madeira, I asked the school doctor to give me a prescription of Desoxyn. He said, "I certainly won't. That's a mind-altering drug. You shouldn't be taking it." I did what I always did when I had a medical question—I called Hy. Hy said, "Well he's silly as hell. The little bit you're taking can't do you any harm at all. Forget it. I'll send it to you anyway." It was the only time in ten years of taking Desoxyn that anyone suggested to me that it was dangerous.

Joel subpoenaed the prescription books. The Scarsdale Medical Group, which had control of them, initially resisted complying with the subpoena. Finally Judge Leggett ordered the books turned over; what was left of them, we received. Oddly enough, forty-two prescription slips were missing.

Bill Riegelman went to Albany and got copies of the missing forty-two. Forty-one of them were prescriptions for me. Of these, some even used false names and addresses, but all were intended for me and were signed by Hy. If Hy was the one who tore them out, then he knew long ago that he was giving me something he shouldn't. On Tuesday, March 11, 1980, after Hy had died, and I was sitting in a small cage in the Harrison police station, a package from Hy arrived for me at Madeira. It contained a bottle of Desoxyn.

There is one small sidelight of the trial that still interests me. On March 12, two days after Hy's death, the police returned to Hy's bedroom and took many pictures. Hy's room had an unusual ceiling to it. The center was vaulted, and around the edges there was a deep ledge. Hy used the ledge for years as a sort of hiding place. He kept some of his wallets up in it. If he had traveler's checks left when he came back from a trip he put them up there in one of his wallets. If he cashed a large check, he put what money he wasn't using up there. On March 12 the police found his hiding place and took a picture of it with two dusty wallets lying on the ledge. They had obviously been lying there for a long time so they were left untouched.

On April 3 the police came back to photograph again. This time there was a third wallet in the hiding place. One had recently been returned. Why would anyone who had the wallet legally return it to a hiding place, after Hy's death, and after the house was being prepared for sale? The wallet was taken by the police to be fingerprinted, but apparently everyone at the police station forgot about it for two weeks, and when they got around to dusting it for fingerprints the oil in the leather had risen and wiped out whatever prints there might have been. At least that's what we were told.

I shudder to think what would have been made of the wallet if I had been allowed back in the room between March 12 and April 3, 1980. Someone with the free run of the place, who knew Hy's habits intimately, had stolen from him before he died, or far worse, right after he died.

During the trial Bolen spent considerable time and effort trying to prove that the .32-caliber gun in the case was so hard to shoot that Jean Harris could only have fired it "consciously, knowingly, volitionally, and deliberately" each time it was discharged. He had apparently changed his mind by his summation to the jury. It went like this:

Bolen: She confronts the doctor. She gets the gun. She is in control of the situation now. She controls, she has power. The doctor is in bed. She is further enraged. She now finds herself on the left side of his bed, near that headboard. And in her mind if Herman Tarnower won't deny himself of Lynne Tryforos, she will do it for him. If I can't have him, no one can. Her rage, her frustrations are about to explode. She is going to punish Herman Tarnower. Kill him. Keep him from Lynne Tryforos, and then take her own life. She is now between the two beds. The doctor gets up seated on the edge of the bed. The defendant has the gun out in her hand. The defendant confronts Herman Tarnower with the gun, points it and shoots it, pulls the trigger. . . . The bullet goes through Herman Tarnower's outstretched hand and re-enters his chest. Herman Tarnower falls back a little, recovers and lunges toward Jean Harris at this point. She fires again. The bullet enters the posterior shoulder and as he falls back and while Jean is holding the gun in her left hand, Herman Tarnower, falling back, knocks the left hand with the gun, causing another round to discharge into the cabinet, causing blood from his hand to come in contact with the gun.

Aurnou: Wait a minute. The cabinet is on the other side of the room. That's physically impossible.

Bolen: Your honor, if I may respond, I have positioned the defendant on the left side of the doctor's bed as you look at it near the headboard from which the bullet was recovered.

Aurnou: Then the blood spatter is impossible because that's on the other side of the bed.

The Court: Overruled.

Bolen: Dr. Tarnower falls back on his bed on the sheets. . . . The doctor falls back on his bed, having sustained a wound to his hand, to the chest, to the back, and there is a bullet in the headboard. The defendant retreats, goes around his bed, her bed to the bathroom. All those things that were found strewn in the dressing area, all the things strewn on the floor in the bathroom of the east bathroom, she is throwing, she is tossing. She's enraged. There are only two people who could have thrown all that stuff around, Herman Tarnower and Jean Harris. But unbeknownst to Jean Harris, Herman Tarnower recovers. Do you remember that trail of blood leading starting at the midside of the left side of his bed? He gets up and starts walking ever so slowly, and where does the trail lead you? The trail leads you to in front of his door. . . . The door is opened with the left hand. There is no blood on the handle. The light switch is turned on. We know that. The light is on because Tamilio told us. And he goes into the bathroom. Why does he go in the bathroom? He is a doctor. He doesn't know how badly he has been hurt or where he has been hurt. He now can see, and he now realizes, being a doctor, what a precarious state he's in. And what about that trail of blood leading back out of the bathroom along the right-hand wall, his hand at his right side, blood dripping down, on his pajamas, on the rug, back around his bed? And the defendant sees him, gets the gun. There are two rounds left in it. Two rounds left for her. They meet at the ends of the beds. They are between the beds. The doctor with his right hand bleeding pushes Jean Harris on the bed. You have seen blood on that bed. She falls back. The gun is in her left hand. Her left hand is facing the glass door and as she goes back the gun discharges through the glass window.

At this point Joel objected for the eighth time, and for the first time the judge did not overrule him.

The Court: I think we are getting fairly far away from the evidence now. Pick up with the evidence and the inferences to be drawn therefrom.

When the trial was over I wrote to mother. "The jury sat there for fourteen long weeks, conscientious and patient; American Gothic, looking serious and feeling pure. They did the best they could with their prejudices and myths, and I did the best I could with mine." Through the whole grim experience, one of the most frightening things was that as I told many lawyers what was being done to me, the usual answer was a gentle shrug and, "Well, that's the way it is, Jean. You've got to realize this guy wants to win. That's the name of the game. He doesn't really give a damn if you're guilty or not." Even living, as I do, with the reality of that, I find it difficult to come to terms with. "The law, sir, if this be the law, is not 'a ass,' " as Mr. Bumble said. "The law, sir, is a monster."

Part II

Bedford Hills:
"This Ain't No Tea Party"

> *. . . everything can be taken from a man but one thing: the last of the human freedoms—to choose one's attitude in any given set of circumstances, to choose one's own way.*
>
> Viktor Frankl
> *Man's Search For Meaning*

1.

On February 28, 1981, I was found guilty of murdering Dr. Herman Tarnower. Judge Leggett congratulated the jury on their verdict. "The evidence substantiates the verdict," he assured them. On March 20 I was sentenced to prison for fifteen years to life, with no hope of parole for at least fifteen years. This leaves me with the questionable distinction of being one of the most dangerous women in the state of New York. The average stay in this top security prison is less than three years.

I was given a few moments to remove my jewelry and hug the boys goodbye, and then Vivian and Dolf, who had served as the officers of the court during the trial, drove me to Bedford Hills Correctional Facility. It is a top security prison for women, but as with so many things in the justice system, one is not supposed to call it by its proper name. Vivian and Dolf were both very kind. I don't believe they think I am a murderer. Dolf even brought his children to see me. They didn't handcuff me, and they did everything they possibly could to keep the press away. I was wearing all my own clothes, probably for the last time in my life.

There were crowds of people at the prison gate as we drove up. Dolf went in as quickly as he could and drove up to the medical building where one's term begins. Vivian took me in, hugged me goodbye, and left. Except for the clothes I was wearing I had brought a toothbrush and a book. I was left in the hands of a corrections officer (C.O.) those grim initials that were soon to become the bane of my existence. She quickly took me upstairs and told me to take off all my clothes. She handed me some disinfectant soap and led me to a grim, grimy shower. Having made sure that I washed my hair with the disinfectant, just in case I had lice, she permitted me to dry myself, then handed me a yellow jumper that zipped up the front and came about three inches above my knees. A secondhand, sickly green blouse completed the ensemble, and since they had no shoes my size, I was permitted to wear my own.

The inmates had already eaten dinner at the regular time, 4:15 P.M., and I didn't arrive until 5:30 P.M. so I was brought a tray of mashed potatoes, corn, gravy and some kind of meat. The milk was very welcome. Having drunk my dinner, I was taken to see the chief psychologist. He was civil and told me he would continue the medication I had been given for depression. From his office, I went downstairs to a little room to have my picture taken in my new yellow and green costume.

It was developed and laminated on the spot, so that I would not have to venture any further without my ID. I was now 81 G 98, meaning I was the ninety-eighth prisoner to enter the facility that year, 1981. The G is a code letter which indicates that wherever my criminal life may lead me in New York State, someone will know that I started out at Bedford. I was instructed henceforth to wear the ID at all times. New ones cost $1.50 and I have now bought seven of them because I keep losing them. I am not good at remembering such things. I used to lose keys too. I am constantly being asked, "Harris, let's see your ID." If they know who you are, what purpose does the ID serve?

My next stop was the state store where I was issued:

1 dark green winter coat, very heavy and size 46. They said it was the smallest one they had and I wore it for a year, all ninety-eight pounds of me. The tag which reads "10 percent wool, 90 percent

unidentified fibers" is a treasure I have saved.

1 lightweight coat, dark green

1 dark green jumper

1 yellow jumper

2 dark green slacks, double knit

4 blouses, all used

2 pair of pajamas

1 brown flannel robe

various undergarments

2 pair of shoes

1 pair of boots

When my new wardrobe was complete, and everything had been stamped with my name, 81 G 98, it was all tossed into a large black garbage bag and handed to me. Carrying this bag, or rather dragging it as best I could, I was led to my last stop. I could barely stand up let alone carry a heavy bag. I lifted and dragged and kicked it along. A young C.O. walked casually beside me, making no effort to help. I suppose it's against the rules, and it's a rule, one of the few, that is scrupulously observed.

There was a beautiful moon as we walked along, and the sight of it made a few tears fall. I realized very quickly that I could only survive if I blocked out of my mind anything that reminds me of Hy, or of me, or of happiness.

Finally, I arrived at the reception area where I was to spend the first eight weeks of my sentence. My cell was number 3B. Other prisoners quickly gathered around the open door of the cell to see the notorious Jean Harris. But they were decent. Even kind.

"Remember me, Jean? I was in the cell next to you in Valhalla."
"Hi, Clair."
"How you doin? Don't worry. You be OK. It ain't too bad."
"Thanks, Clair. I'm fine."
"How you doin', Jean?"

"Fine thanks."

"You number 98 ain't you?"

"Yes. Do I get a prize?"

"Naw. I'm number 97. I come in this morning just before you."

"You wanna little cup of tea?"

"Thank you. I'd love one."

One of the ladies with a hot pot and a tea bag went off to brew me a little comfort. Some with a religious bent came by with a Bible to urge me to begin reading it and praying. A few asked if I would tutor them. And last of all came Annabelle, six feet tall and sixty-eight years old, with a stub of a pencil, but no paper, and asked me if I'd write a letter to the judge for her.

"Shit. He gotta understand I was just tryin' to make ends meet."

Before I had hung up my clothes she explained to me how she "bought a little coke for $75 and added a little sugar and sold it for $100."

My new life had begun.

It was dark when I arrived. The only thing about the cell that worried me was whether I could see sky and trees from its window. Hoping to God that I could, I put on my pale yellow, state certified pajamas, made my bed and climbed in. I wrote in my notebook that first morning.

I woke early this morning, and my first thought was of the window. My first glance left a knot in the pit of my stomach. There were trees and sky out there, but a 12 ft high fence with rows of evil looking barbed razor blades stood between me and the view. With a little experimenting I have discovered that if I sit at the end of my bed, and scrunch down against the wall, just so, I can look out at the trees and the sky as God made them. The sun is shining this morning and the picture is beautiful, as only something like that can be. If I sit up straight or raise my head the least little bit, the fences and barbed wire come into view, man-made ugliness intrudes upon the whole picture, and I am reminded at once where I am.

Where I am is a cinder block cage approximately 6½' by 9', with a cot, a sink, a toilet, and a table. Can this possibly be real?

That day I began what would become my "Blue Book," a place to write down experiences and thoughts I knew I didn't want to trouble friends or family with, but which I felt a need to say. This is the second page:

We were awakened today, as I guess we will always be awakened, with "the cracking of the doors," which simply means the partial opening and then banging closed of the metal doors to the cells. You wake with a start. As soon as the doors have been cracked the count is taken. One is to stand at the door and place the palm of her hand in the small window in the door. It is just about large enough to frame one hand. To look down a hallway of disembodied palms pressed against a tiny rectangle of glass in a metal door is the ugliest, grimmest, most dehumanizing sight I have ever seen or imagined. It is macabre. I haven't the words to say. Whatever other rules there may be in this insanity, I will never, never put my hands this way. As long as I am breathing I will be more than a disembodied hand. Christ as my witness, there is absolutely nothing they can threaten me with that will raise my hand to that window.

And so far nothing has.

My state of mind during those early months at Bedford was like an early morning fog in Westchester. I moved slowly, and slept a good deal, and thought very little, partly because I was being given large doses of Elavel, I don't remember how much, and partly because I was still in a state of shock over Hy's death and the obscene public circus that followed it. But through the fog my little wind-up mechanism was still functioning. "Must remember to look your best. It's quite all right to work like a horse, Jean, but for heaven's sake don't look as though you did."

Tragedy and comedy, as I'm constantly observing, are close cousins. I am reminded of that every day, and especially so in here. I remember it again as I look back on my first day here. With the first glance in my prison mirror the terrible thought struck me, "Now that I'm here, where will I go to get my hair fixed? I can remember a deep feeling of relief when someone told me there was a prison beauty parlor. The head of it? Mrs. Smith. One of my first worldly acts as 81 G 98 was to sit down in my cell and write Mrs. Smith a courteous little note asking for a standing appointment, any time at her convenience. She never did respond, but then perhaps she thought the writer was making fun of her, instead of making a fool of herself.

I met Mrs. Smith several weeks later. She stopped to introduce herself to me and to assure me that God loved me and Jesus loved me too. She even called me out of work several times to tell me the same thing. "Jesus love you, Jean. I'm prayin' for you."

I thought this boded well for my hair, but I was mistaken. I was told that a woman named "Cricket" had fixed hair on the outside and was good at haircutting. I needed a haircut, and arrived for my first appointment full of good will and optimism. I asked Mrs. Smith if Cricket could cut my hair. "Oh, Cricket cut hair real good," she said. "But Cricket ain't gonna cut your hair. Think I'll have," she paused and looked around the room, "her cut your hair," she added, pointing to a little Colombian woman, about four-feet-ten-inches tall, with three-inch fingernails and a frightened, nervous, birdlike quality about her.

I introduced myself to Carmelita and with her broken English and my broken Spanish discovered that she had never cut hair before. "I do what you call fingersnails." She may have done windows too, but she wasn't going to do my hair. I thanked her profusely and said I had changed my mind. "I think I'll let it grow." We smiled pleasantly. She looked relieved and so did I. I moved over to another chair and sat for two hours and seventeen minutes until the "escort" came to lead us back to our cells.

A few months later I had gotten to know Cricket and she had assured me she would be happy to cut my hair. She assured me too that she could arrange it. "People ask me all the time. It's no problem. Mrs. Smith lets me do anyone who asks." With hope springing eternal I arrived for my second appointment.

It all started out well. Mrs. Smith told me Jesus loved me, Cricket said, "Hi," wet my hair and sat me down to cut it. I had come prepared for the "escort" this time and started to read. Suddenly the silence in the room made me look up. Though Cricket was bravely and doggedly snipping away, every other woman had gotten up and left the room. Cricket, it turned out, was the only white woman fixing hair that day. Jean Harris was a racist. She had asked for a white woman. The women walked downstairs in tandem looking for the sergeant on duty. Apparently it was duty too chancy, too explosive to handle alone. The first sergeant went to get the second sergeant.

The next thing we knew the two of them marched into the beauty parlor and over to where Cricket was cutting. One sergeant seized Cricket's hand and took the scissors from her. The other one seized the box of curlers that was sitting in front of us. He handed them solemnly to Mrs. Smith, who took them and locked them away.

Cricket managed to convince them that since half of my hair was now long and the other half was short, she should be allowed to finish the haircut. They discussed it for awhile and finally conceded that it might be the best solution. She was, however, forbidden to set my hair. The curlers remained under lock and key.

I have since discovered that getting one's hair cut is part of the art of learning how to "jail." Hair is cut in classroom toilets while friends stand guard, in linen closets, out in the yard with friends standing casually between the cutter, the cuttee, and the C.O., all because scissors are contraband, and yet, going through the proper channels is just too damned unpleasant and complicated. I, for one, now have very long hair which I put quickly into pigtails each morning, and get on with the business of the day. Getting over the beauty-parlor syndrome is one of the good things that has happened to me here.

2.

As for prison discipline, it has little to do with wrongdoing. It has a great deal to do with how people feel about you, or how fearful the staff is of the people who complain about you. Cricket and I had broken no rules, and done nothing wrong. That, however, did not keep two sergeants, two grown men, from abruptly stopping our harmless activity.

It also has a great deal to do with your relationship to the C.O.s. In that area I have been most unwise. Where others walk away, or just scream a casual obscenity, I stop and make a caustic remark, sometimes even rude, never obscene. But while C.O.s can stomach being told to "Go fuck yourself," they cannot cope with being asked, "Does it bother you that what you are doing makes absolutely no sense at all?" or "Rose, go arrest someone who's breaking the law and leave me alone." Even "You'd have loved Auschwitz. Have you ever tried making lamp shades?"

It would be ugly to watch people poking sticks at a caged rat. It is uglier still to watch rats poking sticks at a caged person. When you are the person, when you are the person that I am, at least, you feel little desire to share the experience. You don't want to hurt the people who love you, and you don't want to add "cry baby" to the long list of inappropriate epithets that you have already managed to acquire without earning them. I bitch, but I never whine.

You could call this chapter an incipient Scarsdale Letter if you chose, incubated for five years this time, not ten; but expressing the same frustrated contempt for those capable of committing daily atrocities and obscenities, smiling the smile of the angels all the while. I've grown suspicious of angels in my old age, or dotage, or whatever what I'm in is now called. Slippery bunch, angels, hiding their nasty little sins behind curtsies and complements, bibles and badges.

"You're only as big as the thing it takes to make you angry, Jean." I hear it again, a favorite remonstrance of my mother's each time I chose to take my stand at things others might and did consider trifles. What is large and what is small is something my children and my dearest friends and I do not always agree upon. Their advice when I describe the daily habits of C.O.s is always, "Just smile and walk away." "Ignore the bastards." "Tell the bloody little creeps to have a nice day. It'll drive them crazy." I can't do it.

Call it body chemistry, call it stupid, call it childish, I cannot simply walk away. Deliberate cruelty, patent dishonesty, unspeakable stupidity, when the perpetrators are wearing badges, when they are the rule setters, the dispensers of justice, are not small things. The hypocrisy of the whole sleazy business of prison life is something I will never roll over for. One must be the victim of it to know how truly evil it can be.

I have been given fifteen or sixteen charge sheets for "misbehavior" since coming to Bedford. My sons urge me to do "better." I'm not sure that I know what "better" is. It's all very well to do as the Romans do in Rome. But what do you do in hell? Every day within this grim, ridiculous cinder block pile I play Horatio at small bridges, having easily convinced myself that what stands at risk on the other side is Human Decency, always in capital letters, or even that ephemeral little Tinker Bell called justice. I tilt at windmills. I even tilt at windbags. In short, I go on being all the things I have been urged to be better than. I am grateful that I have had only one heart attack. I am surprised that I haven't had a stroke.

I am neither proud nor ashamed of my prison behavior. It is hardly pragmatic, but for me it was inevitable. It has made me stronger than I have ever been in my life, and it has left me thanking God that I am me, and not one of my keepers. If someone were to touch my shoulder this moment, and say, "You may go now, Jean. But when you leave you will never be you again, never think your thoughts, never remember your memories, love whom you love, trust whom you trust; you may pick any one of your keepers, or any one of the people who sent you here, and become one of them," I wouldn't move an inch, not a millimeter. Does that sound very smug? I wish it didn't.

Reaffirming whatever it is that makes each of us unique can be an awkward, embarrassing, and soul-searing process. It has been for me. But then, as my mother said, "A clay pot sitting in the sun will always be a clay pot. It has to go through the white heat of the furnace to become porcelain." Maybe I'm becoming porcelain. Maybe I'm just becoming brittle.

I had thought that claustrophia would be the most terrifying part of prison, locked for hours in a seven-foot by nine-and-a-half-foot cage. For me it hasn't been. I grew to welcome the jarring clang of that metal door as it separated me from the ugliness on the other side. A cell can become one's haven, the one place to feel clean. But for some women, claustrophobia is a reality, and it is a living hell. Fortunately, the metal door that locks one in is not flush with the floor. There is a five-inch space under it. I know a woman who slept for months on the floor, with her head next to that five-inch space, and her arm partially out in the hall. She kept a small unbreakable mirror nearby, and moving it back and forth under the door she could see up and down the corridor. It gave her some feeling of space.

No, claustrophobia has not been my bête noir. C.O.s have been. The trauma of waking to a daily nightmare in which people whose judgment you have little respect for control you totally is nightmare alley. Nothing in life had prepared me for them. I soon began thanking God for the things I had taken for granted for fifty-seven years, that I had lived with people who could think and act logically, who wished me well, or at least were subtle about wishing me ill; people who judged me after they knew me, not before.

The massive doses of media publicity about Jean Harris, socialite or social climber, power wielding headmistress of the "exclusive Madeira

School," wearer of wildly expensive skirts and blouses, aging mistress, "Queen Jean," had left many of the C.O.s, waiting breathlessly to get their hands on me, salivating over the delicious prospect of "putting her in her place." And this they set out with a vengeance to do.

My first two charge sheets I managed to earn simultaneously. I took off my coat in the yard one day and forgot to bring it in with me. My identification tag was attached to the collar. Six hours later two sergeants brought the coat back to my cell and handed me two charge sheets, one for not taking proper care of state property, and one for not keeping my ID with me at all times. I have watched a woman sitting not seven feet from the officer's bubble cut up a state-issue winter coat and make it into a vest. The C.O.s watched with a total lack of interest. Slacks are cut into shorts, shirts are made sleeveless and fringed, or simply thrown away. As far as I know, no one else has ever been given a charge sheet for simply leaving something on a bench. And they were only warming up.

I learned, too late, the first important rule of prison: "Never let anyone know what is important to you. As soon as you do, that will become the hardest thing to get or to keep." At first there were two things on my "needed" list and they quickly became known. One is anti-depressants prescribed by the psychiatrist who has treated me for more than five years. The other is a glass of milk.

The law of the state of New York stipulates that C.O.s may not interfere with an inmate's medication. Nonetheless, they do, and my first two years at Bedford I was torn between whether it was worse to go without medication or to go through the harassment and hell of trying to get it. That was my daily decision to make, and I started about 7:30 each evening to go through the decision making process. Sometime between 8:30 and 9:30 the nurse arrived with medication.

The system for getting medication is this:

(1) A call is made to your floor to tell the C.O.s in charge that the nurse is in the building and people getting medication should report to her.

(2) The C.O.s announce this by calling "Medication."

(3) Inmates needing medication (it must, of course, be medically prescribed) report to the C.O. station, or "bubble" as it is called, and wait for the door to the stairway to be opened.

(4) Inmates, accompanied by a C.O., walk downstairs, through a lobby, into a dark, airless cul-de-sac where they are stopped by another door.

(5) A second C.O., when she has finished visiting with someone on the phone, ambles slowly to the door, pushing people aside as she goes—there may be as many as twenty women by now yelling, "Open the fucking door." I have waited at this door for as long as six minutes by the clock, with the screams getting louder and more ominous every half minute.

(6) She opens the door.

(7) You proceed down a long tunnel, going past the kitchen and dining areas until you come to another locked door.

(8) A C.O. on the other side of this door finishes his or her phone call, and may make another one before coming to open the door.

(9) The women are still yelling, "Open the fucking door." You walk through the door, proceed seven steps and come to another locked door.

(10) A C.O. opens it and you proceed down another long tunnel to the nurse's station, where you line up for medication.

(11) At least nine people elbow their way ahead of you while the C.O. in charge watches and says and does nothing.

(12) If the C.O. who accompanied you is new, he or she stands next to the nurse's station and watches you swallow your pill, then makes you open your mouth to be sure you swallowed it. This is to keep you from selling the pill to someone else.

(13) If the C.O. is not new, he or she wanders into 112 Lobby nearby and visits while the medication line progresses.

(14) It makes little difference whether a C.O. is watching or not because people who sell their medication can easily hide it from the C.O. if they want to.

(15) When everyone has gotten her medication you retrace your steps stopping at the same four locked doors again.

The process takes anywhere from ten to forty minutes. If you take medication three times a day, as some women do, a considerable slice of your day is gone before it starts. Most inmates and C.O.s don't mind. Life in prison for many is just a question of *how* you're going to waste the day, not *if* you're going to waste it.

But all of the above is merely the way the system is supposed to

work, not necessarily the way it actually does work. My cell for almost
two years was at the end of a long corridor, quite removed from the
C.O.'s bubble. I rarely heard them call, "Medication." I asked friends
whose cells were near the bubble to call me when they heard it, but
the two C.O.s in charge, knowing my anxiety about medication,
rarely called it so that my corridor could hear it. I told them I couldn't
hear them. I asked them if they would push the lever to my cell door,
opening and slamming it to let me know. This involved one of them
moving a hand about six inches to the left and touching a lever. They
refused, though this is the accepted practice for calling inmates.

Consequently, I often ran back and forth to the bubble asking, "Did
you call medication yet?" They would smile with pleasure when they
could tell me, "It's too late. You've missed it. You should have come
when we called," knowing full well I hadn't heard them. Legally, I
could then ask for a special escort to take me down to the medical
building to get the medication I had missed. Sometimes I did this,
sometimes I skipped it and went through a long wretched night of
sleeplessness.

A C.O. is supposed to accompany an inmate when she goes for
medication. The two regulars on my floor were too lazy to walk that far
and simply refused to go. I'm told they were occasionally too drunk to
go but I never saw them drinking. The fact that they often made no
sense at all I chalked up to stupidity and meanness. Sending me off to
get medication without an escort meant sending me quite deliberately into trouble. At eight doors I was stopped and asked:

"Where you goin', Harris?"

"To medication," or "from medication" as the case happened to be.

"Where's the C.O.?"

"She told me to come with the other floor."

"You ain't goin' no place without a C.O."

"What should I do if she won't come?"

"That's your problem."

Sometimes I wasn't stopped until the third door, and then I was
really trapped. I couldn't go forward or backward. I stood until another C.O. happened along and then as a special favor was permitted
to move again. I was a human yo-yo, a pawn in a sick game every night
for two years. I was threatened with charge sheets if I went backward
or forward.

One night·I went all the way to medication and back with three other women and no C.O. For some reason the doors had been left open, the C.O.s were all busy visiting, and they ignored us. I had made it back through the seventh door, the other three women were ahead of me and had walked through the eighth undisturbed, when suddenly a C.O. appeared coming through the same door the other way.

"Where you goin', Harris?"

"I'm going back to my cell."

"What you doin' down here?"

"I went to medication."

"Where's the C.O.?"

"She didn't come. She doesn't like the long walk."

"You can't go for medication without a C.O."

"But she refused to go and I've already been to medication."

"You turn around and walk to the medication window with me."

"But that doesn't make any sense. I've already been and I've taken my medication."

"You turn around and walk back with me and that's a direct order. You refuse a direct order you get a charge sheet."

I already had too many charge sheets so I turned around and went back through the locked doors again, back to the medication window, waited while the C.O. visited a while, then walked back with her to my floor. The other three women had returned to their cells un-molested. This was par for my course every night for almost two years until I moved to Fiske, where I am now, thank God, allowed to have two week's medication at a time. The sound of a voice saying, "Where you think you goin', Harris?" turns my stomach to knots and makes me want to shriek with pain. My distaste for the sick little bastards who asked it night, after night, after night is strong. Having experi-enced both kinds of crime, and both kinds of criminal, I can tell you it is far easier to be robbed of a gold chain than of your sanity.

3·

To be a C.O. one must be eighteen years old, have a high school equivalency certificate, and pass an elementary civil service test. You are given six week's training and then you are ready to start opening and closing doors, at a higher salary than a beginning teacher with a college degree receives. While I cannot speak for men's prisons, certainly duty at Bedford Hills Correctional Facility is not as dangerous as driving a taxi in New York City, or even teaching there, so that isn't a viable excuse. It is unpleasant duty, but much of the unpleasantness they create for themselves.

Not all of it. There are some very decent human beings who choose this line of work, or who do it because they can't get any other kind of work. As a rule they are treated with the same degree of respect that they give others. There are some with college degrees and graduate work, and some who see their jobs as teacher—to correct is to teach—and their efforts are nothing short of heroic. But there are not enough of them. Some of the best are reaching retirement age, and the turnover of C.O.s is constant.

Many C.O.s are from upstate New York, so their first worldly act upon arriving at Bedford is to sign up to leave. Often their moves must be in short hops, from prison to prison, each move bringing them a little closer to home. Until they get where they are within driving distance of home, they share rooms with other C.O.s at local motels, or they sleep in rooms on the prison grounds when those are available. They go home only on days off.

Nothing contributes more to the air of constant confusion in a prison than the C.O. seniority system. Instead of learning one or two posts well, they constantly hopscotch all over the facility, each location with different rules and requirements. In this way they hope to get closer to the spot they eventually want, or at least further away from the spot they don't want. C.O.s bid for their posts, and are given their choice according to seniority. The most popular posts, by and large, are the easiest and/or safest ones, so experienced people take those jobs and the toughest posts go to the youngest and least experienced. They are just this side of childhood. They still have three years to go before they can be trusted to buy a drink legally, but they are in charge of what society considers its most dangerous and difficult members.

If anyone thinks that makes sense, I would be interested to hear why. The C.O. union, however, has made it clear that those are the conditions that will prevail until the state offers incentive wages to stay at the toughest posts. Since seniority already brings with it higher wages I would think that alone would carry with it the requirement of greater experience and know-how. One is constantly aware of the large groups of new C.O.s coming into Bedford.

You can recognize the new recruits in traffic because they are so earnest about making you take all your clothes off, searching carefully in places there obviously aren't any drugs, and assuring you "I'm just following procedure." Bedford, we are told, is a place C.O.s are usually eager to transfer out of, partly because it's downstate and many of the recruits live eight hours away, and partly because the women, for reasons I also don't understand, are allowed to behave very badly without anyone doing much about it.

C.O.s run the prison. "I don't care what the rule is, we gonna do it *my* way" is a familiar refrain. It is a new experience, for someone who has lived in a world where logic and decency still play some role in daily life, to wake up each morning in the clutches of C.O.s

My third charge sheet was for refusing to open my mouth wide enough to see if I had swallowed my pill. When I was asked, I had opened it immediately and as wide as it will open. I have a small mouth and small bone structure. Even having my teeth cleaned is a painful procedure. But as wide as I could open it was not wide enough for the new, eighteen-year-old C.O. in charge. All progress in the medication line stopped while he continued to demand, "Open it wider." I finally suggested he stick his fist down my throat and see if he could open it any wider. For such insolence and disobedience I was given a charge sheet. The hearing for that crime was held in a sergeant's office and was finally dismissed.

When I first arrived at Bedford the regular C.O. on my floor in the morning was a short, stocky woman with a butch haircut. She had already been suspended once for drugs. She was a dyke, synonym for bull dagger, both new terms in my vocabulary, and meaning the lesbian who plays the male role. She went after me daily and threatened me at every turn, including the slightly maniacal threat that if I wore my state-issue raincoat downstairs she would give me a charge sheet. When I insisted, "That doesn't make any sense. You have to give me a reason," she would answer, "This ain't no tea party. You is in jail."

I have written pages and pages of notes about this C.O., long boring descriptions of our senseless conversations, as my level of frustration grew and her enjoyment became more and more expansive. It was my first experience with something bordering on lunacy, at least the first time, if I had come upon it before, that I couldn't walk away from it. Here was lunacy in the driver's seat, senselessly calling the plays, with the power to punish if you didn't hop when the signals were called.

"You go downstairs in that coat you get a chawge sheet." "You go out that door with that cuppa water you get a chawge sheet." "You talk to that girl in lock you getta chawge sheet."

Three other women were sitting on the floor playing pinochle under the door with the woman in lock when that threat was issued. "You go down there without you ID you getta chawge sheet."

Later I learned to laugh or shrug it off, but not right away. I wasted a good deal of energy trying to reason, showing her the book of rules that had been issued to me, asking for logical explanations. Sometimes I'd tell her she was crazy. It took only a few minutes on those occasions before a sergeant called me down to his office. "What did you call the C.O.?"

"I don't remember the exact words but whatever it was it wasn't bad enough. She is like something that has climbed out of the primordial ooze."

"Take it easy Harris. You'll only make it harder on yourself unless you calm down. Walk away from it. Do what she says and don't give her an argument."

People find it wonderfully easy to give that advice. I find it wonderfully hard to follow. In time I could beat her to the line: "I know, this ain't no tea party. I is in jail."

Finally, she was fired and took to the streets. Her life outside must have been grim. It ended in tragedy last year when she was murdered, I'm told, by her sister.

The next charge sheet was for walking from my cell, across the hall and down a few steps to the shower room without a bathrobe. Women are not required to wear bras at Bedford, so it is quite normal procedure to bounce around any part of the grounds with see-through tee shirts on. But the written rules do in fact say you must wear a robe when you leave your cell.

"Harris, go back and put on a robe."

"I'm just going to wash my face and hands, and there's no place to put a robe in there. And anyway, you can't see through this night-gown."

"I'm tellin' ya, go get a robe."

"Go arrest someone," I said, "and leave me alone. Bug out." My charge sheet read, "Harris then refused a direct order and said, Bug to fuck out."

It isn't a saying that rolls easily off the tongue, and even if it were, it wouldn't roll off mine. However, the charge was written and then began the usual "hearings" to decide my guilt. In this case two ser-geants, one male and one female, heard the case, with the usual tape recording of the proceedings and request for any witnesses.

I was required to go back and get the offending nightgown and model it for the two of them. It was a little pink, flowered Lantz model, the kind you wear to college house meetings, and could wear with complete propriety to answer the doorbell. I had described it to the two of them as "opaque." What the hell was "opaque"? I think that's what piqued their curiosity enough to send me back to get it. The part about not wearing a robe was dismissed—that's the part that broke a rule—but telling the C.O. "Bug to fuck out" stuck.

Before this bit of criminal justice was laid to rest, taxpayers had paid at least three hours wages to two sergeants and one C.O. for their services. I have asked many of them, "Doesn't it embarrass you to be part of this Mickey Mouse nonsense?" and the answer is always the same. "I'm just doin' my job." If school principals interpreted their job in the same manner our national SAT scores would be lower than they already are. There wouldn't be time for teaching.

My next charge was really serious and included inciting a riot, using obscene language and hitting another inmate. No Mickey Mouse this time. Now they were out for blood. In all candor, the "starting a riot" probably had some validity to it, and I told them so. I asked Omenia to turn down her radio, which God knows, and I now know, was tantamount to starting a riot. The rules read very clearly and specifically that radios may be played only with earphones. Omenia's had been blasting away for over an hour, but the C.O., like most of the young inmates, loved noise and confusion and had said nothing. (There is now a loudspeaker system, bought and installed at great expense that insures wall to wall mayhem most of the day and evening.)

Omenia's response to my request was to start shouting obscenities and turn the radio up as far as it would go. "Fuckin' old bitch, think she in the Marriott Motel. Think she in a fuckin' old people's home. Fuckin' old bitch think she gonna tell me what to do."

I was full of sweet reasonableness. I was calm. I assured Omenia this was hard for all of us, and that we could make things better by being thoughtful of one another—blah, blah, blah. She was unmoved and unchastened. Furthermore, she was having a splendid time, and I wasn't. Finally, I made my next big mistake. I went to the C.O. and asked her help.

"Look I'm growing a little weary of being called a fuckin' old bitch and having to listen to a blasting radio that isn't supposed to be played without earphones. I need your help."

"Whadda ya think I'm supposed to do?"

"You're supposed to know what the rules of this place are and enforce them."

Finally, most begrudgingly, she followed me back up the corridor. By this time Charlene and a few others had joined in the fun, and were waiting for me in the hall. Charlene, whose cheery "Good morning all you fuckin' scalawags" greeted us every morning, was ready for me.

"Fuckin' old bitch. You ain't nothin'. You can't tell nobody what to do. You shit. You got a number. You just like me."

That was the red flag. I drew myself up tall and announced: "I am not like you. I don't live like you. I don't think like you. I don't speak like you."

I think that as I drew myself up she thought I was going to hit her. She swung first, and hit me on the head, and then the next calamity happened. I fell to the floor—that wasn't the calamity—but in falling I knocked over Omenia's fish bowl—that was. She had placed it in the corridor while she cleaned her cell. A wail went up.

"Oh my gawd, ma fish, ma fish. Look what she done to ma fish. One a them fish dies I'm gonna kill her."

I dragged myself up to a standing position and said, "Omenia, you are a spoiled, thoughtless bitch and it's time you grew up."

She was shocked speechless for an instant. Then, "She can't talk to me like that. My own Mama don't talk to me like that."

The C.O. took me by the arm and told me I must be locked in my cell. My last words before the door clanged shut were said with deep conviction and in my haughtiest manner. "And damn your fish!"

Charlene was locked too, but Omenia just picked up her fish and went on cleaning her cell, refreshed from the interlude, her radio still blaring.

Omenia and I became friends after that, largely because of the fish comment. Somehow it caught her imagination. I heard her on a number of occasions describing the scene to a friend. "And Jean Harris just say, 'And damn yo fish.' Ain't nobody can say it like she done, just 'Damn yo fish,' like she ain't afraid of nobody."

I remained in lock for two days, until after my "hearing." I told them I thought they had a good case for the starting a riot part, but pled innocent to hitting anyone or using obscene language. I was given "counseling" and dismissed. Twice in these hearings I have been asked to spell "counseling."

There were other charges that followed, for walking upstairs with two pieces of bread, (but the C.O. tore that one up) for asking for a second glass of milk; for using the staff toilet in the school building. The last was dismissed because "It really wasn't your fault. The staff toilet is supposed to be kept locked." I told the sergeant I didn't want it dismissed. I wanted a very big thing made of it so the Board of Health would come and take a look at the inmate toilet facilities in the school building. It was dismissed anyway.

The next serious charge was brought by a C.O. whose behavior was so outrageous that she should, by all standards of decency, not be permitted to be a C.O. Our aversion to one another was palpable. She worked in traffic, which put her in a position of great power. "Traffic" is the area one goes through in order to enter the visiting room and to leave it. The C.O. stood between me and my children and friends, and she knew it only too well.

If I wanted to see David or Jim I knew I must be pawed by her. She felt you all over with a "pat frisk" before you entered the visiting room ending with a quick karate chop to the groin. She put you through the most obscene kind of strip search on the way back. Since everything you possess in prison is something that has been handed you by a

C.O. I keep wondering what they are looking for in the "pat frisk" before you go into the visiting room. What are you trying to sneak out? I always get the same answer when I ask. "I don't know but I'll know it when I see it." "But what do you *think* you'll find?" I insisted.

"I ain't paid to think, I'm paid to follow procedure."

The C.O. did far more searching than is required for security purposes. All that infinite capacity to love and forgive which I claim to have inherited from my mother was tested to the breaking point and beyond by her. "That ain't a good squat. Squat again. Now squat and cough. Now take that thing outta your hair and shake your hair. Run your hands through it." If you had to go to the bathroom while you were in the area she held the door wide open with her foot so you were exposed to the world. Then she leaned her back against the wall and stared directly at you until you were through.

The more I loathed her the more she loved it. Her response was almost sexual, and her great hope was to get me to hit her so that she could win the prize for getting Harris in "segregation," Bedford's equivalent of solitary confinement. "Whyn't ya hit me, Harris. Hit me. Come at me, Harris. Hit me right there." Fortunately, hitting is not a reflex with me. I lash out with my tongue, never my hand.

One day when I tried to get past her to go through a doorway to see if there were another C.O. who could search me instead of her, she raced to the door, turned suddenly and threw her arms out spread eagle so that I couldn't get through. "You're not goin' anyplace." I know how trapped rats feel. As she threw her arms out somehow my hand or my arm touched her upper left arm. She had me. "Assault" of an officer, as it has been explained to me in here, need only mean touching the officer.

She wrote me a charge sheet, charging assault for "touching my left upper arm." Found guilty I would go to segregation, locked all but one hour a day under the worst conditions the prison has to offer. The hearing was held before a deputy superintendent. I am grateful the deputy believed me when I told her with an intensity and sincerity I felt in the very center of my being, "If the only thing that stood between me and a bottomless pit were that C.O.'s left upper arm, I would fall happily into the abyss. The thought of touching her revolts me." The charge was dismissed. Happily, this C.O. finally transferred out. But a new and equally unspeakable one was there to fill the gap.

Two other charges are still fresh in my mind. Both I believe played a role in my heart attack. The new C.O., more unbearable than the first one, has since threatened me with a third—my long silk scarf touched her when I took it off so she could search my hair for contraband. "That's assault, you know." After five years of threats and five years of ugliness, one begins to grow weary.

Three years ago I was moved into a new housing unit named Fiske. I was fair game all over again, because in moving I had created a new need—the need to stay at Fiske. I have been put on and off probation since coming here, though I have not broken any rules. Fiske is a large Tudor cottage built over seventy years ago when what is now Bedford Hills Correctional Facility, a top security prison for women, was known as New York State Reformatory for Women. It was named after a Mrs. Fiske who served on the board of trustees of the reformatory.

Fiske was built to be the segregation unit for the girls who misbehaved. When the reformatory became a prison, about fifteen years ago, the building was no longer used. It had been built long before the security precautions of a prison were considered necessary. The doors to the rooms are of wood, not steel, and lock with a separate key. The bedrooms, though cell size, do not have individual sinks and toilets, which are required now if a prisoner is to be locked in for long periods of time.

The building stood empty for fifteen years. When the space crunch came several years ago it was decided that the twenty-six rooms in Fiske were needed, and could be used, but only as an honor cottage for women who could function in prison without steel doors and cinder block walls to contain them. The windows are of steel, and casement in style so one can't escape that way. To add a toilet and sink to each room would have been prohibitively expensive. Instead, the honor cottage concept was born, and I, in spite of my charge sheets, which for the most part the administration had dismissed, was one of the twenty-six women chosen to live in it.

Forty-four thousand dollars were spent to put in a new heating unit, replace some doors, and refurbish the kitchen. That came to less than $1,750 per inmate. We moved out of twenty-six cells that would cost more than $2 million to replicate. We did the cleaning, which involved, besides literally shoveling out the dirt, scraping the accumulated dirt of many years off the floors, with plastic knives and fingernails, buffing and polishing them to a shine, and making our rooms attractive with bright colored sheets for curtains.

The administration was rightfully proud of what it had accomplished, and of the new concept for a top security prison that they had dared to introduce. There is no other top security prison in America that has managed to create twenty-six decent living units for prisoners for $44,000.

Today, one new cell averages between $75,000 and $100,000, and if one counts the interest charges on borrowed money, it approaches $200,000. It was a common sense move, something that takes real courage when you work in any "system." It should have been greeted enthusiastically by taxpayers. But the point of it, and the value of it was largely lost in newspaper articles headlined: JEAN'S PLACE, WALL TO WALL CARPETING, WOMEN CAN COME AND GO AS THEY PLEASE, JEAN HARRIS HELPED TO FOUND IT.

It was damaging to the concept, damaging to me personally, and most important of all, damaging to the truth. "Hey Jean, you gonna let anyone live in *your* house?" The brouhaha has died down now and twenty-six women live in Fiske with a modicum of human decency, in rational surroundings where people take turns, share, do not shriek obscenities, have the same work responsibilities as other inmates outside of Fiske and additional ones in Fiske, keeping it very clean, gardening, cooking, sharing two refrigerators, and keeping them clean—try it, with twenty-six women, it takes real cooperation.

There is no wall to wall carpeting, in fact the floors are terrazzo and have been restored to their original beauty. To live here after the zoolike atmosphere of my former units is to be given back one's humanness. But I am constantly threatened with being removed. "One more charge sheet and you're out."

A year after I moved to Fiske I was given what was, I believe, my fourteenth charge sheet. This one was for "being where she wasn't supposed to be and lying." It was the nadir of my years here, and once again I howled with pain and ended up in the psychiatrist's office.

It started when I had been told to report to the pharmacist's office to pick up medication at 3:00 P.M. At 3:00 P.M. I was helping to finish a quilt in South Forty and didn't watch the clock. Suddenly it was 3:45, too late to go. The next day I watched the clock and left the Children's

Center, where I had been working, to be sure I would be on time. Since the Children's Center is at the far end of the visiting room I went through Traffic as I left, was strip searched, and headed for the pharmacist in the medical building. I arrived at 2:50. "Where you think you're goin' Harris?"

"To pick up medication."

"Who told you to pick it up?"

"I don't remember."

"Where'd you come from?"

"From traffic. I was in the Children's Center."

"Well go on back."

"I've just been strip searched and it doesn't make sense to go back and go through that for ten minutes."

"You can't wait in here."

I should explain that the largest area of the medical building is a waiting room. Waiting is practically all one does there. I have waited on many occasions for over an hour, to make an appointment, or even to get a new screw in my eyeglasses. Today the rules were different. I couldn't wait ten minutes.

"You gotta get outta here. Wait outside."

I walked outside and sat down on a bench just across from the medical building. Within a moment or two a C.O. on duty outside saw me and walked toward me calling,

"You can't sit there. Get moving. You aren't allowed to sit there."

Why the bench is there I don't know. "I'll just be a few minutes," I told him. "I'm waiting for the pharmacy to open."

"Well you can't wait out here. You gotta wait inside."

"I can't wait inside. They told me to wait outside."

"Well I'm tellin' you ya wait inside."

"Will you come in with me please, so they'll know I'm following a direct order?" I walked in and was met by the same C.O.

"I told you to get outta here."

"I know, but the C.O. outside told me to come back in."

I turned to a third C.O. who had opened the door.

"Look, I need to get my medication, and I don't want a charge sheet. I've been given a direct order to go out, and a direct order to come in. Can you tell me what I should do?"

"Search me," she said, and turned and walked away.

Suddenly a fourth voice was heard from a C.O. who was in the officer's bubble around the corner.

"Harris get outta here and go back to your unit. Traffic didn't sent you here. You're a liar."

"I didn't say that. I said that's where I had come from, and I don't remember who told me to pick up my medication."

"Go back to your unit."

It was now 2:56, four minutes until the pharmacy would open. I said, "Are you telling me that I should walk three-fourths of a mile to and from Fiske because I am four minutes early for the pharmacist?"

"I'm telling you to get out of here and go back to your unit."

I turned around and walked back to Fiske, and went without medication for a second night. Such unwarranted harassment was bad enough, but the C.O. had more in store. The next day I was served— very much as one is served with a subpoena—with a charge sheet, charging me with being out of place and lying.

It was five days later, and with the help of a lawyer, that I got my medication. There were three weeks of hearings over this one, with three C.O.s called as witnesses. They were pretty fair in their assessment of what had happened and the charge was dismissed.

It was dismissed, but the memory lingered on, and shortly afterward I received a letter from a deputy superintendent telling me I was now on probation again at Fiske. It becomes tedious, doesn't it? Tedious writing it, tedious reading it, and heaven knows tedious living it. I will add only one more charge sheet, the last one—how I hope it's the last one. The C.O. who had given me the last charge sheet was putting me through my paces in Traffic searching me. I stood there stark naked while she slowly felt the seams of every piece of my clothing—caressing them, knowing there was nothing in them.

"You're a fool." I said. But *I* was the fool. For this dastardly deed I was accused, and found guilty of *Verbally Harassing a Correction Officer*. Two days later I was in intensive care with a heart attack. Three days later I awoke there to find none other than the C.O. I was accused of harassing standing over me, complete with her loaded pistol. She had asked to be my watchdog in the hospital! I reached for Dr. Kay's arm and said, "Get her out of here. I beg you. And don't let her come back in." Whatever he said to her, she followed his instructions and I didn't see her again. She sat in the hall outside the room.

Bedford Hills:

Maggie Strong

She ain't nothing but Maggie Strong
Everything she own she got on

1.

It was Darlene who taught me the poem about Maggie Strong, but I have since heard the children in our summer program jumping rope to it. Darlene sat on the bright yellow toilet cover she had crocheted for me and explained the pecking order of ladies of the evening, from "flatbacks," to hookers, to call girls, the latter being the crème de la crème, and incidentally, much richer than school teachers.

Darlene often perched there on the toilet, which I had disguised with white ruffles and a yellow pillow, and taught me the facts of life. Other facts I gleaned from the casual street talk out in the corridor, sounds of the night and the day that left me feeling a little like E.T.: "One thing my mama taught me, 'Dessa, whatever you do, get a room of your own. Even if it only got a bed and a chair, and one knife and one fork and one spoon, get a room of your own you can go to.' "

"Girl, that's good advice," all the other ladies agreed.

The subject of sex usually has top billing in the corridors of Bedford. For someone known from coast to coast as "the aging mistress" I still had much to learn.

The price of sex surprised me. Even in prison it goes high. Somewhere from long ago I remember hearing the term "a $2 whore." It must have been during the Great Depression. "I'll do anything they want, but I get my $50 up front," Evelyn told me on several occasions. "They" were the C.O.s. She sounded very businesslike about it, almost officious, and no more self-conscious than if she were discussing the price of a sweater she had just made.

I have rarely heard an unkind word about a woman's own pimp, though the word to me means something that crawls out from under rocks.

"Pimps ain't so bad, Jean. You gotta have a pimp. He handle all my business and finance. He's like family. You gotta have someone. I wouldn't work the street without one."

They can be more clear-eyed and objective about someone else's pimp. "You watch. She get outta here, she'll go right back to that lyin' mother-fucker." It is a variation on a theme one hears discussed in the ladies room at the Little Club in Grosse Pointe. "How she stands that son-of-a-bitch I'll never understand!" And it isn't the only thing in this foreign land that is déjà vu.

One summer, years ago, I was walking down Gorky Prospect in Moscow and saw a woman sitting at the curbside selling flowers. Beside her were three pails filled with zinnias. I stopped and stared. Zinnias can't grow in Russia, I thought. They're much too pedestrian. They're too much like home. Russia is the other side of the world, its flowers must be different. But they aren't, and in the weeks that followed, as I traveled over that broad country, I saw them all again and again, zinnias, petunias, begonias, calendulas, asters, and all the other familiar flowers that grew in my garden at home. When you're far away from home, the exotic is expected, the familiar is what surprises: teapots, aprons, and petunias are the things that catch the eye.

I remembered that experience, and I felt it again the first night I spent in prison. I walked into the recreation room at 9:30 P.M., just before lock-in, and there were women in nightgowns and robes, writing letters, ironing a blouse, fixing each other's hair, playing cards, showing pictures of their children. Extraordinary, I thought. They're so remarkably ordinary. This is the dark side of the moon, but the woman here look so ordinary. They're people. They're women. And they're mothers. It was a sobering moment of discovery.

That is not to say that I suddenly saw us all as just folks and girls together. My comfortable, middle-class solipsism that had once left me earnestly believing that deep down we all value the same things, and aspire to the same goals, had been pretty well laid to rest in a courtroom. We may start out alike, and probably do, but life experiences change us almost at once. Certainly the professions we follow taint our concept of truth. Even so, I felt a kinship with people far removed from me that night, and the kinship has remained, although my awareness of our differences has grown deeper. But then loving thy neighbor as thyself was never meant to be an exercise in narcissism, even though it often ends up that way.

It is an alien world in here. One that is difficult to think about let alone to describe. It is virtually impossible to be consistent about what one thinks. One doesn't expect friendship from these women. It is almost beyond the ken of many. They trust no one and value no one—least of all themselves. Their instincts are sometimes very kind, but they're unreliable. You don't know whether they will hug the wounded animal or kick it. They don't know either.

Until the middle of the 1960s, America's picture of a female inmate came only from Hollywood. She was white, sexy, looked like Ida Lupino or Susan Hayward, and like the little girl with the curl in the middle of her forehead, was either very good or very bad. If she was good, she had fallen in love with the likes of George Raft, and from then on it was downhill all the way. If she was bad, she spent most of her time in prison pulling hair, rioting or planning to break out. If she was a good girl she probably died in the riot. If she was a bad girl she finally returned to society a wiser, better woman. She was "reformed." Children were never a problem to movie molls because any fool knew that mommies don't go to prison. Right? Wrong.

2.

Even today there are few good empirical studies about incarcerated women. Perhaps the only way to begin to know them, and then only very gradually, is to live with them. As with any group, one can generalize up to a point. After that, each woman, each background, each problem is unique.

We tend to homogenize criminals, as we homogenize the poor, as men are inclined to homogenize women. I don't want to do that, but statistically there are some qualities and experiences more than half of the women in prison share. Let's look at one of those women. Her name isn't important here: We will call her "Maggie Strong—Everything she own she got on."

We're told, before judging a stranger, to walk a mile in her moccasins. I'm not sure I could make the whole mile in Maggie's moccasins. She's twenty-five years old, minority born, black or Puerto Rican on the East Coast, black, Mexican American, or Indian American on the West Coast. She is poor. I remember hearing a woman say one night, "The only time in my childhood I can remember eating good is when my daddy died. People filled the house with food. There were times when I was a kid I wished my mother would die too, so we could eat good again. It's a awful thing to admit, but it's true."

Maggie is uneducated, has worked at a minimum wage job, has been on welfare some time during her life, grew up without her natural father in the house, is familiar with drugs and alcoholism, may have one parent who spent some time in jail, and started her criminal career as a prostitute. Keep in mind that all around me are exceptions to the rule, but this is "the mean average."

Our Maggie has 2.5 children and wants more. She came from a family of brothers and sisters or half-brothers and half-sisters, anywhere from one to twenty. I know a number of women here from families of ten or more. One acquaintance of mine has fourteen brothers and sisters, "and every one of 'em has done time. . . . My mother died when she was forty-two. She was just played out."

Maggie's first baby was born when she was in her mid-teens. Ninth grade is a popular time to have that first baby. "I wanted something of my own." It is not unusual for mothers here to have children and grandchildren the same age. There is less than a 20 percent chance that Maggie was married when she was arrested, but a 65–75 percent chance that she had children to support. There is less than a 10 percent chance that she was living in that wonderful Dick and Jane world with father, mother, and children all living together under the same roof. It is not unusual for each of her children to have a different father.

Approximately 33 percent of the men in prison are married. Approximately 17 percent of the women in prison are married. The low incidence of intact marriages in our prison population is not a passing statistic. It is deeply significant. Married people go to prison less often than unmarried ones do. If they do go they are less apt to be recidivists. Married people live longer than unmarried people do, too.

The one constant theme in the whole epic of crime is the need people have for one another. Unfortunately, black women have the most limited field from which to find a husband. The death rate for young black men between the ages of fifteen and twenty-five is very high, higher than any other group in the country, and murder is the main cause of death. Many young black males are in prison. The peak age for involvement in serious felonies is twenty-four. Among those lucky enough to survive outside there is presently almost 40 percent unemployment, and to further reduce the number of available husbands, three times as many black men marry white women as white men marry black women. There are many more black women in college than black men, so a black woman who does marry is more apt to "marry down" than "up." The cards are definitely stacked against her in the lower socio-economic level.

For reasons partly of her own making, and partly not, Maggie's lifestyle "right from jump street," as the ladies say, is hectic and unplanned, and provokes one crisis after another. It was hard to keep track of her before she came to prison and it's hard after she leaves. Before her arrest she may have been living with her mother, other family members, a friend—male or female—her children, or even in that room with "one knife and one fork and one spoon."

Some lived with only half of their children because they couldn't provide housing for all. It was not simply a case of casual neglect in many instances. The fact that not all children were living with mother before her arrest is only one indication of the great social and familial disorganization of prison women. Some of them believe, and may well be correct, that the splitting up of their families, and the isolation that followed, was one of the factors that led them to drugs and to crime. Yet, I have never heard one say, "I shouldn't have had all those kids."

There is better than a 60 percent chance that Maggie was abused as a child, physically, sexually, emotionally, or all three. Accurate statistics on this are not easily come by because Maggie, even though she is in prison, does not like to say things that reflect badly on her parents and family. Family loyalty, even when you haven't much of a family life, is strong. It's one thing you can cling to, and lie about, so you have that little something at least. Moreover, not everyone agrees about what child abuse is. One is more apt to learn the truth about these women in informal conversations than from statistical questionnaires.

On one of the cell blocks containing sixty women, one of the inmates announced that she was doing a study about incest for a sociology report for a college course. She assured the women that no names would be used, and no one would be identified in any way, but she would appreciate it if some women who had experienced incest would be willing to talk privately with her. Before lock-in that night sixteen women had agreed to talk with her. How many more could not bring themselves to talk about it there is no way of knowing.

You probably wouldn't like Maggie very much. She has habits and qualities that would make you turn away. She can be adamant and rude one minute, contrite and vulnerable as a little child the next. One of the least just things about justice is that its decisions are colored not only by the deeds done, but by the fact that deeds are often done by people who are unattractive, even disgusting to us. And their pride often seems to require them to put their worst foot forward.

Their voices are loud, earsplitting loud, and the words that bellow forth are more often than not obscene. Maggie's idea of a good book, if she reads at all, may be your idea of garbage, and people's sexual habits are too often her topic of conversation. She likes to visit while standing in the middle of doorways, and when you try to squeeze by you don't know whether she will say "Pardon me," or "That's right, break my fuckin' arm."

Maggie is often narcissistic and quite insensitive to others, sometimes even to her own children. In many cases this is the result of having lived without love herself. And her age plays a role, too. While the average age of women here is twenty-five, there are girls here as young as sixteen. You can be sent to an adult prison when you're sixteen, but when the pregnant sixteen-year-old daughter of an inmate came to visit one day, she was turned away because she wasn't accompanied by an adult.

Some of the inmates are too young and too emotionally impoverished themselves to know how to rise above their own narcissism and care unselfishly about others. Some have little or no idea what parental obligation is. They haven't seen it in action. Unlike Ibsen's Nora, some of the young women at Bedford may live out their lives in a state of perpetual childhood, not because life has made them clingingly dependent, but because it forced them into adult situations before they had practiced being children.

Recently I was chagrined to learn the life story of a young woman here whom I have found particularly tedious and annoying to be around. My schoolteacher mind had said to itself, "She acts like a third grader." I have since learned, from others, that her father deserted the family when she was four years old, and her mother walked out, leaving her with three younger siblings, when she was thirteen. She had been earning her living on the street from the time she was eleven. One of her friends from the street, a man much her senior, agreed to take the younger children in if she would live with him as his wife. She has lived as a wife, mother of one, and stepmother of three since she was thirteen. She is twenty-six years old now; we sang "Happy Birthday" last week, and on a good day she acts thirteen. Sad to say, she was probably better off with a man to support her and keep the family together than she'd have been in the hands of a social agency. The man comes to visit her regularly (her sentence is fairly short), he seems to be devoted to her. One does wonder, though, where society was the day her mother left town.

And then—if we leave Maggie aside for a moment—there's Ramona, a young woman who lived in a cell opposite mine for almost a year. She was first raped by her uncle when she was five years old. She was in her mother's bed at the time. When she didn't stop bleeding, "My mother carried me downstairs and put me behind the stairs and told me to tell the police I never seen the man before." The harassment went on until she was eleven. Then she killed her uncle and spent eighteen months in juvenile detention, and finally took to the streets. She still believes that this is when her life began. She told me one night, remembering with pleasure and pride, "Man, you shoulda seen me then, Jean!

"There was Rack Tack, Pom Pom, Thunderbody, and ma sister Brenda and me. We owned 140th Street. We had that whole block sewed up . . . all girl hustlers there . . . no mother-fuckin pimps. We was like real gangsters. We got respeck. 'This is ours' we tole 'em. We done our little thing . . . we build up our clientele . . . we used to have a ball."

Ramona is not yet thirty years old, she has five children, she doesn't know where they all are, though she has tried to learn, and neither does the Family Court, the Department of Social Services, or the rest of her family. She is in prison for dealing drugs, and chances are good she will never be a person you want to invite to dinner. She will settle down or slow down as she grows older, but only because she is older, not better, by our definition. She told me she returned to her apartment one day to find her sister strangled with the telephone cord. She told me her husband was shot to death "half a block from home. Don't nobody know who done it. Don't nobody care who done it. Ain't nobody fixin' to find out . . . shit, Miz Harris. Killin' ain't nothin'. Killin' goin on all around me." There is no more important lesson for children to learn than the value of life, starting with their own. But how can a mother teach it who has never experienced it herself?

I will remember this woman as long as I live, for many reasons, but perhaps best for her nightly ritual of waiting until everyone had quieted down after 10:00 P.M. lock-in and then calling out "Goodnight all you niggers, whores, and mother-fuckers." Long pause—then, "I'm a nigger . . . I'm a whore . . . I'm a mother-fucker . . . and I am suuuuuuum body!" Sing me a sadder song than that. Tell me about the birth of the blues.

There are many women here who grew up on the street from puberty, selling themselves and selling drugs. It's a familiar refrain, not a complaint, "I been on the street all my life." They have children now, but they still giggle and push and poke each other like youngsters. They hid their faces when we showed them a movie of the birth of a baby. It frightened them. Some wanted to know what menopause was, and another asked hesitantly if men menstruate. One very pregnant young lady insisted she had never "been with a man." She got pregnant from eating kidney beans. Another explained why she wouldn't have a Cabbage Patch doll in her house. "You know how they make them dolls? Take sperm from a sperm bank and cross 'em with cabbages. Gotta adopt them babies. I wouldn't have one in my house. Wake up some morning and there be a cabbage standin' over me, callin' me 'Mama!' "

Not long ago I would have thought these women "worldly," but they are babes in arms. And the hardest part of teaching them is unteaching what they have already learned. They cling tenaciously to their ignorance. "My truths are as good as your truths. If they aren't, then we aren't equal."

They have been shortchanged in so many ways, and in the past twenty-five years society at large has further shortchanged them by supporting a kind of anarchial individualism which preaches that the way one person lives is just as good as the way anyone else lives. Carried to its logical conclusion, it is a crippling notion, one to which prison inmates subscribe at the top of their voices, and which keeps many of them from learning and growing into responsible adults. To them they are not shameful because the way they live is what they know. One grows up accepting what is acceptable in one's culture. These women have conformed to the life that was thrown their way, and they have ended up as adults demanding the attention they missed as children.

Turning back to Maggie, one finds that there is much about her you would recognize in yourselves. She wants "a lot of good stuff," she wants a moment's peace. She wants to be loved. And in her inept, sometimes valiant way she wants to be "a good mother." Perhaps it is for the children to define what one is.

If, as Edward C. Banfield declares in his book, *The Unheavenly City Revisited*, class can be defined on the basis of people's behavior toward their own future, Maggie is definitely lower class . . . and more and more people are joining her instead of the other way around. She has lived her life for the present, following the line of least resistance, doing what seems easiest to her, rarely investing herself in tomorrow. The immediate rewards of doing the right thing aren't even enticing, and tomorrow will never come. It is easy for her to take what we consider risks because she has no stake in the future. And yet she is terrified of things you and I consider everyday stuff. She won't walk in the field across from Fiske because, "It got snakes in there!" She is not overly concerned if her fourteen-year-old daughter has a baby, but she "Don't want her takin' no trains alone all the way out here to Bedford." She'll give herself to anyone who pays the going rate, but she doesn't want to be seen in bra and pants, and she has a fit when she sees me in mine or in my bare feet.

Maggie is an acquisitive person. She sees little intrinsic worth in herself so she judges herself by the number and value of things she has. She is a disinterested student and an enthusiastic spender. Whatever money is in her commissary fund she spends as soon as she is allowed to. She knows the names of many perfumes, and likes to show others that she recognizes a particular scent. I have personally never known women so perfume conscious. The C.O.s share this interest. Flashy things give her pleasure for a moment, but she finds it difficult to relax and enjoy small, simple things, in many cases because she doesn't notice them. Her first reaction is often, "Why didn't I get more?" instead of "How good to have this much." I wonder sometimes if even gratitude is a luxury for the well-heeled, the financially relaxed. Homemade gives her little pleasure. She wants Bloomingdale's. To her, homemade says "I am poor." "Who needs it?" She lives on the margin of life, buying respectability, even stealing it, if it is the only way she can imagine achieving it.

Maggie's hatred of the state, "the system" is prodigious. It may be what feeds, clothes, and houses her, out of prison as well as in, but it never gives her enough. It makes her wait in long lines and say "Mother may I?" and "feel like a piece of shit" in the process, and she hates it. She hates it because it is there, and she has to go to it. She hates it because it is there, and it lets her go to it. It is a faceless monster on which to vent her rage.

One day in the high school equivalency class (GED), I saw a woman scribbling wildly on a brand new dictionary. Instinctively I said, "Oh Verona stop! That's a beautiful book. It's terrible to deface it." She looked directly into my eyes, and in short, clipped, tight-lipped words she said, "Dis book don't belong to you Miss Jean Harris. Dis book belong to da state and I can do any fuckin' thing I want to it." And she went on digging the pencil into it.

Consistency is not one of Maggie's strong points. She is acquisitive on the one hand and wasteful, even profligate, on the other. Three of the state blouses that I presently wear are ones I found, two in the garbage can, one tied in knots and thrown out a window into 114 Yard. I had picked it up thinking it would make a good rag for the hospital kitchen where I worked at the time, and where cleaning was a particular problem because there were never any dishcloths or dishrags. Opening it up I found a perfectly usable blouse, except the hem was out. Of the two in the garbage can, one also had a ragged hem, and the other was torn under the arm. I soaked them in disinfectant, mended them, and wore them. Many women here don't know how to thread a needle. And few staff members try to teach them. Sewing or mending doesn't occur to Maggie, or if it does her next thought is, "I don't know how. I can't."

Money is to spend, clothes are to wear until they are dirty and torn. Looking ahead, even to the extent of having a clean blouse to wear tomorrow, is something many of the women do not do. It is a skill which must be taught and learned, by rote or by everyday example. They were never taught. Not to throw garbage out of the windows is something else they have not been taught, outside of prison, or in. The yards here are littered with paper, orange peels, banana peels, paper cups, tin cans. When I commented to a staff member that in three years I had never heard a C.O. tell a woman not to throw garbage out of her window, or make her pick it up when she did, he said, "What's so bad about throwing garbage out the window? Where I grew up everybody does it."

Logic, at least what I grew up believing was logic, is not something one can fall back on in prison. To try to explain that beautiful is better than ugly, that a fresh green yard is better than the local dump is like telling them "Cleanliness is next to Godliness," and even I don't buy that anymore. That some people have pretty yards because they plant them, and till them and rake and weed and water and trim them, is not a fact to them. People have pretty yards because they are white and rich—and anyway "What good is flowers? You can't eat 'em."

Surprisingly, considering the lack of caring, supportive men in her life, Maggie is not a feminist, let alone the militant feminist one might expect. She clings to the myth of "happily ever after." She associates feminism, if she thinks about it at all, with white middle class, and since she is as racist as any whites I know that alone would settle feminism's hash. But she also associates feminism with man-hating, and however badly she has been treated by men, she doesn't hate them.

Her fondest wish is to find a good one to support her and her children. Poverty is the bogy man in her life. I spent a summer afternoon in the prison yard with four women who had been asked to read Ibsen's *A Doll's House* for a college English class they were unprepared for, but taking anyway. The story made no sense to them at all. Would I please explain it?

But no amount of explaining would convince them that Nora wasn't some kind of a nut to walk away from all that good stuff her husband had provided for her. So what if he called her "My little sparrow" and treated her like a brainless child, and put his own interests first? He didn't get drunk, or womanize, or smack her across the room. No one in her right mind would walk away from all that. "He could call me any fuckin' thing he want to as long as he payin' the bills." Darlene had the last word. "She musta been havin' her period. She be back in the morning." Others have probably suspected as much.

In her own way, "Maggie Strong" asks profound questions about life. Why do I live this way? What is justice? What is fair? How can I make it better for my children? She is not unaware of the moral inconsistencies in her own life and in the lives around her. And she responds to many of her trials with admirable courage and resilience. She wants to believe in something, preferably God, and praises Him highly, just in case there is one.

It is not unusual for her to tell you that she has had a "religious experience" in prison. "The hand of God have touched me, Jean. I feel the hand of God." How long the warmth of that touch lasts when she returns to the cold reality of life outside of prison, I have no way of knowing. I have gone to Bible classes with her from time to time, but I am not comfortable in them. They are too emotionally charged for me one minute, and I feel like a voyeur the next.

Some mothers in prison use religion as they use motherhood, as a smoke screen to help them get out. But then there are those in the upper middle classes who use religion and motherhood to make their way socially. Which use is the more reprehensible morally and ethically I leave for others to decide. There is no question that for many women here, religion is their answer to the meaning of life, their source of strength, their hope for years to come. Unlike them, I cannot lose myself in the rhythm and the words of their songs. I'm too busy being afraid I might cry.

Of all the great variety of qualities and characteristics that Maggie Strong has, there is only one the public knows or cares about. She is in prison, and that separates her from the rest of womankind in a way that nothing else can.

More than 500,000 people are in prison in America today, and many millions are in jail. Only 4 percent of those inmates are women. In New York State, where over 35,000 people are in prison, only 3.3 percent are women. When we remember that there are over seven million more women than men in this country the statistic is all the more striking. In fact, few statistics can point up the great differences between men and women more clearly. We can give them unisex haircuts, dress them in pants, even conceive their babies in petrie dishes, but men and women will remain very different breeds. They are biologically different, they experience the world in different ways, and they certainly experience prison differently.

Women come to prison with signs of physical injury more often than men do. They have misused their bodies in just about every conceivable way. I know a brand new mother whose arms look as though they have been through a meat grinder. "Oh, that's where I tried to kill myself when I was a kid," she shrugs. She is now nineteen. I have seen many scarred backs and faces, the results of battering by husband or lover. I have seen bodies terribly scarred by drugs, even missing an arm where the needle was dirty and no one treated the infection until it was too late. Maggie's health is especially poor for a young person. She has bad teeth, and ill-fitting false teeth. She is frequently the victim of asthma, drug abuse, alcoholism, seizures, hypertension, diabetes, heart disorders, gastro-intestinal disorders, and genito-urinary infections. Tuberculosis is beginning to be seen more frequently again. And of course, there is AIDS, how much we are never told.

Poverty, poor nutrition, prostitution, the stresses of raising kids with little or no money, lack of good obstetrical and gynecological care, have all taken their toll. Many have never been to a dentist. Routine Pap smears and breast examinations are foreign to them. The day I had the required gynecological exam when I first entered Bedford, I was waiting in line in the hallway when a young women, half dressed and clutching her state clothes to her breast came running frantically out of the doctor's office. "My Gawd! My Gawd! Son of a bitch touchin' me all over . . . feelin' my private parts . . . I'm gettin' outta here."

Being touched and examined for medical reasons was a whole new experience for her. She was used to being paid for sexual favors. To her, the doctor was just another damned member of the system, using her and trying to get something for nothing. Everybody else has used her. It was a reasonable, if slightly paranoid, conclusion to decide that he was too. The embarrassed doctor and the amused nurse never did get her back into the office while I was there.

Maggie has a predisposition toward impulsive, emotional behavior, with little patience to develop skills or the motivation to work toward goals. She is inclined to live in a fantasy world. She has had more education than the average male inmate, or at least more years of school, but she is still limited intellectually. It is difficult for her to think logically. She lives in a world of non sequiturs. There is a 30 to 35 percent chance that she suffers from a definite mental disorder. Sixteen percent of the women in Bedford's educational programs in 1981 had been hospitalized for psychiatric disorders.

That's the last time anyone counted and published the result that I know of. There is a high frequency of mental disorders in male prisons too, but women are at least three times more likely to be given large doses of psychotropic drugs once they enter prison.

Women express their anger and frustration less physically than men do, but their tongues never stop. Using obscenities is against the rule at Bedford, but little or nothing is done to enforce the rule. To do so might be a constructive first step toward rehabilitation, but it's easier to "let 'em yell." There is little effort made to encourage or require the women to "be a little nicer," which, fatuous as it may sound, is probably the most and best that we can expect of anyone.

Women fight institutionalism and those who inflict it upon them, more consistently than men do. The chance that a C.O. will be attacked in a women's prison is slight compared with its happening in a men's prison, but the chance that a C.O. will be insulted daily in the most obscene possible way is far greater in a women's prison. A majority of C.O.s that I know would prefer to take their chances with ice picks and handmade knives in Attica than with the daily noise and turmoil and trauma of Bedford. There are days when I would agree.

Maggie's need for a family becomes apparent in prison. She and the other women in prison quickly adopt inmate cultures that imitate family patterns. It's a kind of role playing. There are power plays in a women's prison too, but it is my observation that they are more noise than substance. If a woman wants to run all the politically oriented committees in this facility she can do it almost by default. Sad to say, most women aren't interested. They want a small place somewhere to feel accepted and safe. Every floor, indeed every corridor here, has at least one "family unit" with a "Mommy" at its center. One hears someone calling "Mommy" here all day long.

Perhaps the make-believe family is a response to prison deprivation, or perhaps it's something they lacked outside as well. Psychologists don't agree on the reasons, but they acknowledge the prevalence of the phenomenon. And "Mommy" is not a name that a woman can give herself, or that is lightly bestowed. There has to be an unspoken, intuitive consensus. "Mommy" is not necessarily older than the others, or even softer and quieter in manner. In fact, she is often self-centered and demanding. But she is special to the others in some way, and she commands their respect. She cooks for her group, when the small stove units on each floor are working, and can produce a full course meal under the most impossible conditions.

Her strong right arm, or one of her "family," make very sure her pots sit on the burners first. Rice is the main course, "black rice" with octopus meat is very popular. When nothing else works she can produce toasted cheese sandwiches on the ironing board with the help of the iron. Whatever the menu, five or six women share it with her. "Mommy" cooks, but she doesn't lift heavy things or do heavy cleaning. I have seen some of the most unlikely inmates, women who themselves have three or four children, get up and run errands for "Mommy!"

Obviously, homosexuality also is a fact of prison life for women as well as men. But, in a female prison, it can be a touchy subject. I had a next-cell neighbor who came complete with mustache and beard (her daughter born of a raping died at the age of six). Her family had wanted a boy and fed her hormones from the time she was an infant. She was an intelligent, articulate woman, "Light, bright and almost white," as she described herself. She made no bones about what her "affectional preferences" were. The women shunned her. Most, not all of them want their homosexuality a little more subtle than that.

I have no statistics on the subject to offer, and neither, as far as I know does anyone else. This much I'm pretty sure of. The "affectional preference" of the majority of women in prison is a man. If they are sloppy and casual about their sex lives, and they are, it's because that's the way they have been brought up and because they are trapped in an untolerable position at the height of their sexual drive. Sex, they have been told, is about all they're good for, and by now they're pretty well convinced. They will go back to a man as soon as they can. Until then, except for an occasional C.O. or a conjugal visit, which most of them can't avail themselves of because they didn't "conjugate" before prison, another woman is the best they have. They hate knowing they have lived their lives "being used" but when nothing else is possible, they use one another. For some, homosexuality is a biological fact. For most it is simply one more indication of the unspeakable loneliness and emptiness of their lives.

3.

The first question most people ask me as they look around the visiting room and point to a particular woman is "What did she do?" It's important, but it's a question I never ask. Sooner or later it comes out in conversation, in a moment of regret, in a moment of bravado, in a moment of seeking my help to write a letter to a lawyer or a judge. That I describe Maggie's life should not for a moment suggest that I think a rotten childhood and horrendous family life is reason to forgive one all her trespasses. Quite the contrary.

I would be far more demanding of these young women if I were their keeper. I would expect far more of them than the behavior many of them presently produce. They would all be learning, to the best of their ability, to read, write, and speak the English language, and to support themselves at an honest trade when they leave here.

And they would be out on work release far sooner than they presently are, earning their keep. Alas, the public punishes them by helping them to perpetuate the qualities that sent them here in the first place. While some outsiders believe, "Why the hell should they get a job? My cousin can't find a job and he didn't commit a crime," many inmates are happy to encourage the same kind of thinking. I've heard them say, "They put me here. It's their job to take care of me. Long as I'm here I ain't liftin' nothin' heavier than a spoon." As Della said recently, "The state suppose to be takin' care a me, and the state doin' a shabby ass job of it."

Some of the women at Bedford were living responsible lives before they came here. Many were not. But whatever went before, most of the people who go to jail are guilty of breaking some law. Contrary to popular myth you don't find the halls ringing with cries of "I was framed." I've heard more say, "I was lucky. I coulda gotten twenty-five to life." What they did is rarely what they go to prison for.

Approximately 95 percent of the men and women in New York State prisons plea bargained. People plea bargain as a rule, to get less punishment than they think they will get if they go to trial, and are found guilty of the crime they actually committed. For those who know the ropes, it's usually a good deal. The Harris rule of thumb, based upon the women I know personally, is, those who went to trial are serving the longest sentences, even though it is often the innocent who insist upon a trial.

Judges and district attorneys, by determining what plea bargain compromise they will accept, are essentially the jury in most cases. Defendants, in accepting a lesser punishment, voluntarily waive their right to stand trial. This also obviates the need for appeals, and saves everyone time and money—at least in the short run. Unfortunately, the only way we can think of to make it better for those who don't go to trial is to make it worse for those who do go to trial.

Trials are often presented to defendants as a threat rather than a constitutional right. I know three women who were offered probation if they would plea bargain, but insisted on their innocence and a trial. They were found guilty and sentenced to fifteen years to life. That doesn't make any sense at all, but it happens.

The average stay in Bedford is two years and seven months. Because the sentences for homicide and murder are usually the longest, almost 40 percent of the women here at a particular time are here for homicide. Statistics from a prison change constantly as the inmates change constantly. These figures from Judy Grossman, then Program Research Specialist for the New York Department of Corrections, give a quick picture of the crimes for which the 345 women sent to Bedford in 1982 were convicted.

OFFENSE	Number	Percent
Murder	9	3
Manslaughter	45	13
Robbery	74	21
Assault	22	6
Burglary	15	4
Grand larceny, non-auto	39	11
Forgery	31	9
Drugs	57	17
Weapons	13	4
All other felonies	38	11
Youthful offender	2	1
	345	100

PRIORS	Number	Percent
None	83	24
Prior arrest	42	12
Prior conviction	61	18
Prior commitment	159	46
	345	100

In a second report of Grossman's "Comparison of Male and Female Inmates Under the Department's Custody as of June 1, 1983," men made up 97.2 percent of all those incarcerated in New York State prisons, and women made up 2.8 percent. Men are younger when they are committed, over 21 percent were under twenty-one, while 11 percent of the women were under twenty-one. A slightly larger percentage of men than women had graduated from high school, though this figure varies from year to year. A larger percentage of males dropped out in elementary school than women. More women began to drop out when they reached puberty. A larger percentage of men (35.1 percent) were committed for robbery than women (20.3 percent), but a larger percentage of women (15 percent) were in for drugs than men (9.3 percent). There was a slight difference in the percentage of men that had been convicted of murder (11.2) than women (10.5 percent), but 8.3 percent of the men had been convicted of homicide and 19.4 percent of the women. Of the men in prison for murder, 18 percent had no prior arrest record. Of the women in prison for homicide, 51 percent had no prior arrest record.

OFFENSE	Male Percent	Female Percent
Murder	11.2	10.5
Homicide	8.3	19.4
Robbery	35.1	20.3
Burglary	13.3	4.2
Assault	3.6	6.9
Grand larceny, non-auto	1.4	4.0
Sex offense	6.5	.4
Drugs	9.3	15.0
Forgery	.8	6.6
Weapons	4.3	2.5
All other felonies	3.4	6.3

There are many theories and perceptions about why people commit crimes. I've heard everything from "He stole my shit," to "My kid was hungry." The notion that prisons are filled with "bad seed" has a certain popularity again in some circles. I personally believe there is no such thing, only damaged seed.

Every woman here who did whatever she did, had a reason for doing it. Sometimes it was irrational and unplanned, sometimes it was premeditated. Whichever was the case, I believe, in more cases than not, she was strongly influenced, directly or indirectly by economic considerations. She may have been hungry or frantic or angry or frustrated or just plain greedy, but money touched the offense in some way. The fact that prisons are, and have always been, filled with the poor instead of the rich is not simply a great cosmic coincidence.

The general public likes to believe that crime is a cultural thing, something those rotten people up in Harlem do. The fact is there is far more white collar crime than street crime, at least in dollar value stolen.

The American system of economics urges people to want, more than it urges them to work. "Childhood," as David Reisman once remarked, "is now a time in which one is a consumer trainee." Unfortunately, Maggie and her kids go through the same training program as the children on Manhattan's Upper East Side. And you can't have it both ways. If you need people to "want," you have to figure out how they can "get." Some people settle for socially unacceptable ways. I have heard Daniel Bell discuss the very basic contradictions of capitalism which requires the discipline of highly trained technicians to produce its wares, and a large, self-indulgent group of consumers to use them. Unfortunately, we have a larger group of the latter than the former.

Wassily Leontief won the Nobel Prize in economics essentially because he has explained to those who will listen how interconnected our lives are. There can't be a plan for the rich, and a plan for the poor, and a plan for the middle class, each an entity unto itself. We are all interconnected. What each of us does affects a stranger. I think of my favorite line from Loren Eiseley's *The Immense Journey*, "one could not pluck a flower without troubling a star." The enormous, interlinked complexity of life is where I think we begin to fathom the causes of crime.

People often forget that the main victims of crime and violence are the same people who fill our prisons, the poor and minorities, black women more than any other group. According to sociologist Michael Harrington, "In the late seventies, black people were murdered in the United States at a rate eight times that of whites, raped 2½ times more frequently, robbed three times more than whites, and suffered 1½ times more aggravated assault." The problem seems much worse to some of us today because street crime, like drugs, finally moved to the suburbs. Would we really care about it if crime were all just down in Harlem?

In the cases of homicide, the final tragedy is usually the culmination of years of family fighting, alcoholism, and drugs. I know one "hit" woman who killed for pay, but she is an aberration even in here. About 24 percent of all the women here are first offenders. Fifty-one

percent of women convicted of homicide are first offenders. According to a study made by Elaine Lord, superintendent of this facility,
long-termers are often noncriminal types, and their prison behavior is
significantly better than that of inmates serving less than five years.
Seventy percent of the homicide cases at Bedford were plea bargained, which accounts for the great discrepancies in sentences of
woman guilty of the same crime, anywhere from three years to
twenty-five years to life.

Felicia had a cell near mine for the first year that I was here. She
had killed her youngest child and served eighteen months. She returned home and killed her second child, for which she was given
three years. She spent much of her time knitting sweaters and making
little things for the children she had killed. She was not in the mental
ward, nor was she treated in any special way. A longer prison term
was not the answer, but certainly more intelligent medical and psychiatric treatment might have saved the second child. It might even have
saved the first. There are women here for killing children they had in
their care as foster mothers too, fairly convincing proof that foster
parents are not always well screened.

It's also an indication that prisons have become our mental hospitals. Dora told me last Saturday night in a very matter of fact way,
"They're just mad at me because I killed my three children and
dismembered the two-year-old." She had approached me to find out
why she isn't being permitted to work in the Children's Center.

There are so many who come to prison because they are mentally
incompetent to take care of themselves outside, and nobody and no
agency knows what to do with them. In 1965 there were more than
85,000 people in mental institutions in the state of New York. Today
that number is 23,000. The effectiveness of Thorazine over the years
convinced people in high places that we could safely release many
people who had been held for many years in "asylums." It was considered a kindness, and so it was for some, but the release from large
institutions was meant to be accompanied by the establishment of
small community centers where those same people could go for support and medical help. Few communities wanted them, and the
promises of the 1960s were not kept. Today many of those people, or
people like them who would once have been institutionalized, now
wander the streets and sleep in doorways, and end up in prison. Their

frustrations are beyond anything I can imagine. As one of the ladies tried to explain to me, "That ain't what I'm sayin'. You don't know what I'm sayin'. You don't know shit about it. That ain't what I didn't do wrong. Ahm facin' the wall with my back to it."

I keep thinking of Ringo, big, fat, jolly, dangerous Ringo. I'm not sure when she earned the nickname, but we'll say her given name is Annette. She came to prison originally with a short sentence for a minor felony. As the pressures of prison closed in upon her, she repeatedly attacked the C.O.s and gradually managed to more than double her original sentence. This is not too unusual. Here again the public pictures everyone getting out early. I know four women, without even asking around, who doubled or more than doubled their original sentence after they came to prison. Not everyone can relax and roll over in a cage.

I knew Ringo for almost four years, and even a casual observer could see the deterioration in her in the course of those years. I have heard her shriek for hours, wild, senseless obscenities. I have seen her spit at people passing her cell, and throw containers of urine at them. I have seen her throw an iron at a woman's head, and seem disappointed when it didn't connect, and puzzled why anyone would make a fuss about it. "Shit, it weren't even hot." Finally all of the other fifty-nine members of floor 114A and B, myself included, signed a petition to the superintendent asking that for safety's sake, our own and hers as well, she be removed from regular population.

That same night, at dinner, a woman who is just about as mentally stable as Ringo approached me as I stood in the food line. "Ya know my friend Ringo can end up at Marcy State now (for the criminally insane). If she ends up in Marcy you gonna be dead. You just say somebody ain't right in the head around here, you gonna be dead. I will personally see you are dead. Just tell me right now where you want the body sent." She repeated the threat on several occasions, always within the hearing of at least one C.O., and once two C.O.s. They didn't bat an eyelash, and neither did I. The few ladies who seemed interested in giving it a try soon learned that death threats were no threat to me at all. They soon stopped.

When it was time to take her to Marcy, and she went back and forth many times, it took three big men to get Ringo into the back of the police car, even when she was handcuffed and chained hand and foot.

I saw it. She became a super strong, battling human animal. At times, when she grew better, she came back up to the floor. She was proud of the accomplishment and sure that she was now on the right road. I think of all the sad moments I have witnessed in this terrible place, nothing matches the poignancy of an afternoon with Ringo and Mabel. Mabel is here for arson, and she too has good days and bad, good months and bad. She had set her cell on fire for the third time that morning and six C.O.s had been called to take her to Satellite, where the most serious mentally ill are kept and watched. Ringo grabbed her around the waist and refused to let go. "Don't take her. Don't take her," she screamed. "I'll watch her. I'll take care of her. Look at me. I made it. She can make it too. She'll be all right." She had to be pried away from Mabel. A few weeks later Ringo had cracked up again too, and joined Mabel over in Satellite.

In time Ringo maxed out—that is she had served her maximum sentence, and all the extra time as well, and she was let go. She was up at Marcy at the time and was released from there, ostensibly to a mental institution in the Bronx. But it wasn't prison anymore, and apparently she was able to walk away with little or no trouble. A few months after she had left, I turned on the TV to hear the morning news. "Annette Seaman, twenty-seven-year-old bag woman, is being sought for the stabbing of a woman in a Penn Station washroom." She had turned in her cage for the floor of Penn Station, and the pressures of life had closed in. The innocent victim of the stabbing will live, but she has suffered. Ringo had even been heard to threaten to commit a new crime so "I can go back to Bedford. That's the place they treat me best." When we begin to fear that life in prison is better than life outside of prison, the important response is not to make prisons worse, but to make life outside better. Ringo is back at Bedford now. Before she arrived she had already broken a C.O.'s nose at Riker's. I don't like this big, confused woman. I don't want to share living quarters with her again. I don't want to listen to her obscenities. But I believe she is as much a victim of something as the woman in the washroom at Penn Station.

Drug crimes, which millions of Americans commit every day, give birth to some of the most appalling cases of injustice in this prison, probably in others as well. Sharmaine was arrested for selling thirteen ounces of cocaine, a crime she admits to. She plea bargained and served three years before going out on work release. Rita was a maid in a New York whorehouse. Twice the madame gave her a package and asked her to give it to "the men in the car out front." Twice she did it and twice the men gave her a $10 tip. The men in the car were agents. Rita, a woman who speaks almost no English, was arrested and offered one to three if she would "take a plea." She refused, went to trial and was found guilty on both counts, and was sentenced to fifteen to life on *each* count, the terms to be served *consecutively*, not concurrently, thirty years to life for a woman who neither used, bought, or sold drugs. She lost her two appeals, was able to get the sentences down to "concurrently," and then, after serving almost five years, with the help of friends, not lawyers, she was finally granted clemency.

Aida came from Colombia "on a business trip" with her husband. She had never been to the United States before. They were both arrested at the airport. Her husband was tried and convicted as a drug dealer and given fifteen to life. Aida was offered five years probation and exportation to Colombia, her home and her children's and grand-children's home. The only problem was Aida spoke no English, and didn't know until almost three years after her trial that she had been offered probation. She is here for fifteen to life. There is no more concern for the public's welfare in many of these cases than there is for the inmates'. While the public rails against the choices of who shall and shall not be returned to society by parole boards, their disgust cannot possibly match that of inmates who watch the revolving door from the inside, and who can usually call every case that will soon be returned to prison.

Women who steal are motivated by many things. Economic pressure obviously plays a lead role, whether the money is needed to pay doctors, support a drug habit, or feed the children, one doesn't always know. Some women steal strictly to satisfy their acquisitive urges. "Yeah, Jean, I'll get a job. I can always get a job, but I'll never make enough money to buy the things I want. I like pretty clothes and a big car. Sooner or later I'll be passin' bad checks again." I know two women in here with sons in Ivy League colleges who paid those bills writing bad checks to others. I said to one of them, "Are your children angry with you because of what you've done?" She looked me right in the eye and said, "My kids have known all their lives I been out hustlin' for them."

I know Annie too, who was given two years in a top security prison for lying about a $167.00 welfare check. She was offered one to three if she would plea bargain. Sister Elaine said to her, "Oh Annie, why didn't you take the plea?" and Annie said, "Because I didn't cash that check, Sister. I think my cousin done, but I ain't sure." She left three young children outside with her mother, and had a fourth baby while she was in here. Her mother and the baby died just weeks before Annie was to be released. Sister tried every possible way to get her released a few weeks early, but society wanted its full pound of flesh, and for that pound it spent close to $80,000 to punish a woman for lying about a $167.00 check—which I personally don't think she signed.

And then there's also Sandy. She was expressing her contempt for another woman who apparently was not treating her with the deference she considered her due. "That girl ain't nothin'. She shit. I see a cockroach. I step on it. She see one, she just live with it. My family own property. My daddy own his own home. He drive a big car." And then, drawing herself up to her full height, she added proudly, "My family and me is criminals by choice!" I don't think there are many woman quite like her here but she's real, she's in the chips, and her sentence isn't a long one. For her, prison is simply a calculated business risk, one she has studied closely.

It is sad to see the obvious pride of accomplishment that some of the women feel about their various underground talents. The fact that they get caught seems to take none of the satisfaction and glamour away. One of the young women, Shotsie, I came to know rather well. She was a full-blooded Apache Indian, born on Prince Edward Island. Her parents died when she was young, and she spent the next ten years of her life being passed from foster homes to institutions.

She decided after we had worked together in west wing kitchen one day, "I wish you'd been my mother," and started calling me "Ma." She has batted around from pillar to post, with only a sister as family, and no one caring enough about her to say "No" and mean it. Now she can't cope with "No." She's in here this time for not reporting to her parole officer. Many women come back for that reason, or some other parole violation.

You ask them, "Why?" and there's a pause and then they say lamely, "I don't like no one tellin' me what to do." Every move they make in prison someone is telling them what to do, but they manage to forget this when they're outside. Some of them commit a crime, are given a suspended sentence, and then go to prison two or three times for not reporting to their probation officer. They constantly spite themselves. Alfa Mae came here with a three-year sentence and so far has served eight years for attacking the guards and breaking parole.

Shotsie came to me one day looking very sad because she had just been told that if she weren't out of prison by September her three very cute children, ages one, two, and three, would be put up for adoption. They were then in foster homes, much loved by families that wanted to adopt them. We talked about the children for a while. I asked her how she could support them when she got out, and what would be best for the children. Her face lit up when we talked about money. "You know what I did outside, Ma? I robbed hotel rooms. And I'm good at it too. You wouldn't believe the money I made.

"I had almost $15,000 in the bank when they busted me. My partner didn't get caught because he wasn't with me on my last job. He said it wasn't planned good enough and he was right. I was tryin' to keep the $15,000 and get enough money to get bail for my sister. It's not so easy doin' what I do. It's a nine-to-five job and I practiced picking locks for a long time before I really got in the business.

"My sister taught me everything I know, so I owed her the bail. We'd rent a room in a fancy hotel, wait until people went downstairs, and be in and out before they got back. We'd stay more than a month in one place, and clean it out. We even reported we was robbed too."

Pointing out to her that if she is good at picking locks she might also be very good at repairing watches, or working with computers made little impression. She left and came back twice that I know of. The last time she told me she had given up the children and all three were well adopted. There will undoubtedly be more picked locks, more children, more prison.

Miriam claims she is the best female jewel thief in the state of New York and would have spent "A lot more time in prison if my father hadn't bought off a couple DAs." Tested at the age of five, both of these women would probably have shown high IQs. Now all the brightness is wasted and counter-productive. And they aren't ashamed, only temporarily inconvenienced. Money is what they want, and lots of it, fast. They don't see any viable alternatives. A young mother, twenty-two, said to me one day, "I know it would be good to go straight for the baby, but Jean, I was out there livin' on $100,000 a year. How'm I gonna go out and live on the ten or twelve thousand a year I could make honestly?" She has created for herself what she considers an impossible problem to solve. Easy money whether from welfare checks or the drug trade is certainly the root of much evil. How do you stop and go back to "the right stuff"?

There is still another reason that some go to prison, though how prevalent it is no one can know. Taking a poll or slipping a question-naire under the cell door would serve no purpose. I know of only two cases. For the payment to her of a large sum of money, Angela "took the fall." The guilty person would have gotten life. Her record was clean, she confessed to a drug crime, took a plea and was sentenced to "three to five." In return, she was given a comfortable home far from New York, money for her two children's school and college, and a guaranteed income for herself. "That may sound good to you," I told her, "but what if you don't get it?" "I already have it," she answered. "It was all in my name before I spent my first night in prison. They kept their promises. I kept mine."

There was a time when the rich could pay others to go to war for them; it stands to reason there are those who will pay others to go to prison for them. The quantity of drug money available for the purpose is so vast, so obscene, it wouldn't be at all painful to "make 'em an offer they couldn't refuse." "Hell, they don't count their money. They weigh it." For their own safety, Angela's children will never know the truth, but they were well provided for while she was here, and were brought to see her frequently. I can't believe mother will live happily ever after for long, but then, she knows who she is doing business with, I don't.

Of all the hundreds of statistics that I have read about women and why they go to prison, I believe the most striking comes from the General Accounting Office of the United States Government, in a publication entitled, "Female Offenders: Who They Are and What Are the Problems Confronting Them?" published August 1979.

Studies have shown that most women enter prostitution for pressing eco-nomic reasons and see it as a viable alternative to scraping by on welfare or poverty level wages. It also tends to be self-reinforcing. Once the woman has a prostitution conviction on her record it becomes more difficult for her to get another job. In addition, bail demands are often so high that the prostitute must get money from her pimp to get her freedom. Consequently recidivism is high.

The woman incarcerated for prostitution suffers more serious consequences than a record. She generally acquires other criminal skills during her confinement. Though most prostitutes spend little time in prison for prostitution, they spend a lot of time in jail. Over thirty percent of the inmates in most women's jails are convicted prostitutes, and they serve longer sentences than other misdemeanants. *For these women, long jail terms become schools for crime; seven out of every ten women in prison for committing a felony were first arrested for prostitution."* (italics mine)

According to statistics published by the United States government, 70 percent of the women in prison for committing a felony were first arrested for prostitution! And yet, knowing that, absolutely nothing is done for her on that first arrest to help preclude the next. She is thrown into a paddy wagon, jeered at, encouraged to be obscene, and given the choice of jail or a fine. Moreover, in New York State prostitutes have lost the right of trial by jury, though conviction for prostitution can cause deportation, summary divorce or loss of child custody. The fine is usually determined by what the traffic will bear, and the police are very savvy about who can afford what. "They should know! They're some of our best customers." The woman pays the money and goes back on the street with a little more of the problem that started her on prostitution in the first place. When she finally commits the felony, suddenly out of nowhere, thousands of dollars in taxpayers' money will be made available to incarcerate her for a year at least. Until then it's strictly a waiting game, since the police know she will turn around and go right back to plying her trade. She is essentially paying the police for the privilege of selling herself. How a system could do less than this to prevent and control crime I truly do not know.

What I do know are many women who started on the road to this place from a street corner in New York City.

"But I never brought the men home! I had a room somewhere else, and the lady downstairs took care a the kids real good when I couldn't be there."

"I keep thinking if only someone at welfare had understood how much I needed help, all this wouldn't have happened. For four years I supported my daughter and me bein' a prostitute. I got arrested seventeen times for loitering during those four years. And I hated the whole deal. I made up my mind I was gonna quit and find another way, but I needed some help. I went and applied for welfare, but they said I'd been workin' steady for four years, no reason I couldn't go on workin'. I applied for a welfare hearing and while they were thinkin' about it a trick got rough an' I killed him. It didn't have to happen. I didn't want it to happen. It just did."

"The police said to me, 'Most girls who works the streets don't take care a your children.' It ain't true. That's one reason we on the street."

4.

How do you pass the time in prison? Options are few, especially in a women's prison. You must keep your eyes and ears open for whatever opportunities may come up. The soap, clothes, furniture, and much of the baked goods used at Bedford are made by incarcerated men. At Bedford we do the laundry for one of the male prisons, nothing more. Here, a woman can clean hallways, lobbies, kitchens, classrooms, toilets and rec rooms, do some cooking in the staff kitchen, take arts and crafts, IBM data processing, electronics, baby-sit with infants in the nursery, go to educational courses starting with Adult Basic Education through what is called college, or go to various self-help courses like Alcoholics Anonymous, Narcotics Anonymous, Down on Violence, Money Addiction, Reality House.

The list doesn't sound too bad, but you must remember that each group is limited in number. Seventy percent of the state's prison population, about 24,000 people, have had a history of drug and/or alcohol abuse, and the Department of Corrections treatment programs can accommodate only two thousand inmates.

Here at Bedford there are high levels of teacher absenteeism in some courses, for whatever reasons, and substitutes don't exist. Obviously, improving one's level of education is an essential first step, but the GED itself, or even a sociology degree from Mercy College, may not open many doors for these women. Reading, writing, and the true discipline of learning get short shrift. The most useful program is the inmate maintenance program. In it a woman can learn something about plumbing, electrical work, bricklaying, virtually all the building skills. They learn by doing, but only fifteen women at a time can avail themselves of it, and there are almost six hundred women here.

There is an electronics course which I am told is a pretty good course when it meets, but many days it doesn't meet. And women are not permitted to put most of what they learn into practice. At Bedford, any inmate possession that needs fixing, like a lamp, hot pot, radio or TV, must be sent out to be fixed, and paid for by women who haven't any money, and who would profit by learning how to fix things themselves.

The rationale behind this obviously satisfies the people who call the plays. It doesn't make any sense to me. There are about five sewing machines in various parts of the facility, some broken, all jealously guarded. For some mysterious reason, sewing machines make "security" very nervous. I was standing next to Phyllis Currey, the then superintendent when I first arrived here, when a group of us asked if we could get some material and make slipcovers for the miserable chairs and sofas in the "honor floor" rec room. She said, "I think it's better if we have it done professionally."

Not only are the number of useful things a prisoner may do limited, the time in which she is permitted to do them is limited still further. She is often physically, forcefully, deliberately not permitted to be on time. She stands in line to get through the door to get in line for the next door, in order to get in line to be fed and to get medication. She stands in line to sign into the clinic and to sign out of the clinic in order to get into the line to the nurse, which will get her into the line to see the doctor—not all in one day, but sometime in the future, at which time she will go through the whole thing all over again.

The only time she can go to the commissary is during the work day. She cannot shop early in the morning, or during lunch or dinner break, or in the evening. She must miss work if she wishes to shop, usually half a day of work. And since she can only shop once every two weeks, at an assigned time, she has no control over what day of work she misses.

There are some C.O.s who will only open a door on the hour and half hour, and since every clock in the facility says a different time, she can often wait for half an hour while she is hurrying to work, until the C.O.'s clock says "go" again. When this happens she doesn't just stop where she is and wait. She must go back to her floor and repeat the whole process again. Unfortunately, for many women this modus operandi is quite satisfactory. If they get to work an hour late, because breakfast is an hour late, or the count is an hour late, or just about anything is an hour late, they get paid anyway—nickels and dimes, but the same amount they would have been paid for working. The message they get is simple, "Work is just another way to kill time . . . it don't mean nothin'."

Before I was moved to Fiske honor cottage, a housing unit the existence of which I thank God for on my knees every day, it was not unusual for me to stop as many as seventy-five times during the day to wait at a locked door. On Fridays it could be as high as ninety, since Friday evenings I go to Bedford Annex to play Bingo with the ladies there, and that has some extra doors. Here was my door schedule:

Doors to meals, 6 and return	18
Doors to work, 7 and return	14 A.M.
	14 P.M.
Doors to medication and return	8
Doors to a visit and return	14
Doors to commissary and return	6
Doors to volunteer work in the annex	<u>16</u>
	90 doors

In prison one works in the moments one can snatch from the system. It suddenly seems easy to understand why prison industries lose money.

I have worked at a number of different positions in here, with varying degrees of success. As soon as an inmate has been checked by doctors and "medically cleared," she is assigned to eight weeks of maintenance work. After that she can, if she wishes, classify into other activities.

I did my first maintenance work in the hospital kitchen. This involved dishing out food, taking it around to patients, and then cleaning the kitchen. The best thing about it for me was that I had to go from one building to another to get to the kitchen, so I got a little exercise and fresh air. For the first two months that I was here I was allowed in the yard twice. Neither inmates nor C.O.s here are fresh-air enthusiasts.

There is a twelve-foot barbed fence around the tiny yard, with rows of razors on top, but we couldn't go out unless a C.O. stood and watched us and the C.O. usually didn't want to go out. Two times I devised outdoor work for myself, raking and washing windows, and earned a fresh-air bonus. Today women are allowed out in the same yard without a C.O. What's "secure" and what is not "secure" changes constantly.

A fellow inmate and I measured the tiles on the floor and figured out that thirty-six lengths of our corridor equaled a mile. We walked back and forth constantly, whenever we weren't locked in our cells, and averaged about four miles a day. A few women joined us from time to time, but soon tired and dropped out. Most of them thought we were a little crazy. The C.O.s couldn't quite decide whether they should forbid us or encourage us. As long as my friend was here I exercised regularly. She challenged and goaded and shamed me into it. After she left I grew lazy.

The inside as well as the outside rules have changed now. Today you can only walk one-half the length of the corridor so a mile is seventy-two miserable lengths. "Security" is the great prison dumping ground. Whatever you do in here, wise or asinine, is always in the name of "security." Last year you could get home-cooked chicken through the package room, but you couldn't have corn on the cob. This year you can have corn on the cob, but you can't have home-cooked chicken.

Last year you could wear your own sweaters in the visiting room, but you couldn't wear your own blouses. Then you couldn't wear anything but prison issue. Now you can wear your own shirts and sweaters, but the sweaters can only be a solid color. Two years ago the state issue was in yellow, blue, and green. This year blue is contraband, and yellow is all right for your own clothes, but not for state issue. I was summarily removed from graduation exercises one year, by a lieutenant, because I was wearing a yellow state-issue jumper. I was made to turn it in to the state store the next day. Yellow state issue was permitted the rest of the inmates for the next year, but not for me.

Two years ago I could not get plain, button down collar shirts through the package room "Because they button on the wrong side. They is men's shirts, can't have men's shirts," even though the label read Saks and the size and the cut made them obviously women's shirts. This year our winter coats were taken from us and replaced with men's winter jackets, obviously cut for men with small waists and very wide shoulders. All in the name of "security." Because C.O. uniforms are blue, almost a black blue, and their raincoats, when they have one, are orange, inmates are not allowed to have anything blue, black, or orange. Makes sense.

The only trouble is they don't teach the C.O.s what is blue, black, or orange. Some of them call anything that isn't dark green "Blue, black, or orange." And by God if they say it's orange, it's orange. Even babies in the nursery are not allowed to have blue booties or a blue bonnet. A scarf with a blue flower in it is "blue." And yet this winter, when I asked for a blanket, I was given a blue one, blue as the C.O.'s shirt.

For the first four years that I was here we were not issued any rain gear by the state, and almost anything that your family sent you in the way of rain gear was contraband. You were allowed only a jacket length, plastic, colorless, see-through raincoat, without a hood. Since all rain gear of that sort comes with a hood you could only keep the jacket if you cut off the hood. Since this is all a matter of security, for reasons that defy all common sense the good people of Westchester were considered safer if the women of Bedford spent rainy days soaked to the skin from the knees down and the neck up.

Since they didn't give us rain gear we were allowed to wear big black plastic garbage bags instead. Thus disguised, no one could see who you were and you couldn't see where you were going. Since the C.O.s themselves often don't have a raincoat, (many of them, I'm told, are stolen when C.O.s are transferred to other facilities) you sometimes found, and still find, C.O.s also covered in big black plastic garbage bags. This apparently passes muster as "security"—inmates and C.O.s alike splashing around in black garbage bags.

The amount of money wasted on these bags costs many times more than the flimsy little ponchos we have finally after four years been issued. They have a hood. Why the hood on a colorless jacket is any more threatening to society than the hood on a khaki-colored poncho no one has yet explained. It is not difficult to understand why rules are soon sneered at in here. They are contradictory; they are foolish, the people asked to enforce them think they are foolish too, and half the people in here don't even know what most of them are. There are literally thousands of xeroxed copies of rules on top of rules on top of rules. They teach contempt for authority, a lesson many of the women have already learned too well.

About six months ago inmates at Bedford were told to turn in all their metal hangers and get plastic ones. One can see the sense in that and only wonder why we had metal ones for as long as we did. We asked family and friends to bring us plastic hangers and this they did. As of June 30 of this year plastic hangers were listed as "contraband" and anyone found with a round plastic hanger would be issued a charge sheet.

The flimsy, flat hangers on which the state blouses are delivered were okay. It takes three of them to hold a bathrobe or jacket, and they snap and break with little more than a touch. When they break they usually break in three pieces, leaving jagged edges on all three pieces, each a potential weapon. These are okay. But a heavy, round, safe, plastic hanger is now *verboten* for reasons of "security." There are many rumors as to why, but we will never be told the real reason, because prisons don't explain. They just make rules.

I have been told that someone brought in round plastic hangers that were hollow, and in which drugs could be hidden. I was told someone had carved the plastic into a dangerous instrument of some kind. If one person does it, thirty-five thousand inmates take the fall. Whatever the reason, the rule temporarily left 600 women with clothes all over the place and no logical place to put them.

It would be a full-time job to keep abreast of the daily rules here. A Kiplinger letter would be an interesting idea for some clever and creative inmate. Sister Elaine Roulet, a Catholic nun who had been on the staff at Bedford for fifteen years, says her last prayer of the day is: "Please God let me forget all of today's rules, so I'll be ready to learn the new ones tomorrow."

A total lack of consistency and judgment is known to play a role in mental illness. There is no way it could not. I have finally come to terms with this by simply not caring what I am allowed to have and what I am not allowed to have. As long as I am permitted to stay at Fiske, and to read and to write, away from the worst of the obscenities, away from some of the constant C.O. harassment, I don't care what else I am allowed to have, what clothes, what food, or what creature comforts. When we were told that we could now wear our own sweaters again (I had given most of mine away to an inmate's daughter when they said we couldn't) I made two new ones for myself. One is a rose colored one into which I knit my initials. Less than two months after it was finished we were told, starting April 1, that any sweater or blouse with a monogram on it would be contraband.

No JSH, not even a J. I suppose 81 G 98 would be okay, but that didn't occur to me until just now. I sent the monogrammed sweater home—wherever that is—and made myself a new one. It is all one color and it doesn't have a monogram. But I have knit into it the Latin words "*Experta credite Illegitimati non carborundum.*" "Take it from one who knows. Don't let the bastards grind you down."

Many of the people who sign up to work in the hospital kitchen, in any prison kitchen for that matter, do so because it is an easy place to steal food. I don't think the patients at Bedford have had much butter on their bread for years. They didn't while I was observing. As soon as food was delivered, the kitchen crew descended upon it like a bunch of Harpies, and suddenly the butter, sugar, tea, meat, and fresh fruit had all but disappeared, into pockets, bags, pants, wherever.

The women on special diets had a treat one night: steaks. Eleven of them were delivered to the kitchen and never seen again. Someone blew the whistle while we were all still in the kitchen, and an official search began. No one was punished because everyone denied taking them, and the steaks were never found. I'm told they were stuffed into the bottom of a garbage bag, and retrieved later. How they tasted I never heard.

Perhaps it is the waste of food here that encourages the women to be so cavalier about taking things. I have never seen such waste in my life. It simply would not be permitted in a private institution, but when the old reliable, not always vigilant taxpayer is paying, no one gives a damn. I have seen four dozen hard-boiled eggs tossed in the garbage, not in the main kitchen, but in the auxiliary kitchens which have no storage facilities: whole loaves of bread thrown out because somebody wanted the plastic bag they came in; cauldrons of cereal and vegetable and soup and cold meats and cheese thrown away.

One day in the hospital, a woman filled four large pitchers with milk, and then noticed that the menu read "iced tea." She poured the milk into the sink, at least two gallons of it, and mixed iced tea. I was particularly sensitive about that since it came at a time when I was literally begging for two three-ounce glasses of milk, and not getting it.

Once in the kitchen, after all the patients had been served, there were a lot of apples left over. I set aside three apples to take back to my cell. Since I didn't want anyone to see them and tell me I couldn't have them, and since I didn't have a bag, I tried wrapping them in my sweater. But every time I picked it up the apples slipped out. Finally one of the women said, "Here, let me show you how." She tied knots in each of the sleeves and slipped the apples down in them. Somehow I managed to drop the apples again. We started to laugh and one of them said, "Oh my gawd, nobody would believe this. Those news-paper people would sure make a headline of this, 'Jean Harris caught stealing apples.' "

A few days after the apple episode, we had finished serving dinner and one of the kitchen crew brought out a box of oranges.

"How come we have so many left?" I asked.

"Dumb mother-fucker—we didn't give 'em no oranges. We got a policy, if they don't ask, we don't give 'em. And ain't nobody asked."

Obviously, if they hadn't seen them they didn't ask for them. It was the people on special diets who were supposed to get the oranges, and the same was true of my ill-gotten apples. I felt as though I had just taken candy from a baby.

"That's a rotten way to do business," I said. "These women are sick."

"Oh my," one of them taunted, "you want to give 'em to the pa-tients? Shit. Well come and get 'em. Shit! You think you in one a your country clubs. Dumb bitch."

The confrontation was inevitable, but not very bright on my part. I spent the rest of the eight-week stint trying to hang on to my teeth.

Alfreda, the only friend I found in the kitchen, said to me later, "You gotta remember, Jean, some a these women never has it so good. They come off the street in rags. They don't own nothin' but what's on their backs. They got no money for things in the commissary. Stealin' is their way a livin'. Some of 'em comes in here on purpose. Ain't no better place to go." That didn't make them any more desirable com-pany as far as I was concerned. I graduated from the kitchen with no regrets.

5·

My first "regular" job was as a teacher's aide in the high school equivalency class. I had thought of working in the library until I discovered that it was not a library but simply a collection of old books, arranged at random on shelves, with no system, no card catalogue, no legitimate sign-out procedure. There were ninety-three copies of *Roots*, geography books that predated the Second World War, and hundreds of gothic novels. I didn't have the know-how, or the authority to change it, and I saw no value in it as it was. We have since acquired a new librarian, and after monumental effort on her part, and that of some of the inmates, it is indeed a library, growing better all the time.

The classroom I went to work in was a double room with anywhere from forty to forty-seven students in it, morning and afternoon, a different group each time. When I arrived, and for most of the time that I worked there, there was only one teacher for all subjects. There had been an English teacher previously, but for over a year the math teacher had taught alone. Students came and went constantly. They still do. Ethel is transferred to Albion; Charlene gets parole; Tootsie "max's out," Dawn's "in lock." Each student works at her own speed, in workbooks. Grammar, fractions, and percentages are the hardest subjects. Some go as far as beginning algebra. There are no reading assignments at all. Graduation comes when you get 225 on the GED graduation equivalency exam.

If a student has a question, she raises her hand, and the teacher goes over to her and answers the question. My function was that of a teacher's aide. The only reason I didn't collect the milk money was because there wasn't any milk, and money in prison is contraband. Teaching to a test, out of workbooks, is a most undesirable way to teach or to learn; but, given the conditions that prevail here, it is the most practical way to approach the job. You don't know whether the class will arrive at 8:00 or 9:00, or anytime in between; you don't know which member will be on "call out" to go to commissary, to get her hair fixed, to see a counselor, to go to the nurse, or to a visit.

The only thing the students have in common, other than their incarceration, is their ability to read at a sixth-grade level or above.

Some spent four years in high school outside, and didn't graduate; some left to hang out or to have a baby in the ninth or tenth grade. Some are just killing time on something they hope will look good to their parole board. They do virtually no work at all, and they disrupt all the others. Some seriously want to work and pass the exam. These women deserve medals for working conscientiously under very difficult conditions, sticking to the job, rising above all the distractions and finally passing. Even under the best conditions, it's hard to go back to school when you remember it as little more than a series of failures. And even when they have passed the GED exam with the magic 225, they are often a long way from being prepared to do college work, that is, honest to God, college-level work. Nevertheless, they are allowed to go on.

The basic requirement seems to be that you qualify for the needed public funds. Some women go on not even knowing what the word "college" means.

"Say, Jean. I need you to tutor me college. I start it next week."

"Sure, Katherine. What course in college?"

"Just college. Tutor me college. I start next week."

I suppose tutoring was the only useful thing I did here for the first two years. It was done anywhere an interested woman and I could meet: the classroom, the recreation room, the gym, the yard. At first, many women asked me to "tutor" them. I was the inhouse freak, and being tutored by Jean Harris was something to talk about. I took each student seriously, but soon discovered that "tutoring" meant trying to find them first. You sought them out, you brought the pencils and paper and books. You did the learning. Finally I told them, "I'll tutor you, but only if you get classified into the tutoring time, and you show up when you're supposed to. If you aren't there, I'll leave. I won't go looking for you." I ended up with five earnest pupils.

Louise wanted to know something about geography and reading graphs. They are both included on the GED exam. I brought a map of the United States the first day and asked her to find the state where she was born and the state where she presently lives. She had no idea where to begin to look. I said, "OK, let's start by putting the basic direction on the map, north, south, east, west." She not only did not know where they are, she did not know the names of the Atlantic

Ocean and the Pacific Ocean. Three days after we had been talking about the map of the United States, she said, as though a light had gone on, "Oh, this map don't have all that Europe stuff on it, do it?"

At first Edna wanted to know about fractions. She had gone through the third grade and couldn't read or write. She is thirty-two years old and has three children. Fractions reduced her to tears. Where she had even heard of them I'm not quite sure. We went back to the sounds of the letters.

The attention span of most of the women was very short. Even as we sat together reading a short story they would flip the pages ahead and say, "Man this is sure a long short story." Nowhere that I can think of would films be a more valuable learning tool. But my suggestion of the classics through movies, or almost anything through movies, has been put to work only in the Children's Center. I urged the education department to set up an audiovisual room. There should be one and it should be scheduled every moment the school building is open. So far no one but me seems to think so. Consequently, when anyone does show a film, half of the period is spent trying to track down the equipment, and setting it up. Use of, and care of, audiovisual material would be an excellent class in itself. I'm sometimes quite torn here, wondering if I serve an idea better by my silence than by words.

Selena was my prize pupil. She had been here for thirteen years when we began to work together. She still hadn't passed her GED exam, which was sinfully wasteful because she read better than most of the women who had.

"Why, Selena? Why have you let all this time go by?"

"I couldn't stand all the confusion, Jean. It upset me to work there. I went back three different times and tried, but I always left. It upset me to be there."

We spent most of our time just reading together, and talking about what we read. We took turns reading aloud, starting with animal and nature stories because that's what she said she liked, *The Red Pony, Light in the Forest, Misty of Chiconteague.* As we finished *The Red Pony* she said, "That's the first book I've read in thirteen years that ain't trash."

Somehow the subject of satire came up, a new word for Selena, and we read *Animal Farm* together. The idea of animals talking and meaning something more than "I'll huff and I'll puff and I'll blow your

house down" delighted her. The concept of this group of words meaning that group of words fascinated her and the book became her
constant companion. On two different occasions I saw her in the yard
reading parts of the book to her friends. An entry in my journal that
spring noted, "Someone has stolen Selena's copy of *Animal Farm* and
she is heartbroken. I have promised to get her another one but it will
never be quite as special to her as the first copy was. How lovely to
watch a brain open up and welcome a new idea."

At the end of her fourteenth year here Selena got Work Release.
One of the first things she did outside was take the GED exam and
pass it, not because of anything I had taught her. I had only convinced
her that she was capable of passing it. It is that assurance, that they
are people of value and ability, that is so completely missing in some
of their lives. I was sitting in the clinic one day when a woman came
up to me and kissed me on the cheek.

"I passed the GED, Jean" she told me.

"That's wonderful," I said.

"I just wanted to thank you."

"What are you thanking me for?" I asked. "You did it yourself."

"No I didn't," she answered. "You the one sat beside me and said,
'You can do it, I know you can do it,' and that's how I done it."

Just remembering that makes me cry. It's such a small thing to do
for a person. So little.

It was a combination of frustration and depression, and just plain
boredom that made me decide to leave being a teacher's aide and find
something new. Some people take cruises when all those things set
in. And a slow boat to China, port out, starboard home, would have
been much cheaper than the $40,000 options I was permitted. I was
classified into South Forty in the morning, and the Children's Center
in the afternoon.

The South Forty program was begun in 1968 at one New York
prison, Greenhaven, by William Vanderbilt of the Vanderbilt family.
He was interested in the American prison system from the standpoint
of rehabilitation. He believed, from what he had observed in his visits
to prisons, that much time and talent were wasted there, and not
enough was being done to help prisoners get a decent start on the

outside. Today the program is still active in six New York State prisons, Bedford among them.

It is both publicly and privately funded, and its primary goal is still to help prisoners prepare for re-entry into society, to help them discover where their interests and talents lie, to offer them the chance to develop appropriate skills, and to put them in touch with individuals or groups on the outside who can steer them toward housing and employment.

Today William Vanderbilt's widow still has an interest in the program, and she visits the group from time to time. Here at Bedford, South Forty is a very active, viable prison program. Its staff leader is Maria Sobol, a bright, creative, kind, earth-mother type, whose concern and help reaches into many parts of the prison. Through her, volunteers from the outside maintain an active interest in helping the women learn new skills, further their graduate education, find jobs outside, lobby for Merit Time Legislation and better Work Release Legislation. Perhaps even more important, they maintain a close association with the prison "long-termers." They help the women make the best use of the endless years some of them must spend here, women who are, by actual study, largely the best educated, most constructive, least criminal of all the inmates.

South Forty meets in a large room with a kiln, potter's wheel, several of those precious sewing machines, and large tables where a woman may knit a sweater, make a quilt, sew stuffed animals and dolls, design jewelry, or fashion pottery. Workshops are offered by volunteers from the outside in subjects as varied as tatting and accounting. One volunteer has organized and manages a small boutique outlet on Long Island where prisoners may sell their work.

Much of the newest equipment in the room, including the kiln, was purchased by the inmates themselves with money they earned selling their work. The ceramic artwork of one of the women, who had never done it before coming to Bedford, has had a showing in New York. South Forty is the only program in the prison I know of that encourages women to create, at a professional level, and then helps them to sell their wares and support themselves.

I hope there will be other programs here in which women who want to work can earn more than the $1.55 per day which is the prison's maximum! You start at $.70 per day if you work morning and afternoon. The prison feeds and clothes a prisoner, and provides toothpaste, when it's available, and a bar of very strong soap made by the men in another prison. It also provides toilet paper and sanitary pads, though it is not too unusual for women to run out well before more is doled out. As I write this, women on one of the floors have to go up to the C.O. on duty and ask for a sanitary pad, one at a time, and for a few sheets of toilet paper, each time she needs them. Since the C.O.s are just as likely to be men as women, it can be very awkward for the C.O. as well as the inmate.

I have reached the maximum salary now, $7.76 a week, but with family and friends constantly asking me what I need, I have plenty of shampoo, deodorant, snacks, fresh fruit, tea, books, pens, pencils, and writing paper. Many women here have no one on the outside to visit them or send them packages. And for well over half of the women, cigarettes are like oxygen. Many came in addicted to drugs and alcohol, and cigarettes play a very important role. Earning the maximum prison wage they can buy one carton of cigarettes every month but that leaves little for toiletries or coffee and Cremora. Since some women will spend anywhere from five to twenty-five years in here, that is a mighty meager existence.

It hardly stimulates or motivates. It merely depresses. By selling her sweaters or ceramics, a woman can make as much as several thousand dollars a year. Others, who aren't given to knitting or crocheting, earn a little over the maximum by working seven days a week, all day, in the prison kitchen. Doing this they can earn $10.78 per week. One of the women at Fiske does it and sends money home to her mother. I don't know what her crime was, but it wasn't self-indulgence.

If you are ill, or physically or mentally unable to do prison work, you are given "unemployment" pay which amounts to $.35 per day (it probably costs more than that to keep track of it), or $1.75 per week. It isn't too hard to understand why some women sell their medication instead of taking it.

I consider it a matter of honor to try to live on my income in here, which has made me more of a penny watcher than I was on the outside, if that's possible. I watch every cent and make very sure that I am paid what I am, by law, supposed to be paid. Around Christmas

Jimmy Harris, 1981

Jean with Liza, 1974

David Harris (on right), 1983

Hy at wine bar in his Westchester house, 1979

Jean and Hy on New Year's Day, 1968

Hy in China, 1973

Hy with Zhou-en-Lai, 1973

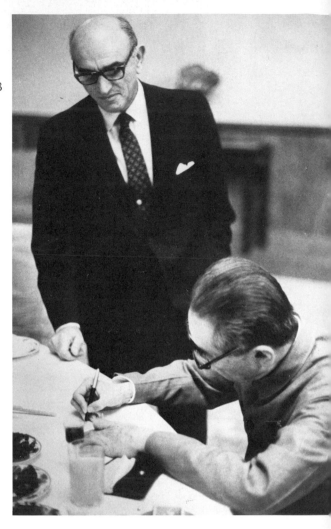

Pond in front of Hy's house in Harrison, where earlier Jean had
brought biology students from the Thomas School, 1971

Joel Aurnou with Jean, 1980

Building 14 A&B, where Jean lived for two years, 1982 and 1983

Jean with children, Christmas, Bedford Hills, 1985

Sister Elaine Roulet in Children's Center, Bedford Hills, 1984

Sister Elaine and Jean in Children's Center, Bedford Hills, 1984

Jean, 1984

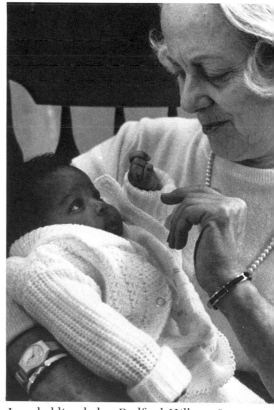

Jean holding baby, Bedford Hills, 1985

Jean, Bedford Hills, 1986

time I sell some of my knitting, but most of it I give away. Being able to do so is probably my greatest source of pleasure in here, to be occasionally the giver instead of the receiver.

A lovely lady named Alice Lacey, who graduated from Madeira before I went there, is one of the kind people who has kept a good many women in here, including me, supplied with yarn. She has sent us pounds and pounds of it, bags full that always remind me of Mother Goose and "Baa, Baa Black Sheep." Other friends and companies have sent us yarn and fabric samples from which beautiful dolls and vests and pillows and handbags are made. They add an important and constructive dimension to some of the lives here.

Bedford Hills:
Sister Elaine and
the Children

*It is not our responsibility to bring hap-
piness to our children. That they will seek
for themselves. It is our responsibility to
recognize our capacity for causing them
pain, and not to call it by another name.*

—Dr. Henry Smith
Harvard magazine

1.

The chasm between me and the other women was wide and deep
when I came to Bedford. In some ways I have bridged the gap. In
many others I have not and never could. I am almost forty years older
than the other women here, and I am considered "rich" because I am
white, and because I have been widely publicized as "social." That my
sons and I lived on a teacher's salary from 1966 until they graduated
from college and found jobs of their own is one of the boring facts
about me that neither the inmates nor the media choose to believe.
That I continue to be mentioned in the media is hard for the women
to forgive, and I can understand why.

It took time, but I have finally come to understand that the only
way for me to be useful to the women in here, and for us to reach one
another, is through their children, and that is the route I have finally
taken. I should add quickly that it was not altruism that led me there,

262

I was looking for a reason to be alive, at least as long as there was even a small hope that I might win a new trial. My move to a full-time job in the Children's Center was a gradual one. Sister Elaine's suggestion that I work on a book of letters from children to their mothers in prison seemed an interesting challenge, and that was the beginning.

I had seen Sister in the visiting room from time to time, but I didn't really meet her until the day that she approached me and asked me about the book. Sister had been a teaching nun for many years, and then the principal of a large Catholic school until she came to Bedford fifteen years ago as a family counselor. Family counseling soon came to include just about any kind of problem an incarcerated woman could have. I had heard her name frequently. When anyone is in particular trouble and needs help at Bedford, Sister is one of the names sure to come into the conversation. Until we were given un- limited phone calls, a woman with three or four children, all in dif- ferent foster homes, or someone with a dying parent, or someone with a legal crisis who absolutely had to get to a phone had one real hope of getting a call through to the outside, and Sister was that hope.

For too many others with a phone on their desk, the big question was "How will it make me look if I let her make the call?" For Sister it is "How can I help?" She never asks "How much do the undeserving deserve?" Of course, if you were having an affair with the C.O. in the phone room you could call every day, two of my acquaintances did. But most of us had to find another route, and in crisis time we ran, and still run to Sister, like children.

Sister rarely says "no" to any plea if there is an outside chance that she can help, and still maintain the necessary discipline of a prison. "My baby doesn't have a crib" is easy. She finds someone to contrib- ute it, drives all over the city to pick it up and deliver it, or buys one herself. "My mother can't get home on the train with the baby and all the baby's stuff" is easy. Sister drives them home.

"My phone has been turned off and I can't get it connected again until the old bill's paid, and my mother's home alone and has a stroke, and I gotta call her each day to see she ain't dead." That's a tough one, but with the help of the phone company that was solved too.

"My baby died and there's no money to bury her, and I really want somethin' nice to bury her in." Sister goes shopping, and Precious goes off to heaven looking her very best.

"My husband's dying and I can't call him collect at the hospital." Husband and wife say goodbye for the last time on the phone in Sister's office. When family members die, a prisoner can go and see them just before they die, if they know when, or they can go to the funeral, but they can't do both. It's a hard decision to make.

"Minnie is in Sag and goin' bananas without no cigarettes." Cigarettes are found.

"They won't give me parole unless I have some place to go and I haven't no place to go." Room is found at Providence House.

"We've got a house, Sister, but we'll lose it if my husband and me are both in prison at the same time, and there's no money coming in. Can you write the judge and ask if we could go at different times? He'll take a longer sentence, anything, if he can just stay out until I get out." With the intervention of Sister and others the judge agrees to let the father stay out until mother's sentence is served.

"We haven't told the girls their daddy is going to prison too. My husband just can't tell 'em. If he brings 'em to you Sister, will you tell 'em? Will you explain?" When the children arrive at Providence House they were so loving, and so obviously adoring of daddy, Sister couldn't bring herself to say the word "prison," either. "You know, the place where mommy is." But they didn't understand and father grew angry with them because they weren't making it easy for him, angry because he loved them so much, and hated whatever it was that he had done. Somehow she makes the hard times easier for others at great emotional cost to herself.

It is hard to catch the spirit and wholeness of Sister Elaine. She is full of love, full of life, full of human frailty, and most of all, full of that one vital quality that no special person can be without, energy. She is spontaneous and funny one moment, full of concern the next, genuinely holy the next, and each quality is real and woven into the texture of the woman she is. Some women here love and are grateful to her; some have little use for her until they need her again. Some seem to feel that her function is to "get stuff for 'em," "She suppose to buy them things. She got the money." And some think she's "letting them play her for a sucker." Hardly. There is little that goes on at Bedford Hills Correctional Facility that Sister doesn't know about. She keeps right on giving. I think this is known as "turning the other cheek," even "Christian" in some circles.

She is the first to see the humor in situations, and especially where she is the dupe. She likes a good joke too, and it isn't always what one would call "nunly." Sister belongs to the order of St. Joseph in Brentwood, Long Island. She put aside the habit years ago and is now stylishly and conservatively dressed by the thrift shop that she runs to support her four Providence Houses. Her sister Jean, her closest relative and closest friend, is now retired from the insurance business and manages the thrift shop. Her biggest challenge is to sell things before Sister Elaine gives them away, no easy job.

One would have to walk a long mile to find a more loving, devout, committed, hard-working nun than Sister, but she is sometimes criticized for not wearing a habit. To put aside the habit is almost as unwise as eschewing a double knit pantsuit when on trial for your life. Sister was invited to a fancy, money-raising dinner party recently, by a large foundation, complete with engraved invitations and all the trappings. Someone followed up her invitation with a phone call telling her to "please wear your habit, and if you don't have one, wear something very conservative." She was polite as always, but when she put down the phone she turned to her secretary and asked her to "please regret for me."

"What shall I tell them?" the girl asked.

"Tell them I haven't anything conservative to wear," she laughed.

Sister's life is a very full one. She rises each morning at 4:30 A.M., dresses, has a quick breakfast, drives the hour's drive from Queens to Bedford, goes to Mass, for which she promptly gives herself a star, heads to the local Boys' Club for a swim, is at the local library when it opens to exchange her pile of books for a new collection, and finally arrives between 8:30 and 9:00 at Bedford. Her letters and her speech reflect the breadth of her interests and of her reading.

She may begin with an apt quotation from the gospels, or a little street wisdom from Mae West. "Too much of a good thing is wonderful!" is a favorite of hers and should probably be needlepointed into her coat of arms. With a twinkle in the eye and all the pleasure of the double entendre, she interprets it to mean, "That was good for yesterday, but it isn't enough for today. Onward and upward." "Here's to the holidays, all 365 of them!"

She enters the prison looking for all the world like a bag lady, with cigarettes for someone in Sag, gifts from the church to use as Bingo prizes for the ladies in the mental ward, toys someone has given her for the Children's Center, a bag full of books, and, if she has any money, a bagel or two for the ladies in the center. Somewhere along the line she has read the newspaper and cut out anything she thinks will be of general interest, or particular interest to a special woman.

Some days here are so bad that Sister earns an extra star for surviving. She keeps a little diary with lists of each day's tasks for which she earns a star, one for going to Mass, one for the stations of the cross, one for fasting on fast days, and more. And there are stars of different colors too, red, gold, and green. It is childlike and amusing, and she enjoys laughing at herself about it, but there's a serious purpose too. There is something of the child still in her, which is why she is so exuberant and loving and trusting.

I saw her pasting stars in her notebook one day in the middle of a particularly hectic morning and asked her, "What's the difference between the blue ones and the red ones, Sister?"

"Oh," she said off-handedly, "I used to give special significance to different colors but now they're all the same. I'm maturing."

As a young girl she had romantic notions of serving in Africa, a female Dr. Schweitzer. "My mother said it was alright with her, and then she asked, 'Where's the mother house for the overseas order?' When I told her Metuchen, New Jersey, she said, 'That's too far away. You've got to pick an order closer to home.' So I didn't go to Africa because Metuchen, New Jersey, was too far away."

Sister's father died when she was very young. She speaks little of him, but she mentions her mother often. I think she carries her somewhere in her conscience, as I do my father. She said recently, "I'm just beginning to appreciate the fact that my mother was a character."

From time to time something will remind her. "Whenever we had to stand in line somewhere my mother would nudge me and say, 'Go to the head of the line and tell 'em your father's dead!' When she sent me to the store she'd always call out, 'Remember to tell 'em your father's dead. They'll take a little off!' It was a constant refrain, 'You can't wear glasses. Your father's dead.' "

She tells this on herself. "Several years ago Marilyn Hill's father dropped dead of a heart attack while he was waiting in line here at the prison to visit her. Months later, Marilyn was preparing to go to the parole board. She was nervous about it and came into my office to talk. As she left I suddenly called after her, 'Tell 'em your father's dead.' You put your arm in your sleeve one day and your mother's hand comes out."

Bedford is not the only place where Sister works. It is simply her daytime job. She is also the founder and prime mover and spirit behind four Providence Houses, two in Brooklyn, one in Queens and a fourth in Westchester. They serve as refuge for battered wives and their children, and also as a temporary haven for women coming out of prison who have nowhere else to go. They are staffed by nuns whom Sister has persuaded to come live in them with her. The nuns, like Sister, work at their regular jobs during the day and share night duty at the houses. It is a fairly onerous duty for a working person, since many of the battered women arrive in the middle of the night. A soup kitchen is presently run at one of the houses in Brooklyn.

The need for help to battered wives in Westchester has prompted the opening of the fourth house in New Rochelle. Even the middle and upper classes bat their wives around. In the daytime each of the houses is capably run by a former Bedford inmate.

Women may stay in the houses for up to six months, but by then they must have found a job and a permanent place to live and move on. With housing what it is today this often means the next stop is a welfare hotel, which is just one step above or below the street. Asking people finally to leave is a hated burden for Sister, and she is presently looking for funds to establish a permanent housing unit for women, with their own rooms and bath and shared cooking facilities, a kind of housing in great demand and virtually nonexistent.

Some women leaving Providence House solve their housing problems by joining another woman they've met while there. A battered woman and a paroled woman can share digs, but two paroled women may not. If caught doing so they are parole violators and are sent back to prison. There are women back in here whose crime for being returned is no more serious than that. Virtually the only friends they have after five years in prison are apt to be other parolees, but they must not "consort." One can see some reasoning behind this, but a case can also be made that it creates as much mischief as it prevents.

If there is one bone of contention between Sister and her co-workers, staff and inmates alike, it is that she is too giving. If she has a dollar she will quickly find someone who needs it, even if the dollar was budgeted for some other place. She would drive a husband crazy. Her handling of money sometimes reminds me a little of Vinnie in *Life with Father*. And yet the bills always get paid. In fact she makes a dollar go further than anyone I know.

For the amount of good it does, and the number of people it touches, the budget of the Children's Center is small. She is constantly trying to do more with the same amount of money, and we are constantly telling Linda Nelson, the staff assistant, "Put it somewhere Sister can't find it so she won't give it away before you need it."

She was standing with the phone in her hand one day, waiting for an outside line, when suddenly, apropos of nothing, Sister turned to us and said, "Am I hard to work for?" There was a pregnant pause when all of us smiled at her, and at one another, and finally someone said, "Well it's hard to keep up with you, Sister, and you're better at performing miracles than balancing a checkbook." But then Sister believes implicitly in miracles, and that's probably what keeps the center going.

2.

I have watched the Children's Center grow from scratch to what is probably the largest program of its kind in the country. One of the early movers in efforts to bring incarcerated mothers and their children together was the Children's Television Workshop (CTW), creators of *Sesame Street*. The first toys to be provided for the visiting room at Bedford came from CTW, so the area was called "Sesame Street." There are many Sesame Streets in prisons and jails around the country.

When I arrived at Bedford in early spring of 1981, there was a small area walled off in the corner of the visiting room, decorated by one of the inmates with bright paintings of "Big Bird" and "Cookie Monster," "Kermit the Frog," and other familiar TV celebrities. The room contained books and toys for visiting children to enjoy while mother visited with family members, or played with the children. The program was run by outside volunteers and was open only on weekends or when a volunteer was available. Some of the inmates worked there on a volunteer basis too, after completing a training program organized and run by CTW.

Until 1980 there had been no toys at all, and no place where children could let off steam. That female prisoners have children simply hadn't occurred to us as a nation. There were no vending machines here either, so a child could be here for hours with nothing to eat or drink. No food could be brought into the visiting room by visitors themselves. You could come at 9:00 A.M. and stay until 3:30 P.M., but you couldn't pack a lunch. "Sit down and keep quiet" were what the child heard most. There were no toys up in the prison nursery either. Families could not send in toys, and the prison didn't provide any. "No frills for inmates" amounted to "punish the children."

Even the first two summer programs organized by Sister Elaine and Brother Tom Grady simply consisted of children visiting mother every day for a week, sitting beside her and talking with her. There was nowhere for them to go and little to do.

In the fall of 1981, a large area for children was established. A wall was put up straight across one end of the visiting room. I watched the room take shape with no idea at the time of what a large role it would play in my life. The original Sesame Street area was renamed the Parenting Office. The rest of the area was the Children's Center. The state of New York established a formal budget for the center, to be administered by Catholic charities in the Brooklyn Diocese with Sister Elaine Roulet as its head.

No one is quicker than Sister to give credit to the many concerned and generous people who have helped to make the Children's Center the special place it is, but there is no question that the spirit that emanates from it is Sister's. Today, five years after its founding, the center averages over 250 child visits per months. That number is inching up toward 300. Six hundred children came during the Christmas holidays, and thanks to a long list of generous friends from all over the country, there were gifts and cookies for all. The center's summer program now serves over 150 children who come for a week to be with their mother, and take part in a day camp program.

At first Sister was asked to be in charge of children's programs in prisons all over the state. Fortunately, she realized the potential of such a program in one facility, and knew that to spread herself that thin would weaken the program. What she has built here at Bedford is a model that few other prisons, if any in the country, have yet been able to emulate. What continues to make the Bedford program unique is the extent to which inmates run the program, and the fact that the state permits inmates to be classified into the Children's Center as a regular job. Happily, more and more states are now beginning to try.

With Sister Elaine to give them the courage and the opportunity, inmates play key roles in the running of the center. There are many different tasks to do, and each member of the group plays several roles. They act as care-givers for the children, plan activities, maintain the toys and games, plan holiday parties, wrap hundreds of gifts at Christmas, team-teach a popular ten week course called "Parenting Through Films," which is now being taught for the fourth time because the demand is so great, and they work as a team for ten weeks in the summer in a unique day camp program that had 158 children in it last summer and will probably have more this summer. One inmate schedules the free buses from all of the boroughs, and monthly weekend visits for children who stay Saturday night one weekend a month with local families who act as their host so that the child can visit both Saturday and Sunday with mother. One inmate works specifically with mothers whose children are in Foster Care; one competent typist handles extensive typing for the center; and still another works in the prison nursery, as sitter and coordinator. And Sister makes us all want to do it.

The Children's Center is one of the few places in the prison where inmates are encouraged to do their own thinking, try new things, and know that if they succeed the feather is in their cap, and if they fail it's their fault and they must try harder. The total, crippling dependence that prison fosters is missing in the Children's Center, and that is because of Sister Elaine. She shares with the inmates many of the

frustrations that come with trying to accomplish something purposeful in a prison setting.

I said to her once, at the end of a particularly unpleasant day, when
every possible roadblock had been thrown in her way, "What keeps
you coming back, Sister? How do you make yourself get up and drive
back to this terrible place?"

"It's very simple," she said. "I am reminded each day how easy it
would have been for me to be sitting on the other side of this desk."

What are the words you think of when you hear "woman in
prison"? Convict? Criminal? Whore? Dangerous? How long would
your list be before you came up with "loving mother"? Many of your
lists would never reach that far, and until I came to prison my list
would have looked very much like yours. Stereotypes are great time-
savers. They save us from thinking, and then exact the price of
thoughtlessness.

Sometimes the price is negligible. Sometimes the price is high.
Because so many of us share the same prejudices and mental pictures
about incarcerated women, their children go unnoticed and neglected
by society, condemned, though quite innocent, to serve their
mother's sentence as surely as she. And the impact of their mother's
imprisonment will stay with them forever.

Seventy percent of the women at Bedford Hills Correctional Facility have children and two-thirds of their children are under ten. To
most of the world, their mother is superfluous, a throw-away person
who must be stashed somewhere at great expense. To her children she
is still "Mama," the most important person in the world.

Our first, and sometimes last, response to imprisoned women and
their children is, "Don't tell me your sad little stories. If you loving
mothers cared so much about your children you wouldn't be in
prison. How much time did you spend with these kids when you were
outside?" In some cases the answer is "very little," and sometimes the
answer is "every minute I could." One way or another the question is
essentially irrelevant. Because their mothers are in prison is not reason enough to be judgmental about, or worse still, unconcerned
about their children.

Incarceration is not proof that a woman is a bad mother, any more
than being outside is proof that she is a good one. The fervent, plead-

ing message in most of the letters children write to their mothers in prison is, "I love you. I need you. I miss you."

"But even if I got mad at you I still love you. You are the best mom."

"When I come up there I'm gonna push you in the nose. Don't you know I miss you so bad."

"I miss kissing you, Mama. God bless you."

"I hear you are going to be out September 29, and I hope the first thing you do is come and get me."

"Without you there's no love here."

Dolores Donovan, a young mother of three, was already working in the center when I arrived. She was paid to work five days a week. She worked seven days a week. If she missed a day in the three years she was here no one can recall it. She was a fixture in the room until her clemency came through, and she left. She should never have been here in the first place, but nobody ever bothered to mention that publicly.

The children who came to Bedford to visit hugged their mother first, and then ran to the center to hug Dolores and ask, "What's the project today? What are we going to make? Can we play musical chairs?"

She knew them all by name, hundreds of them; she knew their mothers. She could remind them if they had spent too much time with a cousin or a friend, and not enough time with the children. And she could do it without arousing anger or resentment. This in itself qualified her for a spot in the State Department. To say anything to anyone in prison without arousing anger or resentment requires a kind of diplomacy few people have, or a kind of trust few people earn. Women come to prison programmed to hate and resent, the people who help them more often than the people who ignore them.

Dolores's own children, two girls and a boy, came to see her sporadically because the relative they stayed with seemed to have a hard time pulling herself together and getting them here. She promised constantly, but often broke the promise. I have seen Dolores many days, going about her job while her eyes searched the doorway at the other end of the room each time she could turn her head in that direction. The look of longing and expectancy and hurt while she waits for the children who don't come, and the look of fear in her eyes when a woman is about to go out and isn't sure whether she will survive the streets or not, are looks you never forget, once you have seen them.

Together, Sister Elaine, and Dolores and I convinced ourselves that the public would be interested in the welfare of the children of prisoners if only someone brought them to the public's attention. What better way to do it than through the children's own words, their letters to their mothers? We began to mention the idea to mothers as they came and went in the center. We asked them if they would share their letters with us. We assured them the names would be changed because identifying individual children or families was not in any way our purpose.

Collecting the letters was a labor of love, because inmates do not all have ready access to one another. Moving about from floor to floor, from cell block to cell block can be a long, tedious, frustrating job. Dolores was much better at it than I. And mothers were not always quick to share. Understandably, they wanted to know our motives, and be sure the letters would be returned, before they were willing to part with them. Some of the letters so generously shared were more than five years old, but still read and treasured. Time stands still in prison. Outside, it goes on.

Between us, Dolores and I know most of the children who wrote the letters you will see here. We have had long talks with their mothers, but we have not discussed the letters with the children, and names are all changed so that no child can be identified. Together we read and reread more than a hundred letters, laughing, crying, and aching for both senders and receivers. For me, the thought of having been here when my sons were young, missing their growing up and the role I played in it is too terrible to imagine. I know from seeing it and sharing it, that for many of the women here, the hardest part of everyday life is being away from their children.

"Look what they wrote about you, ma. They said you was in jail."

"He said you was in jail and I kicked him."

"But prison is for bad people. You're not bad people."

Some children, on the other hand, are almost relieved when they find out. They thought they had been deserted.

"I was gonna hate you ma, 'cause I didn't know where you was at."

If a child's mother dies, or even if she is away because she is sick, the separation, the loss, is traumatic. But knowing of the loss, society rallies, at least for a while, and tries to fill the gap. The neighbors bring in a special dessert, the teacher understands if homework isn't finished, and best friends are kinder than ever.

If mother goes away to prison it's a very different story. Society's reaction can be negative and cruel. The sudden loss is just as real, but added to that is the shame, wondering what classmates will say when they find out, and the fear, wondering what's happening to their mother in "the terrible place."

"If you don't do what they say, do they beat you, Mama?"

"Tell me where is my mother's cage."

Sooner or later someone at school or on the street will mock and scorn. Even a teacher, though she may not recognize it in herself, will look at the child differently when she finds out. When mama goes to prison, grades of her children inevitably go down. Sometimes it's only temporary, and sometimes it's the beginning of dropping out.

How children react to their mother's incarceration depends upon their ongoing relationship with her; the mother's previous arrest record, who tells them, and how supportive the new care-givers are. One mother wrote her children repeatedly and never had a reply. Later she learned that her husband and her mother had told the children she was dead. Try to imagine dealing with that, as the mother, as the child. More than one mother here is faced with decisions better left to Solomon.

One of the mothers who let us see her children's letters came as a child to Bedford to visit her own mother. She sat in the Children's Center one morning, at one of the little tables where the children sit and paint, to reminisce:

"It's hard having a mother in prison, you love her and hate her all at the same time. I kept asking myself, 'Why me? Why did it have to happen to me?' I even began to wonder secretly if I was the reason she was there. Was it something I did that made her break the law? She used to make things for me while she was here and send them to me, and when they came I'd go off alone and cry and cry and cry.

"My mother was killed a year after she left this place, shot on the street. They sent me back to foster homes then, and when I was fifteen I ran away. I was raped by a man on the street. They said he was crazy, and he got sent to some institution. He's my oldest daughter's father. She's eleven now. She hasn't asked much about her father. I guess I'll never tell her. I been married twice and both my husbands were killed. The last one was killed while we were walking out of a restaurant. Somebody started shooting and my husband put a gun in my hand and pushed me down on the sidewalk. He fell on top of me, died there. I got one to three for illegal possession of a gun. How much do you have to be punished to satisfy someone? Sometimes I think one thing more, just one little thing more and I'll go screamin' crazy."

One of her younger daughter's letters ends like this.

"First Daddy got killed, then Pete got killed. When are we gonna be happy?"

Many of the mothers mention the fact that their children suspect they are somehow responsible for what happened. One little girl opened the door the night the police came to arrest her mother. She still says when she comes to visit:

"Oh Mama, if I just didn't open the door. If I just didn't open the door."

Once in prison, an inmate is counted and accounted for all day long. She isn't hard to find; she has three square meals a day and a roof over her head. Her children, on the other hand, who should be cared for and accounted for, are quite a different story.

It is virtually impossible to give an accurate report on where all the inmate children are, because, up to now, no one has acknowledged their existence. While mother is swallowed up in the massive bureaucracy of the criminal justice system for indefinite periods of time, there is not one small bureau that concerns itself with the ongoing welfare, or even the whereabouts of her children. In the state of New York neither the Department of Corrections nor local departments of Social Services can give you the number of children left behind, let alone who is caring for them.

Many policemen even forget to ask a woman if she has children when he arrests her, though, by law, he is required to do so, and to make arrangements for them if they have been left alone. I have asked forty mothers here at random if the police inquired about their children when arresting them. Seventy-five percent said "no." In a survey taken at Rikers Island by the New York State Council on Children and Families 73 percent said "no."

Where children were already living in grandmother's house before their mother was arrested, life can go on for them with some semblance of order. They don't have to change schools and neighborhoods. Something familiar is left for them. They are less at sea. But for many children, whose mother is arrested, life turns upside down. Not only do they lose her, they lose most of the other things they know and love. Overnight, their security, what little they had of it, disappears. They go to live with relatives or strangers, often leaving friends and old neighborhoods behind. They feel rootless, hurt, angry, ashamed, afraid of what worse fate tomorrow may bring.

3.

The first letter shared with us was from an eleven-year-old girl, and her four-year-old brother, Milton:

Dear Mama,
Come home. I love you and anyway don't nobody else want Milton and me. How you doing me and Milton is find. I am not going to do no more for Carol. I no now she is no good. I will like to go back to my old block, but no one is going to take Milton and me. I want you to be home and I no you will like to be home to Mama. I am going to talk to God. I do not like to go to Carol house. I like my old block. Call me and Milton more. I love you and Milton do to.

Almost half of the letters said, "please call me more." The children could not understand why their mother was allowed only two five-minute calls per month. I will never understand it either. Even if all charges were not reversed, which they are, it was in every sense of the word a shortsighted, vindictive, destructive ruling. Now that the phone call restriction has been lifted at Bedford, I pray it will never be reinstated.

In the course of a year approximately 250,000 children all over

America spend some time waiting for their mother to get out of jail or prison. Many more than that have fathers who are incarcerated, but in most cases the child's attachment to his or her mother is much closer, and separation from her is more traumatic. It is a deep, devastating, and complicated thing for a child to handle. There is far more than physical separation to suffer. It is difficult for little children to deal with mother-the-care-giver and mother-the-wrongdoer.

To a child the overwhelming fact is mother's absence, not what she did. Children are unable to integrate the two in one person, so they concentrate on mother's good qualities, and try to play down the bad. They resent relatives who criticize her, "She shouldn't of said that about you, Mama," and they resent the powers that put her in jail.

"Every night before I go to bed, I punch my pillow. I punch it and punch it. I pretend it's a policeman, and I punch it."

Sometimes a mother is able to sit down quietly with her children and explain to them what she did and where she is going. Sometimes children hear it from angry relatives, some from taunting strangers, some know because they witnessed the crime and the arrest, and some learn about it from the media.

Most mothers, understandably, do not try to explain where they are to a child under three. And yet a very young child can be deeply traumatized by the separation if the chief care-giver has been its mother. In a recent study, 8 percent of the mothers said they will never tell their children at any age, "They've been hurt enough." Instead, their children are told:

"Mommy has to go away."

"Mommy is sick."

"Mommy is in the hospital."

"Mommy is at college."

"Mommy's in the army."

Sixty-five percent of the children whose letters we gathered are living with grandmother now. Some know her well. To others she is a stranger. Twenty percent of the children live with sisters or cousins or aunts. Ten percent live with father or a male friend, in most cases only if father or friend has an amenable girlfriend who will play step-mother. For all the mothers we talked with, we found only two stalwart, loyal husbands who were carrying on as best they could, alone. The rest of the children, about 9 percent, are in foster care.

The more children there are in a family, the more likely it is that they will be separated when mother goes to prison. One set of letters that was shared with us spanned seven years, from 1976 to 1983. One could read into them the disintegration of a family. When mother came to prison, three children, two step-sisters and a brother were each sent off to live with a different family member. The older sister, nine when the letters began, had enjoyed a very close relationship with her step-sister, Wilma.

"Mama, why did you let Wilma go to her daddy's house?"

"I opened the door and there was Wilma and I hugged her and hugged her."

"I can't wait to see Wilma."

"I called Wilma and talked to her."

"When you write to Wilma, say hello."

"Do you know where Wilma lives now?"

And finally, "I couldn't really tell you anything about Wilma because she doesn't keep in touch with us anymore."

Given time, each mother makes the best arrangements for her children that she can. Sometimes the best is none too good, and sometimes the best laid plans go awry.

"His girlfriend left him and he says I gotta make other plans. How'm I gonna make other plans?"

"My sister took my three kids, but now her husband's left her and she has to get a job."

"I expected probation, so when they sentenced me I wasn't ready. The kids were home waiting for me and I told the judge 'I gotta talk to my kids and find someone to come and get 'em.' He said 'Well do it fast. You've got five minutes.'"

Sometimes, when police do remember to ask a woman if she has any children, she'll deny having them for fear they'll go to foster care. For black women especially, this is public acknowledgment that she has absolutely no one to turn to, no family at all. In New York State, when children go to foster care mother is not permitted to know their new address. She writes to them through the social worker, and they respond through the social worker.

But whatever explanation the child gets, mother is no longer there.

When a mother is in prison, most of what she learns about her child in foster care comes to her third or fourth hand from the foster mother, to the social worker, to the staff person at Bedford, to the mother. And then it usually comes only after she has asked for it repeatedly. It is not unusual for her to write four, five, and six letters to social agencies and receive no reply. It sometimes takes five or six calls to the agency to reach the social worker, and the mother herself can't make these calls. They must be made by a prison staff person, someone not always easy to reach, even in an emergency. After the struggle to make contact here are some of the actual messages she receives:

"There will be an adoption hearing in May to determine whether Tanya will be adopted by her foster parents. We will try to obtain a court order so that you can be at the hearing too."

"Your mother is unwilling to bring the children up to see you because it would be too upsetting for them to know where you are. She told them you are at college."

"Carleena (age thirteen) has had an abortion and is acting out with boys and drugs. She can no longer be handled by the foster parents. We are moving her into a group home, which we hope will help."

"You are to appear in Family Court on February 22 to extend the children's foster care for twelve more months. They do not think you will be ready to take the children yourself as soon as you get out."

"Your son George is having trouble with the law. The Judge has refused an order for you to be allowed to appear in court with him."

"Miss Clover called to say she is concerned about Shaquanna. She describes her as completely anti-social at school. She expects the school to expel her. She is also expecting her to be held back in 4th

grade. She will begin therapy soon to work on her behavior problems.''

"Onosha says she is being sexually abused by her godmother's son.
Efforts will be made to check this out, and if necessary move her.''

"The social worker is extremely busy and is tired of you constantly
hounding her.''

Letters from a child in foster care are infrequent and treasured even
though they often express unhappiness and dislike of the new family
or of the social worker.

Hi mom, how are you. I'm fine and a little happy. What I mean is my foster
mother hasn't been fare with me. I'm not going to tell you what your Christmas present is.

Ron is the one I can't stand, I actually hate him with passion. . . . He
made up a quick lie, but I knew he was lying so he wasn't fooling nobody but
himself. I can't stand that bald headed weasel. That's why I'll be glad when I
leave this dump. That's why I'm going to do my thing in school this year and
leave. I couldn't stay here another whole year. You know what I mean, my
best friend Richard says the same thing. He said he was gonna go live with
his grandmother . . . oh in the last letter I said I was going to send you a copy
of my report card but now I can't because Claude wouldn't let me. So I'm
going to tell you the grades myself ok. Science 80, English 78, Gym 78 for
Tues, Thurs and 80 for Mon, Wed, Fri, ROTC 91, Lunch this is my favorite
period, European Studies 65, Math 50, Record Keeping 80. Did I do well?
  Love, Rickie

A confusion of generations and roles permeates the letters. The
child is part child and part parent. Often the child is more strength to
his mother than she can be to him. At a time in their lives when they
should be struggling to find their own identity, children who have
mothers in prison have to convince her that she is someone who
matters. They flatter her and advise her and encourage her and ad-
monish her.

"Your 26 going to 27 but still attractive and got your looks. Happy mother's
day Precious.''

"You look beautiful in your new teeth.''

"Dear Mommy, How are you. I miss you very much. Last time I saw you you
looked all right, I didn't mean all right. I mean pretty. Not that either,

beautiful. When are you coming home? I will never forget you. I love you Mommie."

"I liked the picture you sent. I'll show it to all the girls in my class. I know what they will say. Elaine your mother is very pretty."

"Riddle—What has a pretty face? She is something to me. What is it? YOU."

Again and again the children urge their mothers to be good so she can get out sooner. If she doesn't get out sooner, it means to them that she wasn't trying. They warn her not to repeat whatever it was that brought her there; they question how she ever did the deed in the first place, and they assure her they know she will "make it" when she gets out.

One daughter, who writes very loving letters to her mother, stopped almost mid-sentence in one of her letters and asked, "Didn't you realize you could have gotten a job? You didn't have to write bad checks." and then went on with the rest of the letter.

The majority of letters shared with us were from girls. Ten- to fourteen-year-olds wrote most frequently, perhaps because, next to infancy, there is no more tender age than this, no time when mothers are more loved and needed. There are, of course, many children of inmates who do not write. Many letters start out with, "I'm sorry I haven't wrote more." Usually the excuse is homework. This is my favorite one: "I would have rote sooner but I pulled a musel in my neck and i was to tens."

We all experience the pains of loneliness sometime during our lives, but few people know them more intimately than children whose mothers are in prison. Life is hard for most of the children of the world, but the presence of one's mother often compensates for much that is missing. To most children the loss of their mother is devastating. The loss is multiplied when father is a stranger who moves in and out of a child's life rarely or not at all.

"My father sends his regards, and his girlfriend Titi Julia says have a happy new year."

"I guess you wonder where are father is. Margaret says he got married and moved to California."

"I can't count on daddy for anything any more."

"Do you know whatever happened to my real dad? Is Joe my dad? Did he brac out of jail. I miss little Charlie. Tell him I said hi. I still think of you. You are my favorite mom. My favorite dad is Charlie and my favorite brother is little Charlie . . . but could you write and tell me about my real dad please."

Sometimes, after mother has been away a while and grandmother has taken care of them, the younger children become a little confused about who Mama really is. We often hear children in the Children's Center calling them both, "Mama." When they begin to call a foster mother Mama that makes for confusion too, especially to the very young. One child who wrote frequently, solved the problem by beginning his letters quite formally with, "My Dear Mother Brenda."

One of the mothers in Bedford Annex, the mental ward here (I was asked to refer to it as "the housing unit for those women who do not adjust readily to regular population"), told me her children avoided confusion by calling her "Little Self" and her mother, their grandmother, "Big Self."

The woman herself is often quite confused now. She sees her grown children not at all, and rarely gets a letter. It is hard to judge them. She is here for arson, and is often quite removed from reality. "They not treatin' me like I treated them, not payin' much attention."

It is hard to describe how much each letter means to most mothers, how many times each is unfolded and folded again, read and reread. When letters don't come, and children can't visit, and she feels as though her world has forgotten her, a mother will sometimes think of suicide. As with women on the outside, more female inmates try to commit suicide, more male inmates succeed. A mother who wrote home telling of such thoughts received this letter from her ten-year-old daughter.

Dear Mommy what you wrote me I didn't believe it but if you do that I'll die to. Mommy just because I don't write to you that don't mean I don't love you. Because I love you more than anybody, Mommy. I want you to keep writing about God, because I'm busy in Church and praying about you and saying I love you so much, please don't do such a thing like that Mommy. I pray at the night, and Mommy why did you tell grandma to let Wilma go with her father. Mommy I love Wilma and I cry for her too and you too Mommy. I want you to be good over there for we could make a family you me and Wilma. Mommy I miss you and Wilma. Mommy I can't be without you or Wilma. Please try to believe in God Mommy. When I lost Wilma and you

I pray to God and the next day at 1:00 clock Wilma knocked on the door. I went to open it and when I saw Wilma I hugged her and remembered about you and I looked at Manny and kissed him and I remembered about my father and that same day I had go to church and started to scream and cry so hard about my family. Mommy, that same day Cindy's father died in his sleep and I said God what's happying to me. Mommy why did you write that note to grandma. Mommy everybody said they love and miss you remember you got a mother and family that loves you. I love you.

You love God

God loves you.

From your daughter Sharon

Perhaps the most touching thing about all of the children's letters is their bravery, their willingness to forgive, even in the face of something that has hurt them deeply, and which they obviously still don't really understand.

Dear Mommy,

I love you very much. When you left I did not understand why did you leave but you explain to me with the note you sends me. I read the note I started to cry. No one saw me but Myrna and I went to the bathroom and cried more and more and I showed John. And I am taking care of Myrna and Daddy and brother, Jeff and Uncle Herman. Jany and Carlos don't fight no more and I miss you very very very very much. When you come back bring me a souvenir and send me a post card.

Love, Nora

P.S. I miss you very much and for my birthday its two more months and I hope you be home soon.

The problems the letters reflect would take a thick book to catalogue. Two letters from a nine-year-old boy show signs of serious dyslexia. I don't think mother herself realized what a labor of love those two letters must have been. The printing ran together all over the page, looking more like sandpiper prints in the sand than letters of the alphabet. His mother smiled and said, "Oh, that's old Charlie. It's something with his eyes I guess. He hates school. He's in third grade now and he's already talking about quitting."

"Old Charlie" lives with his grandparents and three sisters on Grandpa's retirement pay from the railroad. While mother was in prison she had her fifth child. There is no way that "Old Charlie" will ever get the special understanding and training that a child thus handicapped should have. His frustration will grow greater every year until he can't stand it anymore, and drops out. It is my observation that here in this prison there is a larger percentage of dyslexia than one finds on the outside. Reading problems are common among juveniles who start early to develop a criminal record. To compound the irony, children with dyslexia are often bright. The frustrations of being unable to read, and the low self image that it brings is, I believe, one of the serious causes of juvenile, and ultimately, adult crime.

But the news isn't always bad. Some young scholars write enthusiastically.

"Dear Mom,
   I love you so much. I am almost the smartest girl in my class. Mommy, I am seven years old. I have a trick. A riddle. I am an fruit. You can peel me. What am I?"

"Dear Mama,
   I got my report card Nov. 23. I got 15 ones. That means I am smart."

"Dear Mother,
   I love you. I will be glad when you come home. I am doing good in school. I got a star in school for being good. So I am sending it to you."

Attached to the letter was a much licked star.

Nothing makes mother more aware of the passage of time than letters that say, "Ma, you know I'm not a child any more." Nothing makes her more nervous either. It was such a short time ago that she told her mother the same thing. For grandmother, who has had a surfeit of sadness from one generation, the threat of a new round of boys, and more babies, and more poverty, is a constant and heavy weight on her heart. She lives with the ache of a daughter in prison, and the cold fear, not without reason, that her grandchildren may go the same way. Her answer to what the child thinks are reasonable requests is often a stern "No!" Boys and girls alike write mother asking her to intervene in their behalf, promising her, "I know what I'm doing."

The biggest question is always "When is Mommy coming home?" Sentences vary tremendously from state to state, from upstate to downstate, north to south and east to west. In New York her sentence may be 2 to 4 years, 2½ to 14 years, 3 to 15 years and almost endless other possibilities. There is no way for mother to say when she'll be home. "A year," "two years," "a long time," "pretty soon," mean totally different things to the young.

"Soon is a long time, Mommy."

"You said you were going away for a long time. Well it's been a long time. Why aren't you home?"

For most of the children, the future is embodied in mother's homecoming. The truth is that her homecoming, for many, will be the hardest part of her punishment. Her children have new needs and habits now. She won't be quite the same woman who went away. A house or apartment that she can afford must be found, something she knows will be almost impossible. Her guilt must be left behind so that her children cannot use it to create new tragedies. But to her young children, her homecoming will be the magic hour.

"The day you get out is going to be the specialist day and I'm going to be good all day."

"July 22 would be a good day to come home, Mama. That's my birthday."

A four year old said to his mother, "I know how to get you out of here. I'm Superman. Get on my cape. I'll take you home."

Watching young mothers with their children in the center, we soon discovered that some of them do not know how to go about being a mother, do not know things as elementary as how to pick up a child, or how to play with it, or even to talk to it.

"My son was six months old when I came here. He's four now. I don't know what four-year-olds like, or what they do. I'm anxious to see him, but I'm scared I'll do all the wrong things. I haven't been with him for a whole week since he was six months old."

When the Red Cross volunteered to give its course for instructors on "The Infant from Birth to Two," Dolores and I both took it and qualified as teachers of the course. In time all the pregnant women and new mothers in the facility were required to come down on Wednesdays and take it with us. They were also required to meet once a week with Debby, the visiting nurse, who teaches them the basic biology of childbirth as well as appropriate exercises, and hygiene for mother and baby. In addition, the center sponsored occasional workshops given by outside instructors, and psychologists on the child at various ages and stages of growth. Dr. Spock himself has come to visit and answer questions.

Last spring, under the direction of an inmate, the center organized and offered a course entitled "Parenting Through Films." It is a ten-week course, team-taught by inmates, with each week devoted to a new subject on the growth and care of our children. The first part of the period we show a film, which has been reviewed and evaluated by the Children's Center staff. Following the film, a different inmate staff member leads a general discussion of the week's topic. Thirty women took and completed the course and we have since given it three more times to large groups. The course on infancy and the film course are firsts at Bedford for inmate-organized and inmate-taught courses.

Sister never rests on her laurels, and she doesn't let anyone else do so either. While she is helping us in one direction she is thinking of three other ways to go as well. An encounter one day with one of the many mental patients at Bedford prompted her to say to us soon after I had joined the center, "You know, it isn't just little children who need mothering. The child in all of us needs it. We ought to do something for the women up on Bedford Annex, something to brighten their week. It seems to me their lives are among the bleakest here." Our final decision on what the "something" should be does not indicate any creative genius on our part, but then our options were not plentiful either. We, three of us, began playing Bingo with "the ladies on the annex" every Friday night. The program has been active now for four years. We take some kind of treat for them to eat and drink, and bring cigarettes and needed toiletries as prizes.

At first only five or six women would venture out to the recreation room to join us, and most of those came only to get cigarettes. We didn't care why they came as long as they moved about and socialized a little. We were assured this was better for them than staring into space in their cells. Today, between twenty-five and thirty women play with us each week. Giving them cigarettes bothered me at first, but it doesn't anymore. Some of them are so high strung the cigarette is one of the least harmful things you can give them. There are any number of other options they try when the tension get too tough.

They carve their initials in their arms, or neck, swallow safety pins; one has even swallowed two pair of eyeglasses, the whole thing, piece by piece. They start fights, pick up the large television set and throw it—the repertoire is endless. We have tried with a certain amount of success to wean some of them away from so many cigarettes by getting as much variety as possible into our prizes. We have wrapped up everything that isn't nailed down. I even made enough mittens for everyone one winter. A Marlboro looked better than a mitten to some, but by that time we had become friends and they tried not to hurt my feelings. They took the mittens and traded them later for cigarettes. Cigarettes are prison money.

The summer when I had a heart attack Sister Elaine told the ladies of Bedford Annex she would find a substitute for me until I could return. They told her, "No thanks. We'll wait until Jean comes back." I consider that the height of loyalty and friendship. They sent me many cheerful notes while I was in the hospital, and I appreciated how much effort and kindness went into them.

The week I returned for Bingo, after a month of illness, they had a short, formal ceremony before the game began, at which they presented me with an oil painting of me done by Margie and signed by all. "To a Very Dear Women." Fortunately, I guessed right about who it was. I recognized the pearls.

Nights like this, and many others on Bedford Annex, have probably been among the richest learning experiences of my life. My memories of it are a kaleidoscope of tears and laughter, moments when I felt better because I was there, moments when I wondered what the hell I was doing there. Women I ached for, women I couldn't stand, each one of them my teacher; Minnie who tried to kill herself the night before her five children came to see her for the first time after the doors closed behind her for twenty-five years; Dora who died of AIDS; Candy who has torn her insides apart swallowing bed springs and anything smaller she could find; Sparrow who can't have a baby because "I was raped when I was seven and he tore my insides up real bad"; Koko who thinks, "They're putting cyanide in my food, Jean, but I can eat what you give me because I know you're not tryin' to kill me."

And then there's Pam, the artist, and poet, and realist. We were crowded together at a table one night, eight of us playing Spades.

Suddenly Pam looked up and announced in her deep voice, "Somebody at dis table smells." The game stopped. Everyone looked embarrassed and rather insulted. Finally Anita turned to her and said in her haughtiest tone, "Did it ever occur to you that it might be you?"

"Not me" she answered regally. "Ah never smells." The game continued.

4.

I hadn't given any thought to tiny babies since my children and my godchildren had entered nursery school. But once I began getting involved I was hooked, just as Sister had hoped, I'm sure. I never knew, and still don't know whether some of the things she finds for me to do are because they need doing, or because she is determined to help me find ways to feel useful. She does this for all of us.

It was while we were working over the children's letters that Sister asked me if I would help in a small way in the prison nursery. To say that I agreed is a long way from suggesting that I succeeded. A prison nursery can be a trying place to be, as a mother or as a worker. For babies, however, considering what most of their options are on the outside, it can be a healthy and positive place to get started, and that is the purpose of a prison nursery.

No one knows how many babies are born to incarcerated women in America in any given year because to date it hasn't seemed important enough to anyone to count and write the number down. In the most recent *Source Book of Criminal Statistics*, 1984, published by the United States Department of Justice, there are thousands of statistics.

They tell you about rates of urbanization in the United States, the estimated number of deaths from arson, the basis for wiretaps, public opinion about smoking and the dangers thereof, the number of employees in our correction system, number of arrests for disorderly conduct, public opinion about abortion, even figures on the public's confidence or lack of it in the media; but nowhere in its 693 pages does it suggest that inmates have children waiting for them on the outside, or that a significant number of female inmates give birth while incarcerated. The word divorce is not listed in the criminal index either, though broken homes play a far more important role in crime statistics than such things as smoking, and the public's opinion of the media.

The nursery at Bedford is the only prison nursery in the United States where an imprisoned mother who has given birth while she is incarcerated may keep her baby with her until it is a year old. For that, New York taxpayers should be grateful, and other states should be taking a close look and reevaluating their reasons for not having similar facilities. Of course, being outside with the baby might be better, but in most cases the prison nursery is far better than total separation. The women's jail on Rikers Island has just opened a nursery within the past year.

The history of this nursery goes back to 1901 when what is now a top security prison for women was incorporated as New York State Reformatory for Women, a place for "female vagrants, wayward minors, and youthful offenders." From its inception, young women were allowed to keep their babies with them for a year, even as long as eighteen months if the mother were going out within that time.

Over the years, as the reformatory grew, the nursery grew with it, and sometimes housed as many as forty babies. They lived on an entire floor of the medical building and their mothers cared for them when they were not at their regularly assigned jobs. Other inmates took turns with them them too, since baby care was considered an essential part of each girl's "reformation." I wish we didn't consider that an "old fashioned" notion

Until 1930 women in prison in New York State were not allowed the same privilege as those in reformatories. Through the work of women on the National Committee on Prisons and Prison Labor, and in particular, Dr. Ellen E. Polter, legislation was drafted to permit women in state prisons to keep their babies for a year too. With the strong backing of the New York State Federation of Women's Clubs, and the state Charities Aid Association, the bill was signed into law by then Governor Franklin D. Roosevelt. It is still on the books as Correction Law 611, and virtually unchanged in fifty-six years. It was passed without great difficulty at the time because it was considered the work of nice lady do-gooders, and had no particular political overtones. To try to pass similar legislation today is a very different story.

A woman is excluded from the program if she is not physically able to care for her baby, or if her emotional instability indicates the baby might be in jeopardy. It is a rare occurrence for a woman to be turned down.

Other prisons and jails around the country have nurseries where babies are kept for a week or two after birth, until they can be placed with a family or social agency. Sister Elaine visited one such nursery in the Midwest and found it a bleak, empty room except for six cribs in the middle of it, and not a picture or bright object anywhere in sight. Kansas has recently extended the period an incarcerated woman may keep her baby with her to six weeks. California has tried a mother-child program in a halfway house, but so few women fulfilled all the requirements to get into it that it has been of minimal consequence.

Among the favorite arguments used again and again all over the United States to keep nurseries out of female prisons, or to close the ones that once existed, I have read these from legislative hearings.

"Government isn't in the baby business."
How sad, when the future of government rests in those hands.

"We're not talking about mothers. We're talking about convicted felons."

"A woman in prison doesn't have the same sort of feeling toward her children as a woman in the free world does."

"This dear little baby didn't commit a crime. How can we put her in prison?"

Lila said, "My baby ain't in prison. My baby with her mama."

The main purpose of Bedford's program today is to give infants the healthiest start possible, physically, mentally, and emotionally, and to help them form a strong bond with mother, who in most cases will be their main care-giver in the years ahead. Of the twenty-eight born here in 1981–1982, a third of them left with their mothers, and many others followed within a few months. Traumatic as separation is, there is less separation with the nursery than there would be without it.

It would be difficult for a young mother, with all the other adjustments she has to make when she leaves here, to go out to a year-old baby that had been taken from her at birth and develop the same maternal bond she would feel if she had nursed it through the first year of life. Three of the twenty-eight mothers listed in the above study were returned to Bedford for parole violations, none for a new charge, and 75 percent of the mothers are living with their babies. Two of the twenty-eight are married.

The difficulties involved in the administration of a prison nursery are profound. As with everything else, the more we learn, the more we don't know. Much about human growth and maturation is still obscure. We do know, however, that much of our development occurs far earlier than we once thought, and infancy is a more vital time for future intellectual success and social adjustment than many people still realize. Knowing this increases the need for training young mothers, and fathers as well, and complicates some of the everyday problems in the nursery.

The baby's best interest must share priorities with prison security. What is the baby's best interest varies tremendously from child to child, but few go out to what we still like to think of as a "normal home environment."

Bedford babies are all born in neighborhood hospitals, outside the facility. The only tragedy of that is that to get there a mother must, by law, be handcuffed. I have seen two women in the final stages of labor with their hands chained together and then chained to a big black belt around what was once their waist but is now all baby. They climbed heavily and awkwardly into the prison van to go and give birth. I have seen another young mother, in the middle of a late miscarriage, blood running down both her legs, similarly chained.

She didn't seem angry, only embarrassed by the blood. It is a terrible sight to see, and it is done to women whose crimes are nonviolent as well as violent. It is a pretty good bet that a woman in the final stages of labor cannot outrun the C.O.s who drive her to the hospital, and since she is in a prison car whose doors and windows cannot be opened from the inside, and where there is a strong cage separating her from the driver and rider, the chains are overkill and should be stopped, at least for the mothers. She may also come to in the delivery room handcuffed to the delivery table, always with a uniformed and armed guard sitting beside her. (I have a friend who underwent eight-hour surgery on her spine and woke up chained to the bed. Her offense was nonviolent.)

Whether or not the baby suffers any stigma in the years ahead depends largely on mother and the family. There is nothing on the child's birth certificate to stigmatize it in any way. There is also no follow-up study to find out what happens to these children when they grow up. There has never been money made available to do such a study, which would be a valuable addition to our growing body of knowledge about the needs of infants and children.

I have read of only two Bedford-born children, quite by accident, and sad to say both were in *The New York Times* telling of an arrest. The article did not say the children had spent a year at Bedford, only that each was born while their mother was here, both had been placed in foster homes and both deserted by an alcoholic mother. All other things being equal, the place they were born probably played little role in their lives later on.

Life in the nursery is not an easy ride for the young mothers. It's an emotional time for a woman, and few of her emotional needs are being met. She lavishes love, and whatever things she can get, on her baby, sublimating her own needs that way. Keeping the babies dressed can become a bone of contention. Some of the baby clothes are provided by the state, some by inmate families, and some by kind outsiders. When people send us clothes, obviously they don't send ten or fifteen of anything. One baby gets one thing, one baby gets another. Tempers can get heated about who gets what.

The mother's life experience has been being put down. This they are accustomed to, but if they suspect that anyone is putting down their baby, the air becomes electric and there's trouble. We all try hard to remember not to show even the smallest suggestion of favoritism. And it isn't difficult because the babies are all cute and lovable and funny and charming in their own special ways.

The parenting course that I teach starts with the Red Cross Course curriculum, but whatever the point of departure, the two words I keep coming back to are "love and language." Over and over I tell the young mothers, "The way your children speak is the way they will live, and you are their teacher. They will learn to talk from you. If they spend the first six years of their lives being told, 'Pick up your shit,' they aren't going to start saying, 'Pick up your toys,' just because they've started school. If you do not take the time to talk with your children, use the proper words for things, ask them questions, respond to their questions, they will not learn words. And you can't learn to read without words. School will not be an extension of your family customs. If what they learn at home is completely foreign to what is accepted social behavior and speech outside, you will be sending your children out into a most uncordial world. And it won't have anything to do with being black. It will have to do with not doing your job as a parent." It isn't an exercise in putting down what they do. The point is only to make them realize that they are deciding right now how wide their children's world will be. I find many reasons to praise the mothers, but I don't lie to them.

It was while I was working in the nursery that I first came to know Ma Brown. Her name was Ruth, but I never heard her called anything but "Ma," and "Granny." Before her death last year she had lived in prison for fifty-one years. She had started out in Sing Sing before New York had an official prison for women. She and her husband were found guilty of murder and sentenced to death. Her husband was electrocuted and Ma's head had been shaved in preparation for her own execution when the governor commuted her sentence to life.

She was moved to Bedford, I believe, around the time of the Second World War, and was eventually paroled by then Governor Dewey. She went out for a while but found that she could no longer exist on the outside and asked to be returned, or violated parole, I'm not sure which. As I understand it, if one has been sentenced to life imprisonment she cannot be forced out. She came back to Bedford and for the rest of her life when her parole hearings came up she simply refused to go to them.

She had a daughter outside somewhere, but they had long since lost contact. In time, Ma was moved to the nursery floor and there she lived out most of her adult life. She was a fixture there, loving the babies, caring for them when mother or sitters weren't available, nagging the young mothers to clean up the place, doing far more than her share of cleaning herself. The girls called her "Granny" and "Granny" she was. When Fiske opened, then Superintendent Frank Headley tried hard to persuade her to move here. He brought her up to dinner several times and everyone made a big fuss over her. She was told she could have her pick of rooms, but she wanted no part of it.

Her babies were what kept her alive for so many years, in a life that had little else to convince her it was worth living. She and I chatted frequently when I went upstairs to the nursery to check on which babies had outgrown their sleepers and who needed more little shirts. I finally began taking a complete layette to Ma just in case a baby was born over the weekend. We commiserated over the younger generation and exchanged the news of the day.

Last year, months after Ma's death, Sister called me into her office and I found her as usual with great bags of things piled all over the place. "Would you help me with these?" she asked. "They belonged to Ruth Brown."

They had been stored away in black garbage bags over the years, down in the basement. They included all the simple gifts people had given her over the years for Christmas and birthdays, and the flotsam and jetsam of a poorly spent life. The C.O.s had come to know her in those years and to feel rather protective toward her. I'm sure some of the gifts had been from them.

As old ladies are inclined to do, she saved much and used the same old things over and over again, as though the new things were too grand for her. Unused house dresses were mixed in with old kitchen curtains that she may have brought with her when she came fifty years ago. They were stained and yellow and useless, but a piece of her life that she found need to cling to. Bits of rick-rack carefully removed from something and wound in a ball to be used to decorate something else were there, and masses of small stained fabric, each saved with some purpose in mind but never used again.

Sister had befriended Ma for fifteen years, shopping for her, running small errands, visiting her when she was sick. She seemed the logical person to go through the bags, but it saddened her to do it alone, and it bothered her too. It is intrusive, almost rude to go through the private belongings of someone now dead. One feels like a voyeur, and yet the task must be done. Most of what was there had to be thrown away, but anything usable was put aside and Sister tried to think of someone Ma would like to have given it to.

The most numerous unused gifts were gloves and crosses on chains, large wooden ones, small silver and gold colored ones. The appropriate thing to send women, women you don't know very well but feel in all decency you should care about, varies according to their calling. School teachers get endless bottles of eau de cologne. Nuns, I'm told, get large supplies of white handkerchiefs, and old ladies in prison apparently get gloves and crosses.

Ma had tiny hands. I can't imagine anyone today who could use those gloves. One pair of them is still in a box I keep under my bed of things to use as Bingo prizes. It depresses me to see them each time I open the box, but I can't find anyone to give them to.

5.

The summer program at the Children's Center is our biggest undertaking, and began with Brother Tom Grady and Sister Elaine simply driving children here on their own so the children could see their mothers. In 1980 Sister looked around for a house in this area to rent, so children could stay there for a week and come each day to see their mother. Everything was much too expensive for her budget, which had nothing about a summer program written into it, and anyway, who would rent their house to a bunch of children? A volunteer worker in the center suggested that several children could stay at her house for the week, and the program was born.

In 1981 and 1982 I watched from the sidelines and thought Sister was dreaming when she spoke of having fifteen, and then forty children. In 1983 I played a small role in the program, largely playing games and jumping rope with children. (Today a jump rope is contraband so that game is out.) In 1984 and 1985, along with the other inmate staff members, I played an active role. We had ninety-eight children in the program in 1984, and in 1985, 158 children and sixty-five host families took part, over a nine-week period. We plan on twelve weeks this summer. No other work that I have done in prison has brought me closer to an understanding of these women, and the lives they lead, and the way they lead them, as helping them plan for a week with their children.

The format of the program is simple. Host families are found in the general Bedford area to take a child for a week, from Sunday afternoon until Friday morning. Every day the host family brings the child to the prison to spend the visiting day with mother. A program of games and handwork and music are planned for, but if a mother and child prefer to climb up on the Reader's Roost and share a book, that's all right too.

Lunch is served by the center staff, prepared by them, too, which can be a little complicated at times. This year each mother and her child or children had a small separate table with place card and flowers that Loretta made for them, and everyone lingered longer over their meals than they had when we put everyone at one long table.

Most visits happen on the weekends, and last only a few hours under crowded, noisy conditions. And when they happen mothers are usually torn between wanting to play with her child and wanting to visit with the adult, usually her mother, who brought the child. Many things are left unsaid. The summer program gives mother and child five days of visiting time to themselves, to get to know one another again.

Last year, when many more mothers signed up for the program than we could get hosts for, Sister advertised in various Catholic magazines for teaching nuns who might have some free time during the summer to come and help us, especially with transportation. Children from as far away as Staten Island or Long Island or upstate New York or out of state are given host families first. Others are picked up and taken home each day of their week by nuns, portal to portal, through some of the very worst sections of New York. Moreover, many children had to be picked up in huge housing units where finding little children could be like finding the proverbial needle in the haystack. I thought the nuns would arrive that first morning, hand the car keys to Sister, and bid her a fond farewell. But I was wrong.

For two entire summers now they have arrived smiling, the children clinging happily to them, everyone full of good cheer, even those who had managed to get car sick, or start an argument with a sister or brother along the way. I thought the children would weary of the long drive and drop out before their week with mother was over. Not one has dropped out yet, in fact, last summer we permitted seventeen children to come for two weeks and will do it again this year. Sister would have them all here for the summer if she could figure out how.

Nothing points up the resiliency of a child better than the happy, enthusiastic youngsters who come rushing into mother's arms each summer morning of the program. A beautiful little two-year-old opens her arms wide as she reaches the front gate with all its barbed wire and says happily, "Mommy's house!" The children are picked up, many of them, from the very bowels of poverty.

"Jean, those four kids live with their aunt in one room in a welfare hotel. I'm sure they don't eat right. And where can they play?"

"We drove by the address you gave us twice, and figured it must be a mistake. The whole block is burned out, windows broken. We figured no one could live there. Finally we stopped and I went up to the door. It was the right place. I waited for her in the doorway. The only furniture in the front room is dirty mattresses on the floor." The nuns' descriptions made it easier to understand twelve-year-old Meticia saying, "Oh, Sister. This has been the happiest week of my life."

The mothers' attitude toward the program and their understanding of its purpose have developed in a heartening way. The first few summers the mothers were inclined to think it was social hour for them. We had to remind some of them to be with their children, not just visit with one another. Not so last summer. The warmth and love that filled the room touched even some pretty untouchable by-standers.

Most of the summer program goes on in the Children's Center and the far end of the visiting room, though in the past three years it has, happily, spilled over on to a lovely brick terrace immediately off the visiting room. No inmate or visitor had been allowed on it since it was built. What anyone had in mind when it was added at what must have been a considerable expense I couldn't say.

In 1982 we began asking if we could take the children out on it for a half hour. The answer was "Absolutely, No!" The C.O. in charge of the visiting room couldn't watch the room and the terrace too, so turning the key to the terrace would mean the expense of another C.O. In 1983 with much fanfare, and after considerable unpleasantness and frustration, the door was opened—without another C.O. A half hour of fresh air in the morning and again in the afternoon was timed to the minute. In 1984 and 1985 it was accepted that using the terrace for the summer program was simple common sense.

The children were even allowed a large toy called "The Canal" that held water and in which they could sail little boats. By last summer, the boats were beside the canal, and the children were in it, soaking wet, and having a glorious time. No one complained, and no one felt threatened. Security wasn't compromised and good judgment carried the day. It wasn't easy, but it happened.

Bedford Hills:
Pages from
the Blue Book

My sons, David and Jim, have been close beside me during this whole grim experience, telling me much too little of their own hurts, trying only to assuage mine. For the first seventy-five days that I was imprisoned one of them was here part of every day. I'm still not quite sure how they managed it because they are busy men. For the three weeks that I was in jail, before coming here, David could visit me at night. But here at Bedford visits are from 9:00 to 3:30.

Jim got leave from the Marines for three weeks and spent each day here. David took a three-week vacation in half days and came when Jim wasn't here. Now David comes during a lunch hour because he works near by, and Jim, who has left the Marines and lives and works in New York City, comes on weekends, always with something funny to tell, and sometimes with a sweater that needs mending too.

I keep bits of yarn from the sweaters I've made in a drawer in the Children's Center. I'm almost glad when a hole appears. It makes me feel useful for a few pleasant moments. I have finally convinced them that it means much more to me to know they are out on the golf course or the tennis court on a good day, than lined up outside a top security prison to visit their mother. But they still come often, and always upbeat.

What little kindness I can do the boys is to spare them the grimmest times, to talk much about things and people, but skip some of the things going on in my mind. We laugh a lot together. I am rarely weepy or hand-wringy when they come. I didn't even cry when David came to tell me that Mother had died. He looked so sad, so troubled, I only wanted to reassure him, as Mother would have done. The more introspective moments of my days end up, if they aren't forgotten completely, in the pages of a small blue copy book someone sent me.

At first I wrote only anger and hurts there, where they were safely buried. Then, after Mother died and I wrote less to the family, the blue book became less a whipping boy and more a diary. As I look through it now, it is a little like turning the cylinder of a kaleidoscope. The bits of colored glass don't change, but each design is different, obviously all part of the same.

April 1981

I have, as I am allowed to have, a small lamp in my cell. You can have one as long it is not more than twenty inches high, and can't cost more than $20. Twenty seems to be the magic number. Mine is approved and I have a signed certificate proving it. Tonight I was reading in my cell when a C.O. came by, walked into my cell and turned on the overhead light, a terrible light that I never use. I said, "Don't turn it on, I have plenty of light with the lamp." She said. "You got to have it on. When the door is open you got to have the overhead light on. If you want dat lite out I got to lock your cell door first." Some new Mickey Mouse idiocy becomes a "rule" every day. It disturbs a C.O. almost to distraction to see me sitting quietly in my cell, minding my own business and not breaking any rules. There are some sick people in here in positions of authority. The idea that there might be such a thing as rehabilitation in here is simply false. After someone has been here for a few years, I think returning to a reasonably normal life will be six times harder that it was before.

April 1981

The sink in my room is something of a problem. It doesn't have any spigots. It has buttons to push. Mine do not push easily, to say the least. To get water I brace my feet against the wall, push hard with my right thumb, and then push still harder on my right thumb with my left thumb. This makes it difficult to wash your hands, since there is no stopper. No stoppers allowed. That way inmates can't flood the place . . . at least I guess that's the reasoning, but of course one can always flood if one so desires. As soon as I stop pushing, the water stops, but I can't wash and push at the same time. It's like trying to see if the light really goes out when you close the refrigerator door. The one redeeming feature is I use so much energy pushing, I'm sure it's a little like doing aerobic exercises. It's the best exercise I get.

April 1981

I spend a certain amount of time trying to figure how to get out in the sun. I've raked and washed windows, and moved about as fast as Huck Finn would have in order to stay out a little longer. We are not permitted outside unless there is a C.O. with us, even though there is a twelve-foot fence all around the tiny yard. This morning I asked if I could go out with some of the inmates who were already out.

The C.O. at the desk said, "Sure. Just ask the C.O. out there to open the door for you."

I did as I was asked but the C.O. wouldn't move to open the door. I walked back to tell the first C.O. that the second C.O. wouldn't open the door for us. She left her post and walked down a long hall to the back door of the building and called out, "Why couldn't you open this when you were asked?" She called back, "I don't take no orders from no inmates. You come up here and ask me and I'll open it."

April 20, 1981

We are strip searched every time we have a visit or are in a place where outsiders have been. Any outside programs end with all the inmates standing around like cattle waiting to be strip searched before they are given their IDs back and permitted to leave. I have been to my first and last public program.

I thought I would not be able to stand having visitors at first, because undressing for these disgusting people seemed too denigrating to bear. It doesn't phase me anymore. I feel rather sorry for the idiots who have to make their living this way.

Contraband comes in with little or no trouble hidden in women's vaginas, but there is little or no judgment shown about who the likely perpetrators are. It's much more fun to spend ten minutes going over the seams of my clothing as though I might have sat in the visiting room sewing drugs into them, than to search the women carefully whom they must know are dealing drugs. Everyone else seems to know.

April 26, 1981

Today I moved from the reception area up to a regular housing unit 114B. This is supposed to be a fairly quiet unit but I haven't seen it so far. Most of the women seem to have a vocabulary of about one hundred words—one noun is used in place of just about all others: SHIT. "I told him to pack up his shit and get out." "I ain't eatin this shit." "Well I mean, hell you know the kinda shit I mean." *Fuck* is of course the verb of choice. And *nigger* is used constantly. I thought that had long since become a no no. "These dumb niggers don't know nothin." It is only blacks who use the word.

My move was quite a production because I have so many books. I was supposed to carry everything up by myself but fortunately four of the women volunteered to help and were permitted to. I was greeted in my new pad with friendly hellos, and inquisitive stares. When I arrived in my cell there were no sheets, blankets, or pillows. Charlene said, "Never mind, doll, I have some pillows you can have," whereupon she started pulling things out from under her bed, and came up with two pretty good pillows.

I assured her I didn't want to take two and she said, "That's all right doll, I have five of them." Next, two women came in offering me clean sheets. It wasn't until after dinner that a C.O. came with sheets and towels. They never have enough because everyone squirrels things away. I throw away almost nothing, string, paper, plastic bags, whatever. I'm even saving the little cups that pills are put in. I'm not sure what for, but a use will show up I'm sure.

May 1981

It's fascinating to watch the parade of inmates when classes are passing, to see what they have done to the state uniforms to give them some individuality. Yesterday I saw a Puerto Rican bombshell with bright red hair go mincing by looking like a peeled eel. She had taken in her slacks to the point where they looked painted on. How she gets her foot in and out I can't figure out. She wore a skin tight tee shirt, and cowboy boots to complete the ensemble.

At a Bible study group tonight one of the women looked great in state slacks, pretty brown shoes, and a short smock with a paisley print. I complimented her on her appearance, and she said she owes it all to her yoga class, and thinks I ought to join it. I have now been asked to be on the education committee, the grievance committee, the library committee, the yoga class, the Bible class, and the NAACP. I asked what the NAACP does in prison and was told, "It have a annual banquet."

May 1981

I have been to two Bible study groups to date and I doubt that I will go many more times. I can't tell where the show stops and the truth begins. "When I was on the street I had me plenty a money and a big apartment an all those material things, but I was headed for damnation."

"Praise the Lord." "I tell you I is glad, glad of the day I was busted. I mean I would probably be dead if the cops didn't go and bust me. I praise the Lord, I is here in this place. I is become a child of God!" I guess we all have to pray in our own way.

June 1981

We had the women help to correct papers this morning. We mixed them all up so no one would know who had whose papers. Then we collected them and handed them back to the owners. One large black woman looked at her paper, stood up and in a deep menacing tone said, "All right. Who the one give me this fuckin' C—?" If it's the teacher, and they get anything less than an A, they threaten to quit the class. If it's another student they'll break your arm.

We're working on prefixes and suffixes now and one of the words given them to use in a sentence was "indistinct." *Webster's* first definition is "not clear." One of the women wrote, "I don't know which man it was raped me, so I am indistinct." Like most authors, they write about what they know. Every day I am reminded that the line between tragedy and comedy is the razor's edge.

Amusement at one another's different cultures and sayings is a two-way street. I lost my ID several days ago and this morning someone called and said it had been found. I said, "Hot dog." A black woman standing nearby slapped her leg and laughed. "What kinda sayin' is that, hot dawg, Miz Jean. What do that mean?"

I said, "It's just an old saying that means, I'm glad, or that's great."

She thought a minute and said, "Hot dawg. I'm gonna teach that to my children. That's a good one."

I said, "It sure beats shit," and she agreed.

June 13, 1981

Prison commissary is the "general store." It publishes a mimeographed list of its wares, and then each day it crosses out with yellow markers whatever items it is out of. Most of the time the list is almost one sheet of yellow. I've been told by one of the staff who ran it for a while that it takes in well over $100,000 a year. But it is still slow to pay its bills, and new orders are put in only after items have been missing for weeks.

Vitamins fortified with iron are one of my regular purchases. They are sometimes out of them for four months at a time. And then when they reorder they are apt to reorder eight or ten bottles—for 450 women. They keep as much inmate money and use it for as long as they possibly can before using it for its proper purpose.

I've grown to hate commissary day because it is one more way that C.O.s misuse, or fail to use their authority properly. Getting down to the commissary can be close to dangerous. Every two weeks since I have been here there has been a wild, outrageous, screaming, scratching melee over who will go down first, and who will go down second. The C.O.s do everything they can to encourage the outbursts, first of all by changing the rules for sign-ups constantly.

A woman who follows last week's procedure, and thinks she will be the first, is invariably told she did it wrong and someone else is now going to be first. After all hell breaks loose, the C.O.s stand back, look very superior and say, "Well you're adults now. You'll just have to fight it out."

Apparently no one has ever told them that isn't the way adults are supposed to work things out. The most obnoxious and pushy women always end up going first, and then, having kept everyone else waiting, come back upstairs and settle into an all-day pinochle game. People who have class or purposeful chores to go to end up going last. Absolutely no help is given the women to work out a sensible plan.

Since each of us lives in a numbered cell the order for commissary could easily be rotated so that everyone had a crack at first, but they want no part of my suggestion. The truth is, anyone with a job or class to go to that morning should go first, but they would never buy that. Moreover, when women finish at commissary they should be required to go to their jobs. But they aren't; no one makes them go.

Commissary day is another holiday. Work, these women soon learn, is the least important thing that happens in here. It matters little to C.O.s and it soon matters not at all to many inmates. I have never been anyplace in the entire world, in my entire life, where such God awful work habits were not only taught but virtually forced upon people. Someone as pushy as Jean Harris, who still tries to get to work on time, ends up with charge sheets and a very hard time of it.

June 23, 1981

The women in this place never cease to sadden me. The word *shit* is, quite literally, the only noun they seem to know. It's something you need, eat, pack, unpack, hide, sew, write, read, look at, keep, and throw away. I cannot imagine the frustration one must feel to have something important to think about or say, and have little more to work with than a quacking duck. They are a strange combination of spoiled, self-centered, naughty children, with a little Ethel Waters thrown in.

A large percentage of them are or have been prostitutes, selling themselves all night long on the streets, but they have a fit when they see me walk around in my bare feet, because, "You goin' get something bad on yo feet ef you don get on yo shoes. Look at dat girl! She crazy walkin' roun with bare feet like dat."

The same woman said yesterday, "That big nigger lookin' at me somethin' awful, but ah tell him 'Teddy Bear, you want anything with this girl, get yo fifty dollahs out first.' "

It's amusing to watch the gold chains in here change necks. They go from inmate necks, to C.O. necks, and then, if you're a good girl you can earn them back again. The rules stated in our rule book says no jewelry is to be in here that costs over $50. Obviously, the chains did not cost $50.

June 30, 1981

I suddenly find it hard to believe that this is the last day of June. It isn't that time moves swiftly here, you just lose all sense of time. Except for not going to GED class, Saturday could be Tuesday, and the Fourth of July could be Christmas. No day has any particular significance.

I keep struggling away at a book about the trial, but as I become more aware of the enormity of what was done to me it becomes harder and harder to take down any of the sixteen volumes and reread.

July 3, 1981

Bill Riegelman and Joel Aurnou came to visit today, but it wasn't a social visit. The inevitable clash of lawyers' egos has come between Joel and Herald Fahringer. I don't want Joel as the appeals lawyer; obviously I'm here in part because he made some horrendous mistakes, but, on the other hand, even though he didn't work effectively, he worked hard. All his help would be useful because he knows the testimony pretty well, all fifteen-thousand pages of it, so he could save Herald some time. They both earn more in a month than I did in any one year of my life, but they argue like school boys over who's in charge.

When push comes to shove it is their public images that matter a helluva lot more to them than I do. Bill isn't that way, so he ends up in the middle with everyone damning him. I'm told I must now write a letter telling Joel that Herald is in charge, even though if I say it wrong he may get angry and throw a wrench into the proceedings by not cooperating.

He has all the pictures I want to go over with Herald, and from what I have seen so far, he isn't about to let me have them, even though I paid for them. He also has papers and letters I need. I actually believed that he was genuinely concerned about me and the injustice that has been done me—but where's the concern now? The big question is whose name goes on the appeals papers first.

For the first time since I came here I feel deeply, hopelessly depressed, knowing that the two people I was depending on are arguing among themselves. It makes me realize the whole appeals thing is a sham. Everything I worked for is gone, and I haven't the strength to build over again. I only want the strength to finish a book that will expose the unspeakable dishonesty of my trial, and then the hell with it.

July 9, 1981

Miss Dawson is the C.O. in 14 Lobby, and a very decent lady. She has worked here for years but the ugliness hasn't rubbed off. It hasn't rubbed off on C.O. Cercia, either, over in the school building. How have they stood it all these years? They never raise their voices or make ugly remarks, and they are kind in little ways where many of the others are deliberately unkind.

Dawson has made my Saturday mornings almost bearable by letting me go out in the yard and clean up, and garden a bit before the others go out, or before a C.O. is on guard. The chance of my going over a twelve-foot barbed fence is pretty slim, but that doesn't keep others from acting as though I might. I bring a big black garbage bag with me, and Dawson lets me use a rake, and I clean up the week's garbage from the yard.

It really can look fairly decent without the tuna cans, and grapefruit rinds, and cigarette butts all over the place. I fill the bag, and cultivate my garden a little bit—before Cupcake comes out and makes a point of walking through it and breaking down as many flowers as possible. How sad and bitter she must be inside. There's one section of the garden I have replanted three times. I think I'll just concentrate on the rest of it now and call that stretch of dirt and garbage Cupcake's garden.

She's eighteen years old, and has a baby outside somewhere, and she's like a wild thing, with little or nothing being done to help humanize her. "Rehabilitate" is such a meaningless term for a young thing like her. I don't really believe it gives her pleasure to destroy the garden, but it's something she knows how to do, and there's little else.

July 1981

The garden actually looks pretty today. I wish I could take a picture of it for Mother, but of course cameras aren't allowed. There are lots of wild petunias that apparently come up each year uninvited. God knows how much we need them! There are marigolds from the seeds Glenda saved from last year. She has been the only gardener until now, but after twelve years of it she is growing weary. Now the trowel is passed to me. I wonder how long I will have the heart to do it. There are some zinnias too, my favorite, from some seeds Dawson brought in. We can't get any in through the package room. There is ample space here for flower and vegetable gardens but they are not allowed. Dawson makes ours possible and so far nobody has given out charge sheets for it, but if the spirit moves them to, some day they probably could.

July 10, 1981

I went to the state store this week to return a lot of stuff they had given me that I knew I wouldn't wear—underthings, night things, all the things which we are permitted to get from outside. While I was there I asked the C.O. in charge if she had a panty girdle. "Oh yes," she said. "We have some very nice ones, but you can't get one without a doctor's permission."

I asked the C.O. on my floor if he could make a doctor's appointment for me, and he said, "You can't make a doctor's appointment like that. You got to sign up for nurse's screening first." So I signed up for nurse's screening, and that evening was taken by a C.O. to the medical building.

The nurse on duty was a man. He said very pleasantly, "Well now, Mrs. Harris, what seems to be the matter?"

I said, "I'm fine, but I'm told I have to come to you to get permission to see the doctor to get permission to wear a panty girdle."

He said, again very pleasantly, "Well let's see what we can do to help you. Who is your doctor?"

I said, "I don't have a doctor."

"What do you mean you don't have a doctor. Everybody has a doctor."

"Well, I've gone to about six of them for required checkups, but I don't remember any of their names, except the foot doctor, and a psychiatrist I never want to see again."

"Well, we'll see if we can't find one for you."

He found one for me, checked the appointment calendar and said, "We can get you in to see Dr. Clements on the 20th of July—but I'll tell you what I can do. I can give you written permission to wear a panty girdle between now and the 20th of July."

I thanked him humbly and profusely, and then, troublemaker that I am, I asked him why I needed medical approval to wear a simple pair of pants.

He said, with complete seriousness, "Well you know, Mrs. Harris, women come in here pregnant, and try to hide it by wearing a tight girdle, and that's very unhealthy for mother and baby."

I didn't think it was relevant to mention that I am fifty-eight years old, and not married. He wrote out his permission note and forwarded it to the state store. Two days later the state store called me out of the GED class to report at once to the store. I was given a new, Sears Roebuck panty girdle. In fact, I was cheeky enough to ask if while I was there I might have two. The C.O., with a stern, unsmiling face said, "Don't push your luck, Harris. I really shouldn't even give you this until you see the doctor."

Six state paid employees were directly involved in the acquiring of one flimsy little panty girdle. And still the public doesn't ask "Why in hell should it cost more than $25,000 a year to keep one prisoner in a state prison? A $7 panty girdle ended up costing the taxpayer at least $100. And more than 800 women pass through these portals in the course of a year. Imagine going through that kind of nonsense for hundreds of women.

July 20, 1981

I saw the doctor today, and when I asked him about a panty girdle he said, "Why ask me?" However, he has now given me written permission—just in case I'm pregnant.

July 1981

I was working in the garden today while a woman sat on a nearby bench and watched. Finally she pointed hesitantly to a bright pink petunia and asked bashfully, "Is that a flower?" I assured her it was and turned away before she could see that she had made me cry.

August 1981

There's a little Jewish woman in here with an archetypical Jewish accent . . . all the Jewish jokes you've ever heard sound like her. I'm told there are only five or six Jewish inmates here—by and large they are too ambitious, too well educated—both, one, or none of the above. She gripes and complains and moans and groans constantly "Vy am I in dis place? Oy, vot a rotten place! You vouldn't believe vat a voman said to me dis morning. . . . Da food is making me sick. Oy vot food. Dey call it food . . . it ain't food. I vouldn't give it to a dog."

September 6, 1981

There was a big Labor Day "do" out in 113 Yard this evening, an amateur show, dancing, singing ranging from pretty good to sad. One of the women is really quite clever. She could probably get a job and hold her own in a musical comedy. Most of what they do is "what comes naturally," no discipline, no training. There is no drama or dancing here, and even music is very limited—gospel singing. Imagine almost 450 women here for years and years on end, with so little opportunity to express themselves creatively.

The yard was all in order for the party—the inmate maintenance crew had made it look quite nice. By the time the program was over the yard was a disaster area, cans, wrappers, cigarette butts, and not one single person asked to pick up, only the paid crew to come in later. There is no concept of individual responsibility taught. I find it difficult to cope with the senselessness of that. This place could be fairly decent if everyone performed the simplest functions and had a modicum of courtesy.

September 1981

A lieutenant pulled me aside tonight as I was on my way to medication and said in a very serious tone, "Mrs. Harris, we're having a good deal of trouble with several of your packages."

I said, "Why? What's the matter?"

He said, "Some of them have no address on the outside so they have to be returned to the sender without opening them."

"How do you do that?"

"Return them to the sender without opening them? Just stamp 'return to sender!' I'm just telling you, you better tell your friends to be sure to put an address on the outside, because, by law, we cannot open them if they don't have an address."

"But how will the mail know where to return them to if there isn't any address on the outside?"

"That's what I'm saying, Mrs. Harris. They just return it to the people who sent it."

"But if there isn't any address on it how do they know where to send it? You have to open the package to see if there's a name and address inside."

"I've just told you, Mrs. Harris, the law says you can't open a package that doesn't have an address on the outside."

Finally I said, "OK, just do whatever you have to do with it." God alone knows what was in the packages, or who sent them, or where they finally ended up.

The lieutenant must be a cousin of the C.O. who refuses to let me alphabetize the many names of my visiting list to make it easier for the C.O.s at the gate to find the names when people come to visit me.

"Mrs. Harris" he said, in the sort of tone one uses with a not very bright child after you've explained something simple to them at least five times. "It ain't gonna do no good to put 'em in alphabetical order. These people don't visit you in alphabetical order."

October 1981

I feel deeply depressed today. Every day I grow further away from a world I wanted to leave anyway. I guess the fact that I am determined to stay alive until the truth of the trial has come out is the log that keeps me afloat. The loneliness I feel in here isn't really new, but sometimes it almost consumes me. It makes me ache for Cider— something to hug, something warm.

October 1981

The most frightening thing about prison, the most dangerous, senseless, wicked thing about it is that it is a place where people incapable of understanding or handling authority have it with impunity. They can throw it around, use it as a weapon, a threat, a crutch, a shield, or an entertainment. Such evil little people! I am safer with the inmates. The constant hazing, harassing and humiliating of inmates works to the detriment of each inmate. Many C.O.s hate their jobs and seem to hate themselves for having the job, and their only outlet is to hurt people. We're certainly easy to hurt.

October 19, 1981

It must be after eleven and Ringo has just called out to Odessa to tell her she has written a song.

"Ya wanna hear me sing it Dessa?"

"Yeah, Ringo."

"It's a poem but when I sing it it's a song."

> *We are criminals and we shall be free*
> *For we got problems, yeseree*
> *Criminals are people too*
> *Doo wacka doo wacka doo wacka doo.*
>
> *Tho we try to do are best*
> *Try to live just like the rest*
> *Criminals are people too*
> *Doo wacka doo wacka doo wacka doo.*
>
> *And we try all through the year*
> *to get the hell right out of here*
> *Criminals are people too*
> *Doo wacka doo wacka doo wacka doo.*

"Ya like it, Dessa?"

"Yeah, Ringo. It's great."

"Shall I sing it again?"

"Sure, Ringo. Sing it again."

She's on the third go round at the moment.

November 1981

I have been wonderfully lucky in one respect in here. I seem to be sharing this terrible experience with, quite literally, thousands of kind and concerned people, as well as with the support and affection of dear old friends and acquaintances. My mail would make a fascinating subject for a doctoral thesis. I don't know what its theme would be, but I'm sure it would make some kind of statement. It would be a slice of Americana in the late twentieth century.

Strangely enough, some of the longest, most supportive letters come from men, many written on their business stationery. Almost fifty of them have come from men in prison, terribly lonely men who had read my name in the papers and knew where I was, and wanted someone, anyone, to write them. Only two have come from women in prison. I'm not sure what that proves. I was terribly upset by letters from prison at first, not by what they said, but by the mere fact that I received them.

I felt somehow unclean, appalled that prisoners would write to me.

I threw some away unopened. That feeling is gone now, but I still don't answer them. It would be logistically impossible for me to answer all the mail I get. I'm just beginning to have some small glimpse of how alone many people are. One man wrote, "I've been in prison for eleven years and have never had an outside visitor. I have a cousin who is seventy-one, and she says she sure would come and see me if she could, but she hasn't any way to get here." I did answer him. I couldn't not answer.

December 1981

A kind woman named Laura Haywood has sent me four of Loren Eiseley's books and I am reading them with new pleasure, if pleasure is the word. He was a lonely, rather tormented man and I feel deep empathy for his loneliness. I have known loneliness all my life. I have walked a thousand miles along beaches touched by oceans or lakes or inlets or ponds—loving the beauty of it, loving the freedom of it, feeling clean and whole, but paying the price in loneliness. I have spent a lifetime being alone, rarely if ever initiating any social activity, assiduously minding my own business. Now I read that a woman named Trilling has written a book around her theory that I lived out my life motivated by a burning desire to go to dinner with the right people . . . to climb socially. When will people like Trilling learn what "society" is?

Betsy, a dear young friend of Jim's, has sent me a subscription to *Vogue*, something I never looked at outside, but I guess all the garbage about Mrs. Harris' clothes during the trial made her think I had. I settled into bed last night after all of us were safely locked in our cages, stretched out on my rock hard bed, and started to leaf through the magazine. After the first two flips, there was Diana Trilling, "Social Arbiter of Our Time," talking about, of all things, Jean Harris.

The same sloppy little woman I had seen each day at my trial—the same one I had seen stretched out, full length and shoeless, on one of the court benches quietly snoring—the same woman who kept repeating what a bore the whole thing was, and if it didn't end soon she wouldn't be able to meet her publishing deadline. What could be more boring than two useful people's lives, when there was money to be made, and dinner parties to go to? In all kindness, I thought at first that she was senile. Unfortunately she is simply arrogant and greedy.

As I think about it, Hy wasn't just social climbing most of the time. In fact he had a far better notion of what "society" is than Trilling does, and he carefully avoided it. He would never go to Grosse Pointe with me. Rejection was the last thing in the world he wanted. Hy was simply a poor boy who grew up to be rich, and having become rich, wanted to play golf and tennis instead of stickball. That the rich also play golf and tennis didn't make him a social climber. It was money that excited Hy, not social position. Mrs. Trilling, like many of her ilk, doesn't know that there's a difference.

Is it true that we can only love what we know is good? I believed that Hy was good. But when I learned that he was not, I went on loving him—or at least needing the security of knowing he was there. I hated all the things that made him second rate, and people who brought out the worst in him, people like Arthur and Lynne. Arthur who had all the sensitivity and feeling of a house plant. Did Hy really care for him? Would he have cared as much if Arthur had consistently won at gin instead of consistently lost?

February 1982

Somewhere in Shana's book she apparently wrote that I had a mink coat in my cell, thrown into a pillowcase and used as a pillow. Where she got this idea I can't figure out. I told her once that all my clothes that had been at Hy's house and were used in the trial were still thrown in a plastic bag somewhere in the district attorney's office or the police station. I didn't know where. Somehow she got the story mixed up.

This evening one of the C.O.s came to my cell, most apologetically and said, "Mrs. Harris, I'm sorry to bother you but the deputy superintendent told the sergeant to do this and the sergeant made me do it, and I know it's dumb, but I have to search your room for a mink coat." Maybe the deputy read the book. We both laughed, and I told her, "Be my guest, and if you find it you can have it."

Poor old coat. I wonder where it is. It was referred to all through the trial as a "mink-like coat." Maybe a "mink-like coat" is what I'll get back some day. It had absolutely nothing to do with my trial, but since they had thrown out all the important evidence they had to use something.

April 1982

Today at lunch there was cake for dessert. It comes in tin foil pans. I use these pans for dishes in my room since I try to avoid eating in the zoo as often as possible. I wash them and use them again and again but today I was finally down to one. There were four empty pans sitting on the counter where we are served. C. O. Smith was standing beside them and I asked her politely if I could have two of them. "They're very useful," I added.

She said, "I'm not givin' these to you."

"But I'm allowed to have them and I really do put them to good use."

"I'm givin' you nothin' unless a sergeant give his permission."

I went out to the sergeant in the hall and asked him if I could have the tins and he said, "Yes." I went back to Smith and said "He says it's OK."

"How do I know it's all right. I don't take no inmate's word. He wants to tell me he can come and tell me hisself. I'm givin you nothin' unless the sergeant says."

I went out to the sergeant again and asked if he would step inside and tell Smith it was OK. He followed me back to Smith and said, "It's OK. Give her the pans." Smith said, "It's too late. I just threw 'em all in the garbage." An inmate standing beside her looked pleased. "Fuckin' old bitch. Think she so good cause she from Scarsdale."

April 1982

They're searching cells again for contraband. Three C.O.s are going through one cell at a time, not everyone each time, just certain ones. Georgia's booze will probably be found again. She serves her fifteen days in lock, and then, undaunted, starts another batch. In fact, sometimes, if she is able, she starts the new batch while she is still in lock. Last time they found three gallons of the stuff under her bed.

I told her her timing was bad. She should have sold out to Seagrams and used the income to bring it in from outside. It's a game with Georgia, and with the C.O.s too. We all wonder what happens to the stuff the C.O.s take. They never make a grand gesture and pour it all out while we watch. They always carry it off with them.

"Vats" for making jailhouse booze are the big gallon jars that syrup or mayonnaise or mustard come in—from the kitchen. The base is fruit juice—easy to come by because canned fruit is what we have most often for dessert, gallons and gallons of it. A few raw potatoes pilfered from the kitchen help it to ferment, raisins and rice are useful too. Then after it is well aged for five or six days the ladies get royally drunk.

I must confess I usually can't tell whether they're drunk or sober. Some of them don't make much sense either way. I'm told some frantic women will even drink perfume, but that's a rare occurrence, I'm sure. Just to be sure, we are only allowed three ounces of perfume per month. You can hardly have a good drunk on that.

April 1982

Carmen, one of the older women on this floor, who cooked for "a family on Park Avenue" before she came to Bedford, told me she used to make "a very nice little table wine, Jean. I like a glass of wine with dinner, but the girls would get hold of it and drink it all at one time and get very drunk, so I just don't make it anymore."

The other things searched for are drugs, but they have to use dogs for that, and drugs are rarely hidden in cells. They are all over the facility, in offices, and schoolrooms, and showers, maintenance closets, and probably some under trees too. That way you may lose the stuff when the dogs find it, but you don't end up in Sag because they rarely know whose it is—or can't prove it if they do.

I'm told a very large stash of pot and cocaine was found in the electronics room recently. There were some very long faces for a few days. I guess that's what you call "risk capital" . . . so the mark-up is higher next time. Capitalism flourishes inside as well as outside.

I get nervous if I see a penny on the floor of the visiting room— money is also contraband, but those in the know tell me hundred dollars bills are flashed up in population. In fact, one not overly bright young lady who thought she knew which C.O.s she could trust, asked a C.O. to change a hundred dollar bill for her. She made a bad selection and ended up in Sag for sixty days, and lost the $100 too. I wonder who got it?

April 12, 1982

It's almost 11:00 P.M. and Sharrine, directly across the hall from me, is banging on her door as hard and as loud as she can. She has asked the C.O. for two Tylenol and the C.O. says she can't have it. She should have thought of it before lock-in at 10:00 P.M. Sharrine says she didn't have a headache until now. The C.O. says that's too damned bad.

"You fuckin' bitch. You get me some Tylenol."

"Shut up that noise."

"I ain't makin' no noise. I'm just callin' for some Tylenol."

There are laughs now from different ends of the hall, loud, unnatural laughs, maniacal laughs. This is the kind of excitement they love and sometimes I enjoy it too. Someone else ends up with the charge sheet and you just sit by and are entertained. It breaks the monotony of prison life to have your neighbors shriek and scream. It's almost a letdown when the screaming stops.

She's calling for a sergeant now. "I want the fuckin' sergeant. You get the fuckin' sergeant."

Three times the C.O. has walked down to tell her she won't bring her a Tylenol.

Sharrine picks up two bottles and throws them under her metal door. The glass shatters all over the hall and some of it lands in my cell. "Where's the fuckin' sergeant? I want that Tylenol."

It's 11:00 P.M. now and the shift is changing. Sharrine is quiet, gathering her strength for the next shift. In a little while the noise will start all over again. The guards are sleepy. They want no part of her or her headache. It's now a matter of honor to make her go without the damned Tylenol. To give it to her would be too reasonable. She'll yell until she falls asleep, and not a single inmate will tell her to be quiet. It's better than the late show.

May 1982

I am becoming less of an observer and more of a participant now. We just went out to sign up for commissary, and instead of standing by while everyone else pushed ahead, I stood my ground, fair and square. When a woman in back of me said, "Sign my name and Arlene and Darlene and Williana's too," I said, "We can only sign for ourselves." She gave me a black stare. "If people could sign up for others then the first person up in the morning would decide the whole list."

My modus operandi to date has been to stand by and keep my mouth shut, at least as shut as I could. Now I realize that's just another put down to these women. C.O.s like to say, "Don't expect them to take turns or do anything in an adult way. They don't know any better." That's nonsense. Much of what they do wrong is a test of how far they can go. It reminds me of a prominent little debutante, years ago, using the men's john at the Little Club, probably wondering if anyone would ever tell her that it was unacceptable behavior.

May 1982

It is hard to describe what meals are like here. Inmates who serve the food seem to be picked for their loud voices and rudeness. They slop the food onto a plate and push it into your face. If someone asks, as I used to, "May I have just a small portion, please," they're told to go fuck themselves. If they ask for more than half a pat of butter they are asked, "Who the shit you think you is?" But if the next person in line is a girlfriend or boyfriend, they may be, quite openly, handed a whole pound of butter.

It is a daily occurrence to see women walk upstairs with whole boxes of food from the kitchen, pounds and pounds of meat, butter, eggs, you name it. I have been threatened with a charge sheet for taking two pieces of bread upstairs. "Be my guest," I told the C.O. He wrote the charge sheet and later tore it up.

June 1982

Inmate talking to a friend about her parole officer. "He just a suit-wearin' nobody. He so dumb he play chess with marbles."

I took a tray at lunch today and it had gum all over it and was stuck to the next tray. I took a third tray and it had some rice and other dried food stuck to it. I put the three trays over a ledge behind the tray railing. The women serving yelled, "What the fuck you doin? You can't do that. Who goin pick 'em up?"

I said, "There isn't anywhere else to put them."

"You put 'em where they was," she yelled. "Some dirty person'll use 'em."

August 1982

Today is particularly festive because two women who were granted clemency will be going home. They are both well respected. I don't think anyone begrudges them their moment of happiness. It would be hard to describe the unique emotional experience of watching a woman who has spent 9½ years in a cage, put on her own clothes and walk out, reborn, into a whole new world.

One of the women has worked long hours in here, as many as they would permit her to work, and saved every penny, looking ahead to today. She'll stay with Sister Elaine at Providence House for a while until she gets a job and finds a place of her own, but she'll make it. The other woman, Rica, is Puerto Rican, speaks almost no English, and started out with two consecutive sentences of fifteen to life, the product of Mr. Rockefeller's insane drug laws.

Clemency, from what I have seen of it, is not so much an act of compassion, which the name seems to imply, as it is a way of undoing a great injustice without anyone having to say "I'm sorry." I believe Adela Holzer played a role in Rica's clemency. She was certainly the first to see the terrible injustice that had been done, and to start the wheels turning.

August 1982

Renee, they ought to call her Rastus, is a lazy old bitch. She has nothing, and that's exactly what she has worked for. She shuffles in and out of cells, "borrowing."

"Miz Jean, you got a little coffee? Got some sugar? Got some Cremora? Shit, I can't drink coffee without no Cremora. You sure you ain't got none?"

She is a dyke and cozies up to lonely girls, of which we have more than enough, sweet talks them, and then takes them for every last tea bag, cigarette, Kleenex, and piece of wearable clothing she can manage to get. We were standing in line one day at lunch and a woman walked by she had known on the street.

"Ah knew that girl. Kept me on the street once, bringin' me clothes and all. Shit, they was used clothes. Bringin' me shit. When I get outta here I get me on welfare and find me a nice little girl bring me new things—none of them used shit. Ah like to live nice."

September 1982

The women have asked me to write a letter to the superintendent about the baths and showers on 114A and B. Everyone will sign it. There are two bathtubs for sixty women, and the water hasn't drained properly from them in ten months. There isn't a door or a curtain on either one, and a person bathing in the first tub is in full view of people in the vestibule area. It is virtually impossible to scrub the tubs because by the time the water has seeped out there is a disgusting film of dirt left. In addition, the ceilings over both tubs are beginning to go. Needless to say I haven't taken a bath since I arrived.

The showers aren't much better. There is no proper drainage in them so water sits in areas hard to mop, and collects dirt. One shower has no door at all and the others are broken. The worst thing is the ceilings. The ceiling in all four showers is in such an advanced state of decay that you're showered with debris as well as water. You look up at your peril. Sooner or later someone will lose an eye. In the meantime the hole in the ceiling is so big the area is used to hide contraband in. If you climb up on a chair and reach way back in the hole there's a ledge that's usually full of booze or drugs. If the C.O.s weren't too lazy to pull a chair over and look they'd have quite a haul.

October 1982

Two women tried to escape tonight. It's a rare occurrence, but obviously it does happen. They were two young white women, each with at least twenty year terms. I don't know their whole story. One of them looks like everyone's fresh-faced daughter. The older of the two has a cell kitty-korner to mine. She has apparently been filing a bar on her window for quite some time. She was certainly quiet about it, but then I'm hardly listening for such sounds. They were planning to go out the window tonight and then over the fences. They are both quite capable of going over the fences, by putting a heavy winter coat over the barbed area and climbing over it. They have both done it once before, and both were caught.

Ellie, the younger of the two, had arranged a dummy in her bed so that she wouldn't be missed at count. She planned to hide in Kitty's cell until after count, and then they would take off. Apparently they made the mistake of telling someone, and "someone" told the C.O.s. I suppose for that the "teller" will get some time off. They should have learned from their first experience that you don't share this kind of information. Kitty was apparently picked up after her first escape, when two of her "friends" told the police where she was. The two women who told were released soon after. Who is to say they were less dangerous than Kitty?

It would be interesting to know the crime records of the people released by the system after they involve others. It is my observation that the system doesn't really care which warm bodies it incarcerates as long as it keeps the statistics up. And, of course, it's a matter of honor, "honor" to beat the ones who beat them. Prisons will put up with any kind of anti-social behavior, in fact often encourage it— except escape. That hits them where they live. It messes up their statistics and it's a definite no-no. That the two women released may be more dangerous to society than the two they brought back matters not at all.

The two women who tried the escape are very close friends, possibly a homosexual relationship. For the few months before their attempted escape I saw little of them. They kept very quiet and to themselves. Ellie lost a lot of weight. Both were definitely preoccupied and not quite themselves. They both have a look of suburbia about them—a touch of preppiness, not the pale, sick look of many whites in prison . . . or the empty eyes.

When the C.O. discovered Ellie in Kitty's room they insisted they were lovers and just wanted to spend the night together. Next day the sawed bar in the louvered window was found. They will both be in "solitary" (Sag) for a year.

I suppose if you're young and strong and face twenty years in prison the only logical thing to do is try to escape. But each time it makes the sentence longer. To put someone in jail for twenty years is another kind of insanity. Which is worse I really don't know.

November 1982

I must stop thinking about Hy and God knows stop thinking about me, if I am to survive with any degree of sanity. I'm quite good at it most of the time, and then suddenly I fall over something in the paper or a magazine and a cold chill goes through me and I remember that I'm not really me anymore. I crawled into bed tonight to read *The New York Times*—I still really care what happens in the world which is I suppose a healthy sign. But there in the middle of the first section was a full page ad—Sweet Jesus, a full page ad of a book by Diana Trilling called *Mrs. Harris*.

How could she fill a book? She knows absolutely nothing about me. But then neither did the judge or the jury or the assistant district attorney, and it doesn't seem to matter. There's a picture of me looking sad, at least that's honest. What kind of people are they who print this stuff?

December 1982

I have lost my second appeal. The state Supreme Court, and the Court of Appeals, have both voted unanimously against me. Twelve judges in their infinite wisdom have decided that Jean Harris had a "fair trial." They don't agree with one another as to how and why, and they have written seventy-seven pages and then seventy-five pages explaining why, but whatever their words and the arrangement on the paper it's all one to me.

It is obvious from what they have written that they have no picture in their mind—no accurate picture of the layout of Hy's house, or of times or places or physical evidence. In fact, what they have written is like one of the newspaper articles with little or no bearing on reality. The hardest thing about the criminal justice system, and the whole judicial process, is living with how little truth and reality matter. The truth is whatever some stranger says it is. Bill and Joel keep telling me, "The facts of the case aren't important anymore, Jean." They will always be important to me.

I called my trial a travesty at my sentencing, but I realize now, after two years of studying those thousands of pages of testimony, that "evil" is a more accurate description. The criminal justice system is much as Alan Dershowitz describes it in his recent book *The Best Defense*. It is built on the assumption that most of the people who are indicted are guilty, which is true. For this reason, everyone must be proven guilty by fair means or foul.

As John Connery wrote in *Guilty Until Proven Innocent*, the American system of justice may work for the guilty, but it's a carefully orchestrated nightmare for the innocent. In a recent poll more than 50 percent of the American citizens asked said a defendant is guilty until proven innocent. The burden of proof, they said, is on the defendant. That isn't the law, but it is reality.

December 1982

When you win or lose an appeal in the state courts of New York you don't find out from your lawyer or from a courteous form letter from the court. You find it out, in my case, on the radio or television, or from another inmate who hears it and comes running. In most cases you find it out only if you go to the prison law library every day, not an easy thing to do if you don't work there, and read the daily *Law Journal*, where it is printed.

The press seems to be told first. As the defendant whose life depends on the decision, you are considered rather incidental. Bill and Joel both tried their best to get to me first with the news, but they learned it essentially the same way I did, Bill in the car driving to work. Some women whose lawyers don't take the kind of personal interest mine have blessedly done, and who don't go to the law library because they may not even know about *The New York Law Journal*, may not find out about the outcome of their appeals until long after it is decided. Sometimes they seem to find out almost by accident. Could somebody tell me why this is necessary?

December 1982

We moved to Fiske yesterday, in time to welcome in the new year. The building is a mess, but it has great potential and best of all it is smaller and quieter than the usual prison floors of Bedford. There are twenty-six rooms for prisoners, rooms, not cells. Most of them are the size of a regular cell, about seven by ten, but five of them were used for C.O.s or as offices, and are a little larger. Two of them have walk-in closets, and two of them have two windows.

We drew numbers one to twenty-six to see who would have first, second, etc. choice. I drew eighteen so I ended up in one of the smaller rooms. With a growing collection of books it's a tight squeeze, but I'm just grateful to be here. We will not have to eat in the huge, noisy dining area. Our food will be brought up to us to eat here. Moreover there is a decent kitchen and two refrigerators so we can do our own cooking if we want to. I most certainly don't want to.

Men from Taconic painted the inside of the place, but, like good Russian peasants, didn't use dropcloths, so the floors are a mess, covered with both paint and mud.

The building was actually built almost eighty years ago to be the segregation building for the New York State Reformatory for Women. For those women who had been particularly bad, there were four smaller rooms with tiny walled terraces off the rooms and women in those rooms were not allowed outside. They could get the air in these tiny courts.

Oddly enough, these rooms have become the ones the women covet most. They're now known as the "garden apartments" and two of the little courts have been made very attractive, with rock gardens, even a tiny pond. They were the only four rooms I quite literally prayed I would not have to have. You cannot see the sky from the bedroom, only the brick wall of the courtyard. I didn't have to worry because they were the first ones chosen.

We've started to get the floors cleaned, scraping with plastic knives and fingernails to remove fifteen years of dirt and paint. The building has stood empty for fifteen years. I think the only reason it was never torn down is that it wasn't in anyone's way. It sits at the far southwestern corner of the property, quite literally only feet from the fence. Now that Bedford is a top security prison the building could only be used as a special honor house, or torn down.

There are no toilets or sinks in the bedrooms so inmates cannot be locked into the rooms for any length of time. They have to be trusted to have certain freedom of movement within the building, and they share bathrooms, eight to a bathroom. To put bathrooms in each of these rooms would have cost a fortune, so using the place as an honor house was really the only sensible thing to do.

January 1, 1983

I have carried so many books I feel as though I have moved an entire household. Living here will be a unique experience—but then every move I make these days is a unique experience. We already feel many "jail-house" pressures lifted. There are twenty-six women in the house. It is an interesting building with four different levels. There are two bedrooms, a phone room, and officer's station on the ground floor, thirteen bedrooms on the next level, eight on the next, and two on top, "the penthouse," as we call it.

I am in a small room. But it fits my only requirement—a window that looks out on woods, hills, and sky. I needed a shoe horn to get everything in—a shoe horn and a great deal of ingenuity, but it *is* possible. You have to remember where you put everything or you find yourself moving six boxes under the bed and losing your mind searching. But I'm getting the hang of it.

The building is an old one, happily built before everything attractive was too expensive to use. The floors are terrazzo, the ceiling in the rec room is vaulted with lovely old beams. The downspouts are handmade and copper, really quite lovely, though I doubt that many people have noticed them over the years.

We are never locked into our rooms because each door locks separately—one of the reasons this was designated an honor cottage. The back door is always locked. The front door is locked only during count and at night from 10:00 P.M. until 7:00 A.M.

The C.O.s are most definitely not enthusiastic about Fiske. The name is the original name the building has always had. Mrs. Fiske served on the board of the reformatory and may have contributed funds for the building as well. Mr. Headley, superintendent, has had a small sign made to put over the door saying: Fiske Cottage—but the C.O.s will never refer to it by that name. They call it "Building 119," and whenever you have to write your housing unit's name they prefer that you use a number instead of a name. How telling.

It's not a popular place to work, either. C.O.s who like peace and quiet sign up for it, but there aren't many who like peace and quiet. "How ya stand it up here?" one of them asked me recently. "I like to be where the action is. This place is dead." But that's the best thing about it.

January 11, 1983

I just finished a letter to superintendent Headley asking for permission to start another possible project around here. The day we moved in, the men were just picking up trash around the outside of the building. There were several old paint splattered chairs about to go, and I asked if I could have them. They said, "Sure." They are old "soda fountain chairs." I sanded them down and found one solid maple and another pine. So I gave away the green plastic chair provided for each room, put my two antiques in instead, made seat cushions out of an old sheet, and the effect is very pretty. The heartbreaking part is the men tell me they had already thrown out 175 similar chairs. They were once stock chairs in every room.

I have written Mr. Headley and asked for permission for three of us to go with him or members of his staff through all the attics and basements and storage rooms on the grounds to see what could be salvaged and refinished by the women at Fiske, either to sell to defray expenses of the house, or to use in administrative offices.

Virginia Maddox has already made a handsome frame out of an old wooden washboard which was lying discarded in the field across from Fiske. There's an oil painting hanging, cockeyed and unloved, in the waiting room of the medical building that is quite lovely, and would be up in the thousands to replace. I've tried to convince him it should hang in his office, or over the fireplace at Fiske, someplace where it won't eventually be destroyed—but so far I haven't convinced him. I suppose by now most of the nice things have been tossed or stolen but there must, once, have been some nice things here, not because it was a prison, but because solid woods and copper downspouts were once everyday stuff.

February 1983

The first good thing that has happened to me in three years happened to me this week. One of the women at Fiske was transferred and we drew lots again for her room, one of the larger ones. I drew number one. The women were decent about it and didn't seem angry or annoyed at my good fortune. Only the C.O. was dismayed. She's white and feels comfortably superior to the black women, but struggles with her feelings about me. For two days she refused to give me the key to my new room.

February 1983

I don't fantasize in prison. My thoughts are very concrete—what is wrong?—what logical steps can be taken to make something better? I don't imagine being outside, or living a different life. I long to hug Cider again, but that's as close to fantasy as I come.

May 1983

I was playing spades last night with a young black woman who just turned twenty. She has an ethereal, other worldly quality about her.

Suddenly, apropos of nothing she started talking across the table, in a quiet, sing-song sort of way.

"You went to Smith, didn't you Jean? I went to Mt. Holyoke for a year, but I flunked out. I got early admission to Holyoke through the ABC (A Better Chance) program, but I didn't work when I got there. I was into Buddhism by then, and I had this thing about having a baby, so I left and had a baby. When it was 8½ months old I killed it. They said it was nine months old, but it was 8½. The voices told me to kill her. I wasn't sure that I wanted to, but they said you have to be brave. You have to do it."

She will end up on the street, with many others like her, uncured, and possibly worse than when she came in. Unlike many of the others here, though, she has a nice family that visits her, so she may have a chance. It's very hard to help when you don't know what to do. Until we think up something better I think kindness is more constructive than a prison cell.

One of the young women who left the annex last month was in prison for robbing a bank and a bar. She had walked into the bank with nothing but a paper bag and a note that read, "Please give me all your money. Thank you very much." (She's a well brought up young lady from Long Island.) The teller was terrified, gave her several hundred dollars and she walked away—no gun, no co-conspirator, no get-away car. Since it seemed such a nice easy way to support herself, she tried the same thing in a local bar and was caught.

I had a long talk with her one evening before she left. Her family doesn't want her back. "I'm a nuisance, you know." I gave her the usual "let's think about what kind of a job you might get" and she said, "Oh don't worry about me, Jean. I'll never come back, unless, you know.

"What do you mean? Unless what?"

"Unless somebody makes me mad and then I might have to kill them."

I think at least a third of the women in here could be classified as mentally ill, or mentally incompetent, but everyone gets pretty much the same treatment. We keep writing books about, and wringing our hands about high school, but I think it's in infancy when many of these illnesses begin, and when people can best be helped.

May 1983

I don't know whether our requests and appeals had any bearing on the decision or not, but on an experimental basis we are going to have telephones on every corridor, and we will be allowed to make as many calls as we want to as long as charges are always reversed, and nobody decides to use the phone for illegal purposes. Someone has already had an angry fit, "gone off" as we say at Bedford, and ripped the telephone wires on one corridor right out of the walls. I hope that doesn't happen too many more times.

June 1983

I realize, having lost it, how very fortunate I was most of my life because I lived, worked and played with people capable of logical thought, people who made sense even if you didn't agree with them. One of the C.O.s has only one explanation for any of her idiocies or meannesses: "Cuz dats da way it beez." In fifteen years she should have me well rehabilitated.

August 1983

I've had a pretty garden at Fiske this year, with flowers all over the place, and no feet trampling them down. *Mirabile dictu!* I keep a large bowl of flowers in the recreation room, and in the bathroom on my floor, fix flowers for the chapel, and bring an occasional bouquet to my friend Maggie on the mental ward, when I go there Friday evenings. Maggie has pasted the pages from a Burpee seed catalogue all over the walls of her cell. "Ain't they pretty, Jean?"

I send an occasional bouquet to my old nemesis, Ringo, too. She is in solitary confinement in a building close to Fiske. When she isn't yelling obscenities for the entire facility to hear, and suggesting what kind of an old bitch I am, she whines from the bowels of her cell, "Bring me a flower, Jean. Bring me a flower." I send her some through one of the women who is permitted to enter the Sag area.

I have never known people to whom I would like to give more, and never imagined people who could appreciate less. Jim Harris used to say that giving is a kind of self-indulgence. I always disagreed with him, but now I think he was right.

August 12, 1983

I wonder why anthropologists don't study people in prison more than they apparently do. There are so many cultures here, so many value systems, all living on top of one another, not listening to one another, not understanding one another, and yet somehow pretending that we're all the same, only divided by two things, good and bad. I look at a young woman and wonder, how does her culture cause her to perceive motherhood?

We have studied Samoa more carefully than we have studied imprisoned women. Maybe we're afraid to look too closely at ourselves. Or maybe it's just easier to go on dividing ourselves into "the good and the bad."

The New York Times printed an excerpt from the Nobel lecture of Gabriel García Márquez. Speaking of the people of his native Colombia he wrote:

Poets and beggars, musicians and prophets, warriors and scoundrels, all creatures of that unbridled reality, we have had to ask but little of imagination, for our crucial problem has been a lack of conventional means to render our lives believable. This, my friends, is the crux of our solitude.

And if these difficulties, whose essence we share, hinder us it is understandable that the rational talents on this side of the world, exalted in the contemplation of their own cultures, should have found themselves without a valid means to interpret us. It is only natural that they insist on measuring us with the yardstick that they use for themselves, forgetting that the ravages of life are not the same for all, and that the quest for our own identity is just as arduous and bloody for us as it was for them. The interpretation of our reality through patterns not our own serves only to make us ever more unknown, ever less free, ever more solitary.

Was it Colombia he was talking about, or was it Harlem?

September 1983

Cloretta was sitting beside me today, sewing on a doll she was making to sell. She looked a little dreamy and suddenly she said, "Ya know, when I get out I'm gonna have me a white apartment, all white. Gonna have white walls and white floors and white ceilings. And then I'm gonna get me all white furniture, nothin' but white. And then I'm gonna get me a big black man, black as that old garbage bag over there, stretch him out on that white sofa, jess black on white, so's I can always find him easy."

September 4, 1983

I made the mistake of turning on TV this morning to be told that "Jean Harris has lost her third appeal." All three of my appeal decisions I have learned about from television. For a week or so after I am afraid to turn the TV on for fear there's more that I don't want to hear. My name has stopped being Jean Harris. I am now "Jean Harris, murderer of the famous Scarsdale Diet Doctor."

If you say something enough times it becomes accepted truth. I read somewhere recently that "perception is reality." I think it was in *The New York Times* so it must be true. "Perception is reality." I guess that's why the city has just spent $200,000 to nail pictures of curtains and flowers in the windows of burned out buildings. Twenty families could have decent housing for the year for that. Twenty-five or even thirty families. Perception is reality. God help us.

September 1983

I've been reading some of the recent studies about our schools, Goodlad's study, Ted Sizer's, and Mortimer Adler's. I've also been talking to myself about what's missing. Nobody goes back to address the problem of infant care in America, though every respected pediatric study made in the past fifteen years emphasizes the importance of the first two years of life, and the role those years play in determining a person's intellectual and social adjustment. High school is about fifteen years too late to worry about a curriculum for children who never learned to read, and who gave up trying by the time they were nine.

I'd like to write a book called *Cradle to Crime*—but so far it's just me talking to myself. I read this quotation from Francis Bacon recently, and I find it so true. "There arises from a bad and unapt formation of words a wonderful obstruction to the mind. In other words, stupidity." The boring, endlessly repetitive four letter words that are coin of the realm in here are proof of what he says, and no one tries to change it.

September 1983

It's hard to bring it up without offending. "Who da shit she think she is. She got a number just like us." In some of the classes I've taught I try to approach the subject very gingerly, often by telling them the story of *My Fair Lady*. They are either too young to have heard of it, or the name of the movie turned them off, so they never saw it. The story never fails to amuse them—and my quavering rendition of "The Rain in Spain" is a real show stopper. From there we attack double negatives and four letter words.

There are many kinds of prisons, of the mind as well as the body. Many of these women are trapped in all of them, and the doors are closing on their children too. I doubt that the meek will ever inherit the earth, but the ignorant have a very good crack at it.

October 7, 1983

Judith Clark, one of the Brinks robbers, was sentenced today to seventy-five years in prison without parole, and then whisked away to Bedford Hills Correctional Facility. It would be hard to describe the dither into which this has thrown the Bedford staff. They have been behaving like frightened rabbits for several weeks, and in the process have created in the minds of the young prisoners here a great American folk hero. They think she's great and they haven't even seen her.

Anyone five feet tall who can turn a whole prison on its ear, bring out helicopters, bring special task forces from Albany to test and photograph all the fences, put the guards in bulletproof vests, cause new fences and rolls of razor blades to be installed, and two new ID stations to be set up at the front gate, plus a whole new security detail, armed and driving twenty-four hours a day all along the fence near the building where she is to be housed, has to be a real hotshot in the eyes of the ignorant.

A young black woman sitting in traffic a few days ago allowed as how she thought Judith was probably "a real nice little woman." I was foolish enough to question her statement.

She answered me loud and with deep disdain, "You a great one to talk. You was out there livin' on easy street. She just a young girl tryin' to make her way."

It isn't hard to see how these people are victimized all their lives. They are so easily duped. They fight and resist what might help them, and follow like willing sheep people who care not one damn about them. Come to think of it—who am I to talk?

October 10, 1983

Sister came with the bus today, thrilled because there were forty children on it, all coming to see their mothers. It took more than 2½ hours to process them all through security and two of them, one fourteen years old and one sixteen years old, were not permitted in because they didn't have proper identification. Sister, who knows both of the children and their mothers, literally begged the deputy of security to let them come in, but he refused.

They spent the entire time sitting out in the parking lot, while two mothers waited inside to see them. Only someone very small and very stupid would do such a thing. I have been trying to update the booklet I wrote for people in jail who will be coming to Bedford, and I am trying to find out exactly what the rules are about IDs. If you ask six C.O.s you get six different answers. To date I have been told, "All children, infants included, need IDs." "Any child over thirteen needs an ID," and "Any child sixteen or over needs an ID." Some say a birth certificate is acceptable, others say a birth certificate is not acceptable. Some say the ID must contain a picture, others say it only needs your name and address. I have had friends bring their four children in without being asked for an ID, and I have had another bring in her newborn and be told, "The baby won't get in again unless you have its birth certificate."

October 14, 1983

Today at 10:45 A.M. I was in South Forty. The guard came in and told us, "Count's on." He counted us, left, then returned again to get our prison numbers. "Somebody walked," someone guessed. That was obviously what the staff wanted us to think. Or at least they wanted us to believe that someone was missing.

It was only later that I learned the truth. We were kept locked until 1:00 P.M. right through lunch. The reason? Judith Clark was having a visit with her lawyer—not in the visiting room, but in "a special place." It was in what is called "the Board Room" which is right next door to the inmate payroll office. A friend who works there had reported for work earlier and been told, "You don't have to work today. Judith Clark is having a legal visit." I think that falls under the heading of non sequitur but it seemed logical to the C.O. who said it.

Judith doesn't need to escape to carry on a revolution. Her presence has caused a revolution in here without her raising a little pinkie. No visitors were allowed to leave the visiting room while the lady talked with her lawyer. If they missed a plane or an important meeting—too bad. Judith was talking to her lawyer. Cori couldn't get home for her children's lunch—too bad.

Do they plan to keep this up for seventy-five years? If so we'll soon lose all our volunteers and inmates will be paid for even more work that isn't done. They specialize here already in paid, undone work. And of course visitors for other inmates will be discouraged from coming after they miss a few doctors' appointments, or just panic when told they can't leave.

October 20, 1983

The extra "security" crew that drives back and forth along the fence all day and all night have pretty well destroyed the lawn that was put in last spring and summer at the taxpayers' expense. The keys to new state cars are given to adolescent cowboys and cowgirls, and they play the same games my fifteen- and sixteen-year-old friends used to do once they got their hands on Daddy's car. They "patch out" and drive over the lawn, missing a wide two-lane driveway, land in mud six inches deep, throw the car in reverse and gun it, spraying mud and leaving deep ruts in the lawn.

They broke down a small fir tree—the car's tracks indicated that they had aimed directly at it and driven right over it, at least ten feet in from the road. They wear bulletproof vests and carry guns, and would floor the accelerator and run like hell if they saw anyone suspicious on the other side of the fence. In the meantime they'll probably shoot the deer and neighboring dogs and possibly themselves. This is called "security."

October 23, 1983

Mona was going to the Parole Board on Thursday. She felt sure she'd get parole. No one knows much about her except she has a ten year old son who comes to see her, and they play happily together in the Children's Center. Wednesday night she got in a fight with another inmate. It isn't unusual for inmates to get in fights just before they go out. They're usually frightened and high strung, and there are some inmates who will goad them deliberately. "If I can't get out why should she?"

Thursday the board met and hit her with six more months. Two days later she cracked up completely, went wild, and instead of going out she's now on her way up to Marcy, for the criminally insane. A visitor was coming in the gate today just as Mona was being driven out. A car window was open and Mona was screaming, "Help me, please help me. I'm a person. I'm somebody. Please help me. I'm a black woman, and I'm smart, and I'm somebody. Help me!" The two C.O.s in the front seat looked straight ahead.

October 1983

I think of all the many things that sadden me about these women; one thing that seems most pervasive is their inability to appreciate beauty, their unawareness of it, their inability to recognize it, their willingness to live without it. Perhaps willingness isn't the word—their unawareness of the lack of it.

I like this quotation from Umberto Eco's book *The Name of the Rose*: "For three things occur in creating beauty; first of all integrity or perfection, and for this reason we consider ugly all incomplete things; then proper proportion or consonance, and finally clarity and light, and in fact we call beautiful those things of definite color." Most of the women here like color—all shades of red and purple—but they have little appreciation of light—the light that comes in at the window, the light in the sky.

November 5, 1983

The phones at Fiske have now been "fixed." There was nothing wrong with them—reason enough for a prison administration to have them "fixed." There are three floors at Fiske, and the building is very spread out. Only a C.O. can touch a prison phone, never an inmate. Most of the time a C.O. is on duty in the office on the first floor. If she should be on the third floor or in the kitchen when the phone rings she would have a long way to go to answer the phone. Consequently there was a wall extension placed on each floor. Makes sense. Now the phones have been fixed.

The phones on each floor that were originally just an extension of the first floor phone have each been given a separate number. Now when somebody calls Fiske (and C.O.s make phone calls even more than they lock and unlock doors) it may be on any one of the three different numbers. In the middle of the night the phone on the third floor may ring twelve or fifteen times until some inmate runs down to tell the C.O. to leave her office and run upstairs to answer the phone. Before the call is completed everyone in the house is awake and angry—which may well be the reason the fixing was done. One becomes paranoid enough in here to believe it possible.

If a time-motion expert ever came in to evaluate this place he would probably recommend razing the entire facility and starting over. And the sad thing is—the public doesn't give one small damn that it's paying for the whole ridiculous mess, paying and paying and paying. As long as someone assures them that it's "taking care of the crime problem" they show all the intelligence and concern of lemmings going happily over the abyss.

November 23, 1983

As many as 60 percent of women in prison seek some kind of psychological or psychiatric help. I'm one of them. More than 30 percent of these women at Bedford have some kind of mental disorder, some obviously severe ones. When they get too bad they are put in segregation, where they howl and shriek for hours and days on end. When they are sent up to Marcy, for the criminally insane, they are often returned very quickly, often with the report, "She's just putting on an act. There's nothing much wrong with her."

Thunderbody is much worse now than she was a year ago. She'll probably be that much worse a year from now. Mind-numbing drugs are the main "therapy." Tiger cuts her initials in her arm and swallows pins when she can find any. Lena cuts off all her hair, with little clumps left behind here and there. Sharon pulls a chair right up to a wall and sits and looks at it for hours. "I just want to be alone," she says. Enid has lost eighty-five pounds since she came here a year ago. A member of the staff says, "She's putting on quite an act." Melba has gained over a hundred pounds. More acting. I've seen them all, "acting."

Donna says, "They've killed my parents, you know." Betty tells me in a rather hurt tone, "They're just mad at me because I dismembered my two year old." Carmen says, "I'm five years old now. That's how I learned to use the gun." And Lena, "Crazy Lena" they call her, believes one of the C.O.'s has stolen her dead father's nose, and she's "gonna get him." Tony slips this poem into Sheila's hand Friday night, because it's Sheila's birthday:

> Birds fly high
> And never lose a feather.
> Come to Sheila's party
> And you'll have a soul forever.

November 1983

The Honorable Milton Mollen, presiding judge of the Appellate Division of the Supreme Court for the 2nd Circuit, has granted me permission to appeal my case to his court again. It was Judge Mollen who wrote the seventy-five page refusal to my first appeal. Thanks to Michael Kennedy he has now reconsidered. I guess it will go back first to a judge in Westchester, then if turned down there, to the Supreme Court. The Supreme Court in New York State is not the highest state court. The highest is the Court of Appeals. Why this is so I'm not sure, but it makes about as much sense as all the rest of the system does.

December 1983

I'm beginning to hear and read more and more about prisons for profit, and it certainly has a frightening ring to it. There isn't any question in my mind that they could be run better and less expensively, but if business can be more efficient, isn't there some kind of miracle that could make government more efficient? It could start with higher employment standards, and the ability to fire incompetent people, and better accounting systems to figure out where all the money presently goes. I would venture to guess it is a rare prison in this country that doesn't have a number of the wrong hands in the till.

The public is so accustomed to being fleeced by the system it asks very few questions and no longer has any idea how much things actually should cost. If C.O.s were forbidden to make unnecessary phone calls all day long, and prisoners and C.O.s alike were forced to turn off unnecessary lights, and forbidden to turn the heat up to 85°, we could save a very large wad right there.

Lights that are supposed to go off "automatically in the daytime" shine all day long on the sunniest days to the tune of what must be thousands and thousands of dollars. The heating bill at Fiske alone must be twice what is should be. The quantity of food stolen and thrown away could feed a small nation. There are often five C.O.s in a location where one or at most two would be quite enough. No one ever seems to check to see whether repair jobs are properly done.

I have seen three jobs done here at Fiske that a private citizen would sue the plumber for. The taxpayers just payed and payed and payed, while the job was redone three times. "It ain't my money." Expensive lawsuits could be avoided if C.O.s had to pay for some of the legal hocus-pocus they are responsible for starting. Legal expenses resulting from the inexcusable dental care here could have been easily avoided.

December 1983

With so many children around, there's a feeling of Christmas in the air in spite of where we are. This week the young mothers and I painted a big fireplace and hearth, and made bright stockings of red felt. The fireplace is tacked up in the nursery now, and the stockings are already hung by the chimney with care, one for each of the ten babies. Cutting and sewing and making felt boards and angels are not what the course started out to be, but we seem to cover a little bit of everything now. The mothers are delighted to discover that they can make something pretty, and they keep wanting to make more.

We have four different Christmas buses and parties planned for the Children's Center. We sent letters to friends and companies asking them for toys for the children, and people have been wonderfully generous. One company felt amused to send us something that they shouldn't have, but others were wonderful. A large box arrived last week, unchecked by security for some reason, and brought directly into the center. We opened it to find it full of toy guns, Saturday Night Specials, and policemen's badges. It was good for a momentary laugh, and then we realized that if security saw it they might cancel the rest of the gifts and the parties. We emptied them quickly into a large garbage bag and Sister carried them outside and put them in the trash.

January 12, 1984

I can't remember all the good things anymore. I remember more emptiness now—a lobotomy where my life used to be. I have spent seventeen years of my life carefully, deliberately seeing only the good in Hy, never the bad. Somewhere deep remnants of that good will always be part of me, but I have to look for it now, consciously search, try to remember and bring it back; it doesn't sweep over me as it once did, a sound, a smell, a place, a word, a picture sweeping over me whether I wanted it or not.

I keep getting letters from women, years later, coming forward with new stories I never wanted to hear . . . women who interviewed him after the book, three of them now saying how unattractive they found him, his boasts of many women, his efforts to date them—women he had hurt—sooner or later he hurt them all—a woman he gave the wrong drugs to—a woman who became habituated to a drug he gave her, even strange sick letters from someone who suggests he was one of Hy's men.

I remember now the times he tried to date women while I was sitting there—even at lunch at the White House, until President Carter's private secretary said she'd love to go on a fishing trip with him—if she could bring her boyfriend; the piano player at the fancy little restaurant in Palm Beach; the general's wife at the Waldorf—phone calls in the middle of the night for almost ten years. He could always turn over and go back to sleep—I stayed awake for the rest of the night.

There are moments when I tell myself I don't love him anymore, but a few minutes later it isn't true—it's still there. It's just that part of me is missing now. I can still feel deeply, and care deeply about some things—but without joy. I am deeply concerned about some things—I am still alive in a way, but never again as I once was. The things and people that concern me are real and in living color, but I am in gray—color me gray. The closest thing to intense feeling now is my loathing of some of the C.O.s.

It isn't a constant thing—only when they speak to me to remind me they are still there . . . when they call me "Jean," when they shuffle from place to place, or sit down to the ubiquitous telephone to talk about nothing at all while ten women are made late to work on the other side of the door. How terrible to let loathing use up the energy

338

that love once manufactured. There was so much that I didn't know or even suspect for most of my life. I wish I could have lived out my life safe in that kind of ignorance—still dyeing Easter eggs—still thinking I could reach China if I dug long enough in the sand.

January 1984

When I reread what I have written about many of the women here it sounds as though I feel terribly superior. I don't. I just feel very lucky. Their conversations, and indeed their lives, sound so mind-bendingly boring—so much emptiness, so much unawareness, so much not giving a damn. You can pass two women in the yard having an argument, "What for you went and ate breakfast with that other girl. You said you was goin' have breakfast with me. I sit there waitin' and you go off eatin' breakfast with that little black bitch. She don't know shit—dumb nigger—she don't know if she a pan cake. Why you eating with her stead of me?"

If you passed them half an hour later you would hear snatches of exactly the same: "You tell me you gonna have breakfast with me, then you . . ." I keep wishing I had a tape recorder but that's a no-no.

The tragedy is that their conversations when they come in, and when they go out six years later, aren't very different. They talk about what they don't have, what somebody took from them, what they're going to take from somebody else, and how much they don't like someone. Their insults, after they have gone through the required number of motherfuckers, are childlike. "Motherfuckin' giraffe neck," "Motherfuckin big mouth," "Motherfuckin cupcake nobody," "Dumb dumb upside-down carrot face frog."

Yesterday morning I awoke to this conversation:

"What'd you say?"

"I ain't talkin' to you."

"I say what'd you say?"

"I say I ain't talkin' to you."

"But what'd you say?"

"I say I ain't talkin' to you . . ."

It went on with exactly those words for at least five minutes. I found a quotation I had written down from somewhere about "the infinite capacity of the human brain to withstand the introduction of useful knowledge." I live surrounded by this infinite capacity.

February 1984

Fiske stands within the high fences and roll upon roll of razors that keep society safe. However, it is also in the most likely place to escape if one is so inclined, so most of the population is not permitted to come near it. (It's interesting that the only other building placed so close to escape routes is Segregation—where the most dangerous and difficult inmates are taken, including some who have tried to escape.)

We have special privileges here, like not being locked in our rooms, and having the door to the house open except during count times, and from 10:00 at night until 7:00 in the morning. Our one checkpoint as we go to work each day and return is at a twelve-foot fence at the bottom of our hill, where a gate opens into the regular population area. C.O.s at the gate change from time to time—each one has his own particular idiosyncratic way of doing his job. One of them makes us show our ID and then goes into his little guard house, gets a book with all our pictures in it, and checks the pictures to make sure we are who we say we are. The only trouble is, he does it when we are going out, not when we are coming in. It's like making visitors identify themselves as they leave but not as they enter. Another young man had the duty for weeks, sitting eight hours a day, no one to talk to, getting up only to open and close the gate for twenty-six people, most of whom come and go at the same times. I said to him one day, "You ought to get yourself a good book." He said, "Yeah well there's a problem with that. This ain't my permanent job. I could go get a book, and then they might move me."

February 1984

One of the C.O.s wrote her evaluations today. Mine read, "Jean has been very mature this reporting period." If I ever leave this place, my first two worldly acts will be to stop at the dog pound and adopt a mutt or two, and stop by Pockers and get my evaluation framed.

February 1984

The terrible thing—one of the terrible things about prison is that you begin to get used to it . . . the obscenity of it . . . the noise of it . . . the waste of it. You don't care if today's work is done next week. You don't even know what today's work is. The things that seemed almost funny at first stop being funny and just slide into boring—dear God so boring.

"Ahm biddin' two uptowns."

"Well don't talk so big girl cause I'm biddin' three downtowns."

"Trump that king, girl, I'm going' break yo fuckin' arm."

I keep remembering how exciting—how significant it was—or we all thought it was, when Rhett Butler was permitted to say, on camera, "Frankly my dear, I don't give a damn." Having moved into a world where *fuck* is the subject, the predicate, and the dangling participle it is pleasant to remember a better time and a better place. It is essential to remember them.

"I told that mother-fucker to pack up his shit and get out." It is the Muzak of prison, and it is never turned off.

February 1984

There is a woman here who reminds me of Mr. Dickens's Madame Defarge—or reminds me of my own picture of Madame Defarge, sitting and watching, always watching, and keeping track, remembering every transgression, no matter how small—that one took two pieces of meat—that one put French toast in the toaster and we agreed we wouldn't put French toast in the toaster "because it could clog up the toaster after a while and someone might get electrocuted"—that one took a pound of butter down the hill to her lover, when the butter belongs at Fiske—never mind that we have more than we need . . . there were five cans of grapefruit slices on that table and now there are only four . . . that one left two odd socks in the dryer, that will never do.

She rises early and plants herself at the head of the table in the tiny dining area next to the kitchen. She sits sideways, sipping coffee and smoking, watching in all directions, saying nothing, always watching, always remembering—the eye—the eagle eye. I have begun going into the kitchen through another door, but it's all for naught. She is there. Her presence is felt. You know she is watching, and could tell any interested party what everyone in the house had for breakfast.

I can see her at the gates of hell giving the devil instructions—twenty lashes for her, she left the kitchen door open. Forty lashes for her, she ran the dryer late at night . . . ten for her, she was almost perfect as I. Stop that one—keep an eye on her. She let her pot boil over and didn't wipe the stove. One can only thank God she is an inmate and not a C.O.

March 1984

We are trying to figure out a better way to distribute clothing to the babies here. At the moment a great deal is done by grabbing. We have not put in writing what a basic layette is, or what are the limits of the State's responsibility to the babies. Families cannot send toys through the package room, but until recently the State didn't supply any either. Now, thanks largely to Sister, their nursery is well supplied with toys.

It is hard to exaggerate how important "things" are to these women. They seem to feel they are as good as what they have, and no better. And there's a carry over to their babies. "My baby gotta have the biggest. My baby gotta have the best." They will send a note to Sister requesting, sometimes even demanding a snowsuit for a two week old baby. "Her baby got one. My baby gonna get one too." One rarely sees their babies in shirt and diapers, and nightie, the things my children lived in for their first 6 or 8 months. The babies here are always costumed, always color coordinated, even napping they are curled up in their cribs in fancy stockings and blouses and skirts or dresses. I find it hard to resist the temptation to take it all off and let them enjoy the lovely feeling of no clothes at all. They rarely have the pleasure.

Having a pair of shoes for her baby becomes almost an obsession with some of the women. "My baby gotta have shoes, don't matter if she wear 'em or not. She gotta have shoes. When Dr. Spock himself came to visit he assured the women that their babies were better off without shoes. A few mothers were convinced. Most of them thought it was just one more ploy to do them out of something.

June 3, 1984

Last weekend some inmates broke into the prison commissary and cleaned it out. The women who did it haven't been caught and probably never will be. To go from the commissary carrying what must have been large black garbage bags of stolen goods, any and every inmate involved would have to pass by at least four, and more probably six C.O.s. How in the name of God just one of them didn't look up, stop their phone conversation or gossiping long enough to notice something amiss is hard to figure out, but they managed.

An outside security company, hired to guard the A&P or some such, would at least be fired, if not sued, if the place were robbed, cleaned out right under their noses. But not here. The people on duty just keep shuffling along. The only reaction I heard from a C.O. was, "Geeze these women are dumb. It was such a easy job, if they had any brains they'd a done it a long time ago."

Hundreds of dollars of stuff was apparently stolen: all the cigarettes, canned goods, candy, nuts, and scissors! Small sewing kits are sold here but the scissors are removed. Instead of getting rid of them immediately they were simply dropped in a box to collect there.

There were, from what I've heard, about forty pair in the box when they were stolen.

July 6, 1984

There are moments like yesterday afternoon when I had to leave the Children's Center because I couldn't stand one more moment of all the accumulated sadness in one small room. Everyone was going about her appointed task—mothers and children were visiting quietly—nothing was different. But the unspeakable sadness of it suddenly consumed me. I couldn't speak. I could barely swallow. I left and went hurriedly through traffic. I ran up the hill to Fiske sobbing, and fell on my knees and yanked weeds out of the garden.

August 1984

I can feel anger at Hy now. It comes suddenly and goes as suddenly—but love goes on.

Hy judged a man from the neck up and by the money and power he wielded. He judged woman from the neck down, and by the money and power her husband wielded. As I think of the simple truth of that I am left with no logical explanation at all of what drew him to me, or me to him, or why he turned to me one day and said, quite out of the blue, "I love you, Jean Harris, and you're the second woman I've said that to in my life."

I actually believed him. I had none of the proper qualifications. The only thing about me that I know fascinated him was that I was completely, totally, brutally honest with him. It aggravated him sometimes, it made him laugh sometimes, he resented it sometimes, but it attracted him too, and when we were alone he didn't try to be something he wasn't, so the good things he was were easier to see.

August 22, 1984

I guess the summer program took more out of me than I had realized. I'm too tired to write or to read or to knit. I can't remember ever being so tired. I tried to rake part of the lawn today and after two or three swipes at it, put down the rake and went inside to lie down.

August 23, 1984

I've gotten another charge sheet, and this one has stuck. I was found guilty of "harassing a correction officer." She has driven me almost insane, deliberately and with malice aforethought, and I am called the guilty party. Why should that upset me anymore? It's called justice. She was in traffic the day she wrote me up. She did the strip search on me.

I hadn't even had a visitor—was just working in the Children's Center, but she made me take off everything, squat several times, and then, knowing full well that I had no contraband, and never had had any contraband, she said, "Now take those bands off your hair. Now shake your head. Now run your hands through your hair."

I said to her, "You're a fool." But I was the fool.

Today I spent almost two hours in the lieutenant's office, with the usual "hearing," everything taped, the whole sick charade, and the verdict is "guilty" of harassing a correction officer.

This is a perfect place for sociopaths and sadists. They are not only permitted to ply their trade, they are encouraged to. The only bit of comfort I have is that I am no longer so paranoid as to think she does it only to me. She is despicable to everyone, and hated by everyone—her peers as well as inmates.

September 4, 1984

I'm still in the hospital but getting better. Apparently all the fatigue and depression was the beginning of a heart attack, not old age. Jimmy came to see me that Sunday the twenty-fifth and by the time I reached the visiting room I was perspiring profusely and felt rotten. Jim asked me what was the matter and I said, "You know it will sound crazy but I think I'm having a heart attack." Neither one of us took the idea very seriously. I have never smoked, don't have high blood pressure, or diabetes, or any family history of heart problems so the thought of having a heart attack had never entered my head.

By the time we had sat and talked for a while I felt better and forgot about it. When Jim left I walked into the Children's Center to talk with Sister for a few minutes, and suddenly I heard myself saying again, "You know, I think I'm having a heart attack." Sister said, "You look tired. Go on up and lie down." And I did.

At about 8:30 that night I began to feel a little dizzy and to have some chest pains. The last thing I ever want to do here is go to the medical building. It's the dirtiest building on the facility grounds and one hears little but horror stories of neglect and frustration about it. Finally I decided I should say something and went down to tell the C.O. I didn't feel well and should probably go to the nurse. The roundsman was in the office and offered to drive me down. I felt a little self-conscious in the nurse's office, told her my symptoms and sat while she took my temperature and my blood pressure.

"You're OK," she said. Come in next Wednesday or Thursday and we'll do an EKG. I left her office and stood in the hallway waiting to see if I was supposed to walk back to Fiske or ride.

A C.O. approached me. "Put out your hands. I'm gonna cuff you," he said.

"What do you mean cuff me? What for?"

"Inmates can't ride in a state vehicle unless they're cuffed."

"I rode down without handcuffs. This is ridiculous. I'll walk."

"You're not walkin', you're ridin' and you don't get in the car until you're cuffed."

I started to cry and went on arguing, but it didn't make any difference. I told him I was sick, I told him he was making me sicker. It didn't make any difference. He threatened me with a charge sheet if I didn't stand still, and suddenly the big black belt was around me, the handcuffs were on, and the cuffs were chained to my waist. I was close to hysteria by the time he got me in the car.

Women are driven around the prison grounds for various reasons day and night without anyone mentioning handcuffs. This maggoty little man was getting his kicks. There are many kinds of legal rape in the criminal justice system, and I've endured them all. By the time I reached Fiske I was sicker than I have ever been in my life, and I wanted only to go to my room and hide from everyone.

My first thought when I walked into the room was to try to gather papers together in one place, in one box, so that some of my writing and all my legal papers might somehow get to the boys. C.O.s would pack up all my things if I died, and God knew what would happen to any of them. If I had all the special things in one place there was an outside chance that someone decent would get them to David and Jim.

I emptied a box and sat it in the middle of the floor and began to put things in it. I was in my nightgown now sitting on the floor, and putting things into a box had become a monumental job. I didn't have the strength to do what I wanted done.

I should have had everything in one place all along. Why hadn't I thought of this happening? I leaned against the bed and started to cry. Next to my bed sat a small puppet, a fuzzy little dog I had brought up from the center to sew his ear back on. I reached over and pulled him down on my lap and hugged him and hugged him and cried and cried and cried.

I think it was sometime after 1:00 A.M. when I finally realized I would have to go to the hospital. I was getting sicker by the minute. My shoulders and hands hurt. It was hard to sit up. It was hard to do anything. Even cry. The puppet was still on my lap and I was still on the floor. I finally pulled myself up and walked to Carol's room.

"Can you help me?" I asked her. "I want to call David. I want someone outside to know that I need help."

Carol helped me downstairs and into the phone room, but I couldn't stand up long enough to dial the number. She took me into the officer's bubble and sat me down, then went into the phone room and called David for me. The C.O. called for a car to take me to the hospital.

Suddenly there were five C.O.s in the small office, hovering over me, telling me to put out my hands to be "cuffed." I refused. With more strength than I had had for a week I fought off the officer with the handcuffs. "I didn't go to my mother's funeral because I wouldn't stand over her grave in handcuffs, and by God I'm not going to die in them either." The last thing I remember was a C.O. threatening me with a charge sheet if I didn't immediately put out my hands for the handcuffs.

I came to on the way to the hospital, stretched out on the back seat of a prison van. I tried to scratch my nose but I couldn't. My hands were handcuffed and chained firmly to the heavy belt around my waist. The good people of Westchester were safe in their beds. I came to again on a table in the emergency room. From then on I was in the hands of real people. They were kind. They were competent. They were decent. An armed guard was stationed beside me the entire time that I was in the hospital.

September 6, 1984

However expensive it may be for private citizens to be hospitalized, it is far more expensive for dangerous criminals like me. There is no judgment used as to who is and who is not dangerous. A parole violator sent back to prison for driving without a license will have a twenty-four hour armed guard beside his or her bed. Common sense and common decency are forbidden in the criminal justice system, which is probably just as well because so many of its employees have neither.

I spent the first five days in intensive care, the next few days happily alone in a private room with books and flowers and friends; and then, quite suddenly was well enough to be put into the prison area of the hospital; "no flowers, no knitting, no hardcover books . . . can't have your own comb, can't have, can't have."

Everything went. I'm not sure where. Visitors were suddenly herded into a little room under the staring eyes of C.O.s. The hallways were dirty, very dirty. The walls were dirty, very dirty, the chairs were broken, the look of total and deliberate neglect was made all the more stark by the appearance of the rest of the hospital. For a few days I had felt like a human being again, but it hadn't lasted long.

On my third day in intensive care I woke to see the C.O. who had accused me of harassing her, standing over me, and I reacted as one would in a terrible nightmare.

Dr. Kay was in the room and I reached for his arm and pleaded, "Please, please, get her out of here. There will be one massive heart attack in here if she stays. Please get her out!"

He did, and she sat in the hall for the next eight hours, keeping all the good people of Westchester safe.

Her day wasn't completely wasted, however. She did have the pleasure of bringing a stack of mail for me to look at from a distance and assure me that I couldn't have it until it had gone back to the prison and been opened and inspected by the prison mail room. Sister Elaine finally brought it to me four days later.

The C.O. knew, she had to know, that she had played some role in my heart attack, and knowing it she had chosen to follow me to the intensive care unit.

September 1984

Cassandra, who has the questionable distinction of having told me to go fuck myself more than anyone else on earth, has become almost motherly since my heart attack. In the middle of that loud, loony, wild-eyed woman, there apparently beats a heart. She empties the garbage when it's my turn to do it. She brings me food—she's trying to learn to bake—and she rushes up on Sundays to tell me, "Jean, lunch, come and it's chicken. You better get da hell down there and get some before some mother-fucker steal it." Sometimes it's hard to tell the missionaries from the cannibals.

January 1985

I was called to the medical building this morning to have some lab work done. My blood is checked every now and then because of my heart attack. A young girl ahead of me sat in the technician's office for forty minutes while her arms were poked and prodded to find a vein. The head nurse walked by while I stood waiting outside. "Just my luck," I said, "to get behind somebody who doesn't seem to have any veins." "Three quarters of these women don't have veins," she said. "They collapse, you know, after you've shot enough dope into them." Sometimes a doctor has to be called to take the blood because the lab technician can't do it.

January 1985

I've just finished reading Jerome Bruner's book *In Search of Mind*, and have discovered to my sorrow and to my horror the fate of that

348

splendid Social Studies program, "Man: A Course of Study." I think a strong case could be made that it's one of the finest courses ever devised for a classroom. I would love to teach it in here, to help some of these women realize they are not as far removed from the rest of humanity as they suppose. The films for it are so beautiful. They're silent except for the sounds of nature, so you aren't led passively through what is happening. You have to think your way through. You have to add yourself to what you're seeing.

Bruner, who has taught for years at Harvard, wrote, "The most moving teaching experience I have ever had was that summer in 1965 at the Underwood School in Newton, Massachusetts, where we tried out 'Man: A Course of Study.' "

But only a few years after it was introduced I now learn that the John Birch Society and the "creationists" mounted a strong attack against the course, and eventually the National Science Foundation which had originally financed the making of the course withdrew its funds. It has now agreed to submit all future curriculum proposals to a congressional committee in advance! Education by congressional committee. Just what we needed. So much of what I see in here has to do with education or the lack of it. I wish there were a way to make people believe that. Who would have thought we'd still be fighting the Scopes trial in 1985?

February 1, 1985

Marta is from a small village in Peru. She has lived in America for many years, but she has kept close ties with her family. She has a one to three year sentence, and two children, with no one up here to care for them. Same old story. The man in the picture has left. Consequently her mother and father have left their little village in Peru to come to America for at least a year to take care of their grandchildren. They are peasant people who don't even speak much Spanish. Their native language is Quechua. It must have taken everything they and their daughter possess to get them up here.

Marta said, "Even so far apart we were always a close family. We got nothing now. My mother was in line all day yesterday with my daughter to try to get welfare."

Yesterday the family came to visit her. Madre wore a sweater that Sister complimented her on. "Bonita, sí—from Peru." It was very roughly done—the wool looked casually handloomed. They probably use one size needles and figure out patterns as they go along, not step by step with a book of directions. How frightening it must be to be so far from home, from what is familiar, from a language you understand—no money—no way to earn any. Judges rarely sentence just one person when they send one person to prison. I suppose it's just as well they never know what they have actually done.

February 10, 1985

A woman said to me today, "Prison is a place where you live with women you despise, but you start wondering if you are like them. You strive to remain civilized and unchanged, but gradually you lose ground and you realize it." I hope she's wrong. Are you losing ground if you begin to understand and forgive them? Or are you gaining ground?

February 11, 1985

I've come across another eye-opening statistic. While about .003 percent of the citizens of New York City have had felony arrests, 40 percent of the homeless people in New York have had felony arrests. Yet our President insists that crime and economics don't go together.

February 21, 1985

For at least three years the press dubbed me "murderer"—"snob"—"social climber"—"aging mistress"—"diet doc junkie." That's old news now. Now it would amuse them if I were Florence Nightingale, and Rebecca of Sunnybrook Farm, come to spread light and magic among the poor and downtrodden. They want to hear that I have changed the lives of women whom I have touched, and who have touched me. We are so childish. We want life to be simple, even though we know it isn't. For good or for ill we have touched one another. I would find it hard to stomach some of the conversations I sat through at dinner tables for most of my life. I used to be able to endure them by throwing in a few questions—now I would stand up and shriek. I have probably been changed more than the people I am supposed to be changing.

March 4, 1985

I called my dear friend Dodie tonight, just to see how she is surviving her husband Jim's death, and to chat a while. Her voice is so gentle, her choice of words so ladylike, but always fun, always laced with her special kind of humor. One forgets the sound of such voices in here. One forgets the reality of decency.

April 1985

Do women at Bedford have AIDS? Of course some of them do, but we will never be given an accurate number. *The New England Journal of Medicine* and *The New York Times* have recently reported that AIDS is probably far more prevalent than previously suspected, and that more and more women can be expected to have it, prostitutes and needle users at the top of the list. This is the New York State home for prostitutes and needle users, and probably AIDS. There are constant rumors about who does or doesn't have it and just as constant denials.

Ordinarily when a woman leaves the facility it is the C.O.s who go into her cell and oversee packing her belongings and sending them to the State Store to be checked. If a woman leaves and the C.O.s send inmates into the cell to clean it out, it's a pretty good guess that she had AIDS. This happened recently when a young woman who had looked ghastly for a long time was taken to the hospital and died of pneumonia within hours.

I last saw her walking out of the facility kitchen. The girl had been at Bedford for five years. Does that mean she contracted it here? I don't suppose prisons will ever learn that the one way to stop rumors is to gather people together and tell them the truth. I doubt that it has ever occurred to them. There is a sort of tacit agreement in prison that prisoners don't deserve to be told the truth.

April 7, 1985

It's Easter and I found this wonderful poem in one of Sister's "flaming liberal" publications.

> Liturgical Seasons
>   For all of Retha Jackson's
> thirty years
>   St. Vincent De Paul Thrift Store
> has set her religious holidays.

As surely as any church
calendar
this purple dress with its
faded armpits
means Easter.

March-April 1985 *Broomstick*

June 1985

David brought me a piece of the past today, and where the dickens he found it I can't imagine. I had asked him to bring me some of my own blouses now that we are permitted to wear them. At the rate he's going they'll get here just in time for the rules to change again. He came for a visit today, and was pleased to tell me "I finally brought you some blouses. They're sort of odd, though. They don't look like things you'd wear."

I stopped at the package room after he left, to pick them up. There were four blouses in a paper bag. The first one was blue. We can't wear blue. The second one was striped. We can only wear solid colors. The third one was a short beach robe I hadn't seen since summers in Canada twenty years ago, but the fourth was a treasure! It was a "Beer Jacket." I hadn't seen it or worn it since before the Second World War. It must have been somewhere in the attic with things from the cottage.

I haven't found anyone to share my delight with because there isn't anyone else here old enough to know what one is. In 1939, with a pair of shorts, some saddle shoes, and a Beer Jacket from Best and Co. you were just about as jazzy as you could get. It's a lightweight canvas shirt with four pockets and brass buttons that have a beer keg stamped on them, hence the name. The stylish thing to do was have your friends write all over them. I wasn't stylish. I liked mine plain. No self-respecting teenager in Cleveland Heights would have been without one any more than she would be without blue jeans today.

I was allowed by the C.O. to have it, and for reasons I couldn't begin to explain, having it hanging in my cell adds a dimension to my life that is comforting. It tells me I am still me, whatever that may mean. And that is the most that one can hope for here, not to be destroyed by a world that has done its damnedest to try.

Epilogue

Sister Elaine says I am a different person than I was when I came in. I am older and more knowledgeable; I don't feel very different. I don't respond much differently to the ugliness and meanness around me. But I am more grateful for logic and kindness. Never again will I take them for granted. My own explanation is that few people really knew me when I came here, so it is easy to say that I've changed. The only real difference is that now I am a stranger in two worlds instead of one.

I am still threatened with charge sheets and removal from Fiske, and I still bristle with anger when it happens. The psychiatrist I seek out regularly is kind and says, "That's good. That's healthy. It means you haven't been institutionalized yet." The C.O.s who have come to know me better are civil and have no overt wish to hurt me anymore. Some are genuinely kind. I am less harassed than I was at first, but new C.O.s arrive constantly, and every day without harassment is a gift.

I have finally passed a "stress test" for my heart, after four trips to the hospital, a parade through Grasslands Hospital, trussed up like Paddy's pig, in chains, with endless dread on my part as a prelude to each wretched trip. The last time I went, a nurse sat beside the man across the waiting room from me, explaining everything to him, reassuring him. I sat there in my chains, stared at, the only reassurance being that if I didn't pass the test this time, I would keep going through the whole punishing experience until I did. It's great motivation. It keeps you treading.

I know many things I didn't know six years ago, much of it information I would be glad to give back. The two most frightening things I have learned are a deep contempt for the practice of law, and a deep awareness of the power of money. I am genuinely grateful to every lawyer who has worked in my behalf, but their efforts seem to pall in the face of the reality of what the game of law really is. What I had spent a lifetime believing was the assiduous pursuit of truth, turns out to be merely the assiduous game of one-upmanship.

In a search for truth and justice and decency, one would be as well advised to play Pac Man. That so many of our brightest young people are attracted by the money law generates is frightening to say the least. When the history of the demise of American power is one day written, as it inevitably must be, the plethora of lawyers in our midst will have to be listed as a contributing factor. Our myths have helped to make us strong. Nothing can shatter them like a day in court.

If I were ever permitted to make one change, and only one change, to help raise the level of our criminal justice system to a level many citizens in their innocence believe it now occupies, I would require that lawyers, in each case they prosecute and in each case they defend, be required to put their hands on the Bible and swear, as all witnesses rightly do, to tell the truth so help them God. And they would do it knowing that if their deliberate perjuries could be proven they would be disbarred. If it could be made retroactive, America's glut of lawyers would quickly disappear.

I have learned, too—second only to my new awareness of the clay feet of justice—to understand the power of money, and the explosive impotence of poverty. Money has never been a strong motivating factor in my life. My family was comfortably upper middle class. From the time I left home at twenty-three I have lived, at first on what my husband and I earned, and later on what I alone earned, and nothing more. What I earned was a teacher's salary, on which I learned to make a dollar go a long way, without feeling ill-used or envious of others, though few of my friends had less than I had, and most of them had far more.

The nonsense about "Mrs. Harris being rich" is just that, nonsense, window dressing contrived by media creatures who couldn't think of any other way to make a middle-aged school teacher sound interest-ing. "Make her rich. Everybody likes to read about the rich." The story is so widely accepted now that denying it is almost a waste of time. The women here swoon over my $3 gold earrings, and ask if they're "18 K" or whether my "pearls" are "real."

I said to one of them recently, "Maura, if these pearls were real they'd be worth a king's ransom."

"Oh," she said, "are they real?"

I believe that this idea that I have money helped to send me here, and the political fallout of the public thinking that I am rich helps to keep me here. All of which plays comfortably into the hands of a few very rich who want me here.

But nothing points up the power of money like the absence of it. To live as I now do among many women who possess nothing, quite literally nothing but the state-issued clothes on their backs, is to see impotence incarnate.

I am told that an epilogue is supposed to wrap up a book, make everything neatly relevant, tell you how it all turned out. Yet this story has no denouement; it just keeps happening. And the punch line came long ago; the butler didn't do it and neither did the aging mistress. Many judges in their infinite wisdom have reviewed the case of the People of New York State vs. Jean Harris, and not one has found anything amiss in the endless travesty. "It wasn't a perfect trial," they say, "but it was fair." If you think that you know what soul-searing frustration is, gentle reader, try six years of this.

Hy and I have both paid a terrible price for meeting that long ago evening in December of 1966. Perhaps it is the ultimate selfishness on my part, but I cannot bring myself to be sorry that we met. To do so would be to throw away life and make death the only victor. The only way to celebrate life is to live it and we did. Death is always the way it ends. Timing is the part that breaks the heart.

What family and friends find hardest to understand about me is that for me, the tragedy of Jean Harris is not that she is in prison, but that she was sent to prison. The truth is that there are periods of time when I forget where I am, when I go about my own thoughts and my own activities and none of this exists for me. There is something in my brain that helps to lower a curtain on the ugliness that I am experienc-ing. I am not removed from reality, but it doesn't hurt me twenty-four hours a day. I know that the destruction of Jean Harris was orchestrated quite deliberately by people who go about their lives disguised as decent, and somehow I go on living, and even loving the memory of Hy.

Have I been robbed of my values here? No. Myths, yes. Values, no. I have to live with my values in an alien, jeering world, but maybe that's good. I wrap them around me all the closer to keep out the cold.

Daily I must walk by the Segregation building where Crazy Carrie yells out: "Oh Tarnow, oh Tarnow. I didn't mean to kill ya Tarnow. Old Bitch. Who wanna fuck a ole bitch like that? Look at her, going up that hill. Ole bitch. I hope you fall and break yer fuckin' halo."

But God is good, because in a little while I forget and start to hum a song, and think how lovely the trees are, and how clean the air feels. Air is the one pure thing here. A lovely gift. There are opposite moments too, when for no overt reason a tidal wave of nothingness and emptiness washes over me, consumes me, and I am alone in vast space. Those moments frighten me. They are the only thing here that does frighten me. I look around frantically for something to do that will fill the emptiness, but no book satisfies, nothing fills the space. I am utterly alone. I can't turn on television for fear I will see a dog, or hear a familiar song, or a story about kindness. Those things are quite unbearable.

I don't know how to describe myself now, after almost a year in court and five years in prison. I don't know any more about myself than I did when I started this book. I still don't even know the topic sentence. I am much better at knowing things outside of myself. And these things are what keep me plodding along. I have to believe that this six years of madness did something more useful than titillate the media. I had to be doing something real, something besides slogging through the legal swamp Hy's death sentenced me to. Without that something real I would be nothing more than a wailing wraith by now, quite, quite insane. Perhaps it is the old school teacher in me that saves me. They're a tough breed, I've learned, and I am still one of them.

The first night I spent in Philadelphia, many years ago, I had dinner with members of an old Philadelphia family. I remember only two things about it: dinner was very late, and before we went into the dining room we talked about the Vietnam War, and young people, and education. The host said to me, "My God but you school teachers take yourselves seriously."

It's true. I still believe good teaching will cure almost anything short of the common cold; I still believe that if I wasn't good at anything else I was a good teacher. And I still believe, more strongly than ever, that it is only through our children that we can make a better world.

I have spent most of my life teaching the children of suburbia. My causes (if that's what they could be called) developed as I went along. They were causes that could be advanced with or without the trappings of poverty, but they were genuine nonetheless. Children of all neighborhoods become the product of the goals they are guided to set for themselves, and the skills we teach them to achieve those goals; the ability to work hard, make plans, solve problems, and delay gratification. The young women I see around me here have been horribly shortchanged in their learning of skills. I hope we begin to teach their children better than we taught them. And teaching must begin at birth.

The need for good day-care centers in America cries out so loud I wonder how we could not have responded to it by now. It isn't an impossible dream. Junior high schools and senior high schools would be better places if each one had a day-care center in it, with service in or to the center a requirement for graduation. I wish the Children's Center at Bedford were open to the community too. What better way to serve society?

The only way children of anyone but doctors, lawyers, and real estate tycoons will be able to go to college in the future will be with some form of public or private grant. It may be a blessing in disguise. We've needed something more than a driver's license or an illegitimate baby as rights of passage in America, and now we have it. If every young person who plans to go on to college gave two years, or even four, to teaching children to read, both age groups would be wiser and better for the experience. And a few bright ones might settle for a Toyota instead of a Mercedes and stay on in the classroom. Teaching is catching.

The brightest and the best should be teaching our youngest children. It is a popular notion in this country that the third grade teacher should be just a little brighter than the second grade teacher, and so on up and down the ladder. Not so. Putting all those high IQs into law offices instead of classrooms hasn't improved the practice of law and has diminished our classrooms. For each of our children, black and white, the price of high school and college should be time spent with the young, serving as role models, learning how the human animal learns.

While there are physical and hereditary differences among children, the big differences are the result of how we treat them and teach them. Today, more and more American children are being born into a world that gives them only the back of the hand. I know a beautiful two-year-old whose first two words were "shit" and "fuck." She is bright and she is already doomed to live the way she speaks. You don't have to hit a child to abuse it.

I have worked with both extremes of the socio-economic ladder, and I know that when Jamil and Kisha and Carmen and Muffy and Dee Dee and Christopher do the same things, we don't respond to them in the same way. Many of the problems, inclinations, and actions that send the young poor to group homes or to jail are quite like the actions of the rich which send them to the principal's or the psychiatrist's office, stealing from one another, shoplifting, indulging in promiscuous sex, using drugs and alcohol.

I have stood on the steps of a hospital in Chestnut Hill while a member of the hockey varsity team and student council leader handed her baby over for adoption. I have met with the shopkeepers of Chestnut Hill, and McLean, Virginia, about the rash of shoplifting by the middle school girls. I have talked at length with some of the bistro managers in Georgetown about selling liquor to minors, when they all have fake IDs. I have negotiated with the phone company over a $5,000 bill, run up by girls using a stranger's charge card. I have made arrangements for a sixteen-year-old to be taken to AA five nights a week.

I have had frequent meetings with parents who wanted me to "do something" about the growing drug problems among teenagers, but who weren't about to "do something" themselves. I have had long talks with mother and doctor about a ninth grader who "has never been able to concentrate, Mrs. Harris, since she spent a night at her little friend's house and her little friend's father raped her."

I know that members of the black middle class have a big job ahead of them, because hearing the truth from them will be far more useful to poor blacks than hearing it from me. I know that if we are ever going to wean a growing number of young women away from Aid to Families with Dependent Children (AFDC), it can't be done by taking the money and putting it into Star Wars. It will have to be used to teach good teachers, and teach children personal responsibility.

The present bland, mindless reproducing of children into poverty and ignorance is a form of public cruelty begun in the name of kindness. If we haven't the courage to tell young women who are not prepared to have children and take care of them, that they should limit the number they have, then the least we can do is give better training to the children they do have.

I know there is little informed or considered public agreement as to what prisons are meant to accomplish, which makes it easier for us to be comfortable about their failures. Is the system meant to be a program of punishment of the guilty and preparation of them to return to society, or are prisons simply a tangible expression of public outrage? Is prison the punishment, or is prison the place people are sent to be punished? More than 90 percent of the people who go to prison return, in time, to society.

Warehousing people until their terms are up, handing them $40 and telling them, "Go, and sin no more" is the worst kind of public hypocrisy. Verbatine said, "$40, shit! That's just a round trip ticket to here." You better believe it.

When a sick person is given the wrong medicine or improper medical advice and becomes sicker, the new sickness is described as iatrogenic. Hy taught me that. It is a useful adjective and one that might appropriately be applied to the criminal justice system. Much of what we presently do to punish crime exacerbates crime. Much of America's crime is iatrogenic in nature, made worse by some of the national values we subscribe to.

We preach to the world about American individuality and the importance of each citizen, yet our system of justice is turning more and more to little nests of mandated sentencing, which says everyone in this geographical location is the same, each incidence of lawbreaking the same. There is little common sense or common decency in the judgments made. I have read of a man in this country who is in prison for life without parole because he was found guilty five times of writing bad checks. The checks all together amounted to less than $1,000. The Supreme Court said it was not "cruel and unusual punishment."

A young person can and does go to prison in one of our United States for ten years for something that isn't even a crime in another state. As long as any person who is a nonviolent first offender is in an American prison for long, ungodly sentences, parents in America should be outraged. It isn't enough just to be grateful those children aren't yours.

If I suggest that prisons should be a little more sane it isn't because I believe prisons are a civilized response to lawbreaking. It is only that I accept for now the reality of their existence. Prisons, the very best of them, are primitive and dehumanizing, and should be used to house only the violent and dangerous. Unfortunately, our present investment in them is so immense, and rising so quickly, there is little hope that we will soon stop using them. Making prisons a little less deliberately destructive would be an improvement over what we presently do.

Sister Elaine often says of the Children's Center at Bedford, "The only trouble with this playroom is that people see it and go away feeling good about prison, thinking the whole place is like this. It covers up so much that is ugly and wrong."

A C.O. said of the center one day, "I don't believe in that room. It's wrong. It's like tying a balloon to a coffin." It's far more than that, but there are times when it's that too.

I believe everything that can be reasonably done to help prisoners salvage their family ties should be done. A man or woman who is arrested should be asked immediately if they have children, who is caring for them, and where. The names of the children, their whereabouts, and the names of the care-givers should be part of every incarcerated person's permanent files, and statistics on them should be kept current. No caring parents, however unattractive you may find them, should sit in prison for months wondering where their children are.

This is not uncommon today. I have heard women begging, pleading for the right to make one phone call to find out about a child in the hospital, or a child who has been moved but she doesn't know where.

If children are alone when parents are arrested, then care and housing for them should be provided with the same speed and priority as the arrest of the parent. A child's right to some semblance of security and caring should be inviolate. I hope that soon, in every jail and prison in the country, family visits will be an essential part of the daily program, not a special, once-in-a-while privilege.

Every person in an American prison should be required to try to learn to read and write in English, to compute at an elementary level, and wherever possible, to think logically, especially about personal responsibilities. Little is done here to try to develop a woman's power of moral reasoning. There is little instruction in decision making. There are few intelligent discussions pointing up moral dilemmas and giving inmates opportunities to suggest and reason out solutions.

Never have I overheard a person in authority giving a useful lesson in citizenship to inmates. The crisis of a water shortage has gone by totally unacknowledged here. It is not unusual for some women to take ten minute showers, or to cool their can of soda by letting cold water run on it for an hour or so.

It would be extremely useful if a woman left prison able to turn to something besides prostitution for her livelihood. It is not a calling one would wish on anyone, though why it goes on being illegal is, I suppose, for reasons that lie deep within the psyche of the human male. We have known the part prostitution plays in female criminality for hundreds of years, but we haven't done much more about it than continue to collect fines for it. Decriminalizing might be wise, and making pimping a violent class A felony might be even wiser.

I am told it isn't smart for me to mention that the prohibition of drugs works as well as the prohibition of liquor did, but how can someone who cares about children ignore the subject? The only basic difference I see between the two prohibitions is that where the first bootleggers profited in hundreds of thousands of dollars, the second are profiting in billions of dollars. Legalizing drugs is a frightening prospect, but it would at least leave people with the option of destroying themselves without having to destroy so many others in the process. It would get pushers out of school playgrounds too.

I wanted to say something about alternatives to prison too. There are some intelligent and legitimate ones. But many books are being written about them so there are places you can go to find out about them if you care. It is difficult to end a book that has no ending, but I am very tired, and this is enough.

On second thought, there's one thing more. I think I know the topic sentence now. It's "Work hard and love one another." It doesn't always turn out well, but it's the only way to go.

Appendix

Excerpts from
THE PHYSICIAN AS EXPERT WITNESS
Is Peer Review Needed?
A. Bernard Ackerman, M.D.

I was one of eight pathologists who were called as expert witnesses in the case of The People of New York State *vs*. Jean Harris. Almost nine full days of the fifty days of the trial (nearly 20 percent) were devoted to issues of cutaneous histology. I have read the transcript of the testimony of all of the pathologists and this article summarizes what I perceive to be the crucial aspects of that testimony. The testimony in quotations is verbatim. . . .

Some sense of the importance of the role of "expert" testimony about cutaneous histology in the trial of Jean Harris may be gathered from the written opinion of Justice Mollen on appeal:

An extraordinary amount of expert testimony was offered at trial on a variety of subjects. The major dispute turned out to be whether the bullet which entered and exited Dr. Tarnower's hand went on to cause his chest wound. The People contended that it did and that that fact would suggest that the injury to Tarnower's hand was a 'defensive wound.' The defense argued that the hand and chest wounds had been caused by two separate bullets. Opinions were offered in support of the prosecution's theory, and in contradiction to it, largely depending upon whether the particular expert was able to discern in the slides of the chest wound evidence of cells which were peculiar to the palmar surface of the hand.

During the trial of Mrs. Harris, which began on November 21, 1980, and ended on February 24, 1981, six general pathologists and two dermatopathologists were called to the stand by the defense and by the prosecutor to testify about matters pertaining to histology of the skin. The meaning of those issues in the trial of Jean Harris may be best understood if crucial events and opinions are presented in chronological sequence.

March 10, 1980—Dr. Herman Tarnower dies of bullet wounds. Jean Harris is arrested and charged with murder in the second degree.

March 11, 1980—An autopsy is performed by Drs. Louis Roh, deputy medical examiner, and Gary Paparo, chief medical examiner of Westchester County. Dr. Roh's autopsy report describes four bullet wounds and tells of four separate bullets entering the body of Dr. Tarnower.

March 14, 1980—Preliminary hearing. Dr. Roh testifies that four separate bullets had entered the body of Dr. Tarnower.

March 21, 1980—Dr. Roh issues an autopsy report titled "Histologic Examination" and in the wound in the chest notes only ". . . fresh hemorrhage in subcutaneous tissue and adipose tissue. Dermis shows coagulation necrosis of collagen fibers. A few foci of gun powder deposit are seen in subcutaneous tissue."

March 24, 1980—Grand Jury. Roh testifies that the wound in the hand is consistent with an attempt to defend against a gun being fired and that the victim's wounds are not consistent with a struggle. He again states that four separate bullets entered the body of Dr. Tarnower, but that only three of them were recovered from the body. No bullet was recovered from the hand wound because it was an "in and out, through and through" wound. The fourth bullet was never found.

November 21, 1980—Trial of The People of New York State *vs.* Jean Harris begins at Westchester County Court House, Judge Russell R. Leggett presiding.

December 18, 1980—Dr. Roh is called to the stand by the prosecutor, George Bolen, Assistant District Attorney for Westchester County. Dr. Roh now testifies that only three separate bullets entered the body of Dr. Tarnower. The defense was not given notice of this change of expert testimony.

January 4, 1981—During the presentation of the case for the defense, Mr. Bolen places a telephone call to Dr. Henry Ryan, chief medical examiner for the State of Maine, and learns that the doctor is in Westchester County. That same day Mr. Thomas Lalla, assistant district attorney, visits the law office of Mr. Joel Aurnou, chief counsel for the defense, and learns that a conference is being held there among experts for the defense. Bolen later acknowledges that he surmised that Dr. Ryan was among those at the meeting in Aurnou's office. Aurnou had hired Dr. Ryan as an expert for the defense months earlier.

January 6, 1981—Mr. Bolen telephones Dr. Ryan a second time in Maine, ostensibly to respond to a Christmas card the Bolens had received from Dr. Ryan, who had been a deputy medical examiner of Westchester County. . . .

On Bolen's initiative, they discuss the Harris trial. Bolen asks Dr. Ryan how one can prove that a wound in a palm is defensive and Dr. Ryan tells him that the evidence is suggestive if specialized nerve endings (Meissner's and Vater-Pacini's) are found ectopically in the wound in the skin of the chest. Bolen calls Dr. Roh and tells him to look for pieces of palm skin (apparently not specifically for Meissner's and Pacini's corpuscles) in the histologic sections of the wound in the chest of Dr. Tarnower.

January 8, 1981—Dr. Roh writes an addendum to his histologic report of March 21, 1980, in which he claims to have found "three fragments of tissue in the bullet track in subcutaneous tissue—histologically consistent with stratum corneum, stratum lucidum and portion of stratum granulosum of epidermis of skin." The addendum makes no specific mention of palmar skin.

January 9, 1981—Hearing on a motion for a mistrial. Aurnou asks for a mistrial on the grounds that the prosecutor had invaded the counsels of the defense and violated the defendant's rights by calling an expert hired by the defense in order to learn the strategy of the defense. Bolen admits calling Ryan and discussing signs of the "defensive wound" and the importance of searching for tactile nerve endings from a palm in the wound in the skin of the chest.

Judge Leggett rules against Aurnou's motion for a mistrial. He acknowledges that Bolen had called Dr. Ryan for the specific purpose of discussing the Harris trial, but the Judge holds Ryan responsible for discussing the case with Bolen. Further, the Judge holds that there is no rule that precludes a prosecutor from talking to a defendant's witness. The Judge states, moreover, that he does not find that the prosecutor discussed the strategy of the defense.

Mr. Lalla tells Judge Leggett and Aurnou, in response to Aurnou's

request for a single histologic slide containing the disputed fragments, that no slide may be examined "in any place other than in the
office of the medical examiner" according to the "policy of the medical
examiner's office."

January 14, 1981—Dr. Paparo contacts Dr. Martin H. Brownstein, a
dermatopathologist whose private laboratory is in Great Neck, Long
Island, about examining the tissue sections from the chest wound of
Dr. Tarnower, and on the following January 15, 22, 25 and February 8,
1981 the histologic slides and micrographs are taken by members of
the prosecution to Great Neck for Dr. Brownstein to examine. . . .

January 16, 1981—Dr. Roh is called to the stand by Aurnou. Roh
acknowledges that Bolen called him after speaking to Dr. Ryan and
told him to look for skin from the palm in the skin of the chest wound.
Dr. Roh testifies to finding the fragments and to writing a new report.
He does not know of any nerve corpuscles specific for the skin of a
palm. Roh also testifies that he did not line up the wound in the right
palm with the wound in the chest at the time of the autopsy on March
11, 1980, in order to determine if they could be put into a straight
alignment and, if so, in what relative positions.

Dr. Ryan is called to the stand by Aurnou and confirms the content
of the telephone calls with Mr. Bolen. He disagrees with Dr. Roh
about the wounds in the palm being defensive and, instead, says that
they could have resulted from a struggle. He also disagrees with him
about the fragments being from the epidermis of the palm. Dr. Ryan
says the fragments are connective tissue; that one piece is cartilage,
another consistent with joint capsule; and the third fragment he cannot identify.

Dr. Ryan disagrees with Dr. Roh about the latter's statement of lack
of specificity of Meissner's and Vater-Pacini's corpuscles. Dr. Ryan
says that these corpuscles are virtually specific for the skin of palms
and soles.

January 19, 1981—Dr. J. N. P. Davies, Professor of Pathology at the
Albany Medical School and consultant to the New York State Police
Laboratory, is called to the stand by Aurnou. He disagrees with Dr.
Roh about the three fragments being from the the epidermis of a
palm. For Dr. Davies, one piece is undoubtedly cartilage and another
piece is traumatized fibrous tissue. Davies also disagrees with Roh

about the palmar wound resulting from a defensive posture rather than from a struggle. . . .

January 21, 1981—Dr. Cyril Wecht, former Coroner of Allegheny County, Pennsylvania, takes the stand for the defense. He disagrees with Dr. Roh about the fragments coming from a palm. He diagnoses all three fragments as connective tissue, one piece being cartilage, the other two collagen. . . .

January 23, 1981—Dr. Ackerman is called to the stand by Mr. Aurnou. Using a blackboard he draws diagrams of epidermis from palm and chest skin and explains that the three fragments do not consist of epidermis from the palm, but, because the second fragment is almost certainly cartilage, all three of the closely situated fragments are probably cartilage.

On cross examination, Mr. Bolen raises, for the first time, the possibility that the second fragment with the four nuclei is from the spinous layer of the skin of a palm of Dr. Tarnower. Ackerman rejects that possibility on the ground that a fragment that size from the spinous layer should have many more nuclei, not merely four.

Also on January 23, Mr. Aurnou calls Drs. Alfred Angrist, Professor and Chairman emeritus of the Department of Pathology at Albert Einstein College of Medicine, and Michel Janis, Professor of Pathology at Albert Einstein College of Medicine, to the stand. Both disagree with Dr. Roh that the three fragments consist of epidermis from a palm. Angrist considers the fragments to be cartilage or altered collagen. Janis interprets some of the fragments to be fibrocartilage and insists that none are keratin.

Bolen: "Is it possible that any of these three fragments could be keratin?"

Janis: "Is it possible that any of these three fragments could be keratin? No, it's not possible."

Bolen: "It's not possible at all?"

Janis: "It's not possible at all."

February 4, 1981—Dr. Brownstein writes a report about his findings in the wound of the skin of the chest. He notes small fragments in the subcutaneous tissue, but describes only one of them and concludes on the basis of that one fragment that "there is material in the chest wound that is quite consistent with the type of keratin found on palms and soles." He gives no interpretation for the other two fragments. . . .

February 10, 1981—Dr. Ackerman, at the request of Aurnou, sits at the counsel table in the courtroom to assist counsel and does that for the duration of the trial.

Dr. Roh returns to the stand for the third time, this time called by Bolen. Roh again states that the palmar wound was sustained by Dr. Tarnower in self-defense and that fragments from the palm were carried by the bullet into the wound in the skin of the chest.

Roh projects 23 photomicrographs of skin tissue from the wounds in the palm and chest of Dr. Tarnower and explains his interpretations to the jury. Roh testifies that the largest fragment is from the keratin layer of the palm, the second fragment with the nuclei from the spinous layer of the palm, and the third and smallest fragment from the granular layer of the palm.

February 11, 1981—Dr. Roh is cross-examined by Aurnou. He tells Aurnou that the largest fragment is stratum corneum, the second fragment stratum spinosum close to the granular layer, and the third fragment stratum lucidum close to the granular layer.

Dr. Roh acknowledges to Aurnou that he had left the spinous layer out of his addendum of January 8, 1981, and insists to Aurnou that collagen is a cell with a nucleus, cytoplasm, and cell membrane. He also insists that there are no nuclei in the cells of the granular layer of the epidermis. Aurnou questions Roh about the same 23 photomicrographs that were projected the previous day. Many inconsistencies emerge.

Dr. Roh is inconsistent about whether he had had any discussion with Ackerman in the medical examiner's office on January 21, 1981. Aurnou asks him, "did there occur a dialogue between you and Dr. Ackerman?" and Roh replies, "Yes," but shortly thereafter Roh tells Aurnou that "I didn't say a word. . . . I just listened."

February 12, 1981—Dr. Brownstein is called to the stand by Bolen. Having only commented about one of the fragments in his written report, Brownstein now testifies that two of the fragments are quite consistent with the type of tissue found in the outer layer of the skin of palms and soles. He is not certain of the second fragment with the four nuclei.

Dr. Brownstein disagrees with Dr. Roh on 23 separate issues of fact concerning the three fragments in particular and cutaneous histology in general. Dr. Brownstein admits that he wrote a note in his own hand, presumably to Mr. Bolen, suggesting that good photographic evidence will frighten off the possibility of other dermatopathologists testifying in the case.

Dr. Ackerman is called back to the stand by Aurnou. He disagrees with the testimony of Drs. Roh and Brownstein that the fragments come from epidermis of a palm and reiterates that they consist of connective tissue, probably cartilage.

The defense and the prosecution rest their cases. . . .

February 17, 1981—Judge Leggett charges the jury. He reviews the testimony of every one of the eight pathologists who testified during the trial. His emphasis to the jury is on the question of intent, i.e., did Mrs. Harris intend to kill Herman Tarnower or did she not. The three fragments in dispute are relevant to the question of intent. . . .

Did the testimony and practices of the expert medical witnesses serve the interests of a fair trial by assuring that the jury, who as lay people necessarily rely on the expertness of medical witnesses, was presented with accurate statements of facts for their deliberation and determination of guilt or innocence? To illustrate the gravity of that question, the following progression of facts is highlighted: (italics mine—JH)

1. That by changing his testimony about the number of separate bullets that entered the body of Herman Tarnower from four to three, Dr. Roh created the issue of a "defensive wound." In his autopsy report of March 11, 1980, at the preliminary hearing on March 14, 1980, and before the Grand Jury on March 24, 1980, Dr. Roh stated that four separate bullets had entered the body of the late Dr. Tarnower. On December 18, 1980, during the trial, Dr. Roh changed his testimony from four bullets to three. This change of testimony raised the notion of a "defensive wound" suggesting intent on the part of Mrs. Harris, and created the prosecution's theory of a "defensive wound" rather than a wound suffered during a struggle.

2. That during the trial on January 6 and 7, 1981, during the presentation of the case for the defense, the prosecutor, Mr. Bolen, telephoned Dr. Henry Ryan, whom he knew to be an expert witness for

the defense, and initiated a discussion of the case. Bolen asked Ryan during at least one conversation how one could prove that a bullet had been fired with intent to kill and, in particular, the bullet(s) that went through the right hand and chest of Dr. Tarnower. Ryan advised Bolen that finding specialized nerves from palmar skin in the wound in the skin of the chest would indicate that the late doctor's right palm had been held up in a posture of self-defense.

If Mr. Bolen did not consider his conversations with Dr. Ryan to be improper or unfair, why, during his interrogation by Aurnou and Lalla in the Mistrial Hearing before Judge Leggett on January 19, 1981, did he attempt to explain his calls to Ryan as being little more than social and belated Christmas greetings. . . .

3. That in the midst of the trial Dr. Roh, after a telephone call from Mr. Bolen, changed his findings about the wound in the chest and that his new findings lent support to the prosecution contention of a wound sustained in self-defense. Following the telephone call and instructions from Bolen, Dr. Roh reviewed the histologic sections of skin from the chest wound. Two days after Bolen's telephone conversations with Dr. Ryan and then with himself, Roh wrote an addendum to his original histologic report of March 21, 1980. In the original histologic report, Dr. Roh did not mention any fragments from palmar skin in the skin of the chest wound. In his addendum, Roh wrote that in the bullet track in the subcutaneous tissue there were three tiny fragments of tissue histologically consistent with stratum corneum, stratum lucidum, and stratum granulosum of epidermis of skin, presumably of the palm. He also asserted in that addendum that there was gunpowder near one of the fragments. This supported the prosecution's contention of a wound sustained in self-defense rather than a struggle.

4. That Bolen introduced the issue of the second fragment consisting of cells from the spinous layer when that layer of epidermis was never mentioned in Dr. Roh's addendum. Bolen asked Dr. Ackerman during cross examination on January 23, 1981, if the second fragment with the four nuclei could be from the spinous layer, though Dr. Roh's addendum never mentioned the spinous layer at all. Bolen introduced the spinous layer of the epidermis as an explanation for the second fragment, presumably because Dr. Roh had learned from his

discussion with Dr. Ackerman in the Medical Examiner's office on January 21, 1981, that the normal stratum corneum (including the "stratum lucidum") does not contain nuclei, yet his addendum to the autopsy report had implied that the second fragment with the four nuclei consisted of stratum corneum. Dr. Roh testified incorrectly in court that granular cells in the granular layer do not contain nuclei, so that for him the second fragment with the four nuclei could not possibly consist of granular cells. Furthermore, that second fragment did not contain any granules. On February 10, 1981, Dr. Roh, under direct examination by Bolen, stated that the second fragment consisted of spinous layer of epidermis from a palm and repeated his assertion to Aurnou on cross-examination on February 11, 1981. These changes in Roh's testimony lent validity to the prosecution claim that the wounds in the palm and the chest resulted from a single bullet fired with intent by Mrs. Harris.

5. That the policy of the medical examiner's office did not apply equally to the defense and to the prosecution. . . .

6. That Dr. Brownstein gave testimony about the fragments in court that differed from his written report. On February 4, 1981, after having examined the histologic sections containing the fragments on four separate occasions, to say nothing of reviewing hundreds of photomicrographs of them, Dr. Brownstein wrote a report that addressed itself to only one of the three fragments. Of this fragment he wrote that it "is quite consistent with the type of keratin found on palms and soles." But Dr. Brownstein wrote nothing about the identity of the other two fragments which he had studied on four separate occasions and which had been the object of attention of seven other pathologists. During direct examination by Bolen on February 12, 1981, Dr. Brownstein testified that two of the three fragments were consistent with the stratum corneum from the palm of the late doctor. But Dr. Brownstein told Aurnou on cross-examination that he "could not identify" the second fragment with the four nuclei "with any certainty."

Brownstein admitted to Aurnou that he believed that the three fragments were all of one tissue ("I would like to think that all three [fragments] came from the same piece of tissue"), implying the stratum corneum, but the second fragment had four nuclei so it could not possibly be from stratum corneum. Dr. Roh accounted for the four nuclei in the second fragment by changing his testimony about that fragment from stratum corneum to stratum spinosum. Dr. Brownstein simply stated that he could not identify the second fragment despite the fact that it was considerably larger and better preserved than the third fragment which he said he could identify as stratum corneum.

7. That Dr. Brownstein recommended strategy to "frighten off possibility" of other dermatopathologists testifying. In notes presumably for Mr. Bolen written in Brownstein's own hand and given by the prosecutor to the attorney for the defense, Brownstein wrote that "good photog evidence will frighten off possibility of other dermatopath testify."

Aurnou: "Now, you mentioned that you had come here to help us in a search for the truth; is that correct?"

Brownstein: "That is quite correct."

Aurnou: "Did you ever consider yourself to be an advocate for either side?"

Brownstein: "No."

Aurnou: "You would have had no interest, for example, in discouraging the testimony of any other doctor who might, for example, disagree with you?"

Brownstein: "No way."

Aurnou: "And did you prepare certain notes, in connection with this case?"

Brownstein: "Yes, I did."

Aurnou: "And in your notes, Doctor, did you make the statement in your own handwriting that good photographic evidence will frighten off the possibility of other dermatopathologists who testify?"

Brownstein: "If it is in the notes I probably did write that."

Aurnou: "In a search for truth, Doctor, or as another advocate? Come on, Doctor, give us an answer."

Brownstein: "I was preparing my position and . . ."

Aurnou: "And you hoped to scare off other competent physicians. *That* is in a search for the truth?"

Why did Dr. Brownstein want to "frighten off" other dermatopathologists from testifying in a judicial procedure convened for the purpose of determining the truth? Should a defendant not be permitted, even encouraged, in the spirit of truth and fairness, to have other dermatopathologists examine those same fragments and offer their opinions about them?

8. That critical parts of Dr. Roh's testimony concerning cutaneous histology were, in my opinion, inaccurate. The fragments of tissue in the wound of the chest identified as palmar epidermis by Drs. Roh and Brownstein were offered by the prosecution to suggest that Mrs. Harris had shot Dr. Tarnower with the intention of killing him. Whether these minuscule fragments, the largest 0.2 mm × 0.1 mm according to Brownstein's own measurement, were epithelial, as claimed by Roh and Brownstein, or connective tissue, as contended by the six pathologists who testified for the defense, was crucial to the defense of Mrs. Harris. (See Chronology above.)

This is what Dr. Roh had to say about collagen, the major connective tissue in the body, when he was cross-examined:

Aurnou: "This is your report of March 21, 1980. First of all, you said you found in the dermis of the right chest coagulation necrosis of collagen fibers. Have I quoted you correctly, Doctor?"

Roh: "Correct."

Aurnou: "What is necrosis?"

Roh: "Necrosis means simply the death of a cell."

Aurnou: "Death?"

Roh: "Yes."

Aurnou: "Is collagen alive?"

Roh: "Collagen—"

Aurnou: "Was it ever alive?"

Mr. Bolen: "He was about to answer a question and he went on to the next."

The Court: "I will take the two questions and consider them as one. The way they were framed, they are the same. You can either break it down or you can have it reframed, if you want."

Roh: "Collagen is a cell. If a human being is made out of a cell, if the human being is alive, the collagen cell is alive."

Aurnou: "Isn't it a fact that collagen is not a cell at all, Doctor?"

Roh: "What is it, then?"

Aurnou: "How about a fiber?"

Roh: "A fiber is a cell."

Aurnou: "Doctor, what is a fibroblast?"

Roh: "That's a cell, too."

Aurnou: "What does a fibroblast do with regard to collagen?"

Roh: "Fibroblast is considered as a precursor of the immatured form of the collagen."

Aurnou: "Isn't a fibroblast the cell that makes, spins out, collagen?"

Roh: "Fibroblast becomes collagen fibers."

Aurnou: "Doctor, does collagen have a nucleus, in your opinion?"

Roh: "Collagen fibers, yes."

Aurnou: "What does that consist of, Doctor?"

Roh: "Nucleus?"

Aurnou: "No, Doctor. The particular nucleus of a collagen, as you call it, cell, describe for the jury histologically consistent with accepted medical literature?"

Roh: "Of collagen fibers?"

Aurnou: "Collagen cell, Doctor. You used that term didn't you?"

Roh: "Collagen fiber is a collagen cell. It's made of cells. It has a nucelus in it."

Aurnou: "I am going to try again, Doctor. Isn't it a fact (A) that collagen is a fiber and (B) that it has no nucleus at all?"

Roh: "Yes, they do."

Aurnou: "Now, in all fairness, Doctor, I will ask the question over. Is collagen not the major extracellular component of the—"

Roh: "Cell."

Aurnou: "Of the body. Extracellular, Doctor. Do you understand that means outside the cell, Doctor?"

Roh: "Yes. I would say it's the extracellular portion of the cell."

Aurnou: "Doctor, isn't that a non sequitur? In other words, a thing is either a cell or part of a cell or outside a cell."

Roh: "Anything in the human body is part of the cell."

Aurnou: "Part of the body, Doctor, not part of the cell."

Roh: "The human body is made of cells."

Aurnou: "Are you telling me, then, Doctor, as you understand medicine, as you understand pathology, as you understand histology, that there is no extracellular protein in the body?"

Roh: "Yes, there is. It is part of the cell."

Aurnou at last asked Roh, "Doctor, would you agree or disagree with this sentence: Examination of collagen in connective tissues by light microscopy demonstrates that collagen is deposited as large bundles of regularly oriented fibers which on further examination can be shown to be composed of fibrils and microfibrils?"

Roh: "Yes."

Aurnou: "Doctor, do you know what the criteria are histologically or morphologically for identifying collagen fibers?"

Roh: "That's exactly what you read."

How could Roh exclude the possibility that the three fragments in the wound in the skin of the chest of Dr. Tarnower consisted of connective tissue if he has faulty criteria for recognizing collagen under the microscope?

9. That in my judgment, Dr. Brownstein did not on his own present accurately the morphologic criteria for differentiating epithelial from connective tissue, the criteria upon which the matter of the three fragments turned. This is what Dr. Brownstein had to say about differentiating epithelial from connective tissue when he was cross-examined:

Aurnou: "Well, perhaps you would be kind enough to give us the criteria, for example, Doctor, that differentiate cells of that [epithelial] layer from the connective tissue."

Brownstein: "Oh, yes. In terms of looking under the microscope and looking at cells, for example, if you wanted to decide about a certain fragment, decide whether they come from the outer layers of the skin, the epidermis, or whether they come from the deeper tissues like the connective tissue, collagen or cartilage, there are certain criteria to distinguish them. If we are talking about the outermost layer of the skin, the epidermis, does not have nuclei, this is one of the factors differentiating epidermis from cells like cartilage cells or keratin cells which could have nuclei."

Aurnou: "Would it also be fair for me to suggest to you, Doctor, that the cells from connective tissue are scattered amidst anuclear extracellular material?"

Brownstein: "That is generally true."

Aurnou: "And there is quite a distance, sometimes, between the cells in connective tissue; correct?"

Brownstein: "Correct."

Aurnou: "Now, I would like to turn for just a moment to collagen which we can agree is one of the connective tissues; correct?"

Brownstein: "Yes."

Aurnou: "Is it a living cell?"

Brownstein: "Yes."

Aurnou: "Collagen is a living cell?"

Brownstein: "Collagen is not a cell, no. It is a material that is secreted by a cell."

10. That Dr. Roh stated about a fragment of tissue only micra in diameter: "The major portion of the smallest fragment is lucidum layer, but since there is a transition between the granular layer to the lucidum layer, a small portion of granule was attached to the particular section, the fragment." In my opinion, no human being can make such a determination on a fragment of tissue that minute.

11. That Dr. Roh projected photomicrographs to the jury that he and Dr. Brownstein acknowledged were out of focus when the purpose of the photomicrographs was to convince the jury that three minuscule fragments consisted of "stratum corneum, stratum lucidum, and stratum granulosum."

Aurnou: "And finally, are any of the photomicrographs out of focus, Doctor?"

Roh: "Well, I am not a professional photographer. So some of them are out of focus."

Aurnou: "Tell us about the quality of these photomicrographs, Doctor?"

Brownstein: "The quality was quite satisfactory to make the points, but I would have done things a little differently."

Aurnou: "Well, for one thing, Doctor, would you tell me please if in these photomicrographs you found, among other things, photomicrographs that were out of focus?"

Brownstein: "This is not unusual. Of course, there were areas out of focus."

Aurnou: "I am talking about whole photomicrographs."

Brownstein: "This happens all the time. This is perfectly acceptable."

12. That the histologic sections containing the three fragments were flawed by many technical imperfections:

Aurnou: "Now, with regard to the 20 to 22 [histologic slides] that you saw, Doctor, was there good contrast between the eosinophilic and the basophilic?"

Brownstein: "Satisfactory, but not perfect."

Aurnou: "Was there good contrast?"

Brownstein: "Good is a relative term. I could answer that 'yes'."

Aurnou: "And were there overlays?"

Brownstein: "Yes, there were overlays."

Aurnou: "Were there tears?"

Brownstein: "Yes."

Aurnou: "Were there knife marks?"

Brownstein: "I think there were knife marks, yes."

Aurnou: "Was there dirt?"

Brownstein: "Yes."

Aurnou: "Other artifacts?"

Brownstein: "Yes."

Aurnou: "Folds?"

Brownstein: "Probably."

Aurnou: "Aren't each one of the things that I have listed defects in the slide?"

Brownstein: "It is a defect in minor points of perfection, but we are not talking about perfection here. They still show the evidence with the dirt or with the tears or with anything else."

Aurnou: "Doctor, wouldn't it be helpful in a matter of this importance to have slides . . ."

Brownstein: "They were decent. We are talking about esthetics now rather than essence."

Aurnou: "I am not talking about simply out of focus photomicrographs, I am talking about the original slides which you understand have knife marks on them, tears, artifacts shown clearly, overlays, and so forth."

Brownstein: "Yes."

Aurnou: "Those defects obscure the diagnosis and that is what quality control is all about; is it not, Doctor?"

Brownstein: "Quality control tries to get satisfactory tissue sections, but these were quite satisfactory for the purpose. They weren't ideal, but they show the entire picture."

The difficulties that the technical defects posed for diagnosis of the fragments was communicated to Bolen by Dr. Angrist in this exchange:

Bolen: "What did you determine those fragments to be, sir?"

Angrist: "Well, I can't tell you that I knew exactly what they are, but I know what they are not. They are not ordinary tissue of the palm that I can recognize. At least I cannot recognize them as such. I guess that would be a more appropriate way of putting it."

Bolen: "So you can't recognize them as being tissue, let's say from the palmar surface. Is that correct?"

Angrist: "Correct."

Bolen: "Is it possible they could have been, though?"

Angrist: "Anything is possible. But I doubt it."

Bolen: "Well, what do you think those three fragments were, based upon your years of experience in this area? What do you think they are?"

Angrist: "They are debris. Some of them are dirt. There is a lot of dirt on that slide. But other than that, there were some that were altered tissue with changes in it. . . ."

Bolen: "Did you think any of those tissues might have been cartilage?"

Angrist: "Some of them did mimic cartilage, yes."

Dr. Roh had denied that there were any defects in the histologic sections that his laboratory had prepared.

Aurnou: "Doctor, is there overlay on this slide?"

Roh: "Yes."

Aurnou: "Is that a defect?"

Roh: "It's not a defect. It's the overlay. Defect means absence of something."

Aurnou questioned Roh further.

Aurnou: "Is it a defect in preparation, Doctor?"

Roh: "I don't think it's a very good way of doing it, but you cannot avoid it."

Aurnou: "You cannot avoid it?"

Roh: "It does happen."

13. That Dr. Roh changed his opinion about the findings in the wound in the chest of Dr. Tarnower time after time:

March 21, 1980—Autopsy report. No palmar fragments in the wound in the skin of the chest, only "large amount of fresh hemorrhage" and "coagulation necrosis of collagen fibers."

January 8, 1981—Addendum to the autopsy report. There were "three fragments of tissue in the bullet track in subcutaneous tissue of the chest wound" and "these tiny fragments are . . . histologically consistent with stratum corneum, stratum lucidum, and portion of stratum granulosum of epidermis of skin."

January 16, 1981—In court. "I found a small fragment, tiny fragments of palm tissue in the deep . . . in the skin section taken from the chest." The tissues consistent with palmar skin are "the top three layers of five layers normally present in epidermis."

February 10, 1981—In court. "The largest fragment I found in the chest section is similar or consistent with the histological characteristics with the keratin layer found in the palmar surface. As far as the second fragment is concerned, with the nuclei, it is consistent with the layer found on the upper part of the prickle cell layer, or spinosum layer . . . and the smallest fragment with the fine granules is consistent with the one found in the granule [sic] layer of the palm of the hand."

February 11, 1981—In court. Aurnou: "Doctor, just so we are perfectly clear, I am going to refer to the largest fragment as No. 1. What portion of the skin tissue do you finally determine, in your opinion, that was?"

Roh: "The largest fragment, I determined that was a stratum corneum."

Aurnou: "And the second fragment, the one with the nuclei, that was?"

Roh: "Upper layer of stratum spinosum close to the granular layer."

Aurnou: "And the third and smallest."

Roh: "Stratum lucidum, close to the granular layer." . . .

The role of cutaneous histology in the trial of Jean Harris and its implications for medicine and the law in America should be of concern to the community of physicians. Let it be given careful, reflective, and critical consideration.

A. Bernard Ackerman is Professor of Dermatology and Pathology and Director of Dermatopathology at New York University School of Medicine. Dr. Ackerman prepared at Phillips Academy, Andover, for Princeton University, where his major interests were religion and literature. He received his M.D. in 1962 from The College of Physicians and Surgeons of Columbia University and served residencies in dermatology at the Columbia-Presbyterian Medical Center, the Hospital of the University of Pennsylvania, and the Massachusetts General Hospital. Dr. Ackerman is a prolific writer. In addition to having published more than 150 articles in various journals, he has written several full-length books and numerous chapters in books. His textbook *Histologic Diagnosis of Inflammatory Skin Diseases: A Method by Pattern Analysis* has been hailed as a classic and is now in its third printing. Dr. Ackerman is the founder and Editor-in-Chief of *The American Journal of Dermatopathology.*

Index

PHOTO CREDITS

The publisher gratefully acknowledges permission to reprint the following photographs:

Audrey Topping: Hy at wine bar in his Westchester house; Hy in China; Hy with Zhou-en-Lai; Jean, 1984.

Arty Pomerantz, *New York Post*: Joel Aurnou with Jean.

Peter Byron: Jean with children, Christmas, Bedford Hills; Jean with children in Children's Center, Bedford Hills; Jean holding baby, Bedford Hills; Jean, Bedford Hills.

Ed Lettau: Sister Elaine Roulet in Children's Center, Bedford Hills; Sister Elaine and Jean in Children's Center, Bedford Hills.

Kathleen A. Kavanagh: Jean at Madeira, 1980.